The Sphere Project

Humanitarian Charter and Minimum Standards in Humanitarian Response

Published by:

The Sphere Project
Copyright@The Sphere Project 2011

Email: info@sphereproject.org
Website : www.sphereproject.org

The Sphere Project was initiated in 1997 by a group of NGOs and the Red Cross and Red Crescent Movement to develop a set of universal minimum standards in core areas of humanitarian response: the Sphere Handbook. The aim of the Handbook is to improve the quality of humanitarian response in situations of disaster and conflict, and to enhance the accountability of the humanitarian system to disaster-affected people. The Humanitarian Charter and Minimum Standards in Humanitarian Response are the product of the collective experience of many people and agencies. They should therefore not be seen as representing the views of any one agency.

First trial edition 1998
First final edition 2000
Second edition 2004
Third edition 2011
Second re-print October 2011

ISBN 978-1-908176-00-4

A catalogue record for this publication is available from The British Library and the US Library of Congress.

Distributed for the Sphere Project by Practical Action Publishing and its agents and representatives throughout the world.

Practical Action Publishing, Schumacher Centre for Technology and Development, Bourton on Dunsmore, Rugby, CV23 9QZ, United Kingdom
Tel +44 (0) 1926 634501; Fax +44 (0)1926 634502
Email: sphere@practicalaction.org.uk
Website: www.practicalactionpublishing.org/sphere

Practical Action Publishing (UK Company Reg. No. 1159018) is the wholly owned publishing company of Practical Action and trades only in support of its parent charity objectives.

Designed by: *messaggio studios*, Metz-Tessy, France

Printed by: Belmont Press Ltd, Northampton, United Kingdom

Foreword

This latest edition of the Sphere Handbook, *Humanitarian Charter and Minimum Standards in Humanitarian Response*, is the product of broad inter-agency collaboration.

The Humanitarian Charter and minimum standards reflect the determination of agencies to improve both the effectiveness of their assistance and their accountability to their stakeholders, contributing to a practical framework for accountability.

The Humanitarian Charter and minimum standards will not of course stop humanitarian crises from happening, nor can they prevent human suffering. What they offer, however, is an opportunity for the enhancement of assistance with the aim of making a difference to the lives of people affected by disaster.

From their origin in the late 1990s, as an initiative of a group of humanitarian NGOs and the Red Cross and Red Crescent Movement, the Sphere standards are now applied as the *de facto* standards in humanitarian response in the 21st century.

A word of gratitude must, therefore, be given to all those who have made this happen.

Ton van Zutphen
Sphere Board Chair

John Damerell
Project Manager

Acknowledgements

The revision of the Sphere Handbook has been an extensive, collaborative and consultative process, engaging a considerable number of people around the world – too many to mention individually by name. The Sphere Project acknowledges the breadth of the contributions made and the willingness of organisations and individuals to be involved.

The Handbook revision process was led by a group of focal points for the technical chapters and cross-cutting themes, supported by resource persons for emerging issues, all drawn from the sector, either seconded from humanitarian organisations or directly hired, depending on the level of work envisaged. Consultants led the revision of elements relevant for the Handbook as a whole, and which required substantial new work. Where not stated otherwise, the people listed below were consultants.

Humanitarian Charter: James Darcy, Mary Picard, Jim Bishop (InterAction), Clare Smith (CARE International) and Yvonne Klynman (IFRC)

Protection Principles: Ed Schenkenberg van Mierop (ICVA) and Claudine Haenni Dale

Core Standards: Peta Sandison and Sara Davidson

Technical chapters

▶ **Water supply, sanitation and hygiene promotion**: Nega Bazezew Legesse (Oxfam GB)

▶ **Food security and nutrition**:
- Nutrition: Susan Thurstans (Save the Children UK)
- Food security and livelihoods: Devrig Velly (Action contre la Faim)
- Food aid: Paul Turnbull (WFP) and Walter Middleton (World Vision International)

▶ **Shelter, settlement and non-food items**: Graham Saunders (IFRC)

▶ **Health action**: Mesfin Teklu (World Vision International)

Cross-cutting themes

▶ **Children**: Monica Blomström and Mari Mörth (both Save the Children Sweden)

▶ **Older people**: Jo Wells (HelpAge International)

▶ **Persons with disabilities**: Maria Kett (Leonard Cheshire Disability and Inclusive Development Centre)

▶ **Gender**: Siobhán Foran (IASC GenCap Project)

▶ **Psychosocial issues**: Mark van Ommeren (WHO) and Mike Wessells (Columbia University)

▶ **HIV and AIDS**: Paul Spiegel (UNHCR)

▶ **Environment, climate change and disaster risk reduction**: Anita van Breda (WWF) and Nigel Timmins (Christian Aid)

Sphere companion standards

▶ **Education**: Jennifer Hofmann and Tzvetomira Laub (both INEE)

▶ **Livestock**: Cathy Watson (LEGS)

▶ **Economic recovery**: Tracy Gerstle and Laura Meissner (both SEEP network)

Resource persons

▶ **Early recovery**: Maria Olga Gonzalez (UNDP-BCPR)

▶ **Camp coordination and camp management**: Gillian Dunn (IRC)

▶ **Cash transfer programming**: Nupur Kukrety (Cash Learning Partnership network)

In addition, a number of people were consulted with regard to the civil–military interface, conflict sensitivity and urban settings.

Working groups and **reference groups** were established to support the focal points in their work; while The Sphere Project acknowledges the contribution of all these persons, their individual names are not included herein. However, a full listing of all working group and reference group members can be found on the Sphere website: www.sphereproject.org.

Editors: Phil Greaney, Sue Pfiffner, David Wilson

Revision workshop facilitator: Raja Jarrah

Monitoring and evaluation specialist: Claudia Schneider, SKAT

Sphere Board *(as at 31 December 2010)*

Action by Churches Together (ACT) Alliance (John Nduna) * Agency Coordinating Body for Afghan Relief (ACBAR) (Laurent Saillard) * Aktion Deutschland Hilft (ADH) (Manuela Rossbach) * CARE International (Olivier Braunsteffer) * CARITAS Internationalis (Jan Weuts) * The International Council of Voluntary Agencies (ICVA) (Ed Schenkenberg van Mierop) * International Rescue Committee (IRC) (Gillian Dunn) * InterAction (Linda Poteat) * Intermón Oxfam (Elena Sgorbati) * International Federation of Red Cross and Red Crescent Societies (IFRC) (Simon Eccleshall) * The Lutheran World Federation (LWF) (Rudelmar Bueno de Faria) * Policy Action Group on Emergency Response (PAGER) (Mia Vukojevic) * Plan International (Unni Krishnan) * Save the Children Alliance (Annie Foster) * Sphere India (N.M. Prusty) * The Salvation Army (Raelton Gibbs) * World Vision International (Ton van Zutphen)

Donors

In addition to contributions by the Board organisations listed above, funding for the Handbook revision process was provided by:

Australian Agency for International Development (AusAID) * European Community Humanitarian Office (ECHO) * German Ministry of Foreign Affairs * Spanish Ministry of Foreign Affairs * Swiss Agency for Development and Cooperation (SDC) * United Kingdom Department for International Development (DFID) * United States Department of State Bureau of Refugees and Migration (US-PRM) * United States Agency for International Development Office of Foreign Disaster Assistance (US-OFDA)

Sphere Project staff team

Project Manager: John Damerell
Training and Learning Management: Verónica Foubert
Promotion and Materials Management: Aninia Nadig
Training and Promotion Support: Cécilia Furtade
Administration and Finance: Lydia Beauquis

At various stages during the Handbook revision process, additional team support was provided by Alison Joyner, Hani Eskandar and Laura Lopez.

Contents

The Handbook

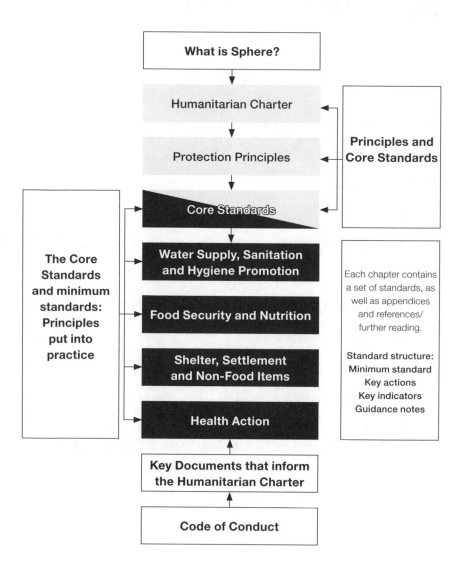

What is Sphere?

Humanitarian Charter

Protection Principles

Core Standards

Water Supply, Sanitation and Hygiene Promotion

Food Security and Nutrition

Shelter, Settlement and Non-Food Items

Health Action

Principles and Core Standards

The Core Standards and minimum standards: Principles put into practice

Each chapter contains a set of standards, as well as appendices and references/ further reading.

Standard structure:
Minimum standard
Key actions
Key indicators
Guidance notes

Key Documents that inform the Humanitarian Charter

Code of Conduct

What is Sphere?

What is Sphere?

The Sphere Project and its Handbook are well known for introducing considerations of quality and accountability to humanitarian response. But what are the origins of the Sphere Project? What are its philosophy and approach? How and why was this Handbook conceived? What is its place in the wider realm of humanitarian action? And who should use it and when? This chapter strives to provide some answers to these key questions. Furthermore, it details the Handbook structure and explains how to use it and how you or your organisation can conform to the Sphere minimum standards.

The Sphere Project philosophy: The right to life with dignity

The Sphere Project – or 'Sphere' – was initiated in 1997 by a group of humanitarian non-governmental organisations (NGOs) and the International Red Cross and Red Crescent Movement. Their aim was to improve the quality of their actions during disaster response and to be held accountable for them. They based Sphere's philosophy on **two core beliefs**: first, that those affected by disaster or conflict have a right to life with dignity and, therefore, a right to assistance; and second, that all possible steps should be taken to alleviate human suffering arising out of disaster or conflict.

Striving to support these two core beliefs, the Sphere Project framed a Humanitarian Charter and identified a set of **minimum standards** in key life-saving sectors which are now reflected in the Handbook's four technical chapters: water supply, sanitation and hygiene promotion; food security and nutrition; shelter, settlement and non-food items; and health action. The **Core Standards** are process standards and apply to all technical chapters.

The minimum standards are evidence-based and represent sector-wide consensus on best practice in humanitarian response. Key actions, key indicators and guidance notes (described in the 'How to use the standards' section below) accompany each standard, providing guidance on how to attain the standard.

The minimum standards describe conditions that must be achieved in any humanitarian response in order for disaster-affected populations to survive and recover in stable conditions and with dignity. The **inclusion of affected populations** in the consultative process lies at the heart of Sphere's philosophy. The Sphere Project, consequently, was one of the first of what are now known as the **quality and accountability** (Q&A) initiatives.

The Humanitarian Charter and the minimum standards are published together as a **Handbook**, the latest edition of which you are reading now. The Sphere Handbook is designed for planning, implementation, monitoring and evaluation during humanitarian response. It is also an effective advocacy tool when negotiating for humanitarian space and for the provision of resources with authorities. Furthermore, it is useful for disaster preparedness activities and contingency planning, with donors increasingly including the standards in their reporting requirements.

Because it is not owned by any one organisation, the Handbook enjoys broad acceptance by the humanitarian sector as a whole. It has become one of the most widely known and internationally recognised sets of standards for humanitarian response and is used as an inter-agency communication and coordination tool.

First published in 2000, the Handbook was revised in 2003 and again in 2009–2010. During each revision process, sector-wide consultations were conducted, involving a wide range of agencies, organisations and individuals, including governments and United Nations (UN) agencies.

The principal users of the Sphere Handbook are practitioners involved in planning, managing or implementing a humanitarian response. This includes staff and volunteers of local, national and international humanitarian agencies. In the context of fund-raising and project proposals, the minimum standards are also frequently referred to.

Other actors, such as government and local authorities, the military or the private sector, are also encouraged to use the Sphere Handbook. It may be useful in guiding their own actions, but also in helping them to understand the standards used by the humanitarian agencies with whom they may interact.

The Handbook: A reflection of Sphere's values

The Handbook structure reflects Sphere's aim to firmly anchor humanitarian response in a rights-based and participatory approach.

Humanitarian Charter, Protection Principles and Core Standards

The Humanitarian Charter, the Protection Principles and the Core Standards articulate Sphere's rights-based and people-centred approach to humanitarian response. They focus on the importance of including the affected population and local and national authorities at all stages of the response. The Protection Principles and Core Standards are grouped together at the beginning of the Handbook so as to avoid repeating them in each technical chapter. Sphere users, including specialists in one particular technical area, must consider them as an integral part of these chapters.

The cornerstone of the Handbook is the **Humanitarian Charter** (accompanied by a descriptive list of key legal and policy documents in Annex 1 on page 356). It provides the ethical and legal backdrop to the Protection Principles, as well as to the Core Standards and minimum standards, thereby setting the stage for their correct interpretation and implementation. It is a statement of established legal rights and obligations and of shared beliefs and commitments of humanitarian agencies, all collected in a set of **common principles, rights and duties**. Founded on the principle of humanity and the humanitarian imperative, these include the right to life with dignity, the right to receive humanitarian assistance and the right to protection and security. The Charter also emphasises the importance of agency **accountability to affected communities**. The Core Standards and minimum standards are an articulation of what these principles and obligations mean in practice.

The Humanitarian Charter explains why both assistance and protection are critical pillars of humanitarian action. To further develop this protection aspect, the Handbook includes a set of **Protection Principles**, which translates several of the legal principles and rights outlined in the Charter into strategies and actions that should inform humanitarian practice from a protection perspective. Protection is a core part of humanitarian action and the Protection Principles point to the responsibility of all humanitarian agencies to ensure that their activities are concerned with the more severe threats that affected people commonly face in times of conflict or disaster.

All humanitarian agencies should ensure that their actions do not bring further harm to affected people (Protection Principle 1), that their activities benefit in particular those who are most affected and vulnerable (Protection Principle 2), that they contribute to protecting affected people from violence and other human rights abuses (Protection Principle 3) and that they help affected people recover from abuses (Protection Principle 4). The roles and responsibilities of humanitarian agencies in protection are, generally, secondary to the legal responsibility of the state or other relevant authorities. Protection often involves reminding these authorities of their responsibilities.

The **Core Standards** are the first set of minimum standards and inform all others. They describe how the processes and approaches taken during a humanitarian response are fundamental to an effective response. A focus on the capacity and active participation of those affected by disaster or conflict, a comprehensive analysis and understanding of needs and context, effective coordination among agencies, a commitment to continually improving performance, and appropriately skilled and supported aid workers are all essential in order to attain the technical standards.

The Protection Principles and Core Standards are grouped together at the beginning of the Handbook so as to avoid repeating them in each technical chapter. They underpin all humanitarian activity and **must be used in conjunction with the technical chapters**. They are critical to achieving the technical standards in a spirit of quality and accountability to the affected populations.

The Core Standards and the minimum standards in four technical chapters

The Core Standards and minimum standards cover approaches to programming and four sets of life-saving activities: water supply, sanitation and hygiene promotion; food security and nutrition; shelter, settlement and non-food items; and health action.

How to use the standards

The Core Standards and minimum standards follow a specific format. They begin with a general and universal statement – the minimum standard – followed by a series of key actions, key indicators and guidance notes.

First, the **minimum standard** is stated. Each standard is derived from the principle that disaster-affected populations have the right to life with dignity. They are qualitative in nature and specify the minimum levels to be attained in humanitarian response. Their scope is universal and applicable in any disaster situation. They are, therefore, formulated in general terms.

Next, practical **key actions** are suggested, to attain the minimum standard. Some actions may not be applicable in all contexts, and it is up to the practitioner to select the relevant actions and devise alternative actions that will result in the standard being met.

Then, a set of **key indicators** serves as 'signals' that show whether a standard has been attained. They provide a way of measuring and communicating the processes and results of key actions. The key indicators relate to the minimum standard, not to the key action.

Finally, **guidance notes** include context-specific points to consider when aiming at reaching the key actions and key indicators. They provide guidance on tackling practical difficulties, benchmarks or advice on priority and cross-cutting themes. They may also include critical issues relating to the standards, actions or indicators and describe dilemmas, controversies or gaps in current knowledge. They do **not** provide guidance as to **how to** implement a specific activity.

Brief **introductions to each chapter** set out the major relevant issues. The technical minimum standards chapters further contain appendices including, for example, assessment checklists, formulas, tables and examples of report forms. Each chapter ends with references and suggestions for further reading. A detailed glossary for each of the Handbook chapters is available on the Sphere website (www.sphereproject.org).

All the chapters are interconnected. Frequently, standards described in one sector need to be addressed in conjunction with standards described in others. As a result, the Handbook contains numerous cross-references.

Conforming with the Sphere minimum standards

The Sphere Handbook is a voluntary code and a self-regulatory tool for quality and accountability, and the Sphere Project does not operate any compliance mechanism. There is no such thing as 'signing up' to Sphere, a Sphere membership or any process of accreditation. The Sphere Project has consciously opted for the Handbook not to be prescriptive or compliance-oriented, in order to encourage the broadest possible ownership of the Handbook.

The Handbook does not offer practical guidance on how to provide certain services (the key actions suggest activities to reach a standard without specifying how to do that). Rather, it explains **what needs to be in place** in order to ensure a life with dignity for the affected population. It is, therefore, up to each implementing agency to choose a system to ensure conformance with the Sphere minimum standards. Some agencies have used purely internal mechanisms, while others have opted for peer review. Some agency networks have used Sphere to evaluate their collective response in particular emergencies.

Conforming with Sphere does not mean meeting all the standards and indicators. The degree to which agencies can meet standards will depend on a range of factors, some of which are outside their control. Sometimes difficulties of access to the affected population, lack of cooperation from the authorities or severe insecurity make standards impossible to meet.

If the general living conditions of an affected population were already significantly below the minimum standards before the disaster, agencies may have insufficient resources to meet the standards. In such situations, providing basic facilities for the entire affected population may be more important than reaching the minimum standards for only a proportion.

Sometimes the minimum standards may exceed everyday living conditions for the surrounding population. Adhering to the standards for disaster-affected populations remains essential. But such situations may also indicate the need for action in support of the surrounding population and for dialogue with community leaders. What is appropriate and feasible will depend on the context.

In cases where the standards cannot be met, humanitarian agencies should:

- describe in their reports (assessment, evaluation, etc.) the gap between the relevant Sphere indicators and the ones reached in practice
- explain the reasons for this and what needs to be changed
- assess the negative implications for the affected population
- take appropriate mitigating actions to minimise the harm caused by these implications.

By committing to the above steps, agencies demonstrate that they are conforming with Sphere's philosophy and its minimum standards even if they are unable to meet them as set out in the Handbook.

The place of Sphere within humanitarian action

The Sphere Handbook is designed for use during humanitarian response in a range of situations including natural disasters, conflict, slow- and rapid-onset events, rural and urban environments, and complex political emergencies in all countries. The term 'disaster' encompasses these situations, and where appropriate, the term 'conflict' is used. 'Population' refers to individuals, families, communities and broader groups. Consequently, we commonly use 'disaster-affected population' throughout the Handbook.

When to use this Handbook

Focusing on the period of **humanitarian response**, the Sphere minimum standards cover activities which meet the urgent survival needs of disaster-affected populations. This phase can range from a few days or weeks to many months and even years, particularly in contexts involving protracted insecurity and displacement. It is, therefore, impossible to assign a particular timeframe to the usefulness of the Sphere standards.

The Handbook does, however, have a specific place within the broader realm of **humanitarian action**, which goes beyond providing immediate relief and covers a spectrum of activities that starts with disaster preparedness, then includes humanitarian response, and finally extends into early recovery. As a reference tool, the Handbook is useful in both the disaster preparedness and the early recovery phases which conceptually 'frame' humanitarian response but in reality need to be considered simultaneously.

Disaster preparedness requires that actors – governments, humanitarian agencies, local civil society organisations, communities and individuals – have the capacities, relationships and knowledge to prepare for and respond effectively to disaster or conflict. Before and during a response, they should start taking actions that will improve preparedness and reduce risk for the future. They should be prepared, at least, to meet the Sphere minimum standards during a future disaster.

Early recovery is the process following relief and leading into long-term recovery and is most effective if anticipated and facilitated from the very outset of a humanitarian response. Recognising the importance of early recovery, the Handbook makes reference to it throughout and as appropriate.

Developments in the humanitarian sector and their implications for Sphere

A number of developments in the humanitarian sector and other relevant areas have arisen over the past few years, encompassing changes in the nature of disasters and conflicts, as well as of humanitarian work. The developments considered during the Handbook revision process include:

- a growing conceptual and operational focus on local and national responses with the awareness that affected populations must be consulted and the response capacities of the crisis-affected state and national agencies and institutions must be reinforced
- more proactive accountability of humanitarian action, in particular accountability to affected populations, but also more proactive coordination, including within the humanitarian reform process (cluster approach), under the auspices of the Inter-Agency Standing Committee (IASC)
- an increased focus on protection issues and responses
- increasing awareness of potentially large-scale forced migration due to climate change-induced disasters and an awareness that environmental degradation increases vulnerability
- the recognition that poor urban populations are growing rapidly and that they have specific vulnerabilities, in particular related to the money economy, social cohesion and physical space

- new approaches to aid, such as cash and voucher transfers and local purchases replacing in-kind shipments of humanitarian assistance
- an increased recognition of disaster risk reduction as both a sector and an approach
- an increased involvement of the military in humanitarian response, a set of actors not primarily driven by the humanitarian imperative, requiring the development of specific guidelines and coordination strategies for humanitarian civil–military dialogue
- an increased involvement of the private sector in humanitarian response requiring similar guidelines and strategies as the civil–military dialogue.

The Sphere Project includes these developments in the Handbook as appropriate – in particular the **emerging issues** of cash transfers, early recovery and civil–military relations.

Understanding the context during humanitarian response

Effective humanitarian response must be based on a comprehensive, contextualised diagnosis (assessment, monitoring and evaluation), in order to **analyse people's needs, vulnerabilities and capacities in each context.**

The Handbook is essentially designed as a tool to recognise different contexts and to adapt response programmes accordingly: it guides practitioners in their reflections around reaching a universally applicable standard in a concrete situation or context, with particular focus on specific vulnerabilities and capacities.

Not all individuals within a disaster-affected population have equal control of resources and power. People are, therefore, impacted differently on the basis of their ethnic origin, religious or political affiliation. Displacement may make vulnerable certain people who in normal situations would not have been at risk. Women, children, older people, persons with disabilities or people living with HIV may be denied vital assistance or the opportunity to be heard due to physical, cultural and/or social barriers. Experience has shown that treating these people as a long list of 'vulnerable groups' can lead to fragmented and ineffective interventions, which ignore overlapping vulnerabilities and the changing nature of vulnerabilities over time, even during one specific crisis.

Relief and recovery efforts must also consider future hazards and vulnerabilities in order to build communities back safer and promote stronger resilience. In many parts of the world, climate change is already beginning to have an impact on patterns of risk; traditional knowledge of hazards, vulnerabilities and capacities needs to be combined with assessments of future climate risks.

In order to do justice to each unique disaster situation and the particular vulnerabilities and capabilities of the affected population, the Handbook addresses a number of **cross-cutting themes**. The themes relating to **children, gender, older people, HIV and AIDS, persons with disabilities,** and **psychosocial support** deal with individual and subgroup vulnerabilities. **Disaster risk reduction** (including **climate change**) and **environment** address vulnerability issues affecting the entire affected population. At the end of this introduction, each theme is described in more detail.

Links with other humanitarian standards

In order to maintain the Sphere Handbook as a single volume of manageable size, the focus remains on the four primary sectors of humanitarian response. Many related sectors which are part of an effective humanitarian response have developed their own standards. A number of them are included in a series of **Sphere companion standards**, published as separate volumes but developed with the same rigor and process of consultation as Sphere – the Inter-Agency Network for Education in Emergencies (INEE) Minimum Standards for Education: Preparedness, Response, Recovery; the Small Enterprise Education and Promotion (SEEP) Network's Minimum Standards for Economic Recovery after Crisis; and the Livestock Emergency Guidelines and Standards (LEGS).

Education in emergencies can be both life-sustaining and life-saving. Provided in safe spaces, it offers a sense of normalcy, psychosocial support and protection against exploitation and harm. It can also be used to communicate messages about safety, life skills and vital health and hygiene information. The INEE Minimum Standards for Education: Preparedness, Response, Recovery were first published in 2004 and updated in 2010, becoming companion standards to Sphere in 2008. They present a framework to ensure critical linkages between education and health, water, sanitation and hygiene, nutrition, shelter and protection and to enhance the safety, quality and accountability of educational preparedness and response.

Small enterprise development and livestock are covered by the SEEP Network's Minimum Standards for Economic Recovery after Crisis and the Livestock Emergency Guidelines and Standards respectively. It is anticipated that these two sets of minimum standards will become Sphere companion standards in 2011.

Used together with this Handbook, the companion standards will improve the quality of assistance provided to people affected by disaster or conflict. Relevant guidance from the INEE, SEEP and LEGS standards has been integrated and is cross-referenced throughout this Handbook.

Agencies, coalitions and networks have established other standards and codes to meet particular operational needs, such as specific agencies' mandates, technical expertise or a perceived gap in guidance. Where relevant, these other standards are referenced in the technical chapters of this Handbook.

The Sphere Project is part of a group of **quality and accountability initiatives** within the sector, having a close working relationship with the Emergency Capacity Building (ECB) Project, which has developed the Good Enough Guide, and the Humanitarian Accountability Partnership (HAP), which deals with compliance issues through its Humanitarian Accountability and Quality Management Standard. Other Q&A initiatives with which Sphere regularly engages are People In Aid, Groupe URD (Urgence, Réhabilitation, Développement), Coordination Sud and the Active Learning Network for Accountability and Performance in Humanitarian Action (ALNAP).

Beyond the Handbook

The Sphere Project's primary and most used tool is this Handbook. It is also available in electronic format on the Sphere website (www.sphereproject.org), where you can get the latest news and updates about the available versions and other resources.

The Handbook exists in numerous languages and is accompanied by various training and promotional materials. These are often adapted to local contexts on the basis of the experience of practitioners. This illustrates the vibrancy of the Sphere community of practice, a sometimes informal, loosely connected and ever-expanding network of practitioners that keep the spirit of Sphere alive. The Sphere Project is founded on the need to help improve the humanitarian response to meet the rights and needs of disaster- or conflict-affected people and to be accountable to them. The Sphere Project has made great progress since its inception, but no Handbook alone can achieve this – only you can.

Outline of the cross-cutting themes

The cross-cutting themes in this Handbook focus on particular areas of concern in disaster response and address individual, group or general vulnerability issues. In this section, each theme is described in some detail.

Children: Special measures must be taken to ensure all children are protected from harm and given equitable access to basic services. As children often form the larger part of an affected population, it is crucial that their views and experiences are not only elicited during emergency assessments and planning but that they also influence humanitarian service delivery and its monitoring and evaluation. Children and young people are prone to the harmful impact of vulnerability in certain situations, such as malnutrition, exploitation, abduction and recruitment into armed groups and fighting forces, sexual violence and lack of opportunity to participate in decision-making. The Convention on the Rights of the Child states that a child is considered to be an individual below the age of 18 years. This definition can differ depending on cultural and social contexts. A thorough analysis of how an affected population defines children must be undertaken, to ensure that no child or young person is excluded from humanitarian assistance.

Disaster risk reduction: This is defined as the concept and practice of reducing disaster risks through systematic efforts to analyse and manage the causal factors of disasters, including through reduced exposure to hazards, lessened vulnerability of people and property, wise management of land and the environment, and improved preparedness for adverse events. Such adverse events include natural disasters like storms, floods, droughts and sea-level rise. As they appear to become increasingly variable and severe, these phenomena are increasingly attributed to global **climate change**.

Environment: The environment is understood as the physical, chemical and biological elements and processes that affect disaster-affected and local populations' lives and livelihoods. It provides the natural resources that sustain individuals and contributes to quality of life. It needs protection and management if essential functions are to be maintained. The minimum standards address the need to prevent over-exploitation, pollution and degradation of environmental conditions and aim to secure the life-supporting functions of the environment, reduce risk and vulnerability and seek to introduce mechanisms that foster adaptability of natural systems for self-recovery.

Gender: Gender refers to the fact that people experience a situation differently according to their gender. **Sex** refers to biological attributes of women and men. It is natural, determined by birth and, therefore, generally unchanging and universal.

The equal rights of women and men are explicit in the human rights documents that form the basis of the Humanitarian Charter. Women and men have the same entitlement to humanitarian assistance and protection, to respect for their human dignity, to acknowledgement of their equal human capacities including the capacity to make choices, to the same opportunities to act on those choices and to the same level of power to shape the outcome of their actions. Humanitarian responses are more effective when they are based on an understanding of the different needs, vulnerabilities, interests, capacities and coping strategies of women and men, girls and boys of all ages and the differing impacts of disaster or conflict upon them. The understanding of these differences, as well as inequalities in women's and men's roles and workloads, access to and control over resources, decision-making power and opportunities for skills development, is achieved through gender analysis. Gender cuts across other cross-cutting themes. The humanitarian aims of proportionality and impartiality mean that attention must be paid to achieving fairness between women and men and ensuring equality of outcome. Historically, attention to gender relations has been driven by the need to address women's and girls' needs and circumstances, as women and girls are typically more disadvantaged than men and boys. However, increasingly, the humanitarian community recognises the need to understand what men and boys face in crisis situations.

HIV and AIDS: Knowing the HIV prevalence in a specific humanitarian context is important to understand vulnerabilities and risks and to plan an effective response. In addition to the most at-risk populations (i.e. men who have sex with men, intravenous drug users and sex workers), who often need to receive specific measures to protect themselves against neglect, discrimination and violence, some contexts may have other vulnerable groups such as refugees, migrants, youth and single mothers. Mass displacement may lead to increased HIV vulnerabilities and risks due to separation of family members and breakdown of community cohesion and of social and sexual norms regulating behaviour. Women and children may be exploited by armed groups and be particularly vulnerable to HIV due to sexual violence and exploitation. During humanitarian emergencies, people may no longer have access to HIV interventions such as prevention programmes and the disruption of anti-retroviral therapy (ART), tuberculosis (TB) treatment and prevention and treatment for other opportunistic infections may occur.

People living with HIV (PLHIV) often suffer from discrimination and stigma and, therefore, confidentiality must be strictly adhered to and protection made available when needed. The sector activities in this Handbook should provide appropriate HIV interventions according to prevalence and context, and not increase people's vulnerabilities and risks to HIV.

Older people: Older men and women are those aged over 60 years, according to the UN, but a definition of 'older' can vary in different contexts. Older people are often among the poorest in developing countries and comprise a large and growing proportion of the most vulnerable in disaster- or conflict-affected populations (for example, the over-80s are the fastest-growing age group in the world) and yet they are often neglected in disaster or conflict management. Isolation and physical weakness are significant factors exacerbating vulnerability in older people in disasters or conflict, along with disruption to livelihood strategies and to family and community support structures, chronic health and mobility problems, and declining mental health. Special efforts must be made to identify and reach housebound older people and households headed by older people. Older people also have key contributions to make in survival and rehabilitation. They play vital roles as carers of children, resource managers and income generators, have knowledge and experience of community coping strategies and help to preserve cultural and social identities.

Persons with disabilities: The World Health Organization (WHO) estimates that between 7 and 10 per cent of the world's population – including children and older people – live with disabilities. Disasters and conflict can cause increased incidence of impairment and subsequent disability. The UN Convention on the Rights of Persons with Disabilities (CRPD) defines disability as an evolving concept that results from the interaction between persons with impairments (which may be physical, sensory, intellectual or psychosocial) and the attitudinal and environmental barriers that hinder their full and effective participation in society on an equal basis with others. It is, therefore, the presence of these barriers that prevent persons with disabilities from fully and meaningfully participating in, or benefiting from, mainstream humanitarian assistance programmes. The new CRPD makes specific reference to the safety and protection of persons with disabilities in conflict and emergency situations (Article 11).

Persons with disabilities face disproportionate risks in disaster situations and are often excluded from relief and rehabilitation processes. Such exclusion makes it more difficult to effectively use and participate in standard disaster support services. Importantly, persons with disabilities are a diverse population including children and older people, whose needs cannot be addressed in a 'one size fits all' approach. Humanitarian responses, therefore, must take into consideration the particular abilities, skills, resources and knowledge of individuals with different types and degrees of impairments. It is also important to remember that persons with disabilities have the same basic needs as everyone else in their communities. In addition, some may also have specific needs, such as replacement of aids or appliances, and access to rehabilitation services. Furthermore, any measures targeting persons with disabilities must not lead to their separation from their family and community networks. Finally, if the rights of persons with disabilities are not taken into consideration in humanitarian responses, a huge opportunity is lost to rebuild communities for all people. It is essential, therefore, to include persons with disabilities in all aspects of relief and recovery. This requires both mainstreamed and targeted responses.

Psychosocial support: Some of the greatest sources of vulnerability and suffering in disasters arise from the complex emotional, social, physical and spiritual effects of disasters. Many of these reactions are normal and can be overcome with time. It is essential to organise locally appropriate mental health and psychosocial supports that promote self-help, coping and resilience among affected people. Humanitarian action is strengthened if at the earliest appropriate moment, affected people are engaged in guiding and implementing the disaster response. In each humanitarian sector, the manner in which aid is administered has a psychosocial impact that may either support or cause harm to affected people. Aid should be delivered in a compassionate manner that promotes dignity, enables self-efficacy through meaningful participation, respects the importance of religious and cultural practices and strengthens the ability of affected people to support holistic well-being.

References

UN Convention on the Rights of the Child: www2.ohchr.org/english/law/crc.htm

UN Convention on the Rights of Persons with Disabilities: www.un.org/disabilities/

WHO on disabilities: www.who.int/disabilities/en/

The
Humanitarian
Charter

The Humanitarian Charter provides the ethical and legal backdrop to the Protection Principles and the Core Standards and minimum standards that follow in the Handbook. It is in part a statement of established legal rights and obligations; in part a statement of shared belief.

In terms of legal rights and obligations, it summarises the core legal principles that have most bearing on the welfare of those affected by disaster or conflict. With regard to shared belief, it attempts to capture a consensus among humanitarian agencies as to the principles which should govern the response to disaster or conflict, including the roles and responsibilities of the various actors involved.

It forms the basis of a commitment by humanitarian agencies that endorse Sphere and an invitation to all those who engage in humanitarian action to adopt the same principles.

The Humanitarian Charter

Our beliefs

1. The Humanitarian Charter expresses our shared conviction as humanitarian agencies that all people affected by disaster or conflict have a right to receive protection and assistance to ensure the basic conditions for life with dignity. We believe that the principles described in this Humanitarian Charter are universal, applying to all those affected by disaster or conflict wherever they may be, and to all those who seek to assist them or provide for their security. These principles are reflected in international law, but derive their force ultimately from the fundamental moral principle of **humanity**: that all human beings are born free and equal in dignity and rights. Based on this principle, we affirm the primacy of the **humanitarian imperative**: that action should be taken to prevent or alleviate human suffering arising out of disaster or conflict, and that nothing should override this principle.

As local, national and international humanitarian agencies, we commit to promoting and adhering to the principles in this Charter and to meeting minimum standards in our efforts to assist and protect those affected. We invite all those who engage in humanitarian activities, including governmental and private sector actors, to endorse the common principles, rights and duties set out below as a statement of shared humanitarian belief.

Our role

2. We acknowledge that it is firstly through their own efforts, and through the support of community and local institutions, that the basic needs of people

affected by disaster or conflict are met. We recognise the primary role and responsibility of the affected state to provide timely assistance to those affected, to ensure people's protection and security and to provide support for their recovery. We believe that a combination of official and voluntary action is crucial to effective prevention and response, and in this regard National Societies of the Red Cross and Red Crescent Movement and other civil society actors have an essential role to play in supporting public authorities. Where national capacity is insufficient, we affirm the role of the wider international community, including governmental donors and regional organisations, in assisting states to fulfil their responsibilities. We recognise and support the special roles played by the mandated agencies of the United Nations and the International Committee of the Red Cross.

3. As humanitarian agencies, we interpret our role in relation to the needs and capacities of affected populations and the responsibilities of their governments or controlling powers. Our role in providing assistance reflects the reality that those with primary responsibility are not always fully able to perform this role themselves, or may be unwilling to do so. As far as possible, consistent with meeting the humanitarian imperative and other principles set out in this Charter, we will support the efforts of the relevant authorities to protect and assist those affected. We call upon all state and non-state actors to respect the impartial, independent and non-partisan role of humanitarian agencies and to facilitate their work by removing unnecessary legal and practical barriers, providing for their safety and allowing them timely and consistent access to affected populations.

Common principles, rights and duties

4. We offer our services as humanitarian agencies on the basis of the principle of humanity and the humanitarian imperative, recognising the rights of all people affected by disaster or conflict – women and men, boys and girls. These include the rights to protection and assistance reflected in the provisions of international humanitarian law, human rights and refugee law. For the purposes of this Charter, we summarise these rights as follows:

▶ *the right to life with dignity*

▶ *the right to receive humanitarian assistance*

▶ *the right to protection and security.*

While these rights are not formulated in such terms in international law, they encapsulate a range of established legal rights and give fuller substance to the humanitarian imperative.

right to life with dignity is reflected in the provisions of international law, and specifically the human rights measures concerning the right to life, to an adequate standard of living and to freedom from torture or cruel, inhuman or degrading treatment or punishment. The right to life entails the duty to preserve life where it is threatened. Implicit in this is the duty not to withhold or frustrate the provision of life-saving assistance. Dignity entails more than physical well-being; it demands respect for the whole person, including the values and beliefs of individuals and affected communities, and respect for their human rights, including liberty, freedom of conscience and religious observance.

6. The **right to receive humanitarian assistance** is a necessary element of the right to life with dignity. This encompasses the right to an adequate standard of living, including adequate food, water, clothing, shelter and the requirements for good health, which are expressly guaranteed in international law. The Sphere Core Standards and minimum standards reflect these rights and give practical expression to them, specifically in relation to the provision of assistance to those affected by disaster or conflict. Where the state or non-state actors are not providing such assistance themselves, we believe they must allow others to help do so. Any such assistance must be provided according to the principle of **impartiality**, which requires that it be provided solely on the basis of need and in proportion to need. This reflects the wider principle of **non-discrimination**: that no one should be discriminated against on any grounds of status, including age, gender, race, colour, ethnicity, sexual orientation, language, religion, disability, health status, political or other opinion, national or social origin.

7. The **right to protection and security** is rooted in the provisions of international law, in resolutions of the United Nations and other intergovernmental organisations, and in the sovereign responsibility of states to protect all those within their jurisdiction. The safety and security of people in situations of disaster or conflict are of particular humanitarian concern, including the protection of refugees and internally displaced persons. As the law recognises, some people may be particularly vulnerable to abuse and adverse discrimination due to their status such as age, gender or race, and may require special measures of protection and assistance. To the extent that a state lacks the capacity to protect people in these circumstances, we believe it must seek international assistance to do so.

The law relating to the protection of civilians and displaced people demands particular attention here:

(i) During **armed conflict** as defined in international humanitarian law, specific legal provision is made for protection and assistance to be given to those not engaged in the conflict. In particular, the 1949 Geneva Conventions and the Additional Protocols of 1977 impose obligations on the parties

to both international and non-international armed conflicts. We
general immunity of the civilian population from attack and repr
particular the importance of the principle of **distinction** betw
and combatants, and between civilian objects and military objectives; the
principles of **proportionality** in the use of force and **precaution** in attack;
the duty to refrain from the use of weapons which are indiscriminate or
which, by their nature, cause superfluous injury or unnecessary suffering;
and the duty to permit impartial relief to be provided. Much of the avoidable suffering caused to civilians in armed conflicts stems from a failure to
observe these basic principles.

(ii) The **right to seek asylum or sanctuary** remains vital to the protection of
those facing persecution or violence. Those affected by disaster or conflict
are often forced to flee their homes in search of security and the means of
subsistence. The provisions of the 1951 Convention Relating to the Status
of Refugees (as amended) and other international and regional treaties
provide fundamental safeguards for those unable to secure protection from
the state of their nationality or residence who are forced to seek safety in
another country. Chief among these is the principle of **non-refoulement**:
the principle that no one shall be sent back to a country where their life,
freedom or physical security would be threatened or where they are likely
to face torture or other cruel, inhuman or degrading treatment or punishment. The same principle applies by extension to internally displaced
persons, as reflected in international human rights law and elaborated in
the 1998 Guiding Principles on Internal Displacement and related regional
and national law.

Our commitment

8. We offer our services in the belief that the affected population is at the centre
of humanitarian action, and recognise that their active participation is essential to
providing assistance in ways that best meet their needs, including those of vulnerable and socially excluded people. We will endeavour to support local efforts to
prevent, prepare for and respond to disaster, and to the effects of conflict, and to
reinforce the capacities of local actors at all levels.

9. We are aware that attempts to provide humanitarian assistance may sometimes have unintended adverse effects. In collaboration with affected communities and authorities, we aim to minimise any negative effects of humanitarian
action on the local community or on the environment. With respect to armed
conflict, we recognise that the way in which humanitarian assistance is provided
may potentially render civilians more vulnerable to attack, or may on occasion
bring unintended advantage to one or more of the parties to the conflict. We are

committed to minimising any such adverse effects, in so far as this is consistent with the principles outlined above.

10. We will act in accordance with the principles of humanitarian action set out in this Charter and with the specific guidance in the Code of Conduct for the International Red Cross and Red Crescent Movement and Non-Governmental Organisations (NGOs) in Disaster Relief (1994).

11. The Sphere Core Standards and minimum standards give practical substance to the common principles in this Charter, based on agencies' understanding of the basic minimum requirements for life with dignity and their experience of providing humanitarian assistance. Though the achievement of the standards depends on a range of factors, many of which may be beyond our control, we commit ourselves to attempting consistently to achieve them and we expect to be held to account accordingly. We invite all parties, including affected and donor governments, international organisations, private and non-state actors, to adopt the Sphere Core Standards and minimum standards as accepted norms.

12. By adhering to the Core Standards and minimum standards, we commit to making every effort to ensure that people affected by disasters or conflict have access to at least the minimum requirements for life with dignity and security, including adequate water, sanitation, food, nutrition, shelter and healthcare. To this end, we will continue to advocate that states and other parties meet their moral and legal obligations towards affected populations. For our part, we undertake to make our responses more effective, appropriate and accountable through sound assessment and monitoring of the evolving local context; through transparency of information and decision-making; and through more effective coordination and collaboration with other relevant actors at all levels, as detailed in the Core Standards and minimum standards. In particular, we commit to working in partnership with affected populations, emphasising their active participation in the response. We acknowledge that our fundamental accountability must be to those we seek to assist.

Protection Principles

How to use this chapter

Humanitarian action consists of two main pillars: protection and assistance. Much of this Handbook, in particular the technical chapters, falls within the remit of assistance, while this chapter focuses on protection. Building on the Humanitarian Charter, it addresses the question of how humanitarian agencies can contribute to the protection of those faced with the threat of violence or coercion. More generally, it is concerned with the role of agencies in ensuring respect for and fulfilment of the rights articulated in the Charter, including access to assistance.

The chapter is divided into two sections:

▪ An introduction, which sets out the general responsibilities of all who are involved in humanitarian response to help protect the affected population and ensure respect for their rights.

▪ Four Protection Principles, which underpin all humanitarian action and encompass the basic elements of protection in the context of humanitarian response. They are accompanied by guidance notes, which further elaborate the role of humanitarian agencies in protection. A reference section includes other standards and materials relating to more specialised areas of protection.

Contents

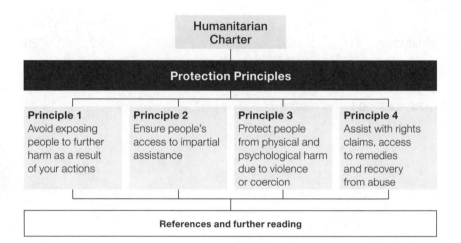

Introduction

Protection and humanitarian response

Protection is concerned with the safety, dignity and rights of people affected by disaster or armed conflict. The Humanitarian Charter summarises some of the most fundamental rights involved in humanitarian response. This chapter is concerned with the way these rights should inform humanitarian practice from a protection perspective and, specifically, the way agencies can avoid exposing the affected population to further harm and how they can help people to achieve greater safety and security.

Core humanitarian protection concerns in this context are freedom from violence and from coercion of various kinds and freedom from deliberate deprivation of the means of survival with dignity.

These concerns give rise to **four basic Protection Principles** that inform all humanitarian action:

1. Avoid exposing people to further harm as a result of your actions
2. Ensure people's access to impartial assistance – in proportion to need and without discrimination
3. Protect people from physical and psychological harm arising from violence and coercion
4. Assist people to claim their rights, access available remedies and recover from the effects of abuse.

In the context of humanitarian response, these four Principles reflect the more severe threats that people commonly face in times of conflict or disaster. The guidance notes address the related responsibilities and options for agencies, as well as particular protection needs.

The four Protection Principles follow from the summary of rights set out in the Humanitarian Charter: the right to life with dignity, the right to humanitarian assistance and the right to protection and security.

;tanding the Protection Principles

ı ıe following is a short guide to interpreting the Protection Principles:

Principle 1 (avoid causing harm) addresses those protection concerns that may be caused or exacerbated by humanitarian response. As stated in the Charter, those involved in humanitarian response must do all they reasonably can to avoid exposing people affected by disaster or armed conflict to further harm, for example by building settlements for displaced people in unsafe areas.

Principle 2 (ensure access to impartial assistance) sets out the responsibility to ensure that humanitarian assistance is available to all those in need, particularly those who are most vulnerable or who face exclusion on political or other grounds. The denial of access to necessary assistance is a major protection concern. This may include (but is not limited to) denial of secure access for humanitarian agencies to provide assistance.

Principle 3 (protect people from violence) is concerned with protection from violence and protection from being forced or induced to act against one's will, e.g. to take up arms, to be forcibly removed from a place or to be prevented from moving, or to be subjected to degrading treatment or punishment. It is concerned with preventing or mitigating physical and psychological harm, including the spread of fear and deliberate creation of terror or panic.

Principle 4 (assist with rights claims, access to remedies and recovery from abuse) refers to the role of humanitarian agencies in helping affected people claim their entitlements and access remedies such as legal redress, compensation or restitution of property. It is also concerned with helping people overcome the effects of rape and, more generally, with helping people recover from the effects of abuse – physical and psychological, social and economic.

Together with the guidance notes, the four Protection Principles describe what humanitarian agencies can and should do to help protect the disaster-affected population. But it is essential to note that the roles and responsibilities of agencies in this context are generally secondary ones. As the Charter states, such roles must be seen in relation to the primary duty of the state or other relevant authorities, e.g. parties to a conflict who control or occupy territory. Such authorities hold formal, legal responsibility for the welfare of people within their territory or control and, more generally, for the safety of civilians in armed conflict.

Ultimately, it is these authorities that have the means to ensure the affected population's security through action or restraint. The key role of agencies may be to encourage and persuade them to do so, and to assist people in dealing with the consequences when the authorities fail in their responsibility.

Putting the Protection Principles into practice

In order to meet the standards of this Handbook, **all** humanitarian agencies should be guided by the Protection Principles, even if they do not have a distinct protection mandate or specialist capacity in protection.

The Principles are not 'absolute': it is recognised that circumstances may limit the extent to which agencies are able to fulfil them. In particular, aspects of Principle 3 may not lie within an agency's capacity. Nevertheless, the Principles reflect universal humanitarian concerns which should guide action at all times.

A number of humanitarian agencies have protection mandates or specific roles concerning vulnerable groups. Several of these agencies carry out protection activities as stand-alone programmes or projects, or framed within 'protection cluster' or 'protection sector' responses with dedicated resources and specialised staff. In 2011, the Global Protection Cluster includes coordination structures with focal points for the following particular areas of concern:

▶ child protection

▶ gender-based violence

▶ housing, land and property

▶ mine action

▶ rule of law and justice.

This list illustrates some of the specific areas of protection. It is not a comprehensive list and it should be recognised that there are many other specific protection concerns.

For a number of these and other protection topics, such as the protection of civilians and internally displaced persons or protection in natural disasters, specific standards and guidelines have been developed as part of initiatives other than Sphere. These are listed in the References and further reading section at the end of this chapter. This chapter is designed to complement such standards.

Different modes of protection activity

The four Protection Principles apply as much to specialist protection activity as to general humanitarian action, though the activities may be different. The protection-related activities of all humanitarian agencies can be classified broadly according to the following three modes of activity, which are inter-dependent and may be carried out simultaneously:

▶ *Preventive:* **Preventing physical threats or rights abuses** from occurring or reducing exposure or vulnerability to such threats and abuses. Preventing protection threats also includes efforts to foster an environment conducive to respect for the rights of women, men, girls and boys of all ages in accordance with international law.

▶ *Responsive:* **Stopping ongoing violations** by responding to incidents of violence and other rights abuses.

▶ *Remedial:* **Providing remedies** to ongoing or past abuses, through reparation and rehabilitation, by offering healthcare, psychosocial support, legal assistance or other services and supports, and helping the affected population to access available remedies and claim their rights.

Advocacy, whether public or private, is a common element linking these three modes of activity. The threats to the affected population arise from deliberate decisions, actions or policies and many of the related protection responses are about attempting to change such behaviours and policies. Advocacy by humanitarian agencies and others, such as human rights organisations, is central to the attempt to influence such change. There may be tensions for humanitarian agencies between 'speaking out' about abuses and the need to maintain an operational presence, and these tensions may dictate whether and how they can undertake advocacy on a given issue.

Where advocacy is pursued, its success generally depends on access to reliable evidence, stakeholder analysis and thorough context analysis. It is thus linked to the assessment standard in the Core Standards (see Core Standard 3 on page 61). As the guidance notes below make clear, any use of evidence such as witness statements that allows the source of information to be identified may be highly sensitive as it may put people at risk, and should be treated with the greatest care (see Protection Principle 1, guidance note 8 on page 35).

Protection Principles

Protection Principle 1: Avoid exposing people to further harm as a result of your actions

Those involved in humanitarian response take steps to avoid or minimise any adverse effects of their intervention, in particular the risk of exposing people to increased danger or abuse of their rights.

This Principle includes the following elements:

▶ The form of humanitarian assistance and the environment in which it is provided do not further expose people to physical hazards, violence or other rights abuse.

▶ Assistance and protection efforts do not undermine the affected population's capacity for self-protection.

▶ Humanitarian agencies manage sensitive information in a way that does not jeopardise the security of the informants or those who may be identifiable from the information.

Guidance notes

Assessing context and anticipating the consequences of humanitarian action for the safety and well-being of the disaster-affected population

1. *Avoid becoming complicit* in abuse of rights. There may be difficult judgements and choices, for example when faced with the decision whether to provide assistance to people who are detained in camps against their will. Such judgements must be made on a case-by-case basis, but they should always be reviewed over time as circumstances change.

2. *Checklist:* When analysing activities, regularly reflect on the following non-exhaustive list of questions, which could serve as a checklist, in terms of both the overall humanitarian response and specific actions:

   - What does the affected population gain by our activities?

- What might be the unintended negative consequences of our activities for people's security, and how can we avoid or minimise these consequences?
- Do the activities take into consideration possible protection threats facing the affected population? Might they undermine people's own efforts to protect themselves?
- Do the activities discriminate against any group or might they be perceived as doing so? Do the activities protect the rights of people who have historically been marginalised or discriminated against?
- In protecting and promoting the rights of such groups, what will be the impact on the relationships within and beyond the community?
- Could the activities exacerbate existing divisions in the community or between neighbouring communities?
- Could the activities inadvertently empower or strengthen the position of armed groups or other actors?
- Could the activities be subject to criminal exploitation?

3. **Consult different segments** of the affected population – or organisations in their trust – in assessing the positive and possible negative consequences of the overall response and specific activities.

4. **The form in which assistance is provided** may render people more vulnerable to attack. For example, valuable commodities like dry food rations may be subject to looting and so can put the recipients at risk of harm and deprivation. Consider providing alternative forms of assistance (e.g. provision of cooked food at kitchens or feeding centres) where this is a significant risk. Affected communities should be consulted on their preferred form of assistance.

5. **The environment in which assistance is provided** should, as far as possible, be safe for the people concerned. People in need should not be forced to travel to or through dangerous areas in order to access assistance. Where camps or other settlements are established, these should be made as safe as possible for the inhabitants and should be located away from areas that are subject to attack or other hazards.

Self-protection of affected populations

6. **Understand the means** by which people try to protect themselves, their families and communities. Support community self-help initiatives (see Protection Principle 3, guidance notes 13–14 on page 40). The ways in which humanitarian agencies intervene should not compromise people's capacity to protect themselves and others – including moving to safer areas and avoiding contact with armed groups.

7. **Subsistence needs:** Help people find safe options for meeting their subsistence needs. This might include, for example, the provision of goods such as water, firewood or other cooking fuel that helps people meet their daily needs without having to undertake hazardous and arduous journeys. This is likely to be a particular issue for older people, women, children and persons with disabilities.

Managing sensitive information

8. **Protection-related data** may be sensitive. Humanitarian agencies should have clear policies and procedures in place to guide their staff on how to respond if they become aware of, or witness, abuses and on the confidentiality of related information. Staff should be briefed on appropriate reporting of witnessed incidents or allegations.

9. **Referring sensitive information:** Consider referring information concerning abuses to appropriate actors with the relevant protection mandate. These actors may be present in other areas than where the information is found.

10. **A policy on referring sensitive information** should be in place and should include incident reports or trends analysis. It should specify how to manage sensitive information and the circumstances under which information may be referred. As far as possible, agencies should seek the consent of the individuals concerned for the use of such information. Any referral of information should be done in a way that does not put the source of information or the person(s) referred to in danger.

11. **Information on specific abuses and violations of rights** should only be collected if its intended use is clear and the detail required is defined in relation to the intended use. Such protection information should be collected by agencies with a protection mandate or which have the necessary capacity, skills, systems and protocols in place. Collecting this information is subject to the condition of informed consent and, in all cases, the individual's consent is necessary for the information to be shared with third parties.

12. **The possible reaction of the government** or other relevant authorities to the collection and use of information about abuses should be assessed. The need for the continuation of operations may have to be weighed against the need to use the information. Different humanitarian agencies may make different choices in this regard.

Protection Principle 2: Ensure people's access to impartial assistance – in proportion to need and without discrimination

People can access humanitarian assistance according to need and without adverse discrimination. Assistance is not withheld from people in need, and access for humanitarian agencies is provided as necessary to meet the Sphere standards.

This Principle includes the following elements:

▶ Ensure access for all parts of the affected population to humanitarian assistance.

▶ Any deliberate deprivation to parts of the population of the means of subsistence should always be challenged on the basis of relevant law and general humanitarian principles, as described in the Humanitarian Charter.

▶ Affected people receive support on the basis of need and are not discriminated against on other grounds.

Guidance notes

Maintaining access

1. *Where the affected population is unable to meet their basic needs* and the relevant authorities are unable to provide the necessary assistance themselves, the latter should not deny access for impartial humanitarian organisations to do so. Such denial may be in violation of international law, particularly in situations of armed conflict.

2. *Monitor access:* Carefully monitor the access of the affected population to humanitarian assistance, especially of the most vulnerable people.

3. *Access to humanitarian assistance and to freedom of movement* are closely linked (see Protection Principle 3, guidance notes 7–9 on page 39). The monitoring of access should consider obstacles, such as checkpoints, blockades or the presence of landmines. In situations of armed conflict, the parties may establish checkpoints, but these barriers should not discriminate between categories of affected people or unduly hinder people's access to humanitarian assistance. Special measures should be taken to ensure equality of access for affected people in remote or inaccessible regions.

4. *Special measures to facilitate the access of vulnerable groups* should be taken, while considering the context, social and cultural conditions and behaviours of communities. Such measures might include the construction of safe spaces for people who have been the victims of abuses, such as rape or trafficking, or putting in place means that facilitate access for persons with disabilities. Any such measures should avoid the stigmatisation of these groups (see Core Standard 3, guidance notes 5–6 on page 63).

Addressing the denial of assistance or of access to subsistence needs

5. *The right to receive humanitarian assistance:* As elaborated in the Humanitarian Charter, the affected population has the right to receive humanitarian assistance. This right is derived from a number of legal norms and rules that are part of international law. More specifically, international humanitarian law contains a number of relevant provisions on access to assistance and on the 'protection of objects indispensable to the survival of the civilian population' (1977 Additional Protocols I and II to the 1949 Geneva Conventions). Humanitarian agencies may consider promoting respect for the relevant laws (see also Protection Principle 3, guidance notes 3–4 on pages 38–39).

Ensuring non-discrimination

6. *Impartiality:* Humanitarian agencies should prioritise the affected people they wish to assist on the basis of their need alone and provide assistance in proportion to need. This is the principle of impartiality affirmed in the Code of Conduct for the International Red Cross and Red Crescent Movement and NGOs in Disaster Relief (see Annex 2 on page 368 and also the Humanitarian Charter on page 19). Humanitarian agencies should not focus uniquely on a particular group (e.g. displaced people in camps) if this focus is at the detriment of another section of the affected population.

7. *Affected people do not need to have a special legal status* in order to receive humanitarian assistance and to be protected.

Protection Principle 3: Protect people from physical and psychological harm arising from violence and coercion

People are protected from violence, from being forced or induced to act against their will and from fear of such abuse.

This Principle includes the following elements:

▶ Take all reasonable steps to ensure that the affected population is not subjected to violent attack, either by dealing with the source of the threat or by helping people to avoid the threat.

▶ Take all reasonable steps to ensure that the affected population is not subject to coercion, i.e. forced or induced to act against their will in ways that may cause them harm or violate their rights (for example the freedom of movement).

▶ Support the affected population's own efforts to stay safe, find security and restore dignity, including community self-help mechanisms.

Guidance notes

Protection from violence and coercion

1. *The primary responsibility to protect people* from threats to their lives and safety rests with governments and other relevant authorities (see the Humanitarian Charter on page 19). In times of armed conflict, the parties engaged in conflict must protect the civilian population and those who have laid down their arms. In analysing the context in terms of the risks and threats for the population, humanitarian agencies should establish who has the legal responsibility and/or the actual capacity to provide protection.

2. *Help minimise other threats:* This includes providing assistance in such a way as to make people more secure, facilitating people's own efforts to stay safe or taking steps (though advocacy or otherwise) to reduce people's exposure to risk.

3. *Monitoring and reporting:* Humanitarian agencies should consider their responsibility to monitor and report grave violations of rights. They should also consider advocating for the rights of affected populations with relevant authorities and actors by reminding them of their obligations. They may use different modes of action including diplomacy, lobbying and public advocacy, keeping in mind the guidance on managing sensitive information (see Protection Principle 1 on page 33).

4. ***During armed conflict,*** humanitarian agencies should consider monitoring the institutions that are specifically protected under international humanitarian law, such as schools and hospitals, and reporting any attacks on them. Agencies should also make efforts to reduce the risks and threats of abductions or forced recruitment that may happen in these locations.

5. ***Where explosives pose a threat to the affected population,*** humanitarian agencies should coordinate with the relevant government authorities and specialised agencies on the removal of landmines and unexploded ordnance. This threat may be particularly present in situations where populations are returning to their home areas following an armed conflict.

6. ***Political, law enforcement and military actors*** play significant roles in protecting people from abuses and violations. Ultimately, it is in the political realm where solutions can be found to the underlying problems that are often at the heart of protection concerns. Security and law enforcement agencies, for example the police and military forces, including peacekeeping forces, can and should play an important role in ensuring the physical security of people at risk. Agencies can alert the relevant actors to ongoing violations. Such interventions with military contingents, their commanding officers or the authorities under whose control these forces operate, may be an essential step in stopping violations by military forces.

Freedom of movement

7. ***People should not be forced to stay*** in, or go to, a place that is not of their choice (such as a camp) nor should any other unreasonable restrictions be placed on their movement. Restrictions to freedom of movement and choice of residence should only be made if there are serious security or health reasons and should be proportional to the aim. At all times, people affected by conflict or disaster have the right to seek asylum.

8. ***Evacuations:*** Humanitarian agencies should only be involved in evacuations as exceptional measures in extreme circumstances, where there is no other way of providing urgent assistance or protection in the face of severe threats to life, security and health.

9. ***Incentives to remain in a dangerous place*** should not be provided to the affected population nor should their return or resettlement be promoted when they do not have full access to all information on the conditions in those areas.

Particular vulnerabilities to violence and coercion

10. ***Vulnerable people:*** Consideration should be given to individual, social and contextual factors in order to identify those most susceptible to certain risks

and threats. Special measures may be needed for those facing particular risks, including women, children, people who have been forcibly displaced, older people, persons with disabilities and religious or ethnic minority groups.

11. *Safe environments for children:* Agencies should provide children with access to safe environments. Families and communities should receive support in their efforts to keep children safe and secure.

12. *Children, especially when separated from their families* or not accompanied by an adult, can be more easily abused or exploited during disasters or conflict. Agencies should take all reasonable steps to prevent children from being recruited into armed forces and, if they are associated with armed forces, work on their immediate release and reintegration.

13. *Women and girls can be at particular risk* of gender-based violence. When contributing to the protection of these groups, humanitarian agencies should particularly consider measures that reduce possible risks, including trafficking, forced prostitution, rape or domestic violence. They should also implement standards and instruments that prevent and eradicate the practice of sexual exploitation and abuse. This unacceptable practice may involve affected people with specific vulnerabilities, such as isolated or disabled women who are forced to trade sex for the provision of humanitarian assistance.

Community-based social support and self-help

14. *Family and community mechanisms of protection and psychosocial support* should be promoted by keeping families together, teaching people how to prevent children from becoming separated from their families, promoting appropriate care for separated children and organising family tracing and reunification processes for separated children and other family members. Wherever possible, keep families together and enable people from a particular village or support network to live in the same area.

15. *Supporting community self-help activities:* Such activities include, for example, women's groups addressing issues of gender-based violence, youth groups collaborating on livelihood supports, parenting groups supporting positive interactions with children and care for parents of young children and of children with special needs, youth groups spreading protective information on threats such as landmines and community groups reaching out to women and men who have lost their partners, older people and persons with disabilities.

> **Protection Principle 4: Assist people to claim their rights, access available remedies and recover from the effects of abuse**
>
> The affected population is helped to claim their rights through information, documentation and assistance in seeking remedies. People are supported appropriately in recovering from the physical, psychological and social effects of violence and other abuses.

This Principle includes the following elements:

▶ Support affected people to assert their rights and to access remedies from government or other sources and provide them with information on their entitlements and available remedies.

▶ Assist affected people in securing the documentation they need to demonstrate their entitlements.

▶ Assist affected people to recover by providing community-based and other psychosocial support.

Guidance notes

Supporting affected people in asserting their rights

1. *The government and other relevant authorities are responsible* for ensuring that the rights of the affected population are respected and fulfilled. Whether through legal systems or other channels, humanitarian agencies should consider supporting affected populations to claim their rights.

2. *Entitlements:* Agencies should inform affected people of their entitlements both within a given aid programme and under the laws and regulations of the country in question. (Re)establishing people's rights to housing, land and property must be given particular attention.

3. *Information and consultation:* The affected population should be informed by authorities and humanitarian agencies in a language and manner they can understand. They should be engaged in a meaningful consultation process regarding decisions that affect their lives, without creating additional risks (see Core Standard 1 on page 55). This is one way of assisting them to assert their rights.

Documentation

4. *Securing or replacing lost documents:* Humanitarian agencies should assist the affected population in securing documentation – or replacing lost documents – in order to access their rights. People generally have rights regardless of possessing particular documentation. But in order to access the full range of entitlements, some form of documentation or identification, such as a birth certificate, marriage certificate, passport or land title, is usually required. Access to property documentation is often particularly important following a disaster but in a number of countries, ownership is not necessarily clearly documented through legal titles and can become a major point of contention. Death certificates need to be organised to avoid unnecessary financial and legal problems for relatives. Death certificates are usually not available when there is unceremonious disposal of corpses, a practice that should be avoided.

5. *Legal documentation* recognised by the government or relevant authorities must not be confused with documents issued by humanitarian agencies, such as registration documents, ration cards or transportation vouchers. Official documentation issued by authorities should not determine who is eligible for assistance from humanitarian organisations.

Access to remedies

6. *People are entitled to seek legal and other redress* from the government and relevant authorities for violations of their rights. This can include compensation for loss or restitution of property. They are also entitled to expect that the perpetrators of such violations will be brought to justice. This can play a major role in restoring trust and confidence among the affected populations. Humanitarian agencies may be able to assist people in accessing justice or refer the issues to agencies that are able to provide such support.

7. *Healthcare and rehabilitation support:* People should be supported in accessing appropriate healthcare and other rehabilitation support following attacks, gender-based violence and related problems (see Essential health services – control of communicable diseases standard 3 on page 316 and Essential health services – child health standards 1–2 on pages 321–323).

8. *Where remedial assistance is available* from non-governmental sources, people should be helped to identify and access such assistance, where appropriate.

Community-based and other psychosocial support

9. *Positive communal coping mechanisms* such as culturally appropriate burials, religious ceremonies and practices, and non-harmful cultural and social practices should be supported.

10. *Activities for children:* Where appropriate, communities should be encouraged to organise structured, supportive educational and protective activities for children through non-formal means such as child-friendly spaces. Community protection mechanisms should include self-help activities that promote psychosocial well-being.

11. *Help organise appropriate psychosocial support* for survivors of violence. Ensure that survivors have access to community social networks and self-help activities. Access to community-based social support should be complemented by access to mental healthcare.

12. *Integrated support system:* Those agencies working on psychosocial support and mental health in various sectors should collaborate to build an integrated system of support for the population (see Essential health services – mental health standard 1 on page 333).

13. *Clinical support:* Establish mechanisms for the referral of severely affected people for available clinical support.

References and further reading

General protection: Background and tools

Caritas Australia, CARE Australia, Oxfam Australia and World Vision Australia (2008), Minimum Agency Standards for Incorporating Protection into Humanitarian Response – Field Testing Version.
www.icva.ch/doc00002448.pdf

Giossi Caverzasio, S (2001), Strengthening Protection in War – A Search for Professional Standards. Ref 0783. International Committee of the Red Cross (ICRC). Geneva.

Inter-Agency Standing Committee (IASC) (2002), Growing the Sheltering Tree – Protecting Rights through Humanitarian Action – Programmes & practices gathered from the field. Geneva. www.icva.ch/gstree.pdf

IASC (2010), Operational Guidelines and Manual for the Protection of Persons Affected by Natural Disasters.

ICRC (2008), Enhancing protection for civilians in armed conflict and other situations of violence. Geneva.
www.icrc.org/eng/resources/documents/publication/p0956.htm

ICRC (2009), Professional standards for protection work carried out by humanitarian and human rights actors in armed conflict and other situations of violence. Geneva. www.icrc.org/web/eng/siteeng0.nsf/htmlall/p0999 or www.unhcr.org/refworld/type,THEMGUIDE,,,4b39cba52,0.html

O'Callaghan, S and Pantuliano, S (2007), Incorporating Civilian Protection into Humanitarian Response. HPG Report 26. Overseas Development Insitute (ODI). London.

Slim, H and Bonwick, A (2005), Protection – an ALNAP guide for humanitarian agencies. ODI. London. www.alnap.org/initiatives/protection.aspx

United Nations Office for the Coordination of Humanitarian Affairs (OCHA) (2009), Aide Mémoire: For the Consideration of Issues Pertaining for the Protection of Civilians. New York.
www.humansecuritygateway.com/showRecord.php?RecordId=33206

Specific standards for protection

Children

ICRC, International Rescue Committee, Save the Children, UNICEF, UNHCR and World Vision (2004), Interagency Guiding Principles on Unaccompanied and Separated Children. Geneva. www.icrc.org/eng/assets/files/other/icrc_002_1011.pdf

UNICEF (2007), Paris Principles and Commitments to Protect Children from Unlawful recruitment or Use by Armed Forces or Groups. Paris. www.un.org/children/conflict/english/parisprinciples.html

UN Disarmament, Demobilization and Reintegration (UN-DDR) (2006), Integrated Disarmament, Demobilisation, and Reintegration Standards. New York. www.unddr.org/iddrs/05/20.php and www.unddr.org/iddrs/05/30.php

Disabilities

Handicap International (2006), Protection – Issues for People with Disabilities and Injuries.

Handicap International (2008), Toolkit on Protection of Persons with Disabilities.

Gender-based violence

IASC (2005), Guidelines for Gender-Based Violence Interventions in Humanitarian Settings – Focusing on the Prevention of and Response to Sexual Violence in Emergencies. Geneva. www.humanitarianinfo.org/iasc/pageloader. aspx?page=content-products-products&productcatid=3

World Health Organization (WHO) (2007), Ethical and safety recommendations for researching, documenting and monitoring sexual violence in emergencies. Geneva. www.who.int/gender/documents/violence/9789241595681/en/index.html

Housing, land and property rights

Principles on Housing and Property Restitution for Refugees and Displaced Persons. E/CN.4/SUB.2/RES/2005/21. "Pinheiro Principles". http://ap.ohchr.org/documents/alldocs.aspx?doc_id=11644

Global Land Tool Network and Early Recovery Cluster (2010), Land and natural disasters – Guidance for Practitioners. UN Human Settlements Programme (UN-Habitat) and Food and Agriculture Organization (FAO). Nairobi. www.unhabitat.org/pmss/listItemDetails.aspx?publicationID=2973

Global Protection Cluster, Housing, Land And Property Area of Responsibility (2009), Checklist of Housing, Land and Property Rights and Broader Land Issues Throughout the Displacement Timeline from Emergency to Recovery. www.internal-displacement.org/8025708F004BE3B1/(httpInfoFiles)/430298C 3C285133DC12576E7005D360D/$file/HC%20Checklist%20on%20HLP%20 and%20Land%20Issues_Final2.pdf

Internal Displacement Monitoring Centre, FAO, OCHA, Office of the UN High Commissioner for Human Rights, UN-Habitat and UNHCR (2007), Handbook on Housing and Property Restitution for Refugees and Displaced Persons. Implementing the 'Pinheiro Principles', IASC. Geneva. www.unhcr.org/refworld/docid/4693432c2.html

Internally displaced persons

Bagshaw, S and Paul, D (2004), Protect or Neglect? Towards a More Effective United Nations Approach to the Protection of Internally Displaced Persons – An Evaluation. Brookings-SAIS Project on Internal Displacement and UNOCHA, Interagency Internal Displacement Division. Washington DC. www.brookings.edu/papers/2004/1123humanrights_bagshaw.aspx

Brookings Institution – University of Bern Project of Internal Displacement (2005), Addressing Internal Displacement: A Framework for National Responsibility. Washington DC. www.brookings.edu/projects/idp/20050401_nrframework.aspx

Global Protection Cluster (2010), Handbook for the Protection of Internally Displaced Persons. www.unhcr.org/refworld/docid/4790cbc02.html

IASC (2004), Implementing the Collaborative Approach to Situations of Internal Displacement – Guidance for UN Humanitarian and/or Resident Coordinators. www.humanitarianinfo.org/iasc/pageloader. aspx?page=content-products-products&productcatid=10

IASC (2010), Framework on Durable Solutions for Internally Displaced Persons. www.brookings.edu/reports/2010/0305_internal_displacement.aspx

UN Economic and Social Council (1998), UN Guiding Principles on Internal Displacement. E/CN.4/1998/53/Add.2. www.idpguidingprinciples.org/ or www.unhchr.ch/Huridocda/Huridoca.nsf/TestFrame/d2e008c61b70263ec12566 1e0036f36e?Opendocument

Mental health and psychosocial support

IASC (2007), IASC Guidelines on Mental Health and Psychosocial Support. www.humanitarianinfo.org/iasc/pageloaderaspx?page=content-products-default

IASC Reference Group on Mental Health and Psychosocial Support (2010), Mental Health and Psychosocial Support (MHPSS) In Humanitarian Emergencies: What Should Protection Programme Managers Know.
www.psychosocialnetwork.net/explore/tags/mhpss/

Mine action

The International Mine Action Standards:
www.mineactionstandards.org/imas.htm#english

Older people

IASC (2008), Humanitarian Action and Older Persons – An essential brief for humanitarian actors. WHO–HelpAge International. www.humanitarianinfo.org/iasc/pageloader.aspx?page=content-products-products&productcatid=24

The
Core Standards

How to use this chapter

The Core Standards are essential process standards shared by all sectors. They provide a single reference point for approaches that underpin all the standards in the Handbook. Each chapter, therefore, requires the companion use of the Core Standards to help attain its own standards.

There are six Core Standards:

> People-centred humanitarian response
>
> Coordination and collaboration
>
> Assessment
>
> Design and response
>
> Performance, transparency and learning
>
> Aid worker performance

Each Core Standard is structured as follows:

- The Core Standard: It is qualitative in nature and specifies the level to be attained in humanitarian response.

- Key actions: These are suggested activities and inputs to help meet the standards.

- Key indicators: These are 'signals' that show whether a standard has been attained. They provide a way of measuring and communicating the processes and results of key actions; they relate to the minimum standard, not to the key action.

- Guidance notes: These include specific points to consider when applying the Core Standard, key actions and key indicators in different situations. They provide guidance on tackling practical difficulties, benchmarks or advice on priority issues. They may also include critical issues relating to the standards, actions or indicators, and describe dilemmas, controversies or gaps in current knowledge.

The key indicators of the Core Standards accommodate wide variations in a user's application and context. Measurable and time-bound specifications for each indicator are highly context- and sector-specific. Users should therefore adapt the key indicators to their particular situation, as appropriate.

A select list of references and further reading is included at the end of this chapter.

Contents

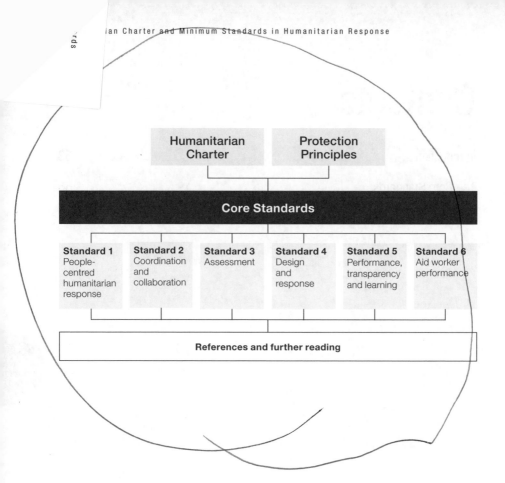

Introduction

The Core Standards describe processes that are essential to achieving all the Sphere minimum standards. They are a practical expression of the principles of the Sphere Humanitarian Charter and are fundamental to the rights of people affected by conflict or disaster to assistance that supports life with dignity. The Core Standards define the minimum level of response to be attained (as signalled by the key indicators) by humanitarian agencies, be they community-based, local, national or international.

The Core Standards are also linked to other key accountability initiatives, promoting coherence and reinforcing a shared commitment to accountability. For example, the Humanitarian Accountability Partnership (HAP) 2010 Standard in Accountability and Quality Management benchmarks and the Core Standards contain complementary requirements. The aid worker performance standard is coherent with People In Aid's Code of Good Practice. *The Good Enough Guide* of the Emergency Capacity Building (ECB) Project, Groupe URD's *Quality Compas* and the Active Learning Network for Accountability and Performance in Humanitarian Action (ALNAP) inform Core Standards 1 and 5 in particular. The Core Standards are a companion to the Foundational Standards in the INEE (Inter-Agency Network for Education in Emergencies) Minimum Standards for Education: Preparedness, Response, Recovery.

The importance of the Core Standards for all sectors

The first Core Standard recognises that the participation of disaster-affected people – women, men, girls and boys of all ages – and their capacity and strategies to survive with dignity are integral to humanitarian response. Core Standard 2 addresses the need for an effective response to be coordinated and implemented with other agencies and governmental authorities engaged in impartial humanitarian action.

Core Standard 3 describes the need for assessments systematically to understand the nature of the disaster, identify who has been affected and how, and assess people's vulnerability and capacities. It acknowledges the critical importance of understanding need in relation to the political, social, economic and environmental context and the wider population. Agencies meeting Core Standard 4 design their response based on an impartial assessment of needs, addressing unmet needs in relation to the context and capacity of affected people and states to meet their own needs.

Core Standard 5 is attained by agencies that continually examine the effectiveness, quality and appropriateness of their response. Agencies adapt their strategies in accordance with monitoring information and feedback from people affected by disaster, and share information about their performance. They invest in unbiased reviews and evaluations and use the findings to improve their policy and practice.

Core Standard 6 recognises that humanitarian agencies have an obligation to disaster-affected people to employ aid workers with the appropriate knowledge, skills, behaviour and attitudes to deliver an effective humanitarian response. Equally, agencies are responsible for enabling aid workers to perform satisfactorily through effective management and support for their emotional and physical well-being.

Vulnerability

Sphere's focus is on meeting the urgent survival needs of people affected by disaster or conflict. However, the Core Standards can also support disaster preparedness and approaches that reduce future risk and vulnerability, enhance capacity and promote early recovery. Such approaches take account of the impact of the response on the natural environment and broader context and are highly relevant to the needs of the host and wider population.

Throughout the Handbook, 'vulnerable' refers to people who are especially susceptible to the effects of natural or man-made disasters or of conflict. People are, or become, more vulnerable to disasters due to a combination of physical, social, environmental and political factors. They may be marginalised by their society due to their ethnicity, age, sex, disability, class or caste, political affiliations or religion. A combination of vulnerabilities and the effect of an often volatile context all contribute to people being vulnerable for different reasons and in different ways. Vulnerable people, like all those affected by disaster, have various capacities to manage and recover from disasters. A thorough understanding of vulnerable people's capacities and the barriers they may face in accessing humanitarian support is essential for a response that meets the needs of those who need it most.

The Core Standards

Core Standard 1: People-centred humanitarian response

People's capacity and strategies to survive with dignity are integral to the design and approach of humanitarian response.

Key actions (to be read in conjunction with the guidance notes)

▶ Support local capacity by identifying community groups and social networks at the earliest opportunity and build on community-based and self-help initiatives (see guidance note 1).

▶ Establish systematic and transparent mechanisms through which people affected by disaster or conflict can provide regular feedback and influence programmes (see guidance note 2).

▶ Ensure a balanced representation of vulnerable people in discussions with the disaster-affected population (see guidance note 3).

▶ Provide information to the affected population about the humanitarian agency, its project(s) and people's entitlements in an accessible format and language (see guidance note 4).

▶ Provide the affected population with access to safe and appropriate spaces for community meetings and information-sharing at the earliest opportunity (see guidance note 5).

▶ Enable people to lodge complaints about the programme easily and safely and establish transparent, timely procedures for response and remedial actions (see guidance note 6).

▶ Wherever feasible, use local labour, environmentally sustainable materials and socially responsible businesses to benefit the local economy and promote recovery.

▶ Design projects, wherever possible, to accommodate and respect helpful cultural, spiritual and traditional practices regarded as important by local people (see guidance note 7).

Progressively increase disaster-affected people's decision-making power and ownership of programmes during the course of a response.

Key indicators (to be read in conjunction with the guidance notes)

- Project strategies are explicitly linked to community-based capacities and initiatives.

- Disaster-affected people conduct or actively participate in regular meetings on how to organise and implement the response (see guidance notes 1–2).

- The number of self-help initiatives led by the affected community and local authorities increases during the response period (see guidance note 1).

- Agencies have investigated and, as appropriate, acted upon complaints received about the assistance provided.

Guidance notes

1. *Local capacity:* Disaster-affected people possess and acquire skills, knowledge and capacities to cope with, respond to and recover from disasters. Active participation in humanitarian response is an essential foundation of people's right to life with dignity affirmed in Principles 6 and 7 of the Code of Conduct for the International Red Cross and Red Crescent Movement and Non-Governmental Organisations (NGOs) in Disaster Relief (see Annex 2 on page 368). Self-help and community-led initiatives contribute to psychological and social well-being through restoring dignity and a degree of control to disaster-affected populations. Access to social, financial, cultural and emotional support through extended family, religious networks and rituals, friends, schools and community activities helps to re-establish individual and community self-respect and identity, decrease vulnerability and enhance resilience. Local people should be supported to identify and, if appropriate, reactivate or establish supportive networks and self-help groups. The extent to which people participate, and how they do so, will be determined by how recently the disaster occurred and by the physical, social and political circumstances. Indicators signalling participation should, therefore, be selected according to context and represent all those affected. The local population is usually the first to react in a disaster and even early in a response some degree of participation is always feasible. Explicit efforts to listen to, consult and engage people at an early stage will increase quality and community management later in the programme.

2. *Feedback mechanisms* provide a means for all those affected to influence programme planning and implementation (see HAP's 'participation' benchmark). They include focus group discussions, surveys, interviews and meetings on 'lessons learnt' with a representative sample of all the

affected population (see ECB's *Good Enough Guide* for tools and guidance notes 3–4). The findings and the agency's actions in response to feedback should be systematically shared with the affected population.

3. *Representative participation:* Understanding and addressing the barriers to participation faced by different people is critical to balanced participation. Measures should be taken to ensure the participation of members of all groups of affected people – young and old, men and women. Special efforts should be made to include people who are not well represented, are marginalised (e.g. by ethnicity or religion) or otherwise 'invisible' (e.g. housebound or in an institution). The participation of youth and children should be promoted so far as it is in their own best interest and measures taken to ensure that they are not exposed to abuse or harm.

4. *Sharing information:* People have a right to accurate and updated information about actions taken on their behalf. Information can reduce anxiety and is an essential foundation of community responsibility and ownership. At a minimum, agencies should provide a description of the agency's mandate and project(s), the population's entitlements and rights, and when and where to access assistance (see HAP's 'sharing information' benchmark). Common ways of sharing information include noticeboards, public meetings, schools, newspapers and radio broadcasts. The information should demonstrate considered understanding of people's situations and be conveyed in local language(s), using a variety of adapted media so that it is accessible to all those concerned. For example, use spoken communications or pictures for children and adults who cannot read, use uncomplicated language (i.e. understandable to local 12-year-olds) and employ a large typeface when printing information for people with visual impairments. Manage meetings so that older people or those with hearing difficulties can hear.

5. *Safe and accessible spaces:* Locate public meeting places in secure areas and ensure they are accessible to those with restricted mobility including to women whose attendance at public events is limited by cultural norms. Provide child-friendly spaces for children to play, learn, socialise and develop.

6. *Complaints:* People have the right to complain to an agency and seek a corresponding response (see HAP's 'handling complaints' benchmark). Formal mechanisms for complaints and redress are an essential component of an agency's accountability to people and help populations to re-establish control over their lives.

7. *Culturally appropriate practices,* such as burials and religious ceremonies and practices, are often an essential element of people's identity, dignity and capacity to recover from disaster. Some culturally acceptable practices

violate people's human rights (e.g. denial of education to girls and female genital mutilation) and should not be supported.

Core Standard 2: Coordination and collaboration

Humanitarian response is planned and implemented in coordination with the relevant authorities, humanitarian agencies and civil society organisations engaged in impartial humanitarian action, working together for maximum efficiency, coverage and effectiveness.

Key actions (to be read in conjunction with the guidance notes)

▶ Participate in general and any applicable sectoral coordination mechanisms from the outset (see guidance notes 1–2).

▶ Be informed of the responsibilities, objectives and coordination role of the state and other coordination groups where present (see guidance note 3).

▶ Provide coordination groups with information about the agency's mandate, objectives and programme.

▶ Share assessment information with the relevant coordination groups in a timely manner and in a format that can be readily used by other humanitarian agencies (see Core Standard 3 on page 61).

▶ Use programme information from other humanitarian agencies to inform analysis, selection of geographical area and response plans.

▶ Regularly update coordination groups on progress, reporting any major delays, agency shortages or spare capacity (see guidance note 4).

▶ Collaborate with other humanitarian agencies to strengthen advocacy on critical shared humanitarian concerns.

▶ Establish clear policies and practice regarding the agency's engagement with non-humanitarian actors, based on humanitarian principles and objectives (see guidance note 5).

Key indicators (to be read in conjunction with the guidance notes)

▶ Assessment reports and information about programme plans and progress are regularly submitted to the relevant coordinating groups (see guidance note 4).

▶ The humanitarian activities of other agencies in the same geographical or sectoral areas are not duplicated.

▶ Commitments made at coordination meetings are acted upon and reported in a timely manner.

▶ The agency's response takes account of the capacity and strategies of other humanitarian agencies, civil society organisations and relevant authorities.

Guidance notes

1. *Coordinated responses:* Adequate programme coverage, timeliness and quality require collective action. Active participation in coordination efforts enables coordination leaders to establish a timely, clear division of labour and responsibility, gauge the extent to which needs are being collectively met, reduce duplication and address gaps in coverage and quality. Coordinated responses, timely inter-agency assessments and information-sharing reduce the burden on affected people who may be subjected to demands for the same information from a series of assessment teams. Collaboration and, where possible, the sharing of resources and equipment optimise the capacity of communities, their neighbours, host governments, donors and humanitarian agencies with different mandates and expertise. Participation in coordination mechanisms prior to a disaster establishes relationships and enhances coordination during a response. Local civil society organisations and authorities may not participate if coordination mechanisms appear to be relevant only to international agencies. Respect the use of the local language(s) in meetings and in other shared communications. Identify local civil society actors and networks involved in the response and encourage them and other local and international humanitarian agencies to participate. Staff representing agencies in coordination meetings should have the appropriate information, skills and authority to contribute to planning and decision-making.

2. *Common coordination mechanisms* include meetings – general (for all programmes), sectoral (such as health) and cross-sectoral (such as gender) – and information-sharing mechanisms (such as databases of assessment and contextual information). Meetings which bring together different sectors can further enable people's needs to be addressed as a whole, rather than in isolation (e.g. people's shelter, water, sanitation, hygiene and psychosocial needs are interrelated). Relevant information should be shared between different coordination mechanisms to ensure integrated coordination across all programmes. In all coordination contexts, the commitment of agencies to participate will be affected by the quality of the coordination mechanisms: coordination leaders have a responsibility to ensure that meetings and information are well managed, efficient and results-orientated. If not, participating agencies should advocate for, and support, improved mechanisms.

3. **Coordination roles:** It is the affected state's role to coordinate the humanitarian response of assisting organisations. Humanitarian agencies have an essential role to play by supporting the state's coordination function. However, in some contexts, alternative coordination mechanisms may be appropriate if, for example, state authorities are themselves responsible for abuse and violations or their assistance is not impartial or if the state is willing to play a coordination role, but lacks capacity. In these situations coordination meetings may be separately or jointly led by the local authorities with the United Nations or NGOs. Many large-scale humanitarian emergencies are now typically coordinated through the 'cluster approach', with groupings of agencies working in the same sector under a lead agency.

4. **Efficient data-sharing** will be enhanced if the information is easy to use (clear, relevant, brief) and follows global humanitarian protocols which are technically compatible with other agencies' data (see Core Standard 3 on page 61). The exact frequency of data-sharing is agency- and context-specific but should be prompt to remain relevant. Sensitive information should remain confidential (see Core Standards 3–4 on pages 61–65).

5. **Military and private sector:** The private sector and foreign and national military are increasingly part of the relief effort and therefore affect coordination efforts. The military bring particular expertise and resources, including security, logistics, transport and communication. However, their activities can blur the important distinction between humanitarian objectives and military or political agendas and create future security risks. Any association with the military should be in the service of, and led by, humanitarian agencies according to endorsed guidelines. Some agencies will maintain a minimum dialogue to ensure operational efficiency (e.g. basic programme information-sharing) while others may establish stronger links (e.g. use of military assets). In all cases, humanitarian agencies must remain clearly distinct from the military to avoid any real or perceived association with a political or military agenda that could compromise the agencies' independence, credibility, security and access to affected populations. The private sector can bring commercial efficiencies, complementary expertise and resources to humanitarian agencies. Information-sharing is required to avoid duplication and to promote humanitarian good practice. Private–humanitarian partnerships must strictly be for the benefit of humanitarian objectives.

Core Standard 3: Assessment

The priority needs of the disaster-affected population are identified through a systematic assessment of the context, risks to life with dignity and the capacity of the affected people and relevant authorities to respond.

Key actions (to be read in conjunction with the guidance notes)

▶ Find and use pre-disaster information about local humanitarian capacity, the affected and wider population, context and other pre-existing factors that may increase people's susceptibility to the disaster (see guidance note 1).

▶ Carry out an initial assessment immediately, building on pre-disaster information to assess changes in the context caused by the disaster, identifying any new factors that create or increase vulnerability (see guidance note 2).

▶ Carry out a rapid assessment as soon as possible, following up with subsequent in-depth assessments as time and the situation allow (see guidance note 3).

▶ Disaggregate population data by, at the very least, sex and age (see guidance note 4).

▶ Listen to an inclusive range of people in the assessment – women and men of all ages, girls, boys and other vulnerable people affected by the disaster as well as the wider population (see Core Standard 1 on page 55 and guidance notes 5–6).

▶ Participate in multisectoral, joint or inter-agency assessments wherever possible.

▶ Gather information systematically, using a variety of methods, triangulate with information gathered from a number of sources and agencies and document the data as they are collected (see guidance note 7).

▶ Assess the coping capacity, skills, resources and recovery strategies of the affected people (see guidance note 8).

▶ Assess the response plans and capacity of the state.

▶ Assess the impact of the disaster on the psychosocial well-being of individuals and communities.

▶ Assess current and potential safety concerns for the disaster-affected population and aid workers, including the potential for the response to exacerbate a conflict or create tension between the affected and host populations (see guidance note 9).

▶ Share assessment data in a timely manner and in a format that is accessible to other humanitarian agencies (see Core Standard 2 on page 58 and guidance note 10).

Key indicators (to be read in conjunction with the guidance notes)

▶ Assessed needs have been explicitly linked to the capacity of affected people and the state to respond.

▶ Rapid and in-depth assessment reports contain views that are representative of all affected people, including members of vulnerable groups and those of the surrounding population.

▶ Assessment reports contain data disaggregated by, at the very least, sex and age.

▶ In-depth assessment reports contain information and analysis of vulnerability, context and capacity.

▶ Where assessment formats have been agreed and widely supported, they have been used.

▶ Rapid assessments have been followed by in-depth assessments of the populations selected for intervention.

Guidance notes

1. *Pre-disaster information:* A collaborative pooling of existing information is invaluable for initial and rapid assessments. A considerable amount of information is almost always available about the context (e.g. political, social, economic, security, conflict and natural environment) and the people (such as their sex, age, health, culture, spirituality and education). Sources of this information include the relevant state ministries (e.g. health and census data), academic or research institutions, community-based organisations and local and international humanitarian agencies present before the disaster. Disaster preparedness and early warning initiatives, new developments in shared web-based mapping, crowd-sourcing and mobile phone platforms (such as Ushahidi) have also generated databases of relevant information.

2. *Initial assessments,* typically carried out in the first hours following a disaster, may be based almost entirely on second-hand information and pre-existing data. They are essential to inform immediate relief needs and should be carried out and shared immediately.

3. **Phased assessments:** Assessment is a process, not a single event. Initial and rapid assessments provide the basis for subsequent in-depth assessments that deepen (but do not repeat) earlier assessment findings. Care should be taken as repeated assessments of sensitive protection concerns such as gender-based violence can be more harmful than beneficial to communities and individuals.

4. **Data disaggregation:** Detailed disaggregation is rarely possible initially but is of critical importance to identify the different needs and rights of children and adults of all ages. At the earliest opportunity, further disaggregate by sex and age for children 0–5 male/female, 6–12 male/female and 13–17 male/female, and then in 10-year age brackets, e.g. 50–59, male/female; 60–69, male/female; 70–79, male/female; 80+, male/female. Unlike the physiologically-related age groupings in the health chapter, these groupings address age-related differences linked to a range of rights, social and cultural issues.

5. **Representative assessments:** Needs-based assessments cover **all** disaster-affected populations. Special efforts are needed to assess people in hard-to-reach locations, e.g. people who are not in camps, are in less accessible geographical areas or in host families. The same applies for people less easily accessed but often at risk, such as persons with disabilities, older people, housebound individuals, children and youths, who may be targeted as child soldiers or subjected to gender-based violence. Sources of primary information include direct observation, focus group discussions, surveys and discussions with as wide a range of people and groups as possible (e.g. local authorities, male and female community leaders, older men and women, health staff, teachers and other educational personnel, traders and other humanitarian agencies). Speaking openly may be difficult or dangerous for some people. Talk with children separately as they are unlikely to speak in front of adults and doing so may put the children at risk. In most cases, women and girls should be consulted in separate spaces. Aid workers engaged in the collection of systematic information from people who have been abused or violated should have the necessary skills and systems to do so safely and appropriately. In conflict areas, information could be misused and place people at further risk or compromise an agency's ability to operate. Only with an individual's consent may information about them be shared with other humanitarian agencies or relevant organisations (see Protection Principle 1 on page 33). It will not be possible to immediately assess all those affected: excluded areas or groups should be clearly noted in the assessment report and returned to at the earliest opportunity.

6. **Assessing vulnerability:** The risks faced by people following a disaster will vary for different groups and individuals. Some people may be vulnerable

due to individual factors such as their age (particularly the very young and the very old) and illness (especially people living with HIV and AIDS). But individual factors alone do not automatically increase risk. Assess the social and contextual factors that contribute to vulnerability, such as discrimination and marginalisation (e.g. low status and power of women and girls); social isolation; environmental degradation; climate variability; poverty; lack of land tenure; poor governance; ethnicity; class or caste; and religious or political affiliations. Subsequent in-depth assessments should identify potential future hazards, such as changing risk patterns due to environmental degradation (e.g. soil erosion or deforestation) and climate change and geology (e.g. cyclones, floods, droughts, landslides and sea-level rise).

7. **Data-gathering and checklists:** Assessment information including population movements and numbers should be cross-checked, validated and referenced to as many sources as possible. If multisectoral assessments are not initially possible, pay extra attention to linkages with other individual sector, protection and cross-cutting assessments. Data sources and levels of disaggregation should be noted and mortality and morbidity of children under 5 years old documented from the outset. Many assessment checklists are available, based on agreed humanitarian standards (see the checklists in the appendices of some technical chapters). Checklists enhance the coherence and accessibility of data to other agencies, ensure that all key areas have been examined and reduce organisational or individual bias. A common inter-agency assessment format may have been developed prior to a disaster or agreed during the response. In all cases, assessments should clarify the objectives and methodology to be used and generate impartial information about the impact of the crisis on those affected. A mix of quantitative and qualitative methods appropriate to the context should be used. Assessment teams should, as far as possible, be composed of a mix of women and men, generalists and specialists, including those with skills in collecting gender-sensitive data and communicating with children. Teams should include people familiar with the language(s) and location and able to communicate with people in culturally acceptable ways.

8. **Assessing capacities:** Communities have capacities for coping and recovery (see Core Standard 1 on page 55). Many coping mechanisms are sustainable and helpful, while others may be negative, with potentially long-term harmful consequences, such as the sale of assets or heavy alcohol consumption. Assessments should identify the positive strategies that increase resilience as well as the reasons for negative strategies.

9. **Assessing security:** An assessment of the safety and security of disaster-affected and host populations should be carried out in all initial and subsequent assessments, identifying threats of violence and any forms of coercion

and denial of subsistence or basic human rights (see Protection Principle 3 on page 38).

10. *Sharing assessments:* Assessment reports provide invaluable information to other humanitarian agencies, create baseline data and increase the transparency of response decisions. Regardless of variations in individual agency design, assessment reports should be clear and concise, enable users to identify priorities for action and describe their methodology to demonstrate the reliability of data and enable a comparative analysis if required.

Core Standard 4: Design and response

The humanitarian response meets the assessed needs of the disaster-affected population in relation to context, the risks faced and the capacity of the affected people and state to cope and recover.

Key actions (to be read in conjunction with the guidance notes)

▶ Design the programme based on an impartial assessment of needs, context, the risks faced and the capacity of the affected population (see Core Standard 3 on page 61).

▶ Design the programme to meet needs that cannot or will not be met by the state or the affected people (see guidance note 1).

▶ Prioritise life-saving actions that address basic, urgent survival needs in the immediate aftermath of a disaster.

▶ Using disaggregated assessment data, analyse the ways in which the disaster has affected different individuals and populations, and design the programme to meet their particular needs.

▶ Design the response so that vulnerable people have full access to assistance and protection services (see guidance note 2).

▶ Ensure that the programme design and approach supports all aspects of the dignity of the affected individuals and populations (see Core Standard 1 on page 55 and guidance note 3).

▶ Analyse all contextual factors that increase people's vulnerability, designing the programme to progressively reduce their vulnerability (see Core Standard 3 on page 61 and guidance note 4).

▶ Design the programme to minimise the risk of endangering people, worsen the dynamics of a conflict or create insecurity or opportunities for exploitation and abuse (see guidance note 5 and Protection Principle 1 on page 33).

▶ Progressively close the gap between assessed conditions and the Sphere minimum standards, meeting or exceeding Sphere indicators (see guidance note 6).

▶ Design programmes that promote early recovery, reduce risk and enhance the capacity of affected people to prevent, minimise or better cope with the effects of future hazards (see guidance note 7).

▶ Continually adapt the programme to maintain relevance and appropriateness (see Core Standard 5 on page 68).

▶ Enhance sustained recovery by planning for and communicating exit strategies with the affected population during the early stages of programme implementation.

Key indicators (to be read in conjunction with the guidance notes)

▶ Programme design is based on an analysis of the specific needs and risks faced by different groups of people.

▶ Programme design addresses the gap between people's needs and their own, or the state's, capacity to meet them.

▶ Programme designs are revised to reflect changes in the context, risks and people's needs and capacities.

▶ Programme design includes actions to reduce people's vulnerability to future hazards and increase their capacity to manage and cope with them.

Guidance notes

1. *Supporting existing capacity:* It is the primary role and responsibility of the state to provide timely assistance and protection to those affected (see Humanitarian Charter, paragraph 2 on page 20). Intervene if the affected population and/or state does not have sufficient capacity to respond (particularly early in the response) or if the state or controlling authorities actively discriminate against certain groups of people and/or affected areas. In all cases the capacity and intentions of the state towards all members of the affected population inform the scale and type of humanitarian response.

2. *Access:* Assistance is provided to those in need without discrimination (see Protection Principle 2 on page 36). People's access to aid and their ability to use and benefit from assistance is increased through the provision of timely information and through design that corresponds with their particular needs and cultural and safety considerations (for example, separate queues for older people or women with children attending food distributions). It is enhanced by the participation of women, men, girls and boys of all ages in the design.

Access is increased through the use of carefully designed targeting criteria and processes that are widely communicated, understood by the community and systematically monitored. Actions described in the technical chapters facilitate equal access through considered design, such as locating facilities in areas that are safe, etc.

3. *The foundation of life with dignity* is the assurance of access to basic services, security and respect for human rights (see Humanitarian Charter on page 19). Equally, the **way** in which humanitarian response is implemented strongly affects the dignity and well-being of the disaster-affected population. Programme approaches that respect the intrinsic value of each individual, support their religious and cultural identity, promote community-based self-help and encourage positive social support networks all contribute to psychosocial well-being and are an essential element of people's right to life with dignity.

4. *Context and vulnerability:* Social, political, cultural, economic, conflict and natural environment factors can increase people's susceptibility to disasters; changes in the context can create newly vulnerable people (see Core Standard 3 on page 61). Vulnerable people may face a number of factors simultaneously (for example, older people who are members of marginalised ethnic groups). The interplay of personal and contextual factors that heighten risk should be analysed and programmes should be designed to address and mitigate those risks and target the needs of vulnerable people.

5. *Conflict sensitivity:* Humanitarian assistance can have unintended negative impacts. Valuable aid resources can increase exploitation and abuse and lead to competition, misuse or misappropriation of aid. Famine can be a weapon of war (e.g. deliberately depopulating an area or forcing asset transfers). Aid can negatively affect the wider population and amplify unequal power relations between different groups, including men and women. Careful analysis and design can reduce the potential for assistance to increase conflict and insecurity (including during natural disasters). Design to ensure equitable distribution and the impartial targeting of assistance. Protect people's safety and dignity by respecting confidential personal information. For example, people living with HIV and AIDS may be stigmatised; survivors of human rights violations must be guaranteed safe and confidential assistance (see Core Standard 3 on page 61).

6. *Meeting Sphere's minimum standards:* The time taken to reach the minimum standards will depend on the context: it will be affected by resources, access, insecurity and the living standards of the area prior to a disaster. Tension may be created if the affected population attains standards that exceed those of the host and/or wider population, or even worsen their conditions. Develop strategies to minimise the disparities and risks by,

for example, mitigating any negative impacts of the response on the wider natural environment and economy and advocating to increase the standards of the host population. Where and when possible, increase the scope of the response to include the host population.

7. **Early recovery and risk reduction:** Actions taken at the earliest opportunity to strengthen local capacity, work with local resources and restore services, education, markets and livelihood opportunities will promote early economic recovery and the ability of people to manage risk after external assistance has ended (see Core Standard 1 on page 55). At the very least, humanitarian response should not harm or compromise the quality of life for future generations and inadvertently contribute to future hazards (through, for example, deforestation and the unsustainable use of natural resources). Once immediate threats to life have been stabilised, analyse present and (multiple) potential future hazards (such as those created by climate change). Design to reduce future risks. For example, take opportunities during the response to invest in risk reduction and 'build back safer'. Examples include building earthquake- and hurricane-resistant houses, protecting wetlands that absorb storm surges and supporting policy development and community-driven initiatives in early warning and disaster preparedness.

Core Standard 5: Performance, transparency and learning

The performance of humanitarian agencies is continually examined and communicated to stakeholders; projects are adapted in response to performance.

Key actions (to be read in conjunction with the guidance notes)

▶ Establish systematic but simple, timely and participatory mechanisms to monitor progress towards all relevant Sphere standards and the programme's stated principles, outputs and activities (see guidance note 1).

▶ Establish basic mechanisms for monitoring the agency's overall performance with respect to the agency's management and quality control systems (see guidance note 2).

▶ Monitor the outcomes and, where possible, the early impact of a humanitarian response on the affected and wider populations (see guidance note 3).

▶ Establish systematic mechanisms for adapting programme strategies in response to monitoring data, changing needs and an evolving context (see guidance note 4).

▶ Conduct periodic reflection and learning exercises throughout the implementation of the response.

▶ Carry out a final evaluation or other form of objective learning review of the programme, with reference to its stated objectives, principles and agreed minimum standards (see guidance note 5).

▶ Participate in joint, inter-agency and other collaborative learning initiatives wherever feasible.

▶ Share key monitoring findings and, where appropriate, the findings of evaluation and other key learning processes with the affected population, relevant authorities and coordination groups in a timely manner (see guidance note 6).

Key indicators (to be read in conjunction with the guidance notes)

▶ Programmes are adapted in response to monitoring and learning information.

▶ Monitoring and evaluation sources include the views of a representative number of people targeted by the response, as well as the host community if different.

▶ Accurate, updated, non-confidential progress information is shared with the people targeted by the response and relevant local authorities and other humanitarian agencies on a regular basis.

▶ Performance is regularly monitored in relation to all Sphere Core and relevant technical minimum standards (and related global or agency performance standards), and the main results shared with key stakeholders (see guidance note 6).

▶ Agencies consistently conduct an objective evaluation or learning review of a major humanitarian response in accordance with recognised standards of evaluation practice (see guidance note 6).

Guidance notes

1. *Monitoring* compares intentions with results. It measures progress against project objectives and indicators and its impact on vulnerability and the context. Monitoring information guides project revisions, verifies targeting criteria and whether aid is reaching the people intended. It enables decision-makers to respond to community feedback and identify emerging problems and trends. It is also an opportunity for agencies to provide, as well as gather, information. Effective monitoring selects methods suited to the particular programme and context, combining qualitative and quantitative data as appropriate and maintaining consistent records. Openness and communication (transparency) about monitoring information increases accountability to the affected population. Monitoring carried out by the population itself further enhances transparency and the quality and people's ownership of the information. Clarity about the intended use and users of the data should determine what is collected and how it is presented. Data should be presented in a brief accessible format that facilitates sharing and decision-making.

2. **Agency performance** is not confined to measuring the extent of its programme achievements. It covers the agency's overall function – its progress with respect to aspects such as its relationships with other organisations, adherence to humanitarian good practice, codes and principles and the effectiveness and efficiency of its management systems. Quality assurance approaches such as Groupe URD's *Quality Compas* can be used to assess overall agency performance.

3. **Impact monitoring:** Increasingly, the assessment of impact (the wider effects of interventions in the short to medium term, positive or negative, intended or unintended) is viewed as both feasible and essential for humanitarian response. Impact assessment is an important emerging field, linking particular humanitarian contributions to changes in populations and the context that are complex and interrelated. The affected people are the best judges of changes in their lives; hence outcome and impact assessment must include people's feedback, open-ended listening and other participatory qualitative approaches, as well as quantitative approaches.

4. **Maintaining relevance:** Monitoring should periodically check whether the programme continues to be relevant to the affected populations. Findings should lead to revisions to the programme as appropriate.

5. **Methods for examining performance:** Different approaches suit different performance, learning and accountability purposes. A variety of methods may be used including monitoring and evaluation, participatory impact assessments and listening exercises, quality assurance tools, audits and internal learning and reflection exercises. Programme evaluations are typically carried out at the end of a response, recommending changes to organisational policies and future programmes. Performance monitoring and 'real-time evaluation' can also be carried out during a response, leading to immediate changes in policy and practice. Evaluations are usually carried out by independent, external evaluators but internal staff members can also evaluate a programme as long as they take an objective approach. This would normally mean agency staff who were not involved in the response themselves. Humanitarian evaluation uses a set of eight dimensions known as the DAC (Development Assistance Committee)

criteria: relevance; appropriateness; connectedness; coherence; coverage; efficiency; effectiveness; and impact.

6. **Sector-wide performance:** Sharing information about each agency's progress towards the Sphere minimum standards with coordination groups supports response-wide monitoring and creates an invaluable source of sector-wide performance data.

Core Standard 6: Aid worker performance

Humanitarian agencies provide appropriate management, supervisory and psychosocial support, enabling aid workers to have the knowledge, skills, behaviour and attitudes to plan and implement an effective humanitarian response with humanity and respect.

Key actions (to be read in conjunction with the guidance notes)

▶ Provide managers with adequate leadership training, familiarity with key policies and the resources to manage effectively (see guidance note 1).

▶ Establish systematic, fair and transparent recruitment procedures to attract the maximum number of appropriate candidates (see guidance note 2).

▶ Recruit teams with a balance of women and men, ethnicity, age and social background so that the team's diversity is appropriate to the local culture and context.

▶ Provide aid workers (staff, volunteers and consultants, both national and international) with adequate and timely inductions, briefings, clear reporting lines and updated job descriptions to enable them to understand their responsibilities, work objectives, organisational values, key policies and local context.

▶ Establish security and evacuation guidelines, health and safety policies and use them to brief aid workers before they start work with the agency.

▶ Ensure that aid workers have access to medical care and psychosocial support.

▶ Establish codes of personal conduct for aid workers that protect disaster-affected people from sexual abuse, corruption, exploitation and other violations of people's human rights. Share the codes with disaster-affected people (see guidance note 3).

▶ Promote a culture of respect towards the disaster-affected population (see guidance note 4).

▶ Establish grievance procedures and take appropriate disciplinary action against aid workers following confirmed violation of the agency's code of conduct.

▶ Carry out regular appraisals of staff and volunteers and provide feedback on performance in relation to work objectives, knowledge, skills, behaviour and attitudes.

▶ Support aid workers to manage their workload and minimise stress (see guidance note 5).

▶ Enable staff and managers to jointly identify opportunities for continual learning and development (see guidance note 6).

▶ Provide appropriate support to aid workers who have experienced or witnessed extremely distressing events (see guidance note 7).

Key indicators (to be read in conjunction with the guidance notes)

▶ Staff and volunteers' performance reviews indicate adequate competency levels in relation to their knowledge, skills, behaviour attitudes and the responsibilities described in their job descriptions.

▶ Aid workers who breach codes of conduct prohibiting corrupt and abusive behaviour are formally disciplined.

▶ The principles, or similar, of the People In Aid Code of Good Practice are reflected in the agency's policy and practice.

▶ The incidence of aid workers' illness, injury and stress-related health issues remains stable, or decreases over the course of the disaster response.

Guidance notes

1. *Management good practice:* People management systems depend on the agency and context but managers and supervisors should be familiar with the People In Aid Code of Good Practice which includes policies and guidelines for planning, recruitment, management, learning and development, transition at the end of a contract and, for international agencies, deployment.

2. *Recruitment procedures* should be open and understandable to all staff and applicants. Such transparency includes the development and sharing of updated and relevant job descriptions for each post and is essential to establish diverse and competent teams. Existing teams can increase their appropriateness and diversity through new recruitment as required. Rapid staff expansion may lead to the recruitment of inexperienced team members who should be supported by experienced staff.

1. *Aid workers' control* over the management and allocation of valuable aid resources puts them in a position of power over the disaster-affected population. Such power over people dependent on assistance and whose protective social networks have been disturbed or destroyed can lead to corruption and abuse. Women, children and persons with disabilities are frequently coerced into sexually abusive situations. Sexual activity can never be demanded in exchange for humanitarian assistance or protection. No individual associated with humanitarian response (aid workers and military, state or private sector personnel) should be party to abuse, corruption or sexual exploitation. The forced labour of adults or children, illicit drug use and trading in humanitarian goods and services by those connected with humanitarian distributions are also prohibited.

1. *Aid workers should respect* the values and dignity of the disaster-affected population and avoid behaviours (such as inappropriate dress) that are culturally unacceptable to them.

1. *Aid workers often work long hours* in risky and stressful conditions. An agency's duty of care to its workers includes actions to promote well-being and avoid long-term exhaustion, injury or illness. Managers must make aid workers aware of the risks and protect them from exposure to unnecessary threats to their physical and emotional health through, for example, effective security management, adequate rest and recuperation, active support to work reasonable hours and access to psychological support. Managers can promote a duty of care through modelling good practice and personally complying with policy. Aid workers also need to take personal responsibility for managing their well-being.

1. *In the early phase of a disaster,* staff capacity development may be restricted. Over time, through performance reviews and feedback from staff, managers should identify and support areas for learning and development. Disaster preparedness also provides opportunities to identify and develop humanitarian-related competencies.

2. *Psychological first aid* should be immediately available to workers who have experienced or witnessed extremely distressing events (see Essential health services – mental health standard 1 on page 333 and References and further reading). Psychological debriefing is ineffective and should not be provided.

References and further reading

Sources

People-centred humanitarian response

Emergency Capacity Building (ECB) Project (2007), Impact Measurement and Accountability in Emergencies: The Good Enough Guide. Oxfam Publishing. Oxford. www.oxfam.org.uk/publications

Human Accountability Partnership (HAP) International (forthcoming), Standard in Accountability and Quality Management. Geneva. www.hapinternational.org/projects/standard/hap_2010_standard.aspx

Inter-Agency Standing Committee (IASC) (2007), IASC Guidelines on Mental Health and Psychosocial Support in Emergency Settings. Geneva.

Coordination and collaboration

Global Humanitarian Platform (2007), Global Humanitarian Principles of Partnership. A Statement of Commitment Endorsed by the Global Humanitarian Platform. Geneva. www.globalhumanitarianplatform.org/pop.html

IASC (2008), Guidance Note on using the Cluster Approach to Strengthen Humanitarian Response. Geneva.

IASC, Global Cluster Approach: http://oneresponse.info/GlobalClusters/Pages/default.aspx

IASC and United Nations Office for the Coordination of Humanitarian Affairs (OCHA) (2008), Civil-Military Guidelines and Reference for Complex Emergencies. New York. http://ochaonline.un.org/cmcs/guidelines

OCHA (2007), Guidelines on the Use of Foreign Military and Civil Defence Assets In Disaster Relief – "Oslo Guidelines". Rev. 1.1. Geneva. http://ochaonline.un.org/cmcs

Assessment

IASC (2003), Initial Rapid Assessment (IRA) Guidance Notes for Country Level. Geneva. www.humanitarianreform.org/humanitarianreform/Portals/1/cluster%20approach%20page ?/clusters%20page ?s ?/health%20cluster/RT/IRA_Guidance_Country%20Level_field_test.doc

IASC (forthcoming), Needs Assessment Task Force (NATF) Operational Guidance for Needs Assessments.

Ushahidi mobile phone-based information gathering and sharing: www.ushahidi.com

Design and response

Conflict Sensitivity Consortium: www.conflictsensitivity.org/

Early Recovery Tools and Guidance: http://oneresponse.info/GlobalClusters/Early%20Recovery/Pages/Tools%20and%20Guidance.aspx

IASC (2006), Women, Girls, Boys and Men: Different Needs – Equal Opportunities (The Gender Handbook in Humanitarian Action). Geneva. http://oneresponse.info/crosscutting/gender/Pages/Gender.aspx

Provention Consortium (2007), Vulnerability and Capacity Analysis Guidance Note 9. Geneva. www.proventionconsortium.org/themes/default/pdfs/tools_for_mainstreaming_GN9.pdf

United Nations International Strategy for Disaster Reduction (UNISDR) (2005), Hyogo Framework for Action 2005–2015: Building the resilience of nations and communities to disasters. Geneva. www.unisdr.org/eng/hfa/docs/Hyogo-framework-for-action-english.pdf

Performance, transparency and learning

Active Learning Network for Accountability and Performance in Humanitarian Action (ALNAP) (2009), 8th Review of Humanitarian Action. Overseas Development Institute (ODI). London. www.alnap.org/initiatives/current/rha/8.aspx

Collaborative Learning Projects (2007), The Listening Project (LISTEN). Cambridge, Mass. www.cdainc.com/cdawww/pdf/other/cda_listening_project_description_Pdf.pdf

Groupe URD (2009), Quality Compas. www.compasqualite.org/en/index/index.php

Organisation for Economic Co-operation and Development (OECD) (1999), Guidance for Evaluation of Humanitarian Assistance in Complex Emergencies. Paris. www.oecd.org/dac

Aid worker performance

People In Aid (2003), The People In Aid Code of Good Practice in the Management and Support of Aid Personnel. London. http://peopleinaid.org

World Health Organization, World Vision International and War Trauma Foundation (forthcoming), Psychological First Aid Guide. Geneva. www.who.int/mental_health/emergencies/en/

Further reading

Assessment and response

Office of the United Nations High Commissioner for Refugees (UNHCR) and World Food Programme (WFP) (2008), Joint Assessment Mission Guidelines. 2nd Edition. Rome. www.unhcr.org/45f81d2f2.html

Children

Action for the rights of children (ARC) (2009), www.arc-online.org/using/index.html

Inter-Agency Network for Education in Emergencies (INEE) and The Sphere Project (2009), Integrating Quality Education within Emergency Response for Humanitarian Accountability: The Sphere–INEE Companionship. Geneva.

Disability

Handicap International, Disability Checklist for Emergency Response. www.handicap-international.de/fileadmin/redaktion/pdf/disability_checklist_booklet_01.pdf

Women's Commission for Refugee Women and Children (2008), Disabilities among Refugees and Conflict-affected Populations: A Resource Kit for Fieldworkers. New York. www.womensrefugeecommission.org/docs/disab_res_kit.pdf

Environment

Joint United Nations Environment Programme and OCHA Environment Unit: www.reliefweb.int/ochaunep

Kelly, C (2005), Guidelines for Rapid Environmental Impact Assessment in Disasters. Benfield Hazard Research Centre, University College London and CARE International. London.

UNHCR and CARE International (2005), Framework for Assessing, Monitoring and Evaluating the Environment in Refugee-related Operations: Toolkit for practitioners and managers to help assess, monitor and evaluate environmental circumstances, using mainly participatory approaches. Geneva. www.unhcr.org/4a97d1039.html

UNHCR and International Union for the Conservation of Nature (2005), UNHCR Environmental Guidelines. Geneva. www.unhcr.org/3b03b2a04.html

Gender

Gender and Disaster Network: http://gdnonline.org

WFP (2009), WFP Gender Policy. www.wfp.org/content/wfp-gender-policy

HIV/AIDS

IASC (2010), Guidelines for Addressing HIV in Humanitarian Settings. Geneva. www.humanitarianinfo.org/iasc/page ?loader.aspx?page ?=content-products-products&sel=9

Older people

HelpAge International: www.helpage.org

IASC (2008), Humanitarian Action and Older Persons – an essential brief for humanitarian actors. Geneva. www.humanitarianinfo.org/iasc/pageloader. aspx?page=content-products-products&sel=24

ODI (2005), Network paper 53: Assisting and protecting older people in emergencies. London. www.odi.org.uk/resources/details. asp?id=357&title=protecting-assisting-older-people-emergencies

Performance, monitoring and evaluation

ALNAP Annual Review (2003), Humanitarian Action: Improving Monitoring to Enhance Accountability and Learning. London. www.alnap.org

ALNAP (2009), Real Time Evaluations of Humanitarian Action (Pilot Version). London. www.alnap.org

Catley, A et al (2008), Participatory Impact Assessment. Feinstein International Center, Tufts University. https://wikis.uit.tufts.edu/confluence/display/FIC/Participatory+Impact+Assessment

Groupe URD (2009), Quality COMPAS Companion Book. www.compasqualite.org/en/index/index.php

OECD (1999), Guidance for the Evaluation of Humanitarian Assistance in Complex Emergencies. Paris. www.oecd.org/dac

Further information on evaluation (including training modules) and approaches to learning can be found on ALNAP: www.alnap.org

Targeting

International Federation of Red Cross and Red Crescent Societies (2003), World Disasters Report 2003 – Chapter 1: Humanitarian ethics in disaster and war. www.ifrc.org/publicat/wdr2003/chapter1.asp

UNISDR (2001), Countering Disasters, Targeting Vulnerability. Geneva. www.unisdr.org/eng/public_aware/world_camp/2001/pdf/Kit_1_Countering_ Disasters_Targeting_Vulnerability.pdf

Minimum Standards in Water Supply, Sanitation and Hygiene Promotion

How to use this chapter

This chapter is divided into seven main sections:

> Water supply, sanitation and hygiene promotion (WASH)
>
> Hygiene promotion
>
> Water supply
>
> Excreta disposal
>
> Vector control
>
> Solid waste management
>
> Drainage

The Protection Principles and Core Standards must be used consistently with this chapter.

Although primarily intended to inform humanitarian response to a disaster, the minimum standards may also be considered during disaster preparedness and the transition to recovery activities.

Each section contains the following:

- **Minimum standards:** These are qualitative in nature and specify the minimum levels to be attained in humanitarian response regarding the provision of water, sanitation and hygiene promotion.

- **Key actions:** These are suggested activities and inputs to help meet the standards.

- **Key indicators:** These are 'signals' that show whether a standard has been attained. They provide a way of measuring and communicating the processes and results of key actions; they relate to the minimum standard, not to the key action.

- **Guidance notes:** These include specific points to consider when applying the minimum standards, key actions and key indicators in different situations. They provide guidance on tackling practical difficulties, benchmarks or advice on priority issues. They may also include critical issues relating to the standards, actions or indicators, and describe dilemmas, controversies or gaps in current knowledge.

If the required key indicators and actions cannot be met, the resulting adverse implications for the affected population should be appraised and appropriate mitigating actions taken.

A needs assessment checklist is included as Appendix 1; guideline notes are provided in Appendices 2–6; and a select list of references and further reading, which points to sources of information on both specific and general issues relating to this chapter, is also provided.

Contents

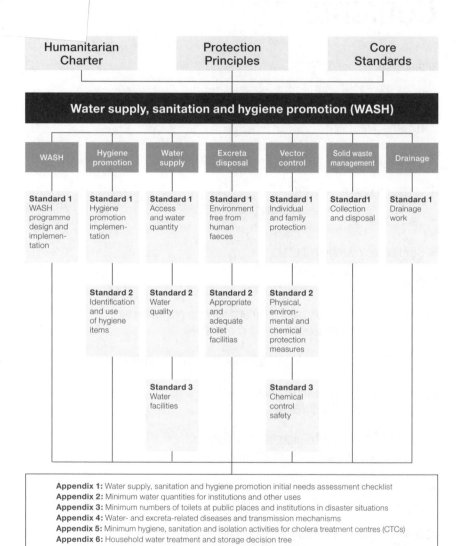

| Humanitarian Charter | Protection Principles | Core Standards |

Water supply, sanitation and hygiene promotion (WASH)

WASH	Hygiene promotion	Water supply	Excreta disposal	Vector control	Solid waste management	Drainage
Standard 1 WASH programme design and implementation	**Standard 1** Hygiene promotion implementation	**Standard 1** Access and water quantity	**Standard 1** Environment free from human faeces	**Standard 1** Individual and family protection	**Standard1** Collection and disposal	**Standard 1** Drainage work
	Standard 2 Identification and use of hygiene items	**Standard 2** Water quality	**Standard 2** Appropriate and adequate toilet facilitias	**Standard 2** Physical, environmental and chemical protection measures		
		Standard 3 Water facilities		**Standard 3** Chemical control safety		

Appendix 1: Water supply, sanitation and hygiene promotion initial needs assessment checklist
Appendix 2: Minimum water quantities for institutions and other uses
Appendix 3: Minimum numbers of toilets at public places and institutions in disaster situations
Appendix 4: Water- and excreta-related diseases and transmission mechanisms
Appendix 5: Minimum hygiene, sanitation and isolation activities for cholera treatment centres (CTCs)
Appendix 6: Household water treatment and storage decision tree

References and further reading

Introduction

Links to the Humanitarian Charter and international law

The minimum standards for water supply, sanitation and hygiene promotion (WASH) are a practical expression of the shared beliefs and commitments of humanitarian agencies and the common principles, rights and duties governing humanitarian action that are set out in the Humanitarian Charter. Founded on the principle of humanity, and reflected in international law, these principles include the right to life and dignity, the right to protection and security and the right to receive humanitarian assistance on the basis of need. A list of key legal and policy documents that inform the Humanitarian Charter is available for reference in Annex 1 (see page 356), with explanatory comments for humanitarian workers.

Although states are the main duty-bearers with respect to the rights set out above, humanitarian agencies have a responsibility to work with disaster-affected populations in a way that is consistent with these rights. From these general rights flow a number of more specific entitlements. These include the rights to participation, information and non-discrimination that form the basis of the Core Standards, as well the specific rights to water, sanitation, food, shelter and health that underpin these and the minimum standards in this Handbook.

Everyone has the right to water and sanitation. This right is recognised in international legal instruments and provides for sufficient, safe, acceptable, physically accessible and affordable water for personal and domestic uses and accessible sanitation facilities. An adequate amount of safe water is necessary to prevent death from dehydration, to reduce the risk of water-related disease and to provide for consumption, cooking and personal and domestic hygienic requirements.

The right to water and sanitation is inextricably related to other human rights, including the right to health, the right to housing and the right to adequate food. As such, it is part of the guarantees essential for human survival. States and non-state actors have responsibilities in fulfilling the right to water and sanitation. In times of armed conflict, for example, it is prohibited to attack, destroy, remove or render useless drinking water installations or irrigation works.

The minimum standards in this chapter are not a full expression of the right to water and sanitation. However, the Sphere standards reflect the core content of the right to water and sanitation and contribute to the progressive realisation of this right globally.

The importance of WASH in disasters

Water and sanitation are critical determinants for survival in the initial stages of a disaster. People affected by disasters are generally much more susceptible to illness and death from disease, which to a large extent are related to inadequate sanitation, inadequate water supplies and inability to maintain good hygiene. The most significant of these diseases are diarrhoeal and infectious diseases transmitted by the faeco-oral route (see Appendix 4: Water- and excreta-related diseases and transmission mechanisms). Other water- and sanitation-related diseases include those carried by vectors associated with solid waste and water. The term 'sanitation', throughout the Sphere Handbook, refers to excreta disposal, vector control, solid waste disposal and drainage.

The main objective of WASH programmes in disasters is to reduce the transmission of faeco-oral diseases and exposure to disease-bearing vectors through the promotion of:

▶ good hygiene practices

▶ the provision of safe drinking water

▶ the reduction of environmental health risks

▶ the conditions that allow people to live with good health, dignity, comfort and security.

Simply providing sufficient water and sanitation facilities will not, on its own, ensure their optimal use or impact on public health. In order to achieve the maximum benefit from a response, it is imperative that disaster-affected people have the necessary information, knowledge and understanding to prevent water- and sanitation-related diseases and to mobilise their involvement in the design and maintenance of those facilities.

The use of communal water and sanitation facilities, for example in refugee or displaced situations, can increase women's and girls' vulnerability to sexual and other forms of gender-based violence. In order to minimise these risks, and to provide a better quality of response, it is important to ensure women's participation in water supply and sanitation programmes. An equitable participation of women and men in planning, decision-making and local management will help to ensure that the entire affected population has safe and easy access to water supply and sanitation services, and that services are appropriate.

Better disaster response in public health is achieved through better preparedness. Such preparedness is the result of capacities, relationships and knowledge developed by governments, humanitarian agencies, local civil society organisations, communities and individuals to anticipate and respond effectively to the impact of likely, imminent hazards. It is based on an analysis of risks and is well linked to early warning systems. Preparedness includes contingency planning, stockpiling of equipment and supplies, emergency services and stand-by arrangements, personnel training and community-level planning training and drills.

Links to other chapters

Many of the standards in the other chapters are relevant to this chapter. Progress in achieving standards in one area often influences and even determines progress in other areas. For a response to be effective, close coordination and collaboration are required with other sectors. Coordination with local authorities and other responding agencies is also necessary to ensure that needs are met, that efforts are not duplicated and that the quality of water and sanitation interventions is optimised.

For example, where nutritional standards have not been met, the urgency to improve the standard of water and sanitation is greater as people's vulnerability to disease will have significantly increased. The same applies to populations where HIV and AIDS prevalence is high or where there is a large proportion of older people or persons with disabilities. Priorities should be decided on the basis of sound information shared between sectors as the situation evolves. Reference is also made, where relevant, to companion and complementary standards.

Links to the Protection Principles and Core Standards

In order to meet the standards of this Handbook, all humanitarian agencies should be guided by the Protection Principles, even if they do not have a distinct protection mandate or specialist capacity in protection. The Principles are not 'absolute': it is recognised that circumstances may limit the extent to which agencies are able to fulfil them. Nevertheless, the Principles reflect universal humanitarian concerns which should guide action at all times.

The Core Standards are essential process and personnel standards shared by all sectors. The six Core Standards cover participation, initial assessment, response, targeting, monitoring, evaluation, aid worker performance, and supervision and support to personnel. They provide a single reference point for approaches that underpin all other standards in the Handbook. Each technical chapter, therefore, requires the companion use of the Core Standards to help attain its own standards. In particular, to ensure the appropriateness and quality of any response, the participation of disaster-affected people – including the groups and individuals most frequently at risk in disasters – should be maximised.

Vulnerabilities and capacities of disaster-affected populations

This section is designed to be read in conjunction with, and to reinforce, the Core Standards.

It is important to understand that to be young or old, a woman or an individual with a disability or HIV does not, of itself, make a person vulnerable or at increased risk. Rather, it is the interplay of factors that does so: for example, someone who is over 70 years of age, lives alone and has poor health is likely to be more vulnerable than someone of a similar age and health status living within an extended family and with sufficient income. Similarly, a 3-year-old girl is much more vulnerable if she is unaccompanied than if she were living in the care of responsible parents.

As WASH standards and key actions are implemented, a vulnerability and capacity analysis helps to ensure that a disaster response effort supports those who have a right to assistance in a non-discriminatory manner and who need it most. This requires a thorough understanding of the local context and of how a particular crisis impacts on particular groups of people in different ways due to their pre-existing vulnerabilities (e.g. being very poor or discriminated against), their exposure to various protection threats (e.g. gender-based violence including sexual exploitation), disease incidence or prevalence (e.g. HIV or tuberculosis) and possibilities of epidemics (e.g. measles or cholera). Disasters can make pre-existing inequalities worse. However, support for people's coping strategies, resilience and recovery capacities is essential. Their knowledge, skills and strategies need to be supported and their access to social, legal, financial and psychosocial support advocated for. The various physical, cultural, economic and social barriers they may face in accessing these services in an equitable manner also need to be addressed.

The following highlight some of the key areas that will ensure that the rights and capacities of all vulnerable people are considered:

▶ Optimise people's participation, ensuring that all representative groups are included, especially those who are less visible (e.g. individuals who have communication or mobility difficulties, those living in institutions, stigmatised youth and other under- or unrepresented groups).

▶ Disaggregate data by sex and age (0–80+ years) during assessment – this is an important element in ensuring that the WASH sector adequately considers the diversity of populations.

▶ Ensure that the right to information on entitlements is communicated in a way that is inclusive and accessible to all members of the community.

₁mum standards

₁. ᵥᵥᵤter supply, sanitation and hygiene promotion (WASH)

The aim of any WASH programme is to promote good personal and environmental hygiene in order to protect health, as shown in the diagram below. An effective WASH programme relies on an exchange of information between the agency and the disaster-affected population in order to identify key hygiene problems and culturally appropriate solutions. Ensuring the optimal use of all water supply and sanitation facilities and practising safe hygiene will result in the greatest impact on public health.

Hygiene promotion is vital to a successful WASH intervention. The focus on hygiene promotion is general and specific. In general terms, hygiene promotion is integral to all of the sections and is reflected in the indicators for water supply, excreta disposal, vector control, solid waste management and drainage. More specifically, the focus narrows on two hygiene promotion standards in this chapter and relates to particular hygiene promotion activities.

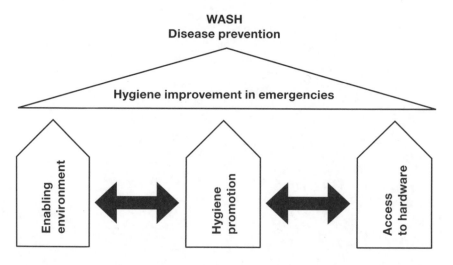

WASH
Disease prevention

Hygiene improvement in emergencies

Enabling environment

Hygiene promotion

Access to hardware

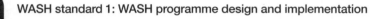

WASH standard 1: WASH programme design and implementation

WASH needs of the affected population are met and users are involved in the design, management and maintenance of the facilities where appropriate.

Key actions (to be read in conjunction with the guidance note)

▶ Identify key risks of public health importance in consultation with the affected population (see guidance note 1 and Core Standards 1, 3–4 on pages 55–65).

▶ Provide and address the public health needs of the affected population according to their priority needs (see guidance note 1).

▶ Systematically seek feedback on the design and acceptability of both facilities and promotional methods from all different user groups on all WASH programme activities (see Core Standards 1, 3–4 on pages 55–65).

Key indicators (to be read in conjunction with the guidance note)

▶ All groups within the population have safe and equitable access to WASH resources and facilities, use the facilities provided and take action to reduce the public health risk (see Hygiene promotion standard 2 on page 94).

▶ All WASH staff communicate clearly and respectfully with those affected and share project information openly with them, including knowing how to answer questions from community members about the project.

▶ There is a system in place for the management and maintenance of facilities as appropriate, and different groups contribute equitably (see guidance note 1).

▶ All users are satisfied that the design and implementation of the WASH programme have led to increased security and restoration of dignity.

Guidance note

1. *Assessing needs:* An assessment is needed to identify risky practices that might increase vulnerability and to predict the likely success of both the provision of WASH facilities and hygiene promotion activities. The key risks are likely to centre on physical safety in accessing facilities, discrimination of marginalised groups that affects access, use and maintenance of toilets, the lack of hand-washing with soap or an alternative, the unhygienic collection and storage of water, and unhygienic food storage and preparation. The assessment should look at resources available to the population, as well as local knowledge and practices, so that promotional activities are effective,

relevant and practical. Social and cultural norms that might facilitate and/
or compromise adherence to safe hygiene practices should be identified
as part of the initial and ongoing assessment. The assessment should pay
special attention to the needs of vulnerable people. If consultation with any
group of vulnerable people is not possible, this should be clearly stated in
the assessment report and addressed as quickly as possible (see Core
Standard 3 on page 61).

2. Hygiene promotion

Hygiene promotion is a planned, systematic approach to enable people to take action to prevent and/or mitigate water, sanitation and hygiene-related diseases. It can also provide a practical way to facilitate community participation, accountability and monitoring in WASH programmes. Hygiene promotion should aim to draw on the affected population's knowledge, practices and resources, as well as on the current WASH evidence base to determine how public health can best be protected.

Hygiene promotion involves ensuring that people make the best use of the water, sanitation and hygiene-enabling facilities and services provided and includes the effective operation and maintenance of the facilities. The three key factors are:

1. a mutual sharing of information and knowledge

2. the mobilisation of affected communities

3. the provision of essential materials and facilities.

Community mobilisation is especially appropriate during disasters as the emphasis must be on encouraging people to take action to protect their health. Promotional activities should include, where possible, interactive methods, rather than focusing exclusively on the mass dissemination of messages.

Hygiene promotion standard 1: Hygiene promotion implementation

Affected men, women and children of all ages are aware of key public health risks and are mobilised to adopt measures to prevent the deterioration in hygienic conditions and to use and maintain the facilities provided.

Key actions (to be read in conjunction with the guidance notes)

▶ Systematically provide information on hygiene-related risks and preventive actions using appropriate channels of mass communication (see guidance notes 1–2).

▶ Identify specific social, cultural or religious factors that will motivate different social groups in the community and use them as the basis for a hygiene promotion communication strategy (see guidance note 2).

▶ Use interactive hygiene communication methods wherever feasible in order to ensure ongoing dialogue and discussions with those affected (see guidance note 3).

▶ In partnership with the affected community, regularly monitor key hygiene practices and the use of facilities provided (see guidance note 3 and Core Standard 5, guidance notes 1, 3–5 on pages 69–70).

▶ Negotiate with the population and key stakeholders to define the terms and conditions for community mobilisers (see guidance note 5).

Key indicators (to be read in conjunction with the guidance notes)

▶ All user groups can describe and demonstrate what they have done to prevent the deterioration of hygiene conditions (see guidance note 1).

▶ All facilities provided are appropriately used and regularly maintained.

▶ All people wash their hands after defecation, after cleaning a child's bottom, before eating and preparing food (see guidance note 6).

▶ All hygiene promotion activities and messages address key behaviours and misconceptions and are targeted at all user groups (see guidance note 6).

▶ Representatives from all user groups are involved in planning, training, implementation, monitoring and evaluation of the hygiene promotion work (see guidance notes 1–6 and Core Standard 1, guidance notes 1–5, on page 56–57).

▶ Care-takers of young children and infants are provided with the means for safe disposal of children's faeces (see Excreta disposal standard 1 on page 105 and guidance note 6).

Guidance notes

1. *Targeting priority hygiene risks and behaviours:* The understanding gained through assessing hygiene risks, tasks and responsibilities of different groups should be used to plan and prioritise assistance, so that the information flow between humanitarian actors and the affected population is appropriately targeted and misconceptions, where found, are addressed.

2. *Reaching all sections of the population:* In the early stages of a disaster, it may be necessary to rely on the mass media to ensure that as many people as possible receive important information about reducing health risks.

Different groups should be targeted with different information, education and communication materials through relevant communication channels, so that information reaches all members of the population. This is especially important for those who are non-literate, have communication difficulties and/or do not have access to radio or television. Popular media (drama, songs, street theatre, dance, etc.) might also be effective in this instance. Coordination with the education cluster will be important to determine the opportunities for carrying out hygiene activities in schools.

3. **Interactive methods:** Participatory materials and methods that are culturally appropriate offer useful opportunities for affected people to plan and monitor their own hygiene improvements. It also gives them the opportunity to make suggestions or complaints about the programme, where necessary. The planning of hygiene promotion must be culturally appropriate. Hygiene promotion activities need to be carried out by facilitators who have the characteristics and skills to work with groups that might share beliefs and practices different from their own (for example, in some cultures it is not acceptable for women to speak to unknown men).

4. **Overburdening:** It is important to ensure that no one group (e.g. women) within the affected population is overburdened with the responsibility for hygiene promotion activities or the management of activities that promote hygiene. Benefits, such as training and employment opportunities, should be offered to women, men and marginalised groups.

5. **Terms and conditions for community mobilisers:** The use of outreach workers or home visitors provides a potentially more interactive way to access large numbers of people, but these workers will need support to develop facilitation skills. As a rough guide in a camp scenario, there should be two hygiene promoters/community mobilisers per 1,000 members of the affected population. Community mobilisers may also be employed as daily workers, on a contract or on a voluntary basis, and in accordance with national legislation. Whether workers have paid or volunteer status must be discussed with the affected population, implementing organisations and across clusters to avoid creating tension and disrupting the long-term sustainability of systems already in place.

6. **Motivating different groups to take action:** It is important to realise that health may not be the most important motivator for changes in behaviour. The need for privacy, safety, convenience, observation of religious and cultural norms, social status and esteem may be stronger driving forces than the promise of better health. These triggering factors need to be taken into account when designing promotional activities and must be effectively incorporated into the design and siting of facilities in conjunction with the

engineering team. The emphasis should not be solely on individual behavioural change but also on social mobilisation and working with groups.

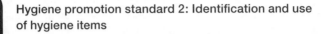

Hygiene promotion standard 2: Identification and use of hygiene items

The disaster-affected population has access to and is involved in identifying and promoting the use of hygiene items to ensure personal hygiene, health, dignity and well-being.

Key actions (to be read in conjunction with the guidance notes)

▶ Consult all men, women and children of all ages on the priority hygiene items they require (see guidance notes 1, 3–4).

▶ Undertake a timely distribution of hygiene items to meet the immediate needs of the community (see guidance notes 2–3).

▶ Carry out post-distribution monitoring to assess use of and beneficiary satisfaction with distributed hygiene items (see guidance notes 3 and 5).

▶ Investigate and assess the use of alternatives to the distribution of hygiene items, e.g. provision of cash, vouchers and/or non-food items (NFIs) (see Food security – cash and voucher transfers standard 1 on page 200).

Key indicators (to be read in conjunction with the guidance notes)

▶ Women, men and children have access to hygiene items and these are used effectively to maintain health, dignity and well-being (see guidance notes 1, 7 and 9).

▶ All women and girls of menstruating age are provided with appropriate materials for menstrual hygiene following consultation with the affected population (see guidance notes 5 and 8).

▶ All women, men and children have access to information and training on the safe use of hygiene items that are unfamiliar to them (see guidance note 5).

▶ Information on the timing, location, content and target groups for an NFI distribution is made available to the affected population (see guidance notes 3–5).

▶ The safety of affected populations and staff is prioritised when organising an NFI distribution (see Protection Principle 1, guidance notes 1–3 on pages 33–34).

Guidance notes

1. **Basic hygiene items:** A basic minimum hygiene items pack consists of water containers (buckets), bathing and laundry soaps, and menstrual hygiene materials.

List of basic hygiene items

10–20 litre capacity water container for transportation	One per household
10–20 litre capacity water container for storage	One per household
250g bathing soap	One per person per month
200g laundry soap	One per person per month
Acceptable material for menstrual hygiene, e.g. washable cotton cloth	One per person

2. **Coordination:** Discuss with the shelter cluster and the affected population whether additional non-food items, such as blankets, which are not included in the basic hygiene items are required (see Non-food items standard 1 on page 269).

3. **Timeliness of hygiene items distribution:** In order to ensure a timely distribution of hygiene items, it may be necessary to distribute some key generic items (soap, jerrycans, etc.) without the agreement of the affected population and come to an agreement concerning future distributions following consultation.

4. **Priority needs:** People may choose to sell the items provided if their priority needs are not appropriately met and so people's livelihoods need to be considered when planning distributions.

5. **Appropriateness:** Care should be taken to avoid specifying products that would not be used due to lack of familiarity or that could be misused (e.g. items that might be mistaken for food). Where culturally appropriate or preferred, washing powder can be specified instead of laundry soap.

6. **Replacement:** Consideration should be given for consumables to be replaced where necessary.

7. **Special needs:** Some people with specific needs (e.g. incontinence or severe diarrhoea) may require increased quantities of personal hygiene items such as soap. Persons with disabilities or those who are confined to bed may

need additional items, such as bed pans. Some items may require adaptation for sanitary use (such as a stool with a hole or commode chair).

8. **Menstrual hygiene:** Provision must be made for discreet laundering or disposal of menstrual hygiene materials.

9. **Additional items:** Existing social and cultural practices may require access to additional personal hygiene items. Subject to availability, such items (per person per month) could include:

   - 75ml/100g toothpaste
   - one toothbrush
   - 250ml shampoo
   - 250ml lotion for infants and children up to 2 years of age
   - one disposable razor
   - underwear for women and girls of menstrual age
   - one hairbrush and/or comb
   - nail clippers
   - nappies (diapers) and potties (dependent on household need).

3. Water supply

Water is essential for life, health and human dignity. In extreme situations, there may not be sufficient water available to meet basic needs and in these cases supplying a survival level of safe drinking water is of critical importance. In most cases, the main health problems are caused by poor hygiene due to insufficient water and by the consumption of contaminated water.

Water supply standard 1: Access and water quantity

All people have safe and equitable access to a sufficient quantity of water for drinking, cooking and personal and domestic hygiene. Public water points are sufficiently close to households to enable use of the minimum water requirement.

Key actions (to be read in conjunction with the guidance notes)

▶ Identify appropriate water sources for the situation, taking into consideration the quantity and environmental impact on the sources (see guidance note 1).

▶ Prioritise and provide water to meet the requirements of the affected population (see guidance notes 2 and 4).

Key indicators (to be read in conjunction with the guidance notes)

▶ Average water use for drinking, cooking and personal hygiene in any household is at least 15 litres per person per day (see guidance notes 1–7).

▶ The maximum distance from any household to the nearest water point is 500 metres (see guidance notes 1, 2, 5 and 6).

▶ Queueing time at a water source is no more than 30 minutes (see guidance note 6).

Guidance notes

1. *Water sources selection:* The following factors should be considered in water source selection: availability, proximity and sustainability of sufficient

quantity of water; whether treatment is needed; and its feasibility, including the existence of any social, political or legal factors concerning the source. Generally, groundwater sources and/or gravity-flow supplies from springs are preferable, as they require less treatment and no pumping. In disasters, a combination of approaches and sources is often required in the initial phase. All sources need to be regularly monitored to avoid over-exploitation.

2. **Needs:** The quantities of water needed for domestic use is context based, and may vary according to the climate, the sanitation facilities available, people's habits, their religious and cultural practices, the food they cook, the clothes they wear, and so on. Water consumption generally increases the nearer the water source is to the dwelling. Where possible, 15 litres per person per day (l/p/d) can be exceeded to conform to local standards where that standard is higher.

Basic survival water needs

Survival needs: water intake (drinking and food)	2.5–3 litres per day	Depends on the climate and individual physiology
Basic hygiene practices	2–6 litres per day	Depends on social and cultural norms
Basic cooking needs	3–6 litres per day	Depends on food type and social and cultural norms
Total basic water needs	7.5–15 litres per day	

For guidance on minimum water quantities needed for institutions and other uses, see Appendix 2: Minimum water quantities for institutions and other uses. For emergency livestock water needs, refer to Livestock Emergency Guidelines and Standards (see References and further reading).

3. **Measurement:** Household surveys, observation and community discussion groups are more effective methods of collecting data on water use and consumption than the measurement of water pumped into the pipeline network or the operation of hand pumps.

4. **Quantity/coverage:** In a disaster, and until minimum standards for both water quantity and quality are met, the priority is to provide equitable access to an adequate quantity of water even if it is of intermediate quality. Disaster-affected people are significantly more vulnerable to disease; therefore, water access and quantity indicators should be reached even if they are higher than the norms of the affected or host population. Particular attention should be

paid to ensure the need for extra water for people with specific health conditions, such as HIV and AIDS, and to meet the water requirement for livestock and crops in drought situations. To avoid hostility, it is recommended that water and sanitation coverage address the needs of both host and affected populations equally (see Appendix 2: Minimum water quantities for institutions and other uses).

5. *Maximum numbers of people per water source:* The number of people per source depends on the yield and availability of water at each source. The approximate guidelines are:

250 people per tap	based on a flow of 7.5 litres/minute
500 people per hand pump	based on a flow of 17 litres/minute
400 people per single-user open well	based on a flow of 12.5 litres/minute

These guidelines assume that the water point is accessible for approximately eight hours a day only and water supply is constant during that time. If access is greater than this, people can collect more than the 15 litres/day minimum requirement. These targets must be used with caution, as reaching them does not necessarily guarantee a minimum quantity of water or equitable access.

6. *Queueing time:* Excessive queueing times are indicators of insufficient water availability due to either an inadequate number of water points or inadequate yields at water sources. The potential negative results of excessive queueing times are reduced per capita water consumption, increased consumption from unprotected surface sources and reduced time for other essential survival tasks for those who collect water.

7. *Access and equity:* Even if a sufficient quantity of water is available to meet minimum needs, additional measures are needed to ensure equitable access for all groups. Water points should be located in areas that are accessible to all, regardless of, for example, gender or ethnicity. Some hand pumps and water carrying containers may need to be designed or adapted for use by people living with HIV and AIDS, older people, persons with disabilities and children. In situations where water is rationed or pumped at given times, this should be planned in consultation with the users including women beneficiaries.

Water supply standard 2: Water quality

Water is palatable and of sufficient quality to be drunk and used for cooking and personal and domestic hygiene without causing risk to health.

Key actions (to be read in conjunction with the guidance notes)

▶ Undertake a rapid sanitary survey and, where time and situation allow, implement a water safety plan for the source (see guidance notes 1–2).

▶ Implement all necessary steps to minimise post-delivery water contamination (see guidance notes 3–4 and Hygiene promotion standard 1 on page 91).

▶ For piped water supplies, or all water supplies at times of risk of diarrhoeal epidemics, undertake water treatment with disinfectant so that there is a chlorine residual of 0.5mg/l and turbidity is below 5 NTU (nephelolometric turbidity units) at the tap. In the case of specific diarrhoeal epidemics, ensure that there is residual chlorine of above 1mg/l (see guidance notes 5–8).

▶ Where household-level water treatment is proposed, ensure that it is accompanied by appropriate promotion, training and monitoring (see guidance notes 3 and 6).

Key indicators (to be read in conjunction with the guidance notes)

▶ There are no faecal coliforms per 100ml of water at the point of delivery and use (see guidance notes 2, 4–7).

▶ Any household-level water treatment options used are effective in improving microbiological water quality and are accompanied by appropriate training, promotion and monitoring (see guidance notes 3–6).

▶ There is no negative effect on health due to short-term use of water contaminated by chemicals (including carry-over of treatment chemicals) or radiological sources, and assessment shows no significant probability of such an effect (see guidance note 7).

▶ All affected people drink water from a protected or treated source in preference to other readily available water sources (see guidance notes 3 and 6).

▶ There is no outbreak of water-borne or water-related diseases (see guidance notes 1–9).

Guidance notes

1. *A sanitary survey and water safety plan:* A sanitary survey is an assessment of conditions and practices that may constitute a public health risk. It covers possible sources of contamination to water at the source in transport and in the home, defecation practices, drainage and solid waste management. Community mapping is a particularly effective way of identifying where the public health risks are and thereby involving the community in finding ways to reduce these risks. Note that while animal excreta is not as harmful as human excreta, it can contain micro-organisms, such as cryptosporidium, giardia, salmonella, campylobacter, caliciviruses and other common causes of human diarrhoea, and therefore presents a significant health risk. WHO recommends the use of its water safety plan (WSP), which is a holistic approach covering hazard identification and risk assessment, an improvement/upgrade plan, monitoring of control measures and management procedures, including the development of supporting programmes (see References and further reading).

2. *Microbiological water quality:* Faecal coliform bacteria (>99 per cent of which are *E. coli*) are an indicator of the level of human and/or animal waste contamination in water and the possibility of the presence of harmful pathogens. If any faecal coliforms are present, the water should be treated.

3. *Promotion of protected sources:* Merely providing protected sources or treated water will have little impact unless people understand the health benefits of this water and therefore use it. People may prefer to use unprotected sources, e.g. rivers, lakes and unprotected wells, for reasons such as taste, proximity and social convenience. In such cases, technicians, hygiene promoters and community mobilisers need to understand the rationale for the preferences so that their consideration can be included in promotional messages and discussions.

4. *Post-delivery contamination:* Water that is safe at the point of delivery can nevertheless present a significant health risk due to recontamination during collection, storage and drawing. Steps that can be taken to minimise such risk include improved collection and storage practices and distribution of clean and appropriate collection and storage containers (see Water supply standard 3 on page 103). Water should be routinely sampled at the point of use to monitor the extent of any post-delivery contamination.

5. *Water disinfection:* Water should be treated with a residual disinfectant such as chlorine if there is a significant risk of source or post-delivery contamination. This risk will be determined by conditions in the settlement, such as population density, excreta disposal arrangements, hygiene practices and the prevalence of diarrhoeal disease. In the case of a threat or the

existence of a diarrhoea epidemic, all drinking water supplies should be treated, either before distribution or in the home. For water to be disinfected properly, turbidity must be below 5 NTU, although for short-term emergency use, water of higher turbidity can be adequately disinfected with double chlorine dosage after filtration until turbidity reduction is achieved (see Appendix 6: Household water treatment and storage decision tree).

6. *Household-level water treatment:* When use of a centrally operated water treatment system is not possible, point-of-use water treatment (PoUWT) at household level can be used as an option. The different types of PoUWT options shown to reduce diarrhoea and improve the microbiological quality of stored household water include boiling, chlorination, solar disinfection, ceramic filtration, slow sand filtration and flocculation/disinfection. The most appropriate PoUWT option for any given context depends on existing water and sanitation conditions, water quality, cultural acceptability and the implementation feasibility of any of the options. Successful PoUWT should include the provision of adequate materials and products and appropriate training for the beneficiaries. Introducing an untested water treatment option in a disaster situation should be avoided. In areas with anticipated risk, pre-placement of PoUWT products should be considered to facilitate a quick response. The use of locally available products should be prioritised if continued use in the post-disaster phase is desired. Effective use of PoUWT requires regular follow-up, support and monitoring and this should be a prerequisite to adopting it as an alternative water treatment approach.

7. *PoUWT using chlorine:* Double-dose chlorination can be considered for higher turbidity where there is no alternative water source. This should be attempted only for short periods of time and after educating users to reduce turbidity by filtering, settling and decanting before treatment (see Appendix 6: Household water treatment and storage decision tree).

8. *Chemical and radiological contamination:* Where hydrogeological records or knowledge of industrial or military activity suggest that water supplies may carry chemical or radiological health risks, the risks should be rapidly assessed by carrying out a chemical analysis. A decision that balances short-term public health risks and benefits should then be made. Furthermore, a decision to use possibly contaminated water for longer-term supplies should be made on the basis of a more thorough assessment and analysis of the health implications.

9. *Palatability:* Taste is not in itself a direct health problem (e.g. slightly saline water does not pose a health risk), but if the safe water supply does not taste good, users may drink from unsafe sources and put their health at risk. To avoid this, hygiene promotion activities are needed to ensure that only safe supplies are used.

10. **Water quality for health centres:** All water for hospitals, health centres and feeding centres should be treated with chlorine or another residual disinfectant. In situations where water is likely to be rationed by an interruption of supply, sufficient water storage should be available at the centre to ensure an uninterrupted supply at normal usage levels (see Appendices 2: Minimum water quantities for institutions and other uses and 5: Minimum hygiene, sanitation and isolation activities for cholera treatment centres).

Water supply standard 3: Water facilities

People have adequate facilities to collect, store and use sufficient quantities of water for drinking, cooking and personal hygiene, and to ensure that drinking water remains safe until it is consumed.

Key actions (to be read in conjunction with the guidance notes)

▶ Provide the affected population with appropriate water collection and storage facilities (see guidance note 1 and Hygiene promotion standard 2 on page 94).

▶ Actively encourage the participation of all affected individuals and vulnerable people in siting and design of water points and in the construction of laundry and bathing facilities (see guidance note 2).

▶ Include, at water distribution points and community laundry facilities, private washing basins and laundry areas for women to wash and dry undergarments and sanitary cloths (see guidance note 2 and Hygiene promotion standard 2 on page 94).

Key indicators (to be read in conjunction with the guidance notes)

▶ Each household has at least two clean water collecting containers of 10–20 litres, one for storage and one for transportation (see guidance note 1 and Hygiene promotion standard 2, guidance note 1 on page 95).

▶ Water collection and storage containers have narrow necks and/or covers for buckets or other safe means of storage, for safe drawing and handling, and are demonstrably used (see guidance note 1).

▶ There is at least one washing basin per 100 people and private laundering and bathing areas available for women. Enough water is made available for bathing and laundry (see guidance note 2).

▶ Water at household level is free from contamination at all times (see guidance note 1).

▶ All people are satisfied with the adequate facilities they have for water collection, storage, bathing, hand washing and laundry (see guidance note 2).

▶ Regular maintenance of the installed systems and facilities is ensured and users are involved in this where possible (see guidance note 3).

Guidance notes

1. *Water collection and storage:* People need vessels to collect water, to store it and to use it for drinking, cooking, washing and bathing. The vessels should be clean, hygienic, easy to carry and appropriate to local needs and habits in terms of size, shape and design. Children, persons with disabilities, older people and people living with HIV and AIDS may need smaller or specially designed water carrying containers. The amount of storage capacity required depends on the size of the household and the consistency of water availability, e.g. approximately four litres per person would be appropriate for situations where there is a constant daily supply. Promotion and monitoring of safe collection, storage and drawing is an opportunity to discuss water contamination issues with vulnerable people, especially women and children.

2. *Communal washing and bathing facilities:* People require spaces where they can bathe in privacy and with dignity. If this is not possible at the household level, separate central facilities for men and women will be needed. Where soap is not available, commonly used alternatives, such as ash, clean sand, soda or various plants suitable for washing and/or scrubbing, can be provided. Washing clothes, particularly children's clothes, is an essential hygiene activity; cooking and eating utensils also need washing. The number, location, design, safety, appropriateness and convenience of facilities should be decided in consultation with the users, particularly women, adolescent girls and persons with disabilities. The location of facilities in central, accessible and well-lit areas with good visibility of the surrounding area can contribute to ensuring the safety of users.

3. Maintenance of water systems: It is important that the affected population is made aware of and provided with all necessary means to maintain and sustain the systems provided.

4. Excreta disposal

Safe disposal of human excreta creates the first barrier to excreta-related disease, helping to reduce disease transmission through direct and indirect routes. Safe excreta disposal is, therefore, a major priority and in most disaster situations should be addressed with as much speed and effort as the provision of a safe water supply. The provision of appropriate facilities for defecation is one of a number of emergency responses essential for people's dignity, safety, health and well-being.

Excreta disposal standard 1: Environment free from human faeces

The living environment in general and specifically the habitat, food production areas, public centres and surroundings of drinking water sources are free from human faecal contamination.

Key actions (to be read in conjunction with the guidance notes)

▶ Implement appropriate excreta containment measures immediately (see guidance note 1).

▶ Carry out rapid consultation with the affected population on safe excreta disposal and hygienic practices (see Hygiene promotion standard 1, guidance notes 1–6 on pages 92–93).

▶ Carry out concerted hygiene promotion campaign on safe excreta disposal and use of appropriate facilities (see Hygiene promotion standard 1, guidance notes 1–6 on pages 92–93).

Key indicators (to be read in conjunction with the guidance notes)

▶ The environment in which the affected population lives is free from human faeces (see guidance notes 1–2).

▶ All excreta containment measures, i.e. trench latrines, pit latrines and soak-away pits, are at least 30 metres away from any groundwater source. The bottom of any latrine or soak-away pit is at least 1.5 metres above the water table (see guidance note 3).

▶ In flood or high water table situations, appropriate measures are taken to tackle the problem of faecal contamination of groundwater sources (see guidance note 3).

▶ Drainage or spillage from defecation systems does not contaminate surface water or shallow groundwater sources (see guidance note 3).

▶ Toilets are used in the most hygienic way possible and children's faeces are disposed of immediately and hygienically (see guidance note 4).

Guidance notes

1. *Safe excreta disposal:* Safe excreta disposal aims to keep the environment free from uncontrolled and scattered human faeces. Immediately after a disaster and while an excreta disposal management plan is put in place, consider implementing an initial clean-up campaign, demarcating and cordoning off defecation areas, and siting and building communal toilets. Based on context, a phased approach to solving the sanitation problem at hand is most effective. Involve all groups from the disaster-affected population in the implementation of safe excreta disposal activities. Where the affected population has not traditionally used toilets, it will be necessary to conduct a concerted hygiene promotion campaign to encourage safe excreta disposal and to create a demand for more toilets. In urban disasters where there could be damage to existing sewerage systems, assess the situation and consider installing portable toilets or use septic and/or containment tanks that can be regularly desludged. Due consideration should be given to desludging, handling, transportation and final disposal of the sludge.

2. *Defecation areas:* In the initial phase and where land is available, mark off a defecation field and/or construct trench latrines. This will only work if the site is correctly managed and maintained and the affected population understands the importance of using the facilities provided and where they are located.

3. *Distance of defecation systems from water sources:* The distance of soak pits, trench latrines and/or toilets from water sources should be at least 30 metres and the bottom of the pits should be at least 1.5 metres above the groundwater table. These distances need to be increased for fissured rocks and limestone, or decreased for fine soils. In some disaster response, groundwater pollution may not be an immediate concern if it is not to be directly used for drinking. Instead, household-level water treatment or other options should be adopted (see Water supply standard 2, guidance note 6 on page 102). In flooded or high water table environments, it may be necessary to build elevated toilets or septic tanks to contain excreta and prevent it contaminating the environment. It is also imperative that drainage or spillage

from septic tanks does not contaminate surface water and/or groundwater sources.

4. **Containment of children's faeces:** Give particular attention to the disposal of children's faeces, as they are commonly more dangerous than those of adults (excreta-related infection among children is frequently higher and children may not have developed antibodies to infections). Parents and care-givers should be provided with information about safe disposal of infants' faeces, laundering practices and the use of nappies (diapers), potties or scoops for effectively managing safe disposal.

Excreta disposal standard 2: Appropriate and adequate toilet facilities

People have adequate, appropriate and acceptable toilet facilities, sufficiently close to their dwellings, to allow rapid, safe and secure access at all times, day and night.

Key actions (to be read in conjunction with the guidance notes)

▶ Consult and secure the approval of all users (especially women and people with limited mobility) on the siting, design and appropriateness of sanitation facilities (see guidance notes 1–4 and Protection Principles 1–2 on pages 33–36).

▶ Provide the affected people with the means, tools and materials to construct, maintain and clean their toilet facilities (see guidance notes 6–7).

▶ Provide an adequate supply of water for hand washing and for toilets with flush and/or hygienic seal mechanisms, and appropriate anal cleansing material for use in conventional pit latrines (see guidance notes 7–8).

Key indicators (to be read in conjunction with the guidance notes)

▶ Toilets are appropriately designed, built and located to meet the following requirements:

- they can be used safely by all sections of the population, including children, older people, pregnant women and persons with disabilities (see guidance note 1)
- they are sited in such a way as to minimise security threats to users, espe-cially women and girls, throughout the day and the night (see guidance note 3 and Protection Principle 1, guidance notes 1–6 on pages 33–34).

- they provide a degree of privacy in line with the norms of the users (see guidance note 3)
- they are sufficiently easy to use and keep clean and do not present a health hazard to the environment. Depending on the context, the toilets are appropriately provided with water for hand washing and/or for flushing (see guidance notes 7–8)
- they allow for the disposal of women's menstrual hygiene materials and provide women with the necessary privacy for washing and drying menstrual hygiene materials (see guidance note 9)
- they minimise fly and mosquito breeding (see guidance note 7)
- they are provided with mechanisms for desludging, transport and appropriate disposal in the event that the toilets are sealed or are for long-term use and there is a need to empty them (see guidance note 11)
- in high water table or flood situations, the pits or containers for excreta are made watertight in order to minimise contamination of groundwater and the environment (see guidance note 11).

▶ A maximum of 20 people use each toilet (see guidance notes 1–4 and Appendix 3: Minimum numbers of toilets at public places and institutions in disaster situations).

▶ Separate, internally lockable toilets for women and men are available in public places, such as markets, distribution centres, health centres, schools, etc. (see guidance note 2 and Protection Principles 1–2 on pages 33–36).

▶ Toilets are no more than 50 metres from dwellings (see guidance note 5).

▶ Use of toilets is arranged by household(s) and/or segregated by sex (see guidance notes 2–5).

▶ All the affected population is satisfied with the process of consultation and with the toilet facilities provided and uses them appropriately (see guidance notes 1–10).

▶ People wash their hands after using toilets and before eating and food preparation (see guidance note 8).

Guidance notes

1. *Acceptable facilities:* Successful excreta disposal programmes depend on an understanding of people's varied needs and their participation. It may not be possible to make all toilets acceptable to all groups. Special toilets may need to be constructed for children, older people and persons with disabilities, e.g. toilets with seats or hand rails or provision of bed pans, potties or commodes. The type of sanitation facility adopted depends on the time of the intervention, the preferences and cultural habits of the intended users,

the existing infrastructure, the availability of water (for flushing and water seals), the soil formation and the availability of construction materials. Different excreta disposal types for different phases of a disaster response are listed in the table below.

Possible alternatives for safe excreta disposal

	Safe excreta disposal type	Application remarks
1	Demarcated defecation area (e.g. with sheeted-off segments)	First phase: the first two to three days when a huge number of people need immediate facilities
2	Trench latrines	First phase: up to two months
3	Simple pit latrines	Plan from the start through to long-term use
4	Ventilated improved pit (VIP) latrines	Context-based for middle- to long-term response
5	Ecological sanitation (Ecosan) with urine diversion	Context-based: in response to high water table and flood situations, right from the start or middle to long term
6	Septic tanks	Middle- to long-term phase

2. **Public toilets:** In public places, toilets are provided with established systems for proper and regular cleaning and maintenance. Disaggregated population data are used to plan the number of women's cubicles to men's using an approximate ration of 3:1. Where possible, urinals should be provided (see Appendix 3: Minimum numbers of toilets at public places and institutions in disaster situations).

3. **Family toilets:** Family toilets are the preferred option where possible. One toilet for a maximum of 20 people should be the target. Where there are no existing toilets, it is possible to start with one for 50 people and lowering the number of users to 20 as soon as possible. In some circumstances, space limitations make it impossible to meet these figures. In such cases, advocate strongly for extra space. However, it should be remembered that the primary aim is to provide and maintain an environment free from human faeces.

4. **Shared facilities:** Households should be consulted on the siting and design, and the responsible cleaning and maintenance of shared toilets. Generally, clean latrines are more likely to be frequently used. Efforts should be made to provide people living with chronic illnesses such as HIV and AIDS with

easy access to a toilet as they frequently suffer from chronic diarrhoea and reduced mobility.

5. **Safe facilities:** Inappropriate siting of toilets may make women and girls more vulnerable to attack, especially during the night. Ensure that women and girls feel and are safe when using the toilets provided. Where possible, communal toilets should be provided with lighting, or households provided with torches. The input of the community should be sought with regard to ways of enhancing the safety of users (see Protection Principles 1–2 on pages 33–36).

6. **Use of local building material and tools:** The use of locally available material for construction of latrines is highly recommended. It enhances the participation of the affected population to use and maintain the facilities. Providing the population with construction tools will also support this aim.

7. **Water and anal cleansing material:** Water should be provided for toilets with water flush and/or hygienic seal mechanisms. For a conventional pit toilet, it may be necessary to provide toilet paper or other material for anal cleansing. Users should be consulted on the most culturally appropriate cleansing materials and their safe disposal.

8. **Hand washing:** Users should have the means to wash their hands with soap or an alternative (such as ash) after using toilets, after cleaning the bottom of a child who has been defecating, and before eating and preparing food. There should be a constant source of water near the toilet for this purpose.

9. **Menstruation:** Women and girls of menstruating age, including schoolgirls, should have access to suitable materials for the absorption and disposal of menstrual blood. Women and girls should be consulted on what is culturally appropriate. Latrines should include provision for appropriate disposal of menstrual material or private washing facilities (see Hygiene promotion standard 2, guidance notes 2 and 8 on pages 95–96).

10. **Desludging:** When appropriate, and depending on the need, desludging of toilets/septic tanks and excreta containers, including siting of final sewage disposal point, needs to be considered right from the start.

11. **Toilets in difficult environments:** In flood or urban disasters, the provision of appropriate excreta disposal facilities is usually difficult. In such situations, various human waste containment mechanisms, such as raised toilets, urine diversion toilets, sewage containment tanks and the use of temporary disposable plastic bags with appropriate collection and disposal systems, should be considered. These different approaches need to be supported by hygiene promotion activities.

5. Vector control

A vector is a disease-carrying agent and vector-borne diseases are a major cause of sickness and death in many disaster situations. Mosquitoes are the vector responsible for malaria transmission, which is one of the leading causes of morbidity and mortality. Mosquitoes also transmit other diseases, such as yellow fever, dengue and haemorrhagic fever. Non-biting or synanthropic flies, such as the house fly, the blow fly and the flesh fly, play an important role in the transmission of diarrhoeal disease. Biting flies, bedbugs and fleas are a painful nuisance and in some cases transmit significant diseases such as murine typhus, scabies and plague. Ticks transmit relapsing fever, while human body lice transmit typhus and relapsing fever. Rats and mice can transmit diseases, such as leptospirosis and salmonellosis, and can be hosts for other vectors, e.g. fleas, which may transmit Lassa fever, plague and other infections.

Vector-borne diseases can be controlled through a variety of initiatives, including appropriate site selection and provision of shelter, water supply, excreta disposal, solid waste management and drainage, provision of health services (including community mobilisation and health promotion), use of chemical controls, family and individual protection, and effective protection of food stores. The nature of vector-borne disease is often complex and addressing vector-related problems may demand specialist attention. However, there is often much that can be done to help prevent the spread of such diseases with simple and effective measures, once the disease, its vector and their interaction with the population have been identified.

Vector control standard 1: Individual and family protection

All disaster-affected people have the knowledge and the means to protect themselves from disease and nuisance vectors that are likely to cause a significant risk to health or well-being.

Key actions (to be read in conjunction with the guidance notes)

▶ Raise the awareness of all affected people who are at risk from vector-borne diseases about possible causes of vector-related diseases, methods of transmission and possible methods of prevention (see guidance notes 1–5).

▶ Help the affected population to avoid exposure to mosquitoes during peak biting times by using all non-harmful means (such as bed nets, repellant lotions, etc.) that are made available to them (see guidance note 3).

▶ Pay special attention to the protection of high-risk groups such as pregnant and feeding mothers, babies, infants, older people, those with restricted mobility and the sick (see guidance note 3).

▶ Carry out control of human body lice where louse-borne typhus or relapsing fever is a threat (see guidance note 4).

▶ Ensure that bedding and clothing are aired and washed regularly (see guidance note 4).

Key indicators (to be read in conjunction with the guidance notes)

▶ All populations have access to shelters that do not harbour or encourage the growth of vector populations and are protected by appropriate vector control measures (see guidance notes 3–5).

▶ All populations at risk from vector-borne disease understand the modes of transmission and take action to protect themselves (see guidance notes 1–5).

▶ All people supplied with insecticide-treated mosquito nets use them effectively (see guidance note 3).

▶ All food stored at the household level is protected from contamination by vectors such as flies, insects and rodents (see guidance note 4).

Guidance notes

1. **Defining vector-borne disease risk:** Decisions about vector control interventions should be based on an assessment of potential disease risk, as well as on clinical evidence of a vector-borne disease problem. Factors influencing this risk include:

   - immunity status of the population, including previous exposure, nutritional stress and other stresses. Movement of people (e.g. refugees, internally displaced people (IDPs)) from a non-endemic to an endemic area is a common cause of epidemics
   - pathogen type and prevalence, in both vectors and humans
   - vector species, behaviours and ecology
   - vector numbers (season, breeding sites, etc.)
   - increased exposure to vectors: proximity, settlement pattern, shelter type, existing individual protection and avoidance measures.

2. *Indicators for vector control programmes:* Commonly used indicators for measuring the impact of vector control activities are vector-borne disease incidence rates (from epidemiological data, community-based data and proxy indicators, depending on the response) and parasite counts (using rapid diagnostic kits or microscopy).

3. *Individual malaria protection measures:* If there is a significant risk of malaria, the systematic and timely provision of protection measures is recommended, such as insecticide-treated materials, e.g. tents, curtains and bed nets. Impregnated bed nets have the added advantage of giving some protection against body and head lice, fleas, ticks, cockroaches and bedbugs. Long-sleeved clothing, household fumigants, burning coils, aerosol sprays and repellents are among other protection methods that can be used against mosquitoes. It is vital to ensure that users understand the importance of protection and how to use the tools correctly so that the protection measures are effective. Where resources are scarce, they should be directed at individuals and groups most at risk, such as children under 5 years old, non-immunes and pregnant women.

4. *Individual protection measures for other vectors:* Good personal hygiene and regular washing of clothes and bedding are the most effective protection against body lice. Infestations can be controlled by personal treatment (powdering), mass laundering or delousing campaigns and by treatment protocols as newly displaced people arrive in a settlement. A clean household environment, together with good waste disposal and good food storage (cooked and uncooked), will deter rats, other rodents and insects (such as cockroaches) from entering houses or shelters.

5. *Water-borne diseases:* People should be informed of health risks and should avoid entering bodies of water where there is a known risk of contracting diseases such as schistosomiasis, Guinea worm or leptospirosis (transmitted by exposure to mammalian urine, especially that of rats – see Appendix 4: Water- and excreta-related diseases and transmission mechanisms). Agencies may need to work with the affected population to find alternative sources of water or ensure that water for all uses is appropriately treated.

> ### Vector control standard 2: Physical, environmental and chemical protection measures
>
> The environment where the disaster-affected people are placed does not expose them to disease-causing and nuisance vectors, and those vectors are kept to a reduced level where possible.

Key actions (to be read in conjunction with the guidance notes)

▶ Settle the displaced populations in locations that minimise their exposure to vectors, especially mosquitoes (see guidance note 1).

▶ Clear and/or modify vector breeding and resting sites where practicable (see guidance notes 2–4).

▶ Undertake intensive fly control in high-density settlements when there is a risk or the presence of a diarrhoea epidemic (see guidance note 2).

▶ Provide working referral mechanisms for people infected with malaria for early diagnosis and treatment (see guidance note 5).

Key indicators

▶ The population density of mosquitoes is kept low to avoid the risk of excessive transmission levels and infection (see guidance note 4).

▶ Fewer people are affected by vector-related health problems (see guidance notes 1–5).

Guidance notes

1. *Site selection* is important in minimising the exposure of the affected population to the risk of vector-borne disease. This should be one of the key factors when considering possible sites. With regard to malaria control, for example, camps should be located 1–2 kilometres upwind from large breeding sites, such as swamps or lakes, whenever an additional clean water source can be provided (see Shelter and settlement standard 2, guidance notes 5–9 on pages 256–257).

2. *Environmental and chemical vector control:* There are a number of basic environmental engineering measures that can be taken to reduce the opportunities for vector breeding. These include the proper disposal of human and animal excreta (see Excreta disposal section on page 105), proper disposal of refuse in order to control flies and rodents (see Solid waste management section on page 117), drainage of standing water, and clearing unwanted

vegetation cover around open canals and ponds to control mosquitoes (see Drainage section on page 121). Such priority environmental health measures will have some impact on the population density of some vectors. It may not be possible to have sufficient impact on all the breeding, feeding and resting sites within a settlement or near it, even in the longer term, and localised chemical control measures or individual protection measures may be needed. For example, spraying infected spaces may reduce the number of adult flies and prevent a diarrhoea epidemic, or may help to minimise the disease burden if employed during an epidemic.

3. **Designing a response:** Vector control programmes may have no impact on disease if they target the wrong vector, use ineffective methods or target the right vector in the wrong place or at the wrong time. Control programmes should initially aim to address the following objectives: reduce vector population density; reduce human – vector contact; and reduce vector breeding sites. Poorly executed programmes can be counterproductive. Detailed study and, often, expert advice are needed and should be sought from national and international health organisations. In addition, local advice should be sought on local disease patterns, breeding sites, seasonal variations in vector numbers and incidence of diseases, etc.

4. **Environmental mosquito control:** Environmental control aims primarily at eliminating mosquito breeding sites. The three main species of mosquitoes responsible for transmitting disease are *Culex* (filariasis), *Anopheles* (malaria and filariasis) and *Aedes* (yellow fever and dengue). *Culex* mosquitoes breed in stagnant water loaded with organic matter such as latrines, *Anopheles* in relatively unpolluted surface water such as puddles, slow-flowing streams and wells, and *Aedes* in water receptacles such as bottles, buckets, tyres, etc. Examples of environmental mosquito control include good drainage, properly functioning VIP (ventilated improved pit) latrines, keeping lids on the squatting hole of pit latrines and on water containers, and keeping wells covered and/or treating them with a larvicide (e.g. for areas where dengue fever is endemic).

5. **Malaria treatment:** Malaria control strategies that aim to reduce the mosquito population density should be carried out simultaneously with early diagnosis and treatment with effective anti-malarials. Such strategies will include eliminating breeding sites, reducing the mosquito daily survival rate and restricting the habit of biting humans. Campaigns to encourage early diagnosis and treatment should be initiated and sustained. An integrated approach, combining active case finding by trained outreach workers and treatment with effective anti-malarials, is more likely to reduce the malaria burden than passive case finding through centralised health services (see Essential health services – control of communicable diseases standard 2, guidance note 3 on page 315).

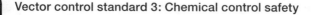

Vector control standard 3: Chemical control safety

Chemical vector control measures are carried out in a manner that ensures that staff, the disaster-affected population and the local environment are adequately protected and that avoids creating chemical resistance to the substances used.

Key actions (to be read in conjunction with the guidance note)

▶ Protect chemical handling personnel by providing training, protective clothing, bathing facilities and restricting the number of hours they spend handling chemicals (see guidance note 1).

▶ Inform the disaster-affected population about the potential risks of the substances used in chemical vector control and about the schedule for application. Provide the population with protection during and after the application of poisons or pesticides, according to internationally agreed procedures (see guidance note 1).

Key indicators (to be read in conjunction with the guidance note)

▶ Accepted international standards and norms are followed in the choice of quality, storage and transport of chemicals for vector control measures. No adverse reactions are reported or observed due to vector control chemicals (see guidance note 1).

▶ All vector control chemicals are accounted for at all times (see guidance note 1).

Guidance note

1. *National and international protocols:* There are clear international protocols and norms, published by WHO, which should be adhered to at all times. These are protocols for both the choice and the application of chemicals in vector control, including the protection of personnel and training requirements. Vector control measures should address two principal concerns: efficacy and safety. If national norms with regard to the choice of chemicals fall short of international standards, resulting in little or no impact or endangering health and safety, then the agency should consult and lobby the relevant national authority for permission to adhere to the international standards.

6. Solid waste management

Solid waste management is the process of handling and disposal of organic and hazardous solid waste which, if unattended appropriately, can pose public health risks to the affected population and can have a negative impact on the environment. Such risks can arise from the breeding of flies and rodents that thrive on solid waste (see Vector control section on page 111) and the pollution of surface- and groundwater sources due to leachate from mixed household and clinical or industrial waste. Uncollected and accumulating solid waste and the debris left after a natural disaster may also create an ugly and depressing environment, which might help discourage efforts to improve other aspects of environmental health. Solid waste often blocks drainage channels and leads to an increased risk of flooding, resulting in environmental health problems associated with stagnant and polluted surface water. Waste pickers, who gain a small income from collecting recyclable materials from waste dumps, may also be at risk of infectious disease from hospital waste mixed with household waste.

Solid waste management standard 1: Collection and disposal

The affected population has an environment not littered by solid waste, including medical waste, and has the means to dispose of their domestic waste conveniently and effectively.

Key actions (to be read in conjunction with the guidance notes)

▶ Involve the affected population in the design and implementation of the solid waste disposal programme (see guidance note 1).

▶ Organise periodic solid waste clean-up campaigns (see guidance note 1).

▶ Consider the potential for small-scale business opportunities or supplementary income from waste recycling (see guidance note 3).

▶ In conjunction with the affected population, organise a system to ensure that household waste is put in containers for regular collection to be burned or buried in specified refuse pits and that clinical and other hazardous wastes are kept separate throughout the disposal chain (see guidance note 3).

▶ Remove refuse from the settlement before it becomes a health risk or a nuisance (see guidance notes 2–6).

▶ Provide additional waste storage and collection facilities for host families, reflecting the additional waste accumulation in disaster situations.

▶ Provide clearly marked and appropriately fenced refuse pits, bins or specified area pits at public places, such as markets and fish processing and slaughtering areas (see guidance notes 3–6).

▶ Ensure there is a regular refuse collection system in place (see guidance notes 3–6).

▶ Undertake final disposal of solid waste in such a manner and place as to avoid creating health and environmental problems for the host and affected populations (see guidance notes 6–7).

▶ Provide personnel who deal with the collection and disposal of solid waste material and those involved in material collection for recycling with appropriate protective clothing and immunisation against tetanus and hepatitis B (see guidance note 7).

▶ In the event that the appropriate and dignified disposal of dead bodies is a priority need, coordinate with responsible agencies and authorities dealing with it (see guidance note 8).

Key indicators (to be read in conjunction with the guidance notes)

▶ All households have access to refuse containers which are emptied twice a week at minimum and are no more than 100 metres from a communal refuse pit (see guidance note 3).

▶ All waste generated by populations living in settlements is removed from the immediate living environment on a daily basis, and from the settlement environment a minimum of twice a week (see guidance notes 1–3).

▶ At least one 100-litre refuse container is available per 10 households, where domestic refuse is not buried on-site (see guidance note 3).

▶ There is timely and controlled safe disposal of solid waste with a consequent minimum risk of solid waste pollution to the environment (see guidance notes 4–6).

▶ All medical waste (including dangerous waste such as glasses, needles, dressings and drugs) is isolated and disposed of separately in a correctly designed, constructed and operated pit or incinerator with a deep ash pit, within the boundaries of each health facility (see guidance notes 4–7).

Guidance notes

1. **Planning and implementation:** Solid waste disposal should be planned and implemented in close consultation and coordination with the affected population and relevant agencies and authorities. This should start in the beginning of the intervention before a solid waste problem becomes a major health risk to the affected population. Depending on the context, periodic clean-up campaigns need to be organised in consultation with the population and responsible local authorities.

2. **Burial of waste:** If waste is to be buried on-site in either household or communal pits, it should be covered daily with a thin layer of earth to prevent it attracting vectors such as flies and rodents where it might become their breeding ground. If children's faeces/nappies are being disposed of, they should be covered with earth directly afterwards. Disposal sites should be fenced off to prevent accidents and access by children and animals. Care should be taken to prevent any leachate contaminating the groundwater.

3. **Refuse type and quantity:** Refuse in settlements varies widely in composition and quantity, according to the amount and type of economic activity, the staple foods consumed and local practices of recycling and/or waste disposal. The extent to which solid waste has an impact on people's health should be assessed and appropriate action taken if necessary. Household waste should be collected in refuse containers for disposal in a pit for burying or incineration. Where it is not possible to provide refuse containers for each household, communal refuse containers should be provided. Recycling of solid waste within the community should be encouraged, provided it presents no significant health risk. Distribution of commodities that produce a large amount of solid waste from packaging or processing on-site should be avoided.

4. **Medical waste:** Poor management of healthcare waste exposes the population, healthcare workers and waste handlers to infections, toxic effects and injuries. In a disaster situation, the most hazardous types of waste are likely to be infectious sharps and non-sharps (wound dressings, blood-stained cloth and organic matter such as placentas, etc.). The different types of waste should be separated at source. Non-infectious waste (paper, plastic wrappings, food waste, etc.) can be disposed of as solid waste. Contaminated sharps, especially used needles and syringes, should be placed in a safety box directly after use. Safety boxes and other infectious waste can be disposed of on-site by burial, incineration or other safe methods (see Health systems standard 1, guidance note 11 on page 300).

5. **Market waste:** Most market waste can be treated in the same way as domestic refuse. Slaughterhouse and fish-market waste may need special

treatment and facilities to deal with the liquid waste produced and to ensure that slaughtering is carried out in hygienic conditions and in compliance with local laws. Slaughter waste can often be disposed of in a large covered pit next to the abattoir or fish processing plant. Blood, etc., can be run from the abattoir or fish processing plant into the pit through a slab-covered channel (which should help reduce fly access to the pit). Water should be made available for cleaning purposes.

6. **Controlled tipping and/or sanitary landfill:** Large-scale disposal of waste should be carried out off-site through either controlled tipping or sanitary landfill. This method is dependent upon sufficient space and access to mechanical equipment. Ideally, waste that is tipped should be covered with earth at the end of each day to prevent scavenging and vector breeding.

7. **Staff welfare:** All involved in the collection, transport, disposal and recycling of solid waste should be provided with protective clothing, including at minimum gloves but ideally overalls, boots and protective masks. When necessary, immunisation against tetanus and hepatitis B should also be provided. Water and soap should be available for hand and face washing. Staff who come into contact with medical waste should be informed of the correct methods of storage, transport and disposal and the risks associated with improper management of the waste.

8. **Management of dead bodies:** The management and/or burial of dead bodies from natural disasters should be dealt with in an appropriate and dignified manner. It is usually handled by search and recovery teams, in coordination with responsible government agencies and authorities. The burial of people who have died due to communicable diseases also needs to be managed appropriately and in consultation and coordination with health authorities (see Health systems standard 1, guidance note 12 on page 300). Further information on how to deal with appropriate burial of dead bodies can be obtained from the materials in the References and further reading section.

7. Drainage

Surface water in or near settlements may come from household and water point wastewater, leaking toilets and sewers, rainwater or rising floodwater. The main health risks associated with surface water are contamination of water supplies and the living environment, damage to toilets and dwellings, vector breeding, and drowning. Rainwater and rising floodwaters can worsen the drainage situation in a settlement and further increase the risk of contamination. A proper drainage plan, addressing stormwater drainage through site planning and wastewater disposal using small-scale, on-site drainage, should be implemented to reduce potential health risks to the disaster-affected population. This section addresses small-scale drainage problems and activities. Large-scale drainage is generally determined by site selection and development (see Shelter and settlement standard 2, guidance note 5 on page 256).

Drainage standard 1: Drainage work

People have an environment in which health risks and other risks posed by water erosion and standing water, including stormwater, floodwater, domestic wastewater and wastewater from medical facilities, are minimised.

Key actions (to be read in conjunction with the guidance notes)

▶ Provide appropriate drainage facilities so that dwelling areas and water distribution points are kept free of standing wastewater and that stormwater drains are kept clear (see guidance notes 1–2, 4–5).

▶ Seek an agreement with the affected population on how to deal with the drainage problem and provide sufficient numbers of appropriate tools for small drainage works and maintenance where necessary (see guidance note 4).

▶ Ensure that all water points and hand washing facilities have effective drainage to prevent muddy conditions (see guidance note 2).

Key indicators (to be read in conjunction with the guidance notes)

▶ Water point drainage is well planned, built and maintained. This includes drainage from washing and bathing areas as well as water collection points and hand washing facilities (see guidance notes 2 and 4).

▶ There is no pollution of surface water and/or groundwater sources from drainage water (see guidance note 5).

▶ Shelters, paths and water and sanitation facilities are not flooded or eroded by water (see guidance notes 2–4).

▶ There is no erosion caused by drainage water (see guidance note 5).

Guidance notes

1. *Site selection and planning:* The most effective way to control drainage problems is in the choice of site and the layout of the settlement (see Shelter and settlement standards 1–2 on pages 249–254).

2. *Wastewater:* Sullage or domestic wastewater is classified as sewage when mixed with human excreta. Unless the settlement is sited where there is an existing sewerage system, domestic wastewater should not be allowed to mix with human excreta. Sewage is difficult and more expensive to treat than domestic wastewater. At water points and washing and bathing areas, the creation of small gardens to utilise wastewater should be encouraged where possible. Special attention needs to be paid to prevent wastewater from washing and bathing areas contaminating water sources.

3. *Drainage and excreta disposal:* Special care is needed to protect toilets and sewers from flooding in order to avoid structural damage and leakage.

4. *Promotion:* It is essential to involve the affected population in providing small-scale drainage works as they often have good knowledge of the natural flow of drainage water and of where channels should be. Also, if they understand the health and physical risks involved and have assisted in the construction of the drainage system, they are more likely to maintain it (see Vector control section on page 111). Technical support and tools may then be needed.

5. *On-site disposal:* Where possible, and if favourable soil conditions exist, drainage from water points, washing areas and hand washing points should be on-site rather than via open channels, which are difficult to maintain and often clog. Simple and cheap techniques such as soak pits or the planting of banana trees can be used for on-site disposal of wastewater. Where off-site disposal is the only possibility, channels are preferable to pipes. Channels should be designed both to provide flow velocity for dry-weather sullage and to carry stormwater. Where the slope is more than 5 per cent, engineering

techniques must be applied to prevent excessive erosion. Drainage of residuals from any water treatment processes should be carefully controlled so that people cannot use such water and it does not contaminate surface or groundwater sources.

Appendix 1

Water supply, sanitation and hygiene promotion initial needs assessment checklist

This list of questions is primarily for use to assess needs, identify indigenous resources and describe local conditions. It does not include questions to determine external resources needed in addition to those immediately and locally available.

1 General

▶ How many people are affected and where are they? Disaggregate the data as far as possible by sex, age, disability, etc.

▶ What are people's likely movements? What are the security factors for the affected population and for potential relief responses?

▶ What are the current, prevalent or possible water- and sanitation-related diseases? What is the likely extent and expected evolution of problems?

▶ Who are the key people to consult or contact?

▶ Who are the vulnerable people in the population and why?

▶ Is there equal access for all to existing facilities including at public places, health centres and schools?

▶ What special security risks exist for women, girls and vulnerable people?

▶ What water and sanitation practices were the population accustomed to before the disaster?

▶ What are the formal and informal power structures (e.g. community leaders, elders, women's groups)?

▶ How are decisions made in households and in the community?

2 Hygiene promotion

▶ What water and sanitation practices were the population accustomed to before the disaster?

▶ What practices are harmful to health, who practises these and why?

▶ Who still practises positive hygiene behaviour and what enables and motivates them to do this?

▶ What are the advantages and disadvantages of any proposed changes in practice?

▶ What are the existing formal and informal channels of communication and outreach (community health workers, traditional birth attendants, traditional healers, clubs, cooperatives, churches, mosques, etc.)?

▶ What access to the mass media is there in the area (radio, television, video, newspapers, etc.)?

▶ What local media organisations and/or non-governmental organisations (NGOs) are there?

▶ What segments of the population need to be targeted (mothers, children, community leaders, community kitchen workers, etc.)?

▶ What type of outreach system would work in this context (volunteers, health clubs, committees, etc.) for both immediate and medium-term mobilisation?

▶ What are the learning needs of hygiene promotion staff and volunteers?

▶ What non-food items are available and what are the most urgent based on preferences and needs?

▶ How effective are hygiene practices in health facilities (particularly important in epidemic situations)?

3 Water supply

▶ What is the current water supply source and who are the present users?

▶ How much water is available per person per day?

▶ What is the daily/weekly frequency of the water supply availability?

▶ Is the water available at the source sufficient for short-term and longer-term needs for all groups in the population?

▶ Are water collection points close enough to where people live? Are they safe?

▶ Is the current water supply reliable? How long will it last?

▶ Do people have enough water containers of the appropriate size and type?

▶ Is the water source contaminated or at risk of contamination (microbiological or chemical/radiological)?

▶ Is there a water treatment system in place? Is treatment necessary? Is treatment possible? What treatment is necessary?

▶ Is disinfection necessary, even if the supply is not contaminated?

▶ Are there alternative sources of water nearby?

▶ What traditional beliefs and practices relate to the collection, storage and use of water?

▶ Are there any obstacles to using available water supply sources?

▶ Is it possible to move the population if water sources are inadequate?

▶ Is it possible to tanker water if water sources are inadequate?

▶ What are the key hygiene issues related to water supply?

▶ Do people have the means to use water hygienically?

▶ In the event of rural displacement, what is the usual source of water for livestock?

▶ Will there be any environmental effects due to possible water supply intervention, abstraction and use of water sources?

▶ What other users are currently using the water sources? Is there a risk of conflict if the sources are utilised for the new populations?

4 Excreta disposal

▶ What is the current defecation practice? If it is open defecation, is there a designated area? Is the area secure?

▶ What are current beliefs and practices, including gender-specific practices, concerning excreta disposal?

▶ Are there any existing facilities? If so, are they used, are they sufficient and are they operating successfully? Can they be extended or adapted?

▶ Is the current defecation practice a threat to water supplies (surface- or groundwater) or living areas and to the environment in general?

▶ Do people wash their hands after defecation and before food preparation and eating? Are soaps or other cleansing materials available?

▶ Are people familiar with the construction and use of toilets?

▶ What local materials are available for constructing toilets?

▶ Are people prepared to use pit latrines, defecation fields, trenches, etc.?

▶ Is there sufficient space for defecation fields, pit latrines, toilets, etc.?

▶ What is the slope of the terrain?

▶ What is the level of the groundwater table?

▶ Are soil conditions suitable for on-site excreta disposal?

▶ Do current excreta disposal arrangements encourage vectors?

▶ Are there materials or water available for anal cleansing? How do people normally dispose of these materials?

▶ How do women manage issues related to menstruation? Are there appropriate materials or facilities available for this?

▶ Are there any specific facilities or equipment available for making sanitation accessible for persons with disabilities or people immobile in medical facilities?

▶ What environmental consideration should be assessed?

5 Vector-borne diseases

▶ What are the vector-borne disease risks and how serious are they?

▶ Are there traditional beliefs and practices (for example, the belief that malaria is caused by dirty water) that relate to vectors and vector-borne disease? Are any of these beliefs or practices either useful or harmful?

▶ If vector-borne disease risks are high, do people at risk have access to individual protection?

▶ Is it possible to make changes to the local environment (by drainage, scrub clearance, excreta disposal, refuse disposal, etc.) to discourage vector breeding?

▶ Is it necessary to control vectors by chemical means? What programmes, regulations and resources exist for vector control and the use of chemicals?

▶ What information and safety precautions need to be provided to households?

6 Solid waste management

▶ Is accumulated solid waste a problem?

▶ How do people dispose of their waste? What type and quantity of solid waste is produced?

▶ Can solid waste be disposed of on-site or does it need to be collected and disposed of off-site?

▶ What is the normal practice of solid waste disposal for the affected population (compost and/or refuse pits, collection system, bins, etc.)?

▶ Are there medical facilities and activities producing waste? How is this disposed of? Who is responsible?

▶ Where are menstrual pads disposed of and is their disposal discreet and effective?

▶ What is the effect of the current solid waste disposal on the environment?

7 Drainage

▶ Is there a drainage problem, e.g. flooding of dwellings or toilets, vector breeding sites, polluted water contaminating living areas or water supplies?

▶ Is the soil prone to water logging?

▶ Do people have the means to protect their dwellings and toilets from local flooding?

▶ Are water points and bathing areas well drained?

Appendix 2

Minimum water quantities for institutions and other uses

Health centres and hospitals	5 litres per outpatient 40–60 litres per inpatient per day Additional quantities may be needed for laundry equipment, flushing toilets, etc.
Cholera centres	60 litres per patient per day 15 litres per carer per day
Therapeutic feeding centres	30 litres per inpatient per day 15 litres per carer per day
Reception/transit centres	15 litres per person per day if stay is more than one day 3 litres per person per day if stay is limited to day-time
Schools	3 litres per pupil per day for drinking and hand washing (Use for toilets not included: see Public toilets below)
Mosques	2–5 litres per person per day for washing and drinking
Public toilets	1–2 litres per user per day for hand washing 2–8 litres per cubicle per day for toilet cleaning
All flushing toilets	20–40 litres per user per day for conventional flushing toilets connected to a sewer 3–5 litres per user per day for pour-flush toilets
Anal washing	1–2 litres per person per day
Livestock	20–30 litres per large or medium animal per day 5 litres per small animal per day

Appendix 3

Minimum numbers of toilets at public places and institutions in disaster situations

Institution	Short term	Long term
Market areas	1 toilet to 50 stalls	1 toilet to 20 stalls
Hospitals/medical centres	1 toilet to 20 beds or 50 outpatients	1 toilet to 10 beds or 20 outpatients
Feeding centres	1 toilet to 50 adults 1 toilet to 20 children	1 toilet to 20 adults 1 toilet to 10 children
Reception/transit centres	1 toilet to 50 individuals; 3:1 female to male	
Schools	1 toilet to 30 girls 1 toilet to 60 boys	1 toilet to 30 girls 1 toilet to 60 boys
Offices		1 toilet to 20 staff

Source: Adapted from Harvey, Baghri and Reed (2002)

Appendix 4

Water- and excreta-related diseases and transmission mechanisms

Water-borne or water-washed	Cholera, shigellosis, diarrhoea, salmonellosis, etc. Typhoid, paratyphoid, etc. Amoebic dysentery, giardiasis Hepatitis A, poliomyelitis, rotavirus, diarrhoea	Faecal-oral bacterial Faecal-oral non-bacterial	Water contamination Poor sanitation Poor personal hygiene Crop contamination
Water-washed or water-scarce	Skin and eye infections Louse-borne typhus and louse-borne relapsing fever		Inadequate water Poor personal hygiene
Excreta-related helminths	Roundworm, hookworm, whipworm etc.	Soil-transmitted helminths	Open defecation Ground contamination
Beef and pork tapeworms	Taeniasis	Man–animal	Half-cooked meat Ground contamination
Water-based	Schistosomiasis, Guinea worm, clonorchiasis, etc.	Long stay in infected water	Water contamination
Water-related insect vector	Malaria, dengue, sleeping sickness, filariasis, etc.	Biting by mosquitoes, flies	Bite near water Breed near water
Excreta-related insect vectors	Diarrhoea, dysentery	Transmitted by flies and cockroaches	Dirty environment

Appendix 5

Minimum hygiene, sanitation and isolation activities for cholera treatment centres (CTCs)

Essential principles that all health facilities and CTCs must follow:

1. Isolate severe cases
2. Contain all excreta (faeces and vomit)
3. Have only one carer per patient
4. Wash hands with chlorinated water
5. All floors must be washable
6. Disinfect feet when leaving the centre
7. Disinfect clothes of infected people before leaving the centre (by boiling or disinfection)
8. Provide regular cleaning of floors and all areas of the centre
9. Provide separate toilets and bathing areas for patients and carers
10. Prepare food in the centre. If brought from outside, food should be trans-ferred from container at the gate to prevent the container taking cholera-causing micro-organisms (vibrio) out of the centre after use
11. Follow up on the families and relatives of the patient, ensure there are no other cases. Disinfect the house and give hygiene information
12. If people arrive by public transport, disinfect the vehicles
13. Contain and treat run-off from rain and wastewater within the isolation camp area
14. Treat waste within the isolation camp area.

Chlorine solutions for CTCs

Chlorine % for different uses	2% solution	0.2% solution	0.05% solution
	Waste and excreta Dead bodies	Floor Objects / beds Footbaths Clothes	Hands Skin

NB: The solutions should be freshly prepared every day, since light and heat weaken the solution

Appendix 6

Household water treatment and storage decision tree

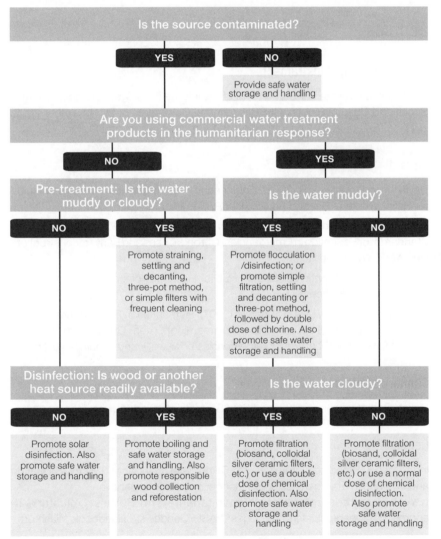

Is the source contaminated?

YES **NO**

NO → Provide safe water storage and handling

Are you using commercial water treatment products in the humanitarian response?

NO **YES**

Pre-treatment: Is the water muddy or cloudy?

Is the water muddy?

NO **YES** **YES** **NO**

YES → Promote straining, settling and decanting, three-pot method, or simple filters with frequent cleaning

YES → Promote flocculation /disinfection; or promote simple filtration, settling and decanting or three-pot method, followed by double dose of chlorine. Also promote safe water storage and handling

Disinfection: Is wood or another heat source readily available?

Is the water cloudy?

NO **YES** **YES** **NO**

NO → Promote solar disinfection. Also promote safe water storage and handling

YES → Promote boiling and safe water storage and handling. Also promote responsible wood collection and reforestation

YES → Promote filtration (biosand, colloidal silver ceramic filters, etc.) or use a double dose of chemical disinfection. Also promote safe water storage and handling

NO → Promote filtration (biosand, colloidal silver ceramic filters, etc.) or use a normal dose of chemical disinfection. Also promote safe water storage and handling

Source: Adapted from IFRC (2008), Household water treatment and safe storage in emergencies manual.

133

References and further reading

Sources

International legal instruments

The Right to Water (articles 11 and 12 of the International Covenant on Economic, Social and Cultural Rights), CESCR, General Comment 15, 26 November 2002. UN Doc. E/C.12/2002/11. Committee on Economic, Social and Cultural Rights.

General

Davis, J and Lambert, R (2002), Engineering in Emergencies: A Practical Guide for Relief Workers. Second Edition. RedR/IT Publications. London.

Inter-Agency Network for Education in Emergencies (INEE) (2010), Minimum Standards for Education in Emergencies, Chronic Crises and Early Reconstruction. New York. www.ineesite.org

Médecins sans Frontières (1994), Public Health Engineering in Emergency Situations. First Edition. Paris.

Walden, VM, O'Reilly, M and Yetter, M (2007), Humanitarian Programmes and HIV and AIDS; A practical approach to mainstreaming. Oxfam GB. Oxford.
www.oxfam.org.uk/what_we_do/emergencies/how_we_work/resources/health.htm

Sanitary surveys

British Geological Survey (2001), ARGOSS manual. London. www.bgs.ac.uk

Gender

Inter-Agency Standing Committee (IASC) (no date), Gender and Water, Sanitation and Hygiene in Emergencies. IASC Gender Handbook. Geneva.
www.humanitarianreform.org/humanitarianreform/Portals/1/cluster%20 approach%20page/clusters%20pages/WASH/Gender%20Handbook_Wash.pdf

Hygiene promotion

Almedom, A, Blumenthal, U and Manderson, L (1997), Hygiene Evaluation Procedures: Approaches and Methods for Assessing Water- and Sanitation-Related Hygiene Practices. The International Foundation for Developing Countries. Practical Action Publishing. UK.

Ferron, S, Morgan, J and O'Reilly, M (2007), Hygiene Promotion: A Practical Manual for Relief and Development. Practical Action Publishing. UK.

Humanitarian Reform Support Unit. WASH Cluster Hygiene Promotion Project. www.humanitarianreform.org/humanitarianreform/Default.aspx?tabid=160

Water supply

Action against Hunger (2006), Water, Sanitation and Hygiene for Populations at Risk. Paris. www.actioncontrelafaim.org/english/

House, S and Reed, R (1997), Emergency Water Sources: Guidelines for Selection and Treatment. Water, Engineering and Development Centre (WEDC), Loughborough University. UK.

Water needs for food security

Food and Agriculture Organization of the United Nations. FAO Water: www.fao.org/nr/water/index.html

Livestock water needs

LEGS (2009), Livestock Emergency Guidelines and Standards (LEGS). Practical Action Publishing. UK. www.livestock-emergency.net/userfiles/file/legs.pdf

Water quality

World Health Organization (WHO) (2003), Guidelines for Drinking-Water Quality. Third Edition. Geneva. www.who.int/water_sanitation_health/dwq/guidelines2/en/

Water safety plan

WHO (2005), Water safety plans: managing drinking-water quality from catchment to consumer. www.who.int/water_sanitation_health/dwq/wsp0506/en/

Excreta disposal

Harvey, P (2007), Excreta Disposal in Emergency, An inter-agency manual. WEDC, Loughborough University, UK. http://wedc.lboro.ac.uk/

Vector control

Hunter, P (1997), Waterborne Disease: Epidemiology and Ecology. John Wiley & Sons Ltd. Chichester, UK.

Lacarin, CJ and Reed, RA (1999), Emergency Vector Control Using Chemicals. WEDC, Loughborough University, UK.

Thomson, M (1995), Disease Prevention Through Vector Control: Guidelines for Relief Organisations. Oxfam GB.

Solid waste

Centre for appropriate technology (2003), Design of landfill sites. www.lifewater.org

International Solid Waste Association: www.iswa.org

Management of dead bodies

WHO (2009), Disposal of dead bodies in emergency conditions. Technical Note for Emergencies No. 8. Geneva. http://wedc.lboro.ac.uk/resources/who_notes/WHO_TN_08_Disposal_of_dead_bodies.pdf

Medical waste

Prüss, A, Giroult, E and Rushbrook, P (eds) (1999), Safe Management of Health-Care Wastes. (Currently under review.) WHO. Geneva.

Drainage

Environmental Protection Agency (EPA) (1980), Design Manual: On-Site Wastewater Treatment and Disposal Systems, Report EPA-600/2-78-173. Cincinnati, USA.

Further reading

General

WHO and Pan American Health Organization (PAHO), Health Library for Disasters: www.helid.desastres.net/en

WHO (2002), Environmental health in emergencies and disasters. Geneva.

Excreta disposal

Harvey, PA, Baghri, S and Reed, RA (2002), Emergency Sanitation, Assessment and Programme Design. WEDC, Loughborough University, UK.

Vector control

UNHCR (1997), Vector and Pest Control in Refugee Situations. Geneva.

Warrell, D and Gilles, H (eds) (2002), Essential Malariology. Fourth Edition. Arnold. London.

WHO, Chemical methods for the control of vectors and pests of public health importance. www.who.int.

Management of dead bodies

PAHO and WHO (2004), Management of Dead Bodies in Disaster Situations. Disaster Manuals and Guidelines Series, No 5. Washington DC. www.paho.org/English/DD/PED/ManejoCadaveres.htm

Medical waste

WHO (2000), Aide-Memoire: Safe Health-Care Waste Management. Geneva.

WHO, Healthcare waste management: www.healthcarewaste.org

WHO, Injection safety: www.injectionsafety.org

Disability and general vulnerability

Jones, H and Reed, R (2005), Water and sanitation for disabled people and other vulnerable groups: designing services to improve accessibility. WEDC, Loughborough University, UK. http://wedc.lboro.ac.uk/wsdp

Oxfam GB (2007), Excreta disposal for physically vulnerable people in emergencies. Technical Briefing Note 1. Oxfam, UK. www.oxfam.org.uk/resources/learning/humanitarian/downloads/TBN1_disability.pdf

Oxfam GB (2007), Vulnerability and socio-cultural considerations for PHE in emergencies Technical Briefing Note 2. Oxfam, UK. www.oxfam.org.uk/resources/learning/humanitarian/downloads/TBN2_watsan_sociocultural.pdf

Minimum Standards in Food Security and Nutrition

How to use this chapter

This chapter is divided into four main sections:

> Food security and nutrition assessment
>
> Infant and young child feeding
>
> Management of acute malnutrition and micronutrient deficiencies
>
> Food security

The fourth section, food security, is subdivided into three sections: food security – food transfers; food security – cash and voucher transfers; and food security – livelihoods.

The Protection Principles and Core Standards must be used consistently with this chapter.

Although primarily intended to inform humanitarian response to a disaster, the minimum standards may also be considered during disaster preparedness and the transition to recovery activities.

Each section contains the following:

- **Minimum standards:** These are qualitative in nature and specify the minimum levels to be attained in humanitarian response regarding the provision of food and nutrition.

- **Key actions:** These are suggested activities and inputs to help meet the standards.

- **Key indicators:** These are 'signals' that show whether a standard has been attained. They provide a way of measuring and communicating the processes and results of key actions; they relate to the minimum standard, not to the key action.

- **Guidance notes:** These include specific points to consider when applying the minimum standards, key actions and key indicators in different situations. They provide guidance on tackling practical difficulties, benchmarks or advice on priority issues. They may also include critical issues relating to the standards, actions or indicators, and describe dilemmas, controversies or gaps in current knowledge.

If the required key indicators and actions cannot be met, the resulting adverse implications for the affected population should be appraised and appropriate mitigating actions taken.

Appendices include checklists for assessments, guidance on measuring acute malnutrition and determining the public health significance of micronutrient deficiencies and nutritional requirements. A select list of references, which points to sources of information on both general issues and specific technical issues and is divided into source material and further reading, is also provided.

Contents

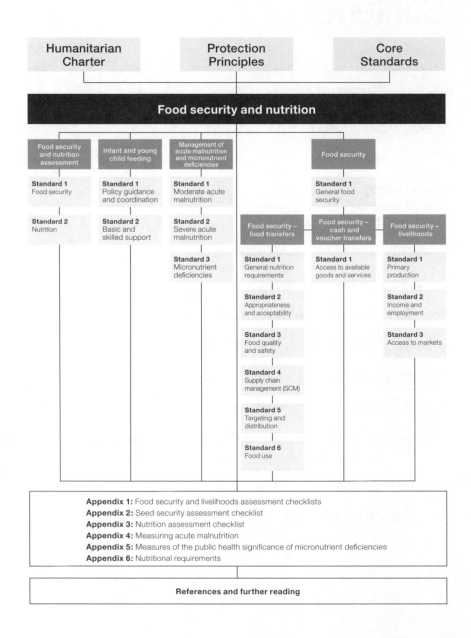

Introduction

Links to the Humanitarian Charter and international law

The minimum standards for food security and nutrition are a practical expression of the shared beliefs and commitments of humanitarian agencies and the common principles, rights and duties governing humanitarian action set out in the Humanitarian Charter. Founded on the principle of humanity, and reflected in international law, these principles include the right to life with dignity, the right to protection and security, and the right to receive humanitarian assistance on the basis of need. A list of key legal and policy documents that inform the Humanitarian Charter is available for reference in Annex 1 (see page 356), with explanatory comments for humanitarian workers.

Although states are the main duty-bearers with respect to the rights set out above, humanitarian agencies have a responsibility to work with the disaster-affected population in a way that is consistent with these rights. From these general rights flow a number of more specific entitlements, including the rights to participation, information and non-discrimination that form the basis of the Core Standards as well as the specific rights to water, food, shelter and health that underpin these and the minimum standards in this Handbook.

Everyone has the right to adequate food. This right is recognised in international legal instruments and includes the right to be free from hunger. When individuals or groups are unable, for reasons beyond their control, to enjoy the right to adequate food by the means at their disposal, states have the obligation to ensure that right directly. The right to food implies the following obligations for states:

- ▶ 'To respect existing access to adequate food' requires states parties not to take any measure that results in the prevention of such access.

- ▶ 'To protect' requires measures by the state to ensure that enterprises or individuals do not deprive individuals of access to adequate food.

- ▶ 'To fulfil' (facilitate) means that states must proactively engage in activities intended to strengthen people's access to and utilisation of resources and means to ensure their livelihoods, including food security.

In the case of disasters, states should provide food to those in need or may request international assistance if their own resources do not suffice. They should also facilitate safe and unimpeded access for international assistance.

The Geneva Conventions and additional protocols include the right to access to food in situations of armed conflict and occupation. It is prohibited to starve civilians as a method of warfare and to attack, destroy, remove or render useless foodstuffs, agricultural areas for the production of foodstuffs, crops, livestock, drinking water installations and supplies, and irrigation works. When one state occupies another by force, international humanitarian law obliges the occupying power to ensure adequate food for the population and to bring in necessary supplies if the resources of the occupied territory are inadequate. States should make every effort to ensure that refugees and internally displaced persons have access at all times to adequate food.

The minimum standards in this chapter reflect the core content of the right to food and contribute to the progressive realisation of this right globally.

The importance of food security and nutrition in disasters

Access to food and the maintenance of an adequate nutritional status are critical determinants of people's survival in a disaster (see The place of Sphere within humanitarian action on page 9). The people affected are often already chronically undernourished when the disaster hits. Undernutrition is a serious public health problem and among the lead causes of death, whether directly or indirectly.

The causes of undernutrition are complex. The conceptual framework (see page 146) is an analytical tool that shows the interaction between contributing factors to undernutrition. The immediate causes of undernutrition are disease and/or inadequate food intake, which result from underlying poverty, household food insecurity, inadequate care practices at household or community levels, poor water, hygiene and sanitation, and insufficient access to healthcare. Disasters such as cyclones, earthquakes, floods, conflict and drought all directly affect the underlying causes of undernutrition. The vulnerability of a household or community determines its ability to cope with exposure to these shocks. The ability to manage the associated risks is determined largely by the characteristics of a household or community, particularly its assets and the coping and livelihood strategies it pursues.

For this chapter the following definitions are used:

▶ *Food security* exists when all people, at all times, have physical, social and economic access to sufficient, safe and nutritious food to meet their dietary needs and food preferences for an active and healthy life. Within this definition of food security, there are three components:

- Availability refers to the quantity, quality and seasonality of the food supply in the disaster-affected area. It includes local sources of production (agriculture, livestock, fisheries, wild foods) and foods imported by traders (government and agencies' interventions can affect availability). Local markets able to deliver food to people are major determinants of availability.
- Access refers to the capacity of a household to safely procure sufficient food to satisfy the nutritional needs of all its members. It measures the household's ability to acquire available food through a combination of home production and stocks, purchases, barter, gifts, borrowing or food, cash and/or voucher transfers.
- Utilisation refers to a household's use of the food to which it has access, including storage, processing and preparation, and distribution within the household. It is also an individual's ability to absorb and metabolise nutrients, which can be affected by disease and malnutrition.

▶ *Livelihoods* comprise the capabilities, assets (including natural, material and social resources) and activities used by a household for survival and future well-being. Livelihood strategies are the practical means or activities through which people use their assets to earn income and achieve other livelihood goals. Coping strategies are defined as temporary responses forced by food insecurity. A household's livelihood is secure when it can cope with and recover from shocks, and maintain or enhance its capabilities and productive assets.

▶ *Nutrition* is a broad term referring to processes involved in eating, digestion and utilisation of food by the body for growth and development, reproduction, physical activity and maintenance of health. The term 'malnutrition' technically includes undernutrition and over-nutrition. Undernutrition encompasses a range of conditions, including acute malnutrition, chronic malnutrition and micronutrient deficiencies. Acute malnutrition refers to wasting (thinness) and/or nutritional oedema, while chronic malnutrition refers to stunting (shortness). Stunting and wasting are two forms of growth failure. In this chapter, we refer to undernutrition and revert to malnutrition specifically for acute malnutrition.

Conceptual framework of the causes of undernutrition

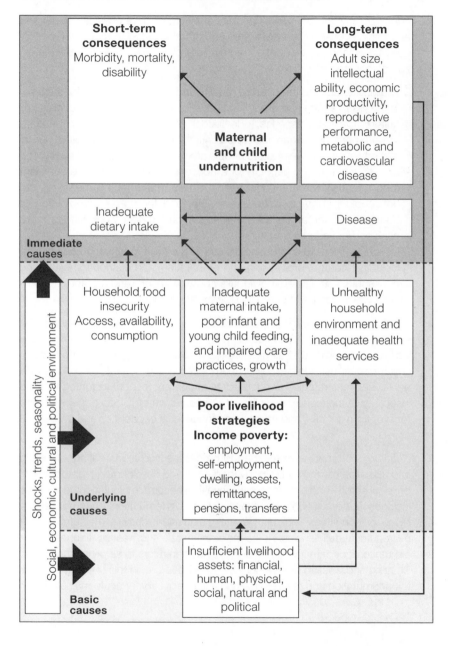

The framework shows that exposure to risk is determined by the frequency and severity of natural and man-made shocks and by their socio-economic and geographical scope. The determinants of coping capacity include the levels of a household's financial, human, physical, social, natural and political assets; the levels of its production, income and consumption; and its ability to diversify its income sources and consumption to mitigate the effects of the risks.

The vulnerability of infants and young children means that addressing their nutrition should be a priority. Prevention of undernutrition is as important as treatment of acute malnutrition. Food security interventions may determine nutrition and health in the short term and their survival and well-being in the long term.

Women often play a greater role in planning and preparation of food for their households. Following a disaster, household livelihood strategies may change. Recognising distinct roles in family nutrition is key to improving food security at the household level. Understanding the unique nutritional needs of pregnant and lactating women, young children, older people and persons with disabilities is also important in developing appropriate food responses.

Better food security and nutrition disaster response is achieved through better preparedness. Such preparedness is the result of the capacities, relationships and knowledge developed by governments, humanitarian agencies, local civil society organisations, communities and individuals to anticipate and respond effectively to the impact of likely, imminent or current hazards. Preparedness is based on an analysis of risks and is well linked to early warning systems. It includes contingency planning, stockpiling of equipment and supplies, emergency services and stand-by arrangements, communications, information management and coordination arrangements, personnel training and community-level planning, drills and exercises.

The main areas of intervention for food security and nutrition in disasters covered in this Handbook are infant and young child feeding; the management of acute malnutrition and micronutrient deficiencies; food transfers; cash and voucher transfers; and livelihoods.

Links to other chapters

Many of the standards in the other chapters are relevant to this chapter. Progress in achieving standards in one sector often influences progress in other sectors. For an intervention to be effective, close coordination and collaboration are required with other sectors. Coordination with local authorities, other responding agencies and community-based organisations is also necessary to ensure that needs are met, that efforts are not duplicated and that the quality of food security and nutrition interventions is optimised.

The conceptual framework for undernutrition (see page 146) identifies poor household environment and inadequate health services among the underlying causes of malnutrition. Responses to prevent and correct malnutrition require the achievement of minimum standards both in this chapter and in the WASH, Shelter and Health chapters. They also require that the Core Standards be achieved and the Protection Principles addressed. In order to ensure food security and nutrition of all groups in a manner that ensures their survival and upholds their dignity, it is not sufficient to achieve only the standards in this chapter of the Handbook.

Reference is made, where relevant, to specific standards or guidance notes in other chapters and to companion and complementary standards.

Links to the Protection Principles and Core Standards

In order to meet the standards of this Handbook, all humanitarian agencies should be guided by the Protection Principles, even if they do not have a distinct protection mandate or specialist capacity in protection. The Principles are not 'absolute': it is recognised that circumstances may limit the extent to which agencies are able to fulfil them. Nevertheless, the Principles reflect universal humanitarian concerns which should guide action at all times.

The Core Standards are essential process and personnel standards shared by all sectors. The six Core Standards cover participation, initial assessment, response, targeting, monitoring, evaluation, aid worker performance, and supervision and support to personnel. They provide a single reference point for approaches that underpin all other standards in the Handbook. Each technical chapter, therefore, requires the companion use of the Core Standards to help attain its own standards. In particular, to ensure the appropriateness and quality of any response, the participation of disaster-affected people – including the groups and individuals most frequently at risk in disasters – should be maximised.

Vulnerabilities and capacities of disaster-affected populations

This section is designed to be read in conjunction with, and to reinforce, the Core Standards.

It is important to understand that to be young or old, a woman or an individual with a disability or HIV, does not, of itself, make a person vulnerable or at increased risk. Rather, it is the interplay of factors that does so: for example, someone who is over 70 years of age, lives alone and has poor health is likely to be more vulnerable than someone of a similar age and health status living within an extended family and with sufficient income. Similarly, a 3-year-old girl is much more vulnerable if she is unaccompanied than if she were living in the care of responsible parents.

As food security and nutrition standards and key actions are implemented, a vulnerability and capacity analysis helps to ensure that the disaster response effort supports those who have a right to assistance in a non-discriminatory manner and who need it most. This requires a thorough understanding of the local context and of how a particular crisis impacts on particular groups of people in different ways due to their pre-existing vulnerabilities (e.g. being very poor or discriminated against), their exposure to various protection threats (e.g. gender-based violence including sexual exploitation), disease incidence or prevalence (e.g. HIV or tuberculosis) and possibilities of epidemics (e.g. measles or cholera). Disasters can make pre-existing inequalities worse. However, support for people's coping strategies, resilience and recovery capacities is essential. Their knowledge, skills and strategies need to be supported and their access to social, legal, financial and psychosocial support advocated for. The various physical, cultural, economic and social barriers they may face in accessing these services in an equitable manner also need to be addressed.

The following highlight some of the key areas that will ensure that the rights and capacities of all vulnerable people are considered:

▶ Optimise people's participation, ensuring that all representative groups are included, especially those who are less visible (e.g. individuals who have communication difficulties, mobility difficulties, those living in institutions, stigmatised youth and other under- or unrepresented groups).

▶ Disaggregate data by sex and age (0–80+ years) during assessment – this is an important element in ensuring that the food security and nutrition sector adequately considers the diversity of populations.

▶ Ensure that the right to information on entitlements is communicated in a way that is inclusive and accessible to all members of the community.

The minimum standards

1. Food security and nutrition assessment

In an acute crisis and for immediate response, multisector initial rapid assessments may be sufficient to decide whether or not immediate assistance is required. Initial rapid assessments are designed to obtain a fast and clear vision of a specific context in time. There will likely be a need to carry out further, more in-depth food security and nutrition assessments which require considerable time and resources to undertake properly. Assessment is a continuous process, particularly in protracted crises, and should inform targeting and decision-making as part of response management.

Ideally, food security and nutrition assessments should overlap and strive to identify the barriers to adequate nutrition, as well as interventions to improve availability, access and optimal utilisation of food intake. Assessment checklists are provided in Appendices 1: Food security and livelihoods assessment checklists, 2: Seed security assessment checklist and 3: Nutrition assessment checklist.

The two food security and nutrition assessment standards follow on from Core Standard 3 (see page 61) and both apply wherever food security and nutrition interventions are planned or are advocated.

Food security and nutrition assessment standard 1: Food security

Where people are at increased risk of food insecurity, assessments are conducted using accepted methods to understand the type, degree and extent of food insecurity, to identify those most affected and to define the most appropriate response.

Key actions (to be read in conjunction with the guidance notes)

▶ Use a methodology which adheres to widely accepted principles and describe it comprehensively in the assessment report (see guidance note 1).

▶ Collect and analyse information at the initial stage of the assessment (see guidance note 2).

▶ Analyse the impact of food insecurity on the population's nutritional status (see guidance note 4).

▶ Build the assessment upon local capacities, including formal and informal institutions, wherever possible (see guidance note 9).

Key indicators (to be read in conjunction with the guidance notes)

▶ Food security and livelihoods of individuals, households and communities are investigated to guide interventions (see guidance notes 3–9).

▶ Assessment findings are synthesised in an analytical report including clear recommendations of actions targeting the most vulnerable individuals and groups (see guidance notes 1–10).

▶ The response is based on people's immediate food needs but will also consider the protection and promotion of livelihood strategies (see guidance note 10).

Guidance notes

1. *Methodology:* The scope of assessments and sampling procedures are important, even if informal. Food security assessments should have clear objectives and use internationally accepted methods. Confirmation via different sources of information (e.g. crop assessments, satellite images and household assessments) is vital to have a consistent conclusion (see Core Standard 3 on page 61 and References and further reading).

2. *Sources of information:* Secondary information may exist about the pre-disaster situation. As women and men have different and complementary roles in securing the nutritional well-being of the household, this information should be disaggregated by sex as much as possible (see Core Standard 3 on page 61 and Appendix 1: Food security and livelihoods assessment checklists).

3. *Food availability, access, consumption and utilisation:* (See definitions for food availability, access and utilisation on page 145.) Food consumption reflects the energy and nutrient intake of individuals in households. It is not practical to measure actual energy content and nutrient details during these assessments. Changes in the number of meals consumed before and after a disaster can be a simple yet revealing indicator of changes in food security. The number of food groups consumed by an individual or household and frequency of consumption over a given reference period reflect dietary diversity. This is a good proxy indicator, especially when

correlated with a household's socio-economic status and also with total food energy intake and diet quality. Tools that can give robust measures on food consumption patterns and problems include seasonal calendars, the Household Dietary Diversity Score, Household Food Insecurity Access Scale or Food Consumption Score.

4. **Food insecurity and nutritional status:** Food insecurity is one of three underlying causes of undernutrition. However, it should not be assumed that this is the sole cause of undernutrition.

5. **Context:** Food insecurity may be the result of wider macro-economic and structural socio-political factors, including national and international policies, processes or institutions that have an impact on the disaster-affected population's access to nutritionally adequate food and on the degradation of the local environment. This is usually defined as chronic food insecurity, a long-term condition resulting from structural vulnerabilities that may be aggravated by the impact of disaster. Local and regional food security information systems, including famine early warning systems and the Integrated Food Security Phase Classification, are important mechanisms to analyse information.

6. **Response analysis:** Food security varies according to people's livelihoods, their location, the market systems, their access to area markets, their social status (including sex and age), the time of year, the nature of the disaster and the associated responses. The focus of the assessment should address how the affected population acquired food and income before the disaster and how they cope now. Where people have been displaced, the food security of the host population must be taken into account. The assessment should also analyse markets, banks, financial institutions or other local transfer mechanisms in the case of cash transfers, and food supply chains, including the risks associated with them (see Protection Principle 1 on page 33). This will help assess the feasibility of cash or food transfer interventions and the design of safe and efficient delivery mechanisms.

7. **Market analysis** should be part of the initial and subsequent assessments. An analysis of markets should include price trends, availability of basic goods and services, the impact of the disaster on market structures and the expected recovery period. Understanding the capacity of markets to provide employment, food, essential items and services after a disaster can help the design of timely, cost-effective and appropriate responses that can improve local economies. Market systems can go beyond short-term needs after a disaster to protect livelihoods by supplying productive items (seeds, tools, etc.) and maintaining demand for employment. Programmes should be designed to support local purchase where possible (see Food security

– food transfers standard 4, guidance notes 2–3 on page 189, Food security
– livelihoods standard 1, guidance note 7 on page 207 and Food security –
livelihoods standard 3, guidance note 2 on page 212).

8. **Coping strategies:** Assessment and analysis should consider the different
    types of coping strategy, who is applying them and when, how well they
    work and the nature of adverse impact (if any). Tools such as the Coping
    Strategies Index are recommended. While strategies vary, there are distinct
    stages of coping. Some coping strategies are normal, positive and could
    be supported. Other strategies, sometimes called crisis strategies, may
    permanently undermine future food security (sale of land, distress migra-
    tion of whole families or deforestation). Some coping strategies employed
    by or forced on women and girls may significantly and adversely impact
    upon their health, psychological well-being and social integration. Coping
    strategies may also affect the environment, such as over-exploitation of
    commonly owned natural resources. Analysis should determine a liveli-
    hood threshold to identify the most appropriate combination of responses
    which ensure that food security is protected and supported before all
    non-damaging options are exhausted (see Protection Principles 1–2 on
    pages 33–36).

9. **Participatory analysis of vulnerability:** Meaningful participation of
    different groups of women and men and appropriate local organisations
    and institutions at all stages of the assessment is vital. Programmes
    should build on local knowledge, be based on need and tailored to the
    local context. Areas subject to recurrent natural disasters or long-running
    conflicts may have local early warning and emergency response systems
    or networks and contingency plans which should be incorporated into any
    assessment. It is critical to engage women in project design and implemen-
    tation (see Protection Principles 2–4 on pages 36–41).

10. **Immediate needs and long-term planning:** Interventions which aim
    to meet immediate food needs can include food transfers and cash and
    voucher transfers. These can be either stand-alone or in combination
    with other livelihoods interventions. While meeting immediate needs and
    preserving productive assets will be the priority at the onset of a crisis,
    responses must always be planned with the longer term in mind, including
    an awareness of the impact of climate change on the environmental resto-
    ration of a degraded environment.

> ### Food security and nutrition assessment standard 2: Nutrition
>
> Where people are at increased risk of undernutrition, assessments are conducted using internationally accepted methods to understand the type, degree and extent of undernutrition and identify those most affected, those most at risk and the appropriate response.

Key actions (to be read in conjunction with the guidance notes)

▶ Compile existing information from pre-disaster and initial assessments to highlight the nature and severity of the nutrition situation (see guidance notes 1–6).

▶ Identify groups with the greatest nutritional support needs and the underlying factors that potentially affect nutritional status (see guidance notes 1–2).

▶ Determine if population-level qualitative or quantitative assessments are needed to better measure and understand anthropometric status, micronutrient status, infant and young child feeding, maternal care practices and associated potential determinants of undernutrition (see guidance notes 1–2).

▶ Consider the opinions of the local community and other local stakeholders on the potential determinants of undernutrition (see guidance note 7).

▶ Include an assessment of national and local capacity to lead and/or support response (see guidance notes 1 and 8).

▶ Use nutrition assessment information to determine if the situation is stable or declining (see guidance notes 7–8).

Key indicators (to be read in conjunction with the guidance notes)

▶ Assessment and analysis methodologies including standardised indicators adhering to widely accepted principles are adopted for both anthropometric and non-anthropometric assessments (see guidance notes 3–6).

▶ Assessment findings are presented in an analytical report including clear recommendations of actions targeting the most vulnerable individuals and groups (see guidance notes 3–6).

Guidance notes

1. *Contextual information:* Information on the causes of undernutrition can be gathered from primary or secondary sources, including existing health and nutrition profiles, research reports, early warning information, health centre

records, food security reports and community groups. Where information is not available for specific areas of assessment or potential intervention, other sources should be consulted such as Demographic Health Surveys, Multi Indicator Cluster Surveys, other national health and nutrition surveys, WHO Nutrition Landscape Information System, WHO Vitamin and Mineral Nutrition Information System, Complex Emergency Database (CE-DAT), Nutrition in Crisis Information System (NICS), national nutrition surveillance systems, and admission rates and coverage in existing programmes for the management of malnutrition. Where representative data are available, it is preferable to look at trends in nutritional status over time rather than the prevalence of malnutrition at a single point in time (see Appendix 3: Nutrition assessment checklist). Nutrition assessment should be considered within broader assessments, especially those focusing on public health and food security. Information on existing nutrition initiatives, their operational capacity and local and national response capacity should be gathered in order to identify gaps and guide response.

2. *Scope of analysis:* In-depth assessment should be conducted following the initial assessment (see Core Standard 3 on page 61) only where information gaps have been identified and where further information is needed to inform programme decision-making, to measure programme outcomes or for advocacy purposes. In-depth nutrition assessment refers to a number of possible assessment approaches including anthropometric surveys, infant and young child feeding assessments, micronutrient surveys and causal analyses. Nutrition surveillance and monitoring systems may also be used.

3. *Methodology:* Nutrition assessments of any type should have clear objectives, use internationally accepted methods, identify nutritionally vulnerable individuals and create an understanding of factors that may contribute to undernutrition. The assessment and analysis process should be documented and presented in a timely report in a logical and transparent manner. Assessment approaches need to be impartial, representative and well coordinated among agencies and governments so information is complementary, consistent and comparable. Multi-agency assessments may be beneficial in assessing large-scale multi-technical and wide geographical areas.

4. *Anthropometric surveys* are representative cross-sectional surveys based on random sampling or exhaustive screening. Anthropometric surveys provide an estimate of the prevalence of malnutrition (chronic and acute). They should report primarily Weight for Height in Z score according to WHO standards (see Appendix 4: Measuring acute malnutrition). Weight for Height in Z score according to the National Center for Health Statistics (NCHS) reference may also be reported to allow comparison with past surveys. Wasting and severe wasting measured by mid upper arm circumference (MUAC) should

be included in anthropometric surveys. Nutrition oedema should be assessed and recorded separately. Confidence intervals for the prevalence of malnutrition should be reported and survey quality assurance demonstrated. This can be done through the use of existing tools (e.g. Standardised Monitoring and Assessment of Relief and Transitions (SMART) methodology manual and tools, or ENA (Emergency Nutrition Assessment) software and EpiInfo software). The most widely accepted practice is to assess malnutrition levels in children aged 6–59 months as a proxy for the population as a whole. However, where other groups may be affected to a greater extent or face greater nutritional risk, assessment should be considered (see Appendix 4: Measuring acute malnutrition).

5. ***Non-anthropometric indicators:*** Additional information to anthropometry is essential, though should be carefully considered and remain limited when attached to anthropometric surveys so as not to undermine the quality of the survey. Such indicators include immunisation coverage rates (especially for measles), Vitamin A supplementation, micronutrient deficiencies and WHO infant and young child feeding (IYCF) indicators. Crude, infant and under-5 death rates may be measured, where appropriate.

6. ***Micronutrient deficiencies:*** If the population is known to have been deficient in Vitamin A, iodine or zinc or suffering from iron deficiency anaemia prior to a disaster, this will likely be exacerbated by the disaster. There may be outbreaks of pellagra, beriberi, scurvy or other micronutrient deficiencies which should be considered when planning and analysing assessments. If individuals with any of these deficiencies are present at health centres, it is likely to indicate lack of access to an adequate diet and is probably indicative of a population-wide problem. Assessment of micronutrient deficiencies may be direct or indirect. Indirect assessment involves estimating nutrient intakes at the population level and extrapolating deficiency risk by reviewing available data on food access, availability and utilisation (see Food security and nutrition assessment standard 1 on page 150), and by assessing food ration adequacy (see Food security – food transfers standard 1 on page 180). Direct assessment, where feasible, involves measuring clinical or sub-clinical deficiency in individual patients or a population sample, e.g. the measurement of haemoglobin during surveys whereby the prevalence of anaemia may be used as a proxy measure of iron deficiency.

7. ***Interpreting levels of undernutrition:*** Determining whether levels of undernutrition require intervention requires detailed analysis of the situation in the light of the reference population size and density, and morbidity and mortality rates (see Essential health services standard 1, guidance note 3 on page 310). It also requires reference to health indicators, seasonal fluctuations, IYCF indicators, pre-disaster levels of undernutrition, levels of

micronutrient deficiencies (see Appendix 5: Measures of the public health significance of micronutrient deficiencies), the proportion of severe acute malnutrition in relation to global acute malnutrition and other factors affecting the underlying causes of undernutrition. A combination of complementary information systems may be the most cost-effective way to monitor trends. Wherever possible, local institutions and populations should participate in monitoring activities, interpreting findings and planning any responses. The application of decision-making models and approaches which consider a number of variables including food security, livelihoods, and health and nutrition may be appropriate (see Food security and nutrition assessment standard 1, guidance note 5 on page 152).

8. **Decision-making:** Assessment findings should inform decisions on responses aimed at managing malnutrition. The decisions to implement general food distribution or other preventative or immediate treatment interventions in the acute phase of a disaster need not await the results of in-depth assessments. Where assessments are conducted, results must inform actions. Decision-making should rely on an understanding of undernutrition as laid out in the conceptual framework, results from nutrition assessments and the existing capacity to respond.

2. Infant and young child feeding

Suboptimal infant and young child feeding practices increase vulnerability to undernutrition, disease and death. The risks are heightened in disasters and the youngest are most vulnerable. Optimal feeding practices that maximise survival and reduce morbidity in children under 24 months are early initiation of exclusive breastfeeding, exclusive breastfeeding for 6 months, continued breastfeeding to 24 months or beyond, and introduction of adequate, appropriate and safe complementary foods at 6 months.

IYCF (infant and young child feeding) is concerned with interventions to protect and support the nutritional needs of both breastfed and non-breastfed infants and young children. Priority interventions include breastfeeding protection and support, minimising the risks of artificial feeding and enabling appropriate and safe complementary feeding. Infants and young children in exceptionally difficult circumstances, such as HIV-prevalent populations, orphans, low birth weight (LBW) infants and those severely malnourished, warrant particular attention. Protection and support of the nutritional, physical and mental health of both pregnant and breastfeeding women are central to the well-being of the mother and child. The particular needs of caregivers who are grandparents, single fathers or siblings must be considered. Cross-sector engagement is essential to protect and meet adequately and in time the broader nutritional needs of infants and young children and their mothers. IYCF is integral to many of the standards in this chapter and overlaps in other chapters.

Infant and young child feeding standard 1: Policy guidance and coordination

Safe and appropriate infant and young child feeding for the population is protected through implementation of key policy guidance and strong coordination.

Key actions (to be read in conjunction with the guidance notes)

▶ Uphold the provisions of the Operational Guidance on infant feeding in emergencies (IFE) and the International Code of Marketing of Breastmilk Substitutes and subsequent relevant World Health Assembly (WHA) resolutions (collectively known as the Code) (see guidance notes 1–2).

▶ Avoid soliciting or accepting donations of breastmilk substitutes (BMS), other milk products, bottles and teats (see guidance note 2).

Key indicators (to be read in conjunction with the guidance notes)

▶ A national and/or agency policy is in place that addresses IYCF and reflects the Operational Guidance on IFE (see guidance note 1).

▶ A lead coordinating body on IYCF is designated in every emergency (see guidance note 1).

▶ A body to deal with any donations of BMS, milk products, bottles and teats is designated (see guidance note 2).

▶ Code violations are monitored and reported (see guidance notes 1–2).

Guidance notes

1. *Policy guidance, coordination and communication:* Key policy guidance documents to inform emergency programmes include the Operational Guidance on IFE and the Code. Additional guidance can be found in the References and further reading section. WHA Resolution 63.23 (2010) urges member states to ensure that national and international preparedness plans and emergency responses follow the Operational Guidance on IFE. Disaster preparedness includes policy development, orientation and training on IFE, identifying sources of Code-compliant BMS and of complementary food. A lead coordinating body on IYCF should be assigned in every emergency. Monitoring and reporting on Code violations is an important contribution to aid accountability. Clear, consistent communication to the affected population and in press releases has a critical influence on the response.

2. **Handling milk and milk products:** Milk and milk products should not be included in untargeted distributions (see Food security – food transfers standard 2, guidance note 5 on page 186). Indications for and management of artificial feeding should be in accordance with the Operational Guidance on IFE and the Code, ideally under the guidance of the designated IFE coordinating body. Donations of BMS, milk products, bottles and teats should not be sought or accepted in emergencies. Any donations that do arrive should be placed under the control of a designated agency and their management determined by the IFE coordinating body.

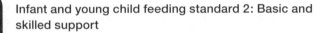

Infant and young child feeding standard 2: Basic and skilled support

Mothers and caregivers of infants and young children have access to timely and appropriate feeding support that minimises risks and optimises nutrition, health and survival outcomes.

Key actions (to be read in conjunction with the guidance notes)

▶ Undertake integrated multisector interventions to protect and support safe and appropriate IYCF (see guidance note 1).

▶ Give priority to pregnant and breastfeeding women to access food, cash and/or voucher transfers and other supportive interventions (see guidance note 1).

▶ Integrate skilled breastfeeding counselling in interventions that target pregnant and breastfeeding women and children aged 0–24 months (see guidance notes 2–7).

▶ Target mothers of all newborns with support for early initiation of exclusive breastfeeding (see guidance note 3).

▶ Support timely, safe, adequate and appropriate complementary feeding (see guidance note 5).

▶ Enable access for mothers and caregivers whose infants require artificial feeding to an adequate amount of an appropriate BMS and associated support (see guidance note 6).

▶ Give special consideration to feeding support of infants and young children in exceptionally difficult circumstances (orphans, acutely malnourished children, LBW infants and those affected by HIV) (see guidance notes 4–7).

Key indicators (to be read in conjunction with the guidance notes)

▶ Measurement of standard WHO indicators for early initiation of breast-feeding, exclusive breastfeeding rate in children <6 months, and continued breastfeeding rate at 1 and 2 years (see guidance notes 2–3, 5–6).

▶ Caregivers have access to timely, appropriate, nutritionally adequate and safe complementary foods for children 6 to <24 months (see guidance notes 5–6).

▶ Breastfeeding mothers have access to skilled breastfeeding support (see guidance notes 1–3).

▶ There is access to Code-compliant supplies of appropriate BMS and associated support for infants who require artificial feeding (see guidance note 5).

Guidance notes

1. **Simple measures and basic interventions** are needed to create a protective and supportive environment for IYCF. Be alert to and investigate reports of difficulties in breastfeeding, complementary feeding and/or practice of artificial feeding in children aged 0–24 months. Non-breastfed infants need urgent support. Support should be prioritised for mothers, caregivers and pregnant and breastfeeding women to meet immediate essential needs. Households with children under 24 months and breastfeeding mothers of all newborns should be registered and linked to food security programmes to ensure access to adequate food. Designated shelters for mothers and caregivers enables access to peer-to-peer and basic IYCF support. Breast-feeding support should be integrated within key services such as reproductive health, primary healthcare, psychosocial services and selective feeding programmes from the outset.

2. **Pregnant and breastfeeding women:** Inadequate nutrient intakes for pregnant and breastfeeding women risk pregnancy complications, maternal mortality, LBW infants and decline in maternal nutritional status associated with lower concentrations of certain nutrients in breastmilk. Low maternal body weight at conception is strongly associated with infant LBW and is a feature of adolescent pregnancy. Pregnant and breastfeeding women should receive daily supplements providing one daily requirement of multiple micronutrients to protect maternal stores and breastmilk content, whether they receive fortified rations or not. Iron and folic acid supplements when already provided should be continued. Women should also receive Vitamin A within six to eight weeks of delivery. Micronutrient supplementation should be in accordance with international recommendations on doses and timing. Referral to psychosocial services may be needed, especially in traumatised populations. Although nutrition support of the adolescent mother is impor-

tant, programmes to prevent adolescent pregnancy are likely to have the most impact on LBW incidence.

3. **Early initiation of exclusive breastfeeding** (within one hour of birth) is a priority intervention to safeguard the health of both the mother and the infant. LBW infants and their mothers will benefit especially from continued skin-to-skin contact at birth and early initiation of exclusive breastfeeding (see Essential health services – child health standard 2, guidance note 1 on page 324).

4. **Breastfeeding:** Exclusive breastfeeding requires an infant to receive only breastmilk and no water, other liquids or solids, with the exception of necessary micronutrient supplements or medicines. It guarantees food and fluid security in infants for the first six months and provides active immune protection. Breastfeeding also protects older infants and children, especially in contexts where water, sanitation and hygiene conditions are lacking, so is important to sustain to 24 months or beyond. Mothers, families, communities and health workers should be reassured of the resilience of breastfeeding; confidence can be undermined by acute emergency situations. Planning and resource allocation should allow for skilled breastfeeding support in managing more difficult situations including stressed populations and acutely malnourished infants under 6 months (see Management of acute malnutrition and micronutrient deficiencies standard 2 on page 169), populations where mixed feeding is common, and infant feeding in the context of HIV (see guidance note 7).

5. **Complementary feeding** is the process of giving other food in addition to breastmilk from the age of 6 months (or to an appropriate breastmilk substitute in non-breastfed infants). During the complementary feeding period (6–24 months), breastfeeding continues to significantly contribute to food and fluid security. Non-breastfed infants need support to make up the nutritional shortfall. Links with food security programmes are essential to support complementary feeding. Where a population is dependent on food aid, a suitable micronutrient-fortified food should be included in the general ration; blanket provision of complementary food may be needed. Clear criteria for the inclusion, use and duration of lipid-based nutrient supplements during the complementary feeding period are needed for different emergency contexts. Ready-to-use therapeutic foods are not a complementary food. Distribution of complementary food should be accompanied with practical guidance and demonstration on their preparation. The use of micronutrient supplementation, including Vitamin A, should be in accordance with the latest recommendations. LBW infants and young children may benefit from iron supplementation. If the population is in a malaria-endemic area, iron supplementation should be targeted to children who are anaemic and iron deficient with appropriate malaria control measures.

6. *Artificial feeding:* Infants who are not breastfed require early identification and assessment by skilled personnel to explore feeding options. Where maternal breastfeeding is not available, donor breastmilk, particularly as wet nursing, has a valuable role, especially in feeding young and LBW infants. Where artificial feeding is indicated, mothers and caregivers need assured access to adequate amounts of an appropriate BMS for as long as is necessary (until infants are at least 6 months old) as well as to the associated essential supports (water, fuel, storage facilities, growth monitoring, medical care, time). Infants under 6 months who are mixed fed should be supported to move to exclusive breastfeeding. Feeding bottles should not be used due to difficulties in cleaning. Programmes that support artificial feeding should monitor the community's IYCF practices using standard indicators to ensure that breastfeeding is not undermined. Morbidity surveillance should be conducted at individual and population levels, with a particular focus on diarrhoea. Low-dose supplemental Vitamin A should be considered for non-breastfed infants under 6 months.

7. *HIV and infant feeding:* Maximising the survival of HIV-free children is a primary consideration in determining the best feeding option for infants born to HIV-infected mothers. Mothers of unknown or negative HIV status should be supported to breastfeed as per general IYCF recommendations for populations (see guidance notes 3–5). For HIV-infected mothers, combining antiretroviral (ARV) interventions with breastfeeding can significantly reduce postnatal HIV transmission. Accelerated access to ARVs should be prioritised (see Essential health services – sexual and reproductive health standard 2 on page 328). The risks to infants associated with replacement feeding are even greater under emergency conditions. This means that breastfeeding offers the greater likelihood of survival for infants born to HIV-infected mothers and for survival of HIV-infected infants, including where ARVs are not yet available. Urgent artificial feeding assistance is needed for infants already established on replacement feeding (see guidance note 6).

3. Management of acute malnutrition and micronutrient deficiencies

Acute malnutrition and micronutrient deficiencies are associated with an increased risk of morbidity and mortality for affected individuals. Therefore, when such prevalence or risk is high, it is necessary to ensure access to services which both correct and prevent undernutrition. The impact of these services will be considerably reduced if the underlying causes of undernutrition are not addressed simultaneously through other interventions to support health, WASH, food transfers and food security.

Moderate acute malnutrition can be addressed in a number of ways. In disasters, supplementary feeding is often the primary strategy for prevention and treatment of moderate acute malnutrition and prevention of severe acute malnutrition. This may be blanket or targeted depending on the levels of acute malnutrition, vulnerable population groups and risk of an increase in acute malnutrition. The indicators in Management of acute malnutrition and micronutrient deficiencies standard 1 refer primarily to targeted supplementary feeding. While there are no defined impact indicators for blanket supplementary feeding, monitoring of coverage, acceptability and rations provided are important.

Severe acute malnutrition is addressed through therapeutic care which can be delivered through a variety of approaches. Community-based management of acute malnutrition should be the preferred approach where conditions permit. Programmes addressing severe acute malnutrition should encompass community mobilisation (including effective communication, active case-finding, referral and follow-up), outpatient treatment for severe acute malnutrition without medical complications and inpatient management for those with medical complications or young infants.

Micronutrient deficiencies are difficult to identify in many contexts. While clinical signs of severe deficiencies may be easiest to diagnose, the greater burden on the health and survival of populations may be sub-clinical deficiencies. Where micronutrient deficiencies are known to have been prevalent in the population, it may be assumed that this could be exacerbated by the disaster. These deficiencies should be tackled using population-wide interventions and individual treatment.

Management of acute malnutrition and micronutrient deficiencies standard 1: Moderate acute malnutrition

Moderate acute malnutrition is addressed.

Key actions (to be read in conjunction with the guidance notes)

- Establish from the outset clearly defined and agreed strategies, objectives and criteria for set-up and closure of interventions (see guidance note 1).

- Maximise access and coverage through involvement of the population from the outset (see guidance note 2 and Core Standard 1 on page 55).

- Base admission and discharge of individuals on assessment against nationally and internationally accepted anthropometric criteria (see guidance notes 3–4 and Appendices 4: Measuring acute malnutrition and 5: Measures of the public health significance of micronutrient deficiencies).

- Link the management of moderate acute malnutrition to the management of severe acute malnutrition and existing health services where possible (see guidance notes 5–6).

- Provide dry or suitable ready-to-use supplementary food rations unless there is a clear rationale for on-site feeding (see guidance note 8).

- Investigate and act on the causes of default and poor response (see guidance notes 5–6).

- Address IYCF with particular emphasis on protecting, supporting and promoting breastfeeding (see guidance note 7).

Key indicators (to be read in conjunction with the guidance notes)

These indicators are primarily applicable to the 6–59 month age group, although others may be part of the programme.

- More than 90 per cent of the target population is within less than one day's return walk (including time for treatment) of the programme site for dry ration supplementary feeding programmes and no more than one hour's walk for on-site supplementary feeding programmes (see guidance note 2).

▶ Coverage is >50 per cent in rural areas, >70 per cent in urban areas and >90 per cent in a camp situation (see guidance note 2).

▶ The proportion of discharges from targeted supplementary feeding programmes who have died is <3 per cent, recovered is >75 per cent and defaulted is <15 per cent (see guidance note 4).

Guidance notes

1. **Programme design** must be based on an understanding of the complexity and dynamics of the nutrition situation. Supplementary feeding can take a targeted or a blanket approach. The decision regarding which approach to take should depend on levels of acute malnutrition and caseload, risk of an increase in acute malnutrition, the capacity to screen and monitor that caseload using anthropometric criteria, available resources and access to the disaster-affected population. Targeted supplementary feeding generally requires more time and effort to screen and monitor individuals with acute malnutrition but requires fewer food resources, whereas a blanket approach generally requires less staff expertise but more food resources. Effective community mobilisation will support the population's understanding and effectiveness of the programme. Links to therapeutic care, health systems, HIV and AIDS and tuberculosis (TB) networks and food security programmes including food, cash or voucher transfers are important. The disaster-affected population should be involved in deciding where to locate programme sites. Consideration should be given to vulnerable people who may face difficulties in accessing sites. Exit strategies or plans for longer-term support should be considered from the outset.

2. **Coverage** refers to individuals who need treatment against those actually receiving treatment. Coverage can be affected by the acceptability of the programme, location and accessibility of programme sites, security situation, frequency of distributions, waiting time, service quality, extent of mobilisation, extent of home visiting and screening, and admission criteria alignment. Programme sites should be close to the targeted population in order to reduce the risks and costs associated with travelling long distances with young children and the risk of people being displaced to them. Methodologies to measure coverage vary in the level of reliability and type of information generated. The method used must be stated when reporting. Current guidance should be consulted when deciding which method is appropriate in the given context. Coverage assessment should be seen as a management tool so should not be left to the end of an emergency support phase.

3. **Admission criteria:** Individuals other than those who meet anthropometric criteria defining acute malnutrition may also benefit from supplementary feeding, e.g. people living with HIV (PLHIV) or TB, discharges from thera-

peutic care to avoid relapse, individuals with other chronic diseases or persons with disabilities. Monitoring and reporting systems will need to be adjusted if individuals falling outside of anthropometric criteria are included.

4. **Discharge criteria** should be according to national guidelines, or international guidelines where no national guidelines are available, and should be specified when reporting performance indicators (see guidance note 5).

5. **Performance indicators** relate to discharged individuals ending treatment. The total number of discharged individuals is made up of all who have recovered, died, defaulted or are non-recovered. Individuals who are referred for complementary services (such as health services) have not ended the treatment and will either continue treatment or return to continue the treatment later. Individuals transferred out to other sites have not ended the treatment and should not be included in performance indicators. Performance-related indicators are as follows:

Proportion of discharges recovered =

$$\frac{\text{Number of individuals recovered}}{\text{Total number of discharged}} \times 100 \text{ per cent}$$

Proportion of discharges died =

$$\frac{\text{Number of deaths}}{\text{Total number of discharged}} \times 100 \text{ per cent}$$

Proportion of discharges defaulted =

$$\frac{\text{Number of defaulters}}{\text{Total number of discharged}} \times 100 \text{ per cent}$$

Proportion of discharges non-recovered =

$$\frac{\text{Number of individuals non-recovered}}{\text{Total number of discharged}} \times 100 \text{ per cent}$$

Individuals admitted after being discharged from therapeutic care should be reported as a separate category in order to avoid biasing results towards better recovery. Children with acute malnutrition secondary to disability, cleft palate or surgical problems, etc., should not be excluded from programme reporting. When reporting, the core group is children aged 6–59 months. In addition to the indicators outlined above when analysing performance, systems should monitor the population's participation, acceptability of the programme (a good measure of this is the default and coverage rate), the quantity and quality of food being provided, coverage, reasons for transfers to other programmes (particularly children whose nutrition status deteriorates to severe acute malnutrition) and number of individuals admitted and in treatment. External factors should also be considered, such as morbidity patterns, levels of undernutrition in the population, level of food insecurity in households and in the population, complementary interventions available to the population (including general food distributions or equivalent programmes) and the capacity of existing systems for service delivery. Causes of defaulting and failure to adequately respond to treatment should be investigated on an ongoing basis.

6. *Health inputs and considerations:* Targeted supplementary feeding programmes are an important contact point for screening and referring for illness. Programmes should take into account the capacity of existing health services and ensure effective provision of antihelminthics, Vitamin A supplementation, iron and folic acid combined with malaria screening and treatment, zinc for treatment of diarrhoea and immunisations (see Essential health services – control of communicable disease standard 2 on page 314 and Essential health services – child health standards 1–2 on pages 321–323). In areas of high HIV prevalence, HIV testing and prophylactic treatment should be available and the quality and quantity of the supplementary food ration should be given special consideration.

7. *Breastfeeding mothers* of acutely malnourished infants under 6 months should be admitted to supplementary feeding, independent of maternal nutrition status. Moderately malnourished mothers can successfully breastfeed and need adequate nutrition support to protect their own nutritional status. Mothers should receive supplementary feeding rations, skilled breastfeeding support on exclusive breastfeeding and advice on safe, nutritious and responsive complementary feeding. Infants under 6 months who are acutely malnourished should be referred appropriately for skilled breastfeeding support and inpatient care as necessary.

8. *Rations:* Dry rations or ready-to-use foods provided on a weekly or bi-weekly basis are preferred to on-site feeding but their composition and size should take into account household food security and the likelihood of sharing.Clear information should be given on how to prepare and store supplementary food in a hygienic manner, how and when it should be consumed (see Food security – food transfers standard 6, guidance note 1 on page 198) and the importance of continued breastfeeding for children under 24 months of age. Vulnerable people, such as those with mobility challenges, may require programme adaptations to meet their specific needs.

Management of acute malnutrition and micronutrient deficiencies standard 2: Severe acute malnutrition

Severe acute malnutrition is addressed.

Key actions (to be read in conjunction with the guidance notes)

▶ Establish from the outset clearly defined and agreed criteria for set-up or increased support to existing services and for scale-down or closure (see guidance note 1).

▶ Include interventions with inpatient care, outpatient care, referral and population mobilisation components for the management of severe acute malnutrition (see guidance note 2).

▶ Maximise access and coverage through involvement of the population from the outset (see guidance notes 1–3 and Core Standard 1 on page 55).

▶ Provide nutritional and medical care according to nationally and internationally recognised guidelines for the management of severe acute malnutrition (see guidance notes 4–8).

▶ Ensure discharge criteria include both anthropometric and non-anthropometric indices (see guidance note 6).

▶ Investigate and act on causes of default and non-response or an increase in deaths (see guidance notes 6–7).

▶ Address IYCF with particular emphasis on protecting, supporting and promoting breastfeeding (see guidance notes 9–10).

Key indicators (to be read in conjunction with the guidance notes)

These indicators are primarily applicable to the 6–59 month age group, although others may be part of the programme.

▶ More than 90 per cent of the target population is within less than one day's return walk (including time for treatment) of the programme site.

▶ Coverage is >50 per cent in rural areas, >70 per cent in urban areas and >90 per cent in camp situations (see guidance note 3).

▶ The proportion of discharges from therapeutic care who have died is <10 per cent, recovered is >75 per cent and defaulted is <15 per cent (see guidance note 6).

Guidance notes

1. **Programme design:** Programmes should be designed to build on and support existing health system capacity wherever possible. The level of additional support required to ensure effective management of severe acute malnutrition should be determined based on existing capacity at health facility and community levels, the numbers and geographical spread of disaster-affected individuals and the security situation. From the start, programmes should consider exit strategies or plans for longer-term support beyond the emergency. Criteria for closure or transition of programmes should consider existing capacity and opportunities to integrate into existing systems.

2. **Programme components:** Programmes addressing the management of severe acute malnutrition should comprise inpatient care for individuals with medical complications and all infants <6 months of age with acute malnutrition and decentralised outpatient care for children with no medical complications. Inpatient care may be through direct implementation or referral. Programmes should also be linked with other services addressing the immediate and underlying causes of undernutrition such as supplementary feeding, HIV and AIDS and TB networks, primary health services and food security programmes including food, cash or voucher transfers. Effective community mobilisation will help to achieve programme acceptance, accessibility and coverage. Outpatient programme sites should be close to the targeted population to reduce the risks and costs associated with travelling long distances with young children and the risk of people being displaced to them.

3. **Coverage:** As with moderate acute malnutrition, coverage can be affected by the acceptability of the programme, location and accessibility of programme sites, general security situation, frequency of distributions, waiting time, service quality, extent of mobilisation, extent of home visiting and screening, and screening and admission criteria alignment. Methodologies to measure coverage vary in the level of reliability and type of information generated. The method used must be stated when reporting. Current guidance should be consulted when deciding which method is appropriate in the given context (see Management of acute malnutrition and micronutrient deficiencies standard 1, guidance note 2 on page 166).

4. **Guidelines:** Where national guidelines exist, they should be adhered to. In the absence of national guidelines or where they do not reach international standards, international guidelines should be adopted. Internationally accepted guidelines can be found in the References and further reading section.

5. **Admission criteria** should be consistent with national and international guidance (see Appendix 4: Measuring acute malnutrition, and References and further reading). Admission criteria for infants <6 months and groups

whose anthropometric status is difficult to determine should include consideration of clinical and breastfeeding status. Individuals who are tested or suspected to be HIV-positive and those who have TB or are chronically ill should have equal access to care if they meet the criteria for admission. PLHIV who do not meet admission criteria often require nutritional support, but this is not best offered in the context of treatment for severe acute malnutrition in disasters. These individuals and their families should be supported through a range of services including community home-based care, TB treatment centres and prevention programmes aimed at mother-to-child transmission.

6. **Discharge criteria and recovery:** Discharged individuals must be free from medical complications, have regained their appetite and have achieved and maintained appropriate weight gain without nutrition-related oedema (e.g. for two consecutive weighings). Breastfeeding status is especially important for infants under 6 months as well as for children to 24 months. Non-breastfed infants will need close follow-up. Discharge criteria should be adhered to in order to avoid the risks associated with premature discharge. Guidelines define limits for the mean length of stay for treatment and are aimed at avoiding prolonged recovery periods. Mean length of stay will differ depending on the guidelines in use and so should be adjusted to national context and guidelines in use. Mean weight gain should be calculated separately for individuals with and without nutritional oedema. HIV, AIDS and TB may result in some malnourished individuals failing to respond to treatment. Options for longer-term treatment or care should be considered in conjunction with health services and other social and community support services (see Essential health services – sexual and reproductive health standard 2 on page 328).

7. **Performance indicators** for the management of severe acute malnutrition should combine inpatient and outpatient care outcomes without double counting (i.e. removing transfers between the two components). Where this is not possible, interpretation of outcome rates should be adjusted accordingly, for example, programmes should expect better indicators where implementing outpatient care alone and should strive for the indicators as outlined for combined care when implementing inpatient care alone. The population of discharged individuals for severe acute malnutrition is made up of those who have recovered, died, defaulted, or not recovered (see Management of acute malnutrition and micronutrient deficiencies standard 1, guidance note 4 on page 167). Individuals who are referred to other services (e.g. medical services) have not ended treatment. Where programmes report for outpatient treatment only, transfers to inpatient care must be reported when assessing performance. Factors such as HIV clinical complexity will affect mortality rates where a proportion of admissions are HIV positive. Though performance indicators have not been adjusted for these situations, their

consideration is essential during interpretation. In addition to discharge indicators, new admissions, number of children in treatment and coverage rates should be assessed when monitoring performance. Causes of re-admission, deterioration of clinical status, defaulting and failure to respond should be investigated and documented on an ongoing basis. The definition of these should be adapted to guidelines in use.

8. *Health inputs:* All programmes for the management of severe acute malnutrition should include systematic treatments according to national or international guidance and established referral for the management of underlying illness such as TB and HIV. In areas of high HIV prevalence, strategies to treat malnutrition should consider both interventions that seek to avoid HIV transmission and those that support maternal and child survival. Effective referral systems for TB and HIV testing and care are essential.

9. *Breastfeeding support:* Infants who are admitted for inpatient care tend to be among the most unwell. Mothers need skilled breastfeeding support as part of nutritional rehabilitation and recovery, particularly for children <6 months. Sufficient time and resources should be provided for this – a designated area (breastfeeding corner) to target skilled support and enable peer support may help. Breastfeeding mothers of severely malnourished infants under 6 months should receive a supplementary ration regardless of their nutritional status unless they meet the anthropometric criteria for severe acute malnutrition in which case they should also be admitted for treatment.

10. *Social and psychosocial support:* Emotional and physical stimulation through play is important for children with severe acute malnutrition during the rehabilitation period. Caregivers of such children often require social and psychosocial support to bring their children for treatment. This may be achieved through mobilisation programmes which should emphasise stimulation and interaction as both treatment and prevention of future disability and cognitive impairment (see Protection Principle 4 on page 41). All caregivers of severely malnourished children should be enabled to feed and care for their children during treatment through the provision of advice, demonstrations and health and nutrition information.

Management of acute malnutrition and micronutrient deficiencies standard 3: Micronutrient deficiencies

Micronutrient interventions accompany public health and other nutrition interventions to reduce common diseases associated with emergencies and address micronutrient deficiencies.

Key actions (to be read in conjunction with the guidance notes)

▶ Train health staff in how to identify and treat micronutrient deficiencies (see guidance notes 1–2).

▶ Establish procedures to respond effectively to the types of micronutrient deficiencies from which the population may be at risk (see guidance note 2).

Key indicators (to be read in conjunction with the guidance notes)

▶ Cases of micronutrient deficiencies are treated according to current best clinical practice (see guidance notes 1–2).

▶ Micronutrient interventions accompany public health interventions to reduce common diseases associated with emergencies such as measles (Vitamin A) and diarrhoea (zinc) (see guidance notes 3–4).

Guidance notes

1. *Diagnosis and treatment of clinical micronutrient deficiencies:* Diagnosis of some clinical micronutrient deficiencies is possible through simple examination. Clinical indicators of these deficiencies can be incorporated into health or nutritional surveillance systems, although careful training of staff is required to ensure that assessment is accurate. Case definitions are problematic and in emergencies can often only be determined through the response to supplementation by individuals who present themselves to health staff. Treatment of micronutrient deficiencies should involve active case-finding and the use of agreed case definitions and guidelines for treatment. Case-finding and treatment should take place both within the health system and within feeding programmes (see Food security and nutrition assessment standard 2, guidance note 6 on page 156). Where the prevalence of micronutrient deficiencies exceeds public health thresholds (see Appendix 5: Measures of the public health significance of micronutrient deficiencies), blanket treatment of the population with supplements may be appropriate. Scurvy (Vitamin C), pellagra (niacin), beriberi (thiamine) and ariboflavinosis (riboflavin) are the most commonly observed epidemics to result from inad-

173

equate access to micronutrients in food aid-dependent populations. With this is mind, deficiencies should be tackled by population-wide interventions as well as individual treatment.

2. **Diagnosis and treatment of sub-clinical micronutrient deficiencies:** Sub-clinical micronutrient deficiencies can have adverse health outcomes but cannot be directly identified without biochemical examination. An exception is anaemia, for which a biochemical test is available which can be undertaken relatively easily in the field (see Food security and nutrition assessment standard 2, guidance note 6 on page 156 and Appendix 5: Measures of the public health significance of micronutrient deficiencies). Indirect indicators can be used to assess the risk of deficiencies in the affected population and determine when an improvement in dietary intake or the use of supplements may be required (see Food security and nutrition assessment standard 2, guidance note 6 on page 156 and Appendix 5: Measures of the public health significance of micronutrient deficiencies).

3. **Prevention:** Strategies for the prevention of micronutrient deficiencies are briefly described in the food security – food transfers section (see Food security – food transfers standard 1 on page 180). Prevention also requires the control of diseases such as acute respiratory infection, measles and parasitic infections such as malaria and diarrhoea that deplete micronutrient stores (see Essential health services – child health standards 1–2 on pages 321–323). Preparedness for treatment will involve the development of case definitions and guidelines for treatment, and systems for active case-finding.

4. **Use of micronutrients in the treatment of common diseases:** Micronutrient supplementation should be integrated in the prevention and treatment of certain diseases. This includes the provision of Vitamin A supplementation alongside measles vaccination and inclusion of zinc with oral rehydration salts (ORS) in guidelines to treat diarrhoea (see Essential health services – child health standards 1–2 on pages 321–323 and Infant and young child feeding standard 2 on page 160).

4. Food security

Food security responses should aim to meet short-term needs, 'do no harm', reduce the need for the affected population to adopt potentially damaging coping strategies and contribute to restoring longer-term food security.

An accurate assessment examines the appropriateness and feasibility of the potential response options (see Food security and nutrition assessment standard 1 on page 150). The food security responses in this section are grouped into standards for general food security, food transfers, cash and voucher transfers, and livelihoods responses.

If food is required, the appropriate form of transfer should be considered and the food basket carefully chosen for both in-kind and voucher transfers. Livelihood responses include primary production, income and employment, and access to market goods and services.

Cash and voucher transfers may be used for a range of goods or services in food security, as well as for other sectors. Understanding the market capacity and the appropriate modality for delivery is critical to designing food security interventions.

Food security standards consider the resources to meet the food needs of both the general population and specific vulnerable people at increased nutritional risk. Until these needs are met, any response aimed at the treatment of malnutrition will have a limited impact since those who recover from malnutrition will return to a context of inadequate food intake and their nutritional status is likely to deteriorate again.

Targeting, delivery and distribution methods should reduce the risk of inclusion and exclusion errors. This includes the risk that food, cash or other assistance is misappropriated by combatants. It is important that food security interventions are not diverted to worsen conflicts.

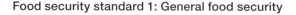

Food security standard 1: General food security

People have a right to humanitarian food assistance that ensures their survival and upholds their dignity, and as far as possible prevents the erosion of their assets and builds resilience.

Key actions (to be read in conjunction with the guidance notes)

▶ Design initial responses to meet immediate needs (see guidance note 1).

▶ Consider taking measures to support, protect and promote food security (see guidance note 2).

▶ Base responses on sound analysis, their benefits, associated risks and costs, and people's coping strategies (see guidance note 3).

▶ Develop transition and exit strategies for all responses to disaster, increase awareness of them and apply them as appropriate (see guidance note 4).

▶ Ensure that beneficiaries have access to appropriate support, including providing necessary knowledge, skills and services (see guidance note 5).

▶ Protect and preserve the natural environment from further degradation in all responses (see guidance note 6).

▶ Monitor to determine the level of acceptance and access to interventions by different groups and individuals and ensure overall coverage of the disaster-affected population without discrimination (see guidance note 7).

▶ Evaluate to measure the effects of responses on the local economy, social networks, livelihoods and the natural environment and ensure the findings are effectively shared and utilised to influence any further interventions (see guidance note 8).

Key indicators (to be read in conjunction with the guidance notes)

▶ All the disaster-affected people in need of food security responses receive assistance that meets their primary needs, prevents erosion of their assets, gives them choice and promotes their dignity.

▶ Households do not use negative coping strategies (see guidance note 3).

▶ The choice of cash, vouchers or a combination of these is based on thorough assessment and analysis (see Food security – cash and voucher transfers standard 1 on page 200).

Guidance notes

1. *Prioritising life-saving responses:* Distribution of food, cash or vouchers or a combination of these is the most common initial response to acute food insecurity. Other types of response should also be considered, including food subsidies, temporary fee waivers, employment programmes, productive support to livelihoods, destocking, fodder provision and support to markets. When markets are functioning and accessible and there are no serious risks of inflation, the priority may be to re-establish normal market arrangements and revitalise economic activities that provide employment (see markets and food security interventions sections in References and further reading). Such strategies could be more appropriate than food distribution if they offer advantages in supporting livelihoods, reducing future vulnerability and upholding dignity. Agencies should take into account what others are doing to ensure that the combined response provides inputs and services that are complementary.

2. *Support, protect and promote food security:* This includes a wide range of responses and advocacy. While meeting immediate needs and preserving productive assets will be the priority during the initial stages of a disaster, responses should be planned with a longer-term perspective and integrated with responses from other sectors. In the short term, it may not be feasible to achieve food security from people's own livelihood strategies. However, existing strategies that contribute to food security and preserve dignity should be supported. Food security responses should prevent further erosion of assets, lead towards recovery of assets lost through disaster and increase resilience to future hazards.

3. *Risks associated with coping strategies:* Coping strategies contributing to food security and dignity should be supported. However, coping strategies may carry costs or incur risks that increase vulnerability (see Food security and nutrition assessment standard 1 on page 150). The risks must be recognised as soon as possible and early interventions undertaken to help people avoid resorting to such strategies. For example, wood distribution and/or fuel-efficient stoves can avoid overuse of natural resources and travel to insecure areas; cash grants can avoid distress sales of assets and land (see Protection Principle 1 on page 33).

4. *Exit and transition strategies* must be considered from the outset, particularly where the response may have long-term implications, e.g. the provision of free services which would normally be paid for, such as veterinary services, may make it difficult to resume paid services. Before closing a programme or making the transition to a new phase, there should be evidence of improvement or that other better-placed actors can take responsibility. In the case of

food, cash and/or voucher transfers, it may mean linking with existing social protection or long-term safety-net systems or advocating with governments and donors to establish systems that address chronic food insecurity.

5. ***Access to knowledge, skills and services:*** Organisational structures should be designed and planned together with users, so that they are appropriate and adequately maintained, where possible beyond the life of the intervention. Some individuals have very specific needs, e.g. children orphaned as a result of AIDS may miss out on the information and skills transfer that takes place within families, which can be provided by appropriate services.

6. ***Environmental impact:*** The natural resource base for production and livelihoods of the disaster-affected population (and host population) should be preserved. Impact on the environment should be considered during assessment and planning of any response. For example, people living in camps require cooking fuel, which may accelerate local deforestation; distribution of food with long cooking times will require more cooking fuel, potentially affecting the environment (see Food security – food transfers standard 2 on page 184). Responses can also help the environment recover from degradation. For example, destocking reduces pressure on pasture during a drought, making more grazing available for surviving livestock. Where possible, responses should build the capacity of people to manage natural resources, particularly when supplying inputs. The risk of a response causing or exacerbating tensions over natural resources, and so fuelling conflict, should be appraised and mitigated (see Protection Principle 1 on page 33).

7. ***Coverage, access and acceptability:*** Beneficiaries and their characteristics should be assessed and their numbers, disaggregated by sex and age, estimated before determining the level of participation of different groups (paying particular attention to vulnerable people). Participation is partly determined by ease of access and the acceptability of activities to participants. Even though some food security responses are targeted at the economically active, they should not discriminate unfairly and should be accessible to vulnerable people and protect dependents, including children. Constraints may limit participation, including reduced capacity to work, heavy workload at home, pregnancy, feeding and caring for children, and illness and disability. Overcoming constraints involves identifying activities within the capacity of the groups or setting-up appropriate support structures. Targeting mechanisms based on self-selection should be established after full consultation with all groups in the population (see Protection Principle 2 on page 36).

8. ***Monitoring and evaluation:*** It is necessary to monitor the wider food security situation in order to assess the continued relevance of an intervention, determine when to phase out specific activities, introduce modifications

or new projects and identify any need for advocacy. The evaluation should be based on established Development Assistance Committee criteria recorded by the OECD, which measure the following: appropriateness, connectedness, coherence, coverage, efficiency, effectiveness and impact.

4.1. Food security – food transfers

The aim of food transfers is to ensure that people have safe access to food of adequate quality and quantity, and have the means to prepare and consume it safely.

General (free) distributions of food are introduced when assessed to be necessary, targeted to those who need the food most, and discontinued when beneficiaries have recovered the ability to produce or access their food through other means. Beneficiaries may require a transition to other forms of assistance, such as conditional transfers or livelihood responses. Supplementary feeding may be needed in addition to any general ration for individuals at risk (e.g. children aged 6–59 months and pregnant or breastfeeding women). This may be blanket or targeted depending on the context (see Management of acute malnutrition and micronutrient deficiencies standard 1 on page 165).

For both general food distributions and supplementary feeding, take-home rations are provided wherever possible. On-site feeding is undertaken only when people do not have the means to cook for themselves (immediately after a disaster or during population movements), where insecurity would put recipients of take-home rations at risk or for emergency school feeding (though take-home rations may be distributed though schools).

Supply chain management (SCM) must be particularly robust and accountable – lives can be immediately at stake and food transfers are often a major proportion of disaster response. Delivery and distribution systems should be monitored at all stages, including at community level, and transparency though effective communication can play a key role. Periodic evaluations should disseminate findings and be discussed with stakeholders, including the affected population and local institutions.

Food security – food transfers standard 1:
General nutrition requirements

Ensure the nutritional needs of the disaster-affected population, including those most at risk, are met.

Key actions (to be read in conjunction with the guidance notes)

▶ Use levels of access to adequate quantity and quality of food to determine if the situation is stable or is likely to decline (see guidance notes 1, 4–5).

▶ Design food transfers on the basis of the standard initial planning requirements for energy, protein, fat and micronutrients, adjusted as necessary to the local situation (see key indicators, guidance note 2 and Appendix 6: Nutritional requirements).

▶ Ensure the population's access to appropriate nutritious foods and nutritional support is protected, promoted and supported (see guidance notes 3–8).

▶ Ensure children aged 6–24 months have access to nutritious, energy-dense complementary foods and pregnant and breastfeeding women have access to additional nutritional support (see guidance note 2).

▶ Ensure households with chronically ill members, including PLHIV, and members with specific impairments or vulnerabilities have access to appropriate nutritious food and adequate nutritional support (see guidance notes 6–8).

Key indicators (to be read in conjunction with the guidance notes)

▶ There is adequate access to a range of foods, including a staple (cereal or tuber), pulses (or animal products) and fat sources, that together meet nutritional requirements (see guidance notes 2–3, 5).

▶ There is adequate access to iodised salt for the majority (>90 per cent) of households (see guidance notes 2–4 and Appendix 6: Nutritional requirements).

▶ There is adequate access to additional sources of niacin (e.g. pulses, nuts, dried fish) if the staple is maize or sorghum (see guidance notes 2–3 and Appendices 5: Measures of the public health significance of micronutrient deficiencies and 6: Nutritional requirements).

▶ There is adequate access to additional sources of thiamine (e.g. pulses, nuts, eggs) if the staple is polished rice (see guidance notes 2–3).

▶ There is adequate access to adequate sources of riboflavin where people are dependent on a very limited diet (see guidance notes 2–3).

▶ There are no cases of scurvy, pellagra, beriberi or riboflavin deficiency (see guidance note 5 and Appendix 5: Measures of the public health significance of micronutrient deficiencies).

▶ The prevalence of Vitamin A deficiency, iron deficiency anaemia and iodine deficiency disorders are not of public health significance (see guidance note 5 and Appendix 5: Measures of the public health significance of micronutrient deficiencies).

Guidance notes

1. *Interpreting access to food:* Access to food can be measured by analytical tools such as the food consumption score or dietary diversity tools. Approaches that consider a number of variables including food security, access to markets, livelihoods, health and nutrition may be appropriate to determine if the situation is stable or declining and if food interventions are necessary (see Food security and nutrition assessment standard 1 on page 150).

2. *Nutritional requirements and ration planning:* The following estimates for a population's minimum requirements should be used for planning general rations, with the figures adjusted for each population as described in Appendix 6: Nutritional requirements:

   - 2,100 kcals/person/day
   - 10 per cent of total energy provided by protein
   - 17 per cent of total energy provided by fat
   - adequate micronutrient intake.

   General food rations can be designed using ration planning tools (e.g. NutVal). Where people have no access to any food at all, the distributed ration should meet their total nutritional requirements. Agreed estimates must be established for the average quantities of food accessible to the affected population (see Food security and nutrition assessment standard 1 on page 150). Rations should then be planned to make up the difference between the nutritional requirement and what people can provide for themselves. Thus, if the standard requirement is 2,100 kcals/person/day and the assessment determines that people within the target population can, on average, acquire 500 kcals/person/day from their own efforts or resources, the ration should be designed to provide 2,100 − 500 = 1,600 kcals/person/day. Aside from the energy content of the diet, consideration of protein, fat and vitamins and minerals in food planning is essential.

If a ration is designed to provide all the energy content of the diet, then it must contain adequate amounts of all nutrients. If a ration is intended to provide only part of the energy requirement of the diet, then it can be designed using one of two approaches. If the nutrient content of the other foods available to the population is **unknown**, the ration should be designed to provide a balanced nutrient content that is proportional to the energy content of the ration. If the nutrient content of the other foods available to the population is **known**, the ration may be designed to complement these foods by filling nutrient gaps. The average planning figures for general rations take into account the additional needs of pregnant and breastfeeding women. Adequate and acceptable food for young children should be included in the general ration, such as fortified blended food (see Infant and young child feeding standard 2 on page 160). Equity should be ensured so that similar food rations are provided to similarly affected populations and population sub-groups. Planners should be aware that different ration scales in adjacent communities may cause tension. Ingestion of excessive amounts of micronutrients can be harmful and ration planning needs to consider this especially if several different fortified food products are to be included.

3. **Preventing acute malnutrition and micronutrient deficiencies:** If the key food indicators are met, then deterioration of the nutrition status of the general population should be prevented, provided adequate public health measures are also in place to prevent diseases such as measles, malaria and parasitic infection (see Essential health services – control of communicable diseases standards 1–2 on pages 312–314). Ensuring the adequate nutrient content of food aid rations may be challenging in situations where there are limited food types available. Options for improving the nutritional quality of the ration include fortification of staple commodities, inclusion of fortified blended foods, inclusion of locally purchased commodities to provide missing nutrients and/or use of food supplementation products such as lipid-based, nutrient-dense, ready-to-use foods or multiple micronutrient tablets or powders. These products may be targeted at vulnerable individuals such as children aged 6–24 or 6–59 months or pregnant and breastfeeding women. Exceptionally, where nutrient-rich foods are available locally, increasing the quantity of food in a general ration to allow more food exchanges may be considered, but cost-effectiveness and impact on markets must be taken into account. Other options that may also be considered for the prevention of micronutrient deficiencies include food security measures to promote access to nutritious foods (see Food security and nutrition assessment standard 1 on page 150 and Food security – livelihoods standards 1–2 on pages 204–208). Micronutrient losses, which can occur during transport, storage, processing and cooking, and the bioavailability of the different chemical forms of the vitamins and minerals should be taken into account.

4. *Monitoring utilisation of food rations:* The key indicators address access to food but do not quantify food utilisation or nutrient bioavailability. Direct measurement of nutrient intake would impose unrealistic requirements for information collection. However, utilisation may be estimated indirectly using information from various sources. These sources might include monitoring food availability and use at the household level, assessing food prices and food availability in local markets, examining food aid distribution plans and records, assessing any contribution of wild foods and conducting food security assessments. Food allocation within households may not always be equitable and vulnerable people may be particularly affected, but it is not usually feasible to measure these aspects. Appropriate distribution mechanisms (see Food security – food transfers standard 5 on page 192), the choice of food and discussion with the affected population may help contribute to improved food allocation within households (see Core Standard 1 on page 55).

5. *Older people* can be particularly affected by disasters. Risk factors which reduce access to food and can increase nutrient requirements include disease and disability, isolation, psychosocial stress, large family size, cold and poverty. Older people should be able to access food sources (including food transfers) easily. Foods should be easy to prepare and consume and should meet the additional protein and micronutrient requirements of older people.

6. *People living with HIV* may face greater risk of malnutrition as a result of a number of factors. These include reduced food intake due to appetite loss or difficulties in eating, poor absorption of nutrients due to diarrhoea, parasites or damage to intestinal cells, changes in metabolism, and chronic infections and illness. The energy requirements of PLHIV increase according to the stage of the infection. PLHIV need to ensure that they keep as well nourished and healthy as possible to delay the onset of AIDS. Milling and fortification of food or provision of fortified, blended or specialist food supplements are possible strategies for improving access to an adequate diet. In some situations it may be appropriate to increase the overall size of any food ration. Consideration should be given to the provision of anti-retroviral therapy (ART) and the supportive role nutrition may play in tolerance and adherence to this treatment.

7. *Persons with disabilities:* Disabled individuals may be at particular risk of being separated from immediate family members and usual caregivers in a disaster. They also may face discrimination affecting food access. Efforts should be made to determine and reduce these risks by ensuring physical access to food, developing mechanisms for feeding support (e.g. provision of spoons and straws, developing systems for home visiting or outreach) and ensuring access to energy-dense and nutrient-dense foods. Specific nutri-

tional risks include difficulties in chewing and swallowing (leading to reduced food intake and choking), inappropriate position or posture when feeding, reduced mobility affecting access to food and sunlight (affecting Vitamin D status), and constipation, which may for example affect individuals with cerebral palsy.

8. ***Caregivers and those they are caring for*** may face specific nutritional barriers, e.g. they may have less time to access food because they are ill or caring for the ill, they may have a greater need to maintain hygienic practices which may be compromised, they may have fewer assets to exchange for food due to the costs of treatment or funerals and they may face social stigma and reduced access to community support mechanisms. It is important that caregivers be supported and not undermined in the care of vulnerable individuals; support offered should address feeding, hygiene, health and psychosocial support and protection. Existing social networks can be used to provide training to selected members of the population to take on responsibilities in these areas (see Protection Principle 4 on page 41).

Food security – food transfers standard 2: Appropriateness and acceptability

The food items provided are appropriate and acceptable to recipients so that they can be used efficiently and effectively at the household level.

Key actions (to be read in conjunction with the guidance notes)

▶ Consult disaster-affected people during assessment and programme design on the acceptability, familiarity and appropriateness of food items, and ensure the results inform decisions on food choices (see guidance note 1).

▶ Assess people's ability to store food, their access to water and fuel, and cooking times and requirements for soaking when selecting food types (see guidance note 2).

▶ When unfamiliar food is distributed, provide instructions on appropriate preparation to people who prepare food, preferably in the local language (see guidance note 1).

▶ If wholegrain cereal is distributed, ensure recipients have either the means to mill/process it at home or access to adequate milling/processing facilities (see guidance note 3).

▶ Ensure disaster-affected people have access to culturally important items, including condiments (see guidance note 4).

Key indicators (to be read in conjunction with the guidance notes)

▶ Programme decisions are based on full participation of all targeted people in the selection of food items (see guidance notes 1 and 4).

▶ Programme design takes into account access to water, cooking fuel and food processing equipment (see guidance notes 2–3).

▶ There is no general distribution of powdered or liquid milk or milk products as single commodities (see guidance note 5).

Guidance notes

1. *Familiarity and acceptability:* While nutritional value is the primary consideration when choosing a food basket, the commodities should be familiar to the recipients and consistent with religious and cultural traditions, including any food taboos for pregnant or breastfeeding women. Vulnerable people should participate in consultations on food choice. If unfamiliar food is used, it should have the potential to be palatable locally. In assessment reports and requests to donors, choices of foods (inclusion and exclusion) should be explained. When disasters prevent access to cooking facilities, ready-to-use foods must be provided (see also Infant and young child feeding standard 2 on page 160). Without cooking facilities, there may be no alternative to providing unfamiliar food and special 'emergency rations' may also be considered.

2. *Food storage and preparation:* People's ability to store food should inform the choice of commodity. For water requirements, see Water supply standard 1 on page 97. A fuel assessment is needed to inform food selection, ensure beneficiaries can cook food sufficiently to avoid health risks and prevent environmental degradation and possibly security risks through excessive wood-fuel collection (see Protection Principle 1 on page 33). Generally, food provided should not require long cooking time or large quantities of water. Milled grain normally reduces cooking time and fuel. For cooking equipment, see Food security – food transfers standard 6 on page 197 and Non-food items standards 3–4 on pages 273–274.

3. *Food processing:* Wholegrain cereal has the advantage of a longer shelf life and may have a higher value to recipients. Where household-level grinding is traditional or where there is access to local mills, wholegrain cereal can be distributed. Facilities can be provided for low-extraction commercial milling: this removes germ, oil and enzymes (which cause rancidity) and greatly increases shelf life, although it also reduces protein content. Milling is a particular concern for maize: milled whole maize has a shelf life of only six to eight weeks so milling should occur shortly before consumption. National laws on import and distribution of wholegrain cereals should be respected.

Milling costs to recipients may be met by cash or vouchers, the less-preferred approach of additional grain, or provision of milling equipment.

4. **Culturally important items:** The assessment should identify culturally important condiments and other food items that are an essential part of daily food habits (e.g. spices, tea) and determine the access people have to these items. The food basket should be designed accordingly, especially where people will depend on food rations for an extended period.

5. **Milk:** There should be no untargeted distribution of free or subsidised infant formula, milk powder, liquid milk or milk products as a single commodity (this includes milk intended for mixing with tea) in a general food distribution or a take-home supplementary feeding programme as their indiscriminate use may cause serious health hazards. Any interventions involving milk should be in accordance with the Operational Guidance on IFE, the International Code of Marketing of BMS and subsequent relevant WHA resolutions (see Infant and young child feeding standards 1–2 on pages 159–160).

Food security – food transfers standard 3: Food quality and safety

Food distributed is fit for human consumption and of appropriate quality.

Key actions (to be read in conjunction with the guidance notes)

▶ Select foods that conform to the national standards of the recipient country and other internationally accepted standards (see guidance notes 1–2).

▶ Distribute food before the expiry date or well within the 'best before' date (see guidance note 1).

▶ Consult recipients about the quality of food distributed and act promptly on the issues that arise (see guidance note 3).

▶ Choose appropriate food packaging that is sturdy, convenient for handling, storage and distribution, and is not a hazard for the environment (see guidance note 4).

▶ Label food packages in an appropriate language; for packaged foods, indicate the date of production, origin, expiry dates for potentially dangerous foods and details of the nutrient content (see guidance note 4).

▶ Transport and store food in appropriate conditions, using best practices in storage management, with systematic checks on food quality (see guidance note 5).

Key indicators (to be read in conjunction with the guidance notes)

▶ All recipients receive food that is 'fit for purpose': for safety, food should not pose a risk to health; for quality, food should match quality specifications and be nutritious (see guidance notes 1–2, 4).

▶ Accountability monitoring tracks all the beneficiaries' complaints received and resolved (see guidance note 3).

Guidance notes

1. *Food quality:* Foods must conform to the food standards of the recipient government and/or the Codex Alimentarius standards with regard to quality, packaging, labelling and 'fitness for purpose'. Food should always be 'fit for human consumption' but should also be 'fit for purpose'. When food does not have the quality to be used in the intended manner, it is unfit for purpose even if it is fit for human consumption (e.g. the quality of flour may not enable baking at household level even if it is safe to consume). For quality testing, samples should be drawn according to the sampling plan and systematically checked by purchasing agencies to ensure quality is appropriate. Whenever required, foods either purchased locally or imported should be accompanied by phytosanitary certificates or other inspection certificates. Random sample testing should be carried out on stocks. Fumigation should use appropriate products and follow strict procedures. When large quantities are involved or there are doubts or disputes about quality, independent quality surveyors should inspect the consignment. Information on age and quality of food consignments may be obtained from supplier certificates, quality control inspection reports, package labels and warehouse reports. Food unfit for purpose should be carefully disposed of (see Food security – food transfers standard 4, guidance note 10 on page 190).

2. *Genetically modified foods:* National regulations concerning the receipt and use of genetically modified foods must be understood and respected. Such regulations should be taken into account when planning food transfers that are expected to use imports.

3. *Complaints and response mechanism:* Agencies should ensure adequate complaints and response mechanisms are in place on food quality and safety for accountability to recipients (see Core Standard 1, guidance note 2 on page 56).

4. *Packaging:* If possible, packaging should allow direct distribution without re-measuring (e.g. scooping) or repacking: appropriate package sizes can help ensure ration standards are met. Food packaging should not carry any messages that are politically or religiously motivated or divisive in nature. Environmental risks can be minimised by the choice of packaging and manage-

ment of empty packages (such as sacks and tins). Ready-to-use foods packaging (such as foil wrappers) may require specific controls for safe disposal.

5. **Storage areas** should be dry and hygienic, adequately protected from weather conditions and uncontaminated by chemical or other residues. They should also be secured against pests such as insects and rodents (see also Food security – food transfers standard 4 on page 188 and Solid waste management standard 1 on page 117).

Food security – food transfers standard 4: Supply chain management (SCM)

Commodities and associated costs are well managed using impartial, transparent and responsive systems.

Key actions (to be read in conjunction with the guidance notes)

▶ Establish a coordinated, efficient SCM system using local capacity where feasible (see guidance notes 1–3).

▶ Ensure a transparent, fair and open procedure for awarding contracts (see guidance notes 1–2, 4).

▶ Build sound relationships with suppliers and service providers and enforce ethical practices (see guidance notes 1–2, 4–5).

▶ Train and supervise staff at all levels of the SCM system to observe food quality and safety procedures (see guidance note 5).

▶ Establish appropriate accountability procedures including inventory, reporting and financial systems (see guidance notes 6–8).

▶ Minimise losses, including theft, and account for all losses (see guidance notes 9–11).

▶ Monitor and manage the food pipeline so that all possible actions are taken to avoid illegal diversions and interruption to distributions and all stakeholders are regularly informed on the performance of the supply chain (see guidance notes 12–13).

Key indicators (to be read in conjunction with the guidance notes)

▶ Food reaches intended distribution points (see guidance notes 1 and 7).

▶ Commodity tracking systems, inventory accounting and reporting systems are in place from the beginning of the intervention (see guidance notes 7–8, 11–13).

▶ SCM assessment reports show evidence of assessment and inventory of local SCM capacities, local food availability and local logistics infrastructure (see guidance notes 2–3).

▶ SCM reporting shows:

- evidence of transparent, fair and open systems for awarding contracts
- evidence of supplier/service provider performance management and reporting
- number and proportion of SCM staff trained
- completeness and accuracy of documentation
- losses are minimised and maintained at less than 2 per cent and all food is accounted for
- regular pipeline analysis and relevant stakeholders informed of food pipeline and supply chain.

Guidance notes

1. ***Supply chain management*** is an integrated approach to logistics. Starting with the choice of commodity, it includes sourcing, procurement, quality assurance, packaging, shipping, transportation, warehousing, inventory management and insurance. SCM involves many different partners, and it is important that activities are coordinated (see Core Standard 2 on page 58). Management and monitoring practices should ensure commodities are safeguarded to distribution points. However, humanitarian agencies are also responsible for the food reaching the targeted beneficiaries (see Food security – food transfers standards 5–6 on pages 192–197).

2. ***Using local services:*** An assessment should be made of the availability and reliability of local capability before sourcing from outside the area. Care must be taken to ensure that sourcing locally does not cause or exacerbate hostilities and do more harm in the community. Reputable local or regional transporters and freight forwarders have valuable knowledge of local regulations, procedures and facilities, and can help to ensure compliance with the laws of the host country and to expedite deliveries. In a conflict environment, the vetting of service providers should be especially rigorous.

3. ***Local sourcing versus importation:*** The local availability of goods, and the implications for local production and market systems of food either being sourced locally or imported, should be assessed, including environmental sustainability (see Food security and nutrition assessment standard 1 on page 150 and Food security – livelihoods standards 1 and 3 on pages 204–211). Markets are stimulated and supported through buying food locally or regionally; this may give farmers an incentive to produce more and help boost the local economy. Where several organisations are involved,

local sourcing should be coordinated as far as possible. Other in-country sources of commodities may include loans or reallocations from existing food programmes (donor agreement may be necessary) or national grain reserves, or loans from, or swaps with, commercial suppliers.

4. *Impartiality:* Fair and transparent contracting procedures are essential to avoid suspicion of favouritism or corruption. Service provider performance should be evaluated and shortlists updated.

5. *Skills and training:* Experienced SCM practitioners and programme managers should be mobilised to set up the SCM system and train staff. Particular types of relevant expertise include contracts management, transportation and warehouse management, inventory management, pipeline analysis and information management, shipment tracking and import management. When training is carried out, it should include staff of partner organisations and service providers and be in the local language.

6. *Food is not used for payment:* The use of food to pay for logistics operations, such as unloading at warehouses and distribution points, should be avoided. If cash payments are not possible and food is used, adjustments should be made on the food amounts sent to distribution points so that originally planned amounts still reach targeted recipients.

7. *Reporting (including logistics cluster and inter-agency):* Most food donors have specific reporting requirements and supply chain managers should be aware of these requirements and establish systems that meet them. Day-to-day management needs include reporting promptly any delays or deviations in the supply chain. Pipeline information and other SCM reports should be shared in a transparent manner.

8. *Documentation:* Sufficient documentation and forms (waybills, stock ledgers, reporting forms, etc.) should be available in the local language at all locations where goods are received, stored and/or dispatched, in order to maintain a documented audit trail of transactions.

9. *Warehousing:* Dedicated warehouses for food are preferable to shared facilities but good management can minimise risks in the latter. When selecting a warehouse, it should be established that no hazardous goods have previously been stored there and there is no danger of contamination. Factors to consider include security, capacity, ease of access, structural solidity (of roof, walls, doors and floor) and absence of any threat of flooding.

10. *Disposal of commodities unfit for human consumption:* Damaged commodities should be inspected by qualified inspectors (such as food safety experts and public health laboratories) to certify them as fit or unfit for human consumption. Disposal should be executed quickly before food becomes

a health hazard. Methods of disposal of unfit commodities include sale for animal feed and burial/incineration authorised and witnessed by relevant authorities. For disposal as animal feed, certification must be obtained for fitness for this purpose. In all cases, unfit commodities must not re-enter the human or animal food supply chain and disposal must not harm the environment or contaminate water sources.

11. **Threats to the supply chain:** In situations of armed conflict or general insecurity, there is a danger of food being looted or requisitioned by warring parties, and the risks to security of transport routes and warehouses must be managed. There is potential for theft at all stages of the supply chain: control systems must be established and supervised at all storage, hand-over and distribution points to minimise this risk. Internal control systems should ensure division of responsibilities to reduce the risk of collusion. Stocks should be regularly checked to detect illegal diversion of food. Measures should be taken not only to ensure the integrity of the supply chain but also to analyse and address broader political and security implications, such as the possibility of diverted stocks fuelling an armed conflict (see Protection Principle 1 on page 33).

12. **Pipeline analysis** should be regularly performed and relevant information on stock levels, expected arrivals and distributions shared among stakeholders involved in the supply chain. Tracking and forecasting of stock levels should highlight anticipated shortfalls and problems in time for solutions to be found. Information-sharing among partners may facilitate loans to prevent pipeline breaks. Pipeline breaks may be unavoidable if resources are inadequate. In such cases, prioritisation of items in the food basket may be necessary when programming resources (i.e. choosing what to buy) with available funds. Stakeholders must be consulted and solutions may include reducing overall ration size or reducing or excluding the food types which beneficiaries have more access to (physically and economically).

13. **Providing information:** Relevant information should be provided to appropriate stakeholders rather than to all stakeholders to avoid misunderstandings. The use of local media, traditional methods of news dissemination and current technologies (mobile phone text messages, email) should be considered as a way of keeping local officials and recipients informed about deliveries and reinforcing transparency.

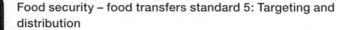

Food security – food transfers standard 5: Targeting and distribution

The method of targeted food distribution is responsive, timely, transparent and safe, supports dignity and is appropriate to local conditions.

Key actions (to be read in conjunction with the guidance notes)

▶ Identify and target recipients of food on the basis of need, consulting appropriate stakeholders (see guidance notes 1–2).

▶ Design efficient and equitable food distribution methods that support dignity in consultation with partner organisations, local groups and recipients. The design process should have the active participation of women and representatives of persons with disabilities, older people and individuals with reduced mobility (see guidance notes 1-4).

▶ Consult local stakeholders on appropriate points for distribution that will ensure easy access and safety for recipients (see guidance notes 5–6).

▶ Inform recipients in advance on the distribution plan and quality and quantity of the food ration (see guidance notes 7–8).

▶ Monitor and evaluate the performance of targeted food distribution (see guidance note 9).

Key indicators (to be read in conjunction with the guidance notes)

▶ Targeting criteria must be based on thorough analysis of vulnerability (see guidance note 1).

▶ Targeting mechanisms are agreed among the disaster-affected population (see guidance notes 1–2).

▶ Existence of relevant alternative distribution models for people with reduced mobility (see guidance notes 3–4).

▶ Recipients should not have to walk more than 10 kilometres to the distribution site, i.e. no more than a four-hour walk (see guidance note 5).

▶ Presence of ration cards, banners and/or signposts specifying the food rations during distributions (see guidance notes 7–8).

▶ Monitoring and/or beneficiary accountability mechanisms (see guidance note 9) track:

- stakeholders' preferences on distribution methods
- information provided to beneficiaries on distribution
- beneficiaries/food receipt: actual versus planned (timeliness, quantity, quality).

Guidance notes

1. **Targeting:** Food should be targeted to the people assessed to be most in need: the most acutely food insecure households and malnourished individuals (see Vulnerabilities and capacities of disaster-affected populations on page 148 and Food security and nutrition assessment standards 1–2 on pages 150–154). Targeting spans throughout the intervention, not just the initial phase. Finding the right balance between exclusion errors (which can be life-threatening) and inclusion errors (which are potentially disruptive or wasteful) is complex; moreover, reducing errors normally increases costs. In acute emergencies, inclusion errors may be more acceptable than exclusion errors: blanket distributions may be appropriate in sudden-onset disasters where all households have suffered similar losses, or where a detailed targeting assessment is not possible due to lack of access. The selection of agents involved in targeting should be based on their impartiality, capacity and accountability. Targeting agents may include local elders, locally elected relief committees, civil society organisations, local NGOs, local governmental institutions, or international NGOs. The selection of women targeting agents is strongly encouraged. Targeting approaches need to be clear and accepted by both recipient and non-recipient populations to avoid creating tensions and doing harm (see Core Standard 1, guidance note 3 on page 57 and Protection Principle 2 on page 36).

2. **Registration:** Formal registration of households to receive food should be carried out as soon as is feasible, and updated as necessary. Information on beneficiaries is essential to design an effective distribution system (the size and demographic profile of a population influences the organisation of distribution), to draw up beneficiary lists, tally sheets and rations cards (if issued) and to identify people with specific needs. In camps, registration is often challenging, especially where displaced people do not have identification documents (see Protection Principle 4, guidance notes 4–5 on page 42). Lists from local authorities and community-generated household lists may be useful, provided an independent assessment proves them accurate and impartial. Women from the disaster-affected population should be encouraged to help in the registration process. Agencies should ensure that vulnerable individuals are not omitted from distribution lists, especially housebound people. While heads of household are normally registered, women should have the right to be registered in their own names: women may utilise trans-

fers more appropriately at household level. If registration is not possible in the initial stages of a disaster, it should be completed as soon as the situation has stabilised; this is especially important when food transfers are required for lengthy periods. A complaints and response mechanism should be established for the registration process (see Core Standard 1, guidance notes 2 and 6 on pages 56–57).

3. **Distribution methods for 'dry' rations**: Most distribution methods evolve over time. A general food distribution is normally in the form of dry rations to be cooked by beneficiaries in their homes. Recipients could be an individual or household ration-card holder, a representative of a group of households, traditional leaders or leaders of a community-based targeted distribution. Conditions on the ground determine the best recipient to select, and changing conditions may change the recipient. The risks inherent in distributions via representatives or leaders should be carefully assessed. The selection of the recipients should consider the impact on workloads and possible risks of violence, including domestic abuse (see Protection Principles 1–2 on pages 33–36). The frequency of distributions should consider the weight of the food ration and the beneficiaries' means to carry it home. Specific action may be necessary to ensure that older people and persons with disabilities can collect their entitlements: other community members may assist but providing weekly or two-week rations may be easier to collect than monthly rations. Attempts to target vulnerable people should not add to any stigma that they already experience: this may be a particular issue in populations with a large number of people living with HIV and AIDS (see Protection Principle 4, guidance notes 1, 9–11 on pages 41–43).

4. **Distribution methods for 'wet' rations:** Exceptionally, a general food distribution can be a cooked meal or ready-to-eat food for an initial period during an acute emergency. These rations may be appropriate when, for example, people are on the move, extreme insecurity and carrying food home would put beneficiaries at risk of theft or violence, high levels of abuse or taxation excludes vulnerable people, major displacement results in people losing their assets (cooking equipment and/or fuel) or leaves them too weak to cook for themselves, local leaders are diverting rations or there are environmental considerations (e.g. to protect a fragile ecological environment by avoiding firewood collection). School meals and food incentives for education personnel may be used as a distribution mechanism in an emergency (see INEE Minimum Standards for Education).

5. **Distribution points and travel:** Distribution points should be established where they are safe and most convenient for the recipients, not based on logistic convenience for the agency (see Protection Principle 3, guidance notes 6–9 on page 39). These should take into consideration terrain and

proximity to other sources of support (potable water, toilets, medical services, shade, shelter, safe spaces for women). Distribution points should avoid areas where people would have to cross military or armed checkpoints or negotiate safe passage. The frequency of distributions and the number of distribution points should take into account the time it takes recipients to travel to distribution points and the practicalities and costs of transporting commodities. Recipients should be able to travel to and from a distribution point within one day; alternative means of distribution should be developed to reach those who cannot and may be isolated (e.g. individuals with mobility difficulties). Walking speeds average 5 km/hour but are slower on poor terrain and on slopes; times vary with age and level of mobility. Access to distribution is a common source of anxiety for marginalised and excluded populations in a disaster situation. Distributions should be scheduled to minimise disruption to everyday activities, at times that allow travel to distribution points during daylight hours for the protection of recipients and to avoid beneficiaries staying overnight, as this carries additional risks (see Protection Principle 1 on page 33).

6. ***Minimising security risks:*** Food distributions can create security risks, including diversion and violence. Tensions can run high during distributions. Women, children, older people and persons with disabilities are at particular risk of losing their entitlements. The risks must be assessed in advance and steps taken to minimise them. These include supervision of the distributions by trained staff and guarding of distribution points by the affected populations themselves. If necessary, the local police may be involved, but they should be sensitised to the objectives of the food transfers. Careful planning of the site layout at distribution points can facilitate crowd control and lower security risks. Specific measures to prevent, monitor and respond to gender-based violence, including sexual exploitation associated with food distribution, should be enforced. These include segregating men and women, for example through a physical barrier or by offering separate distribution times, informing all food distribution teams about appropriate conduct and penalties for sexual abuse, and including female 'guardians' to oversee off-loading, registration, distribution and post-distribution of food (see also guidance note 5 and Protection Principle 2 on page 36).

7. ***Dissemination of information:*** Recipients should be informed about:

   - the quantity and type of ration to be distributed and the reasons for any differences from the plan; ration information should be displayed prominently at distribution sites in formats accessible to people who cannot read or who have communication difficulties (e.g. written in the local language and/or drawn pictorially and/or as oral information) so that people are aware of their entitlements

- the distribution plan (day, time, location, frequency) and any changes
- the nutritional quality of the food and, if needed, special attention required by recipients to protect its nutritional value
- the requirements for the safe handling and use of the foods
- specific information for optimum use of food for children (see Infant and young child feeding standards 1–2 on pages 159–160)
- the appropriate ways for recipients to obtain more information on the programme and the process for complaints.

(See Core Standard 1, guidance notes 4–6 on page 57.)

8. **Changes to the programme:** Changes in the food basket or ration levels caused by insufficient availability of food must be discussed with the recipients, through distribution committees, community leaders and representative organisations. A course of action should be jointly developed before distributions are made. The distribution committee should inform people of changes, the reasons behind them and when normal rations will be resumed. The following options may be considered:

- reduce the rations to all recipients (an equal share of available commodities or a reduced food basket)
- give a 'full' ration to vulnerable individuals and a 'reduced' ration to the general population
- as a last resort, postpone the distribution.

If distribution of the planned ration is not possible, the shortfall is not necessarily corrected in the following distribution (i.e. retroactive provision may not be appropriate).

9. **Monitoring and evaluation** should be carried out at all levels of the supply chain and to the point of consumption (see Core Standard 5 on page 68). At distribution points, check that arrangements for distributions are in place before they take place (e.g. for registration, security, dissemination of information). Random weighing should be carried out on rations collected by households to measure the accuracy and equity of distribution management, with recipients interviewed. Random visits to households can help ascertain the acceptability and usefulness of the ration, and also identify people who meet the selection criteria but are not receiving food. Such visits can also discover if extra food is being received, where it is coming from, what it is being used for and by whom (e.g. as a result of commandeering, recruitment or exploitation, sexual or otherwise). Monitoring should analyse the impact of food transfers on the safety of the beneficiaries. The wider effects of food distributions should also be evaluated, such as implications of the agricultural cycle, agricultural activities, market conditions and availability of agricultural inputs.

Food security – food transfers standard 6: Food use

Food is stored, prepared and consumed in a safe and appropriate manner at both household and community levels.

Key actions (to be read in conjunction with the guidance notes)

▶ Protect beneficiaries from inappropriate food handling or preparation (see guidance note 1).

▶ Disseminate relevant information on the importance of food hygiene to food recipients and promote a good understanding of hygienic practices in food handling (see guidance notes 1–2).

▶ Where cooked food is distributed, train staff in safe storage and handling of food, preparation of food and the potential health hazards caused by improper practices (see guidance note 1).

▶ Consult (and advise where necessary) beneficiaries on storage, preparation, cooking and consumption of food distributed and the implications of targeted provision for vulnerable people and respond to issues that arise (see guidance notes 1–2).

▶ Ensure households have access to appropriate cooking utensils, fuel, potable water and hygiene materials (see guidance notes 1–4).

▶ For individuals who cannot prepare food or cannot feed themselves, ensure access to carers to prepare appropriate food and administer feeding where necessary (see guidance note 5).

Key indicators (to be read in conjunction with the guidance notes)

▶ No cases of health hazards from food distributed.

▶ Raise beneficiaries' awareness of good food hygiene (see guidance notes 1–2).

▶ All relevant staff must be trained on food handling and hazards from improper practices (see guidance note 1).

▶ Full household access to adequate and safe food preparation materials and equipment (see guidance notes 3–4).

▶ Full presence of carers for all individuals with special assistance needs (see guidance note 5).

Guidance notes

1. *Food hygiene:* Disasters may disrupt people's normal hygiene practices. It may be necessary to promote food hygiene and actively support measures compatible with local conditions and disease patterns, e.g. stressing the importance of washing hands before handling food, avoiding contamination of water and taking pest-control measures. Food recipients should be informed about how to store food safely at the household level. Caregivers should be provided with information on the optimal use of household resources for feeding children and safe methods for food preparation (see Hygiene promotion standards 1–2 on pages 91–94). Where community kitchens have been set up to provide hot meals to a disaster-affected population, special attention is needed in selecting the kitchen site, taking into account accessibility, safety and hygiene conditions of the site, cooking and drinking water availability, and eating space.

2. *Sources of information*: Mechanisms are needed for sharing information and collecting feedback from beneficiaries, particularly women (see Core Standard 1, guidance notes 2 and 6 on pages 56–57). For dissemination of instructions about food, schools and safe learning spaces should be considered as suitable locations. Accessible formats or diagrams may be needed for people with different communication requirements (see Core Standard 1, guidance note 4 on page 57).

3. *Fuel, potable water and household items:* When necessary, appropriate fuel should be provided or a wood planting or harvesting programme established, with supervision for the safety of women and children, the main gatherers of firewood (for stoves and fuel, see Non-food items standard 4 on page 274). For water access, quantity, quality and facilities, see Water supply standards 1–3 on pages 97–103. For cooking and eating utensils and water containers, see Non-food items standard 3 on page 273.

4. *Access to food processing facilities* such as cereal grinding mills enable people to prepare food in the form of their choice and also save time for other productive activities. Household-level food processing such as milling can reduce the time and the quantities of water and fuel required for cooking (see Food security – food transfers standard 2, guidance note 2 on page 185).

5. *Specific needs:* Individuals who require assistance with feeding may include young children, older people, persons with disabilities and people living with HIV (see Infant and young child feeding standard 2 on page 160 and Food security – food transfers standard 1, guidance notes 5–7 on page 183). Outreach programmes or additional support and follow-up may be necessary to support some people with reduced capacity to provide food to dependents (e.g. parents with mental illness).

4.2. Food security – cash and voucher transfers

Cash and voucher transfers represent two forms of assistance: cash transfers provide people with money, while voucher transfers provide people with coupons to purchase a fixed quantity of a specified product such as food (commodity-based vouchers) or a fixed monetary value (value-based vouchers). While their objectives and design may differ, cash and voucher transfers share a market-based approach where beneficiaries are provided with purchasing power.

Cash and voucher transfers are used to meet basic food and non-food needs or to purchase assets enabling people to resume economic activity. Unconditional (or non-targeted or 'universal') cash grants have no conditions on how the money should be used, but if basic needs have been identified in the assessment, it is expected that the money will be used to cover these needs. If support to livelihoods or productive activities has been identified as a need, then the cash distributed would be expected to be used for this. Unconditional cash grants may be appropriate at the start of an emergency. Conditional cash grants have the condition that the recipient uses the cash for specific purposes (e.g. to rebuild houses, provide labour, establish or re-establish a livelihood and/or attend health services). Vouchers give access to a range of predetermined commodities (e.g. food, livestock, seeds, tools) or services (e.g. grinding mills, transport, market or stand access, bank loans). Vouchers may have either a cash value or a commodity value, to be used in pre-selected shops, with specified traders or service providers or at fairs. Voucher programmes should refer to the standards for the sector concerned; for example, food voucher programmes should refer to Food security – food transfers standards 1–3 and 6 on pages 180–197.

The choice of appropriate transfers (food, cash or vouchers) requires a context-specific analysis including cost efficiency, secondary market impacts, the flexibility of the transfer, targeting and risks of insecurity and corruption.

Food security – cash and voucher transfers
standard 1: Access to available goods and services

Cash and vouchers are considered as ways to address basic needs and to protect and re-establish livelihoods.

Key actions (to be read in conjunction with the guidance notes)

▶ Consult and involve beneficiaries, community representatives and other key stakeholders in assessment, design, implementation, monitoring and evaluation (see guidance notes 1, 3, 6–7 and Core Standards 1–3 on pages 55–61).

▶ Assess and analyse if people could buy what they need in local markets at prices that are cost-efficient compared with alternative transfers, and analyse the market chain (see guidance note 2).

▶ Choose cash or vouchers or a combination of these based on the most appropriate delivery mechanism and the likely benefits to the disaster-affected population and the local economy (see guidance notes 1–3, 5–6).

▶ Implement measures to reduce risks of illegal diversion, insecurity, inflation, harmful use and negative impacts on disadvantaged groups. Particular care is needed for targeting systems (see guidance notes 4 and 7).

▶ Monitor to assess if cash and/or vouchers remain the most appropriate transfer and if adjustments are needed (see guidance note 8).

Key indicators (to be read in conjunction with guidance notes)

▶ All targeted populations meet some or all their basic food needs and other livelihood needs (e.g. productive assets, health, education, transportation, shelter, transport) through purchase from the local markets (see guidance notes 1–2, 8).

▶ Cash and/or vouchers are the preferred form of transfer for all targeted populations, particularly for women and other vulnerable people (see guidance notes 3–8).

▶ The transfer does not result in anti-social expenditures (see guidance notes 4 and 8).

▶ The transfer does not generate insecurity (see guidance notes 3–4, 8).

▶ The local economy is supported to recover from the disaster (see guidance notes 1–2, 8).

Guidance notes

1. ***Cash and voucher transfers are a tool:*** Cash and vouchers are mechanisms to achieve desired goals, not interventions in themselves. A careful comparative assessment should indicate whether cash and/or vouchers are appropriate or not, and whether they should be used on their own or combined with other responses, such as in-kind support. Cash and voucher transfers can be used at different stages of a disaster. The response should be determined not only by the expected efficiency and effectiveness in meeting beneficiaries' basic needs or re-establishing livelihoods, but also by an expected lower level of associated risks. Cash and vouchers can offer greater choice and flexibility than in-kind responses and this may give recipients a sense of greater dignity. Cash and vouchers may also create positive multiplier effects in local economies, which should be considered during assessments. Cash and vouchers can be used as follows:

   - cash grants – conditional or unconditional transfer of cash in either one or several instalments to meet a range of needs
   - commodity or value-based voucher – transfer of paper or electronic vouchers to be exchanged for specific goods or a range of goods according to the value of the voucher
   - cash for work – transfer of cash as income earned by participating in specified activities (usually activities requiring physical labour).

   Planning, implementation and monitoring should involve local stakeholders such as governments, local authorities, community structures and representatives, cooperatives, associations, local groups and beneficiaries. This will help ensure relevance and sustainability. An exit strategy should be planned with key stakeholders from design onwards.

2. ***Impact on local economies and market systems:*** Market assessment should analyse the situation before and after the disaster, and the competitiveness and integration of the market to respond to current needs. Analysis should also show the roles of different market actors, availability and price of commodities (livelihoods assets, shelter materials, food and others depending on objectives), seasonality and physical, social and economic access by different groups of vulnerable people. Cash and vouchers can be appropriate when markets are functioning and accessible, and when food and other basic items are available in the required amounts and at reasonable prices. Such transfers may stimulate the local economy to a quicker and more sustainable recovery. Market responses can promote local procurement and better use of the capabilities of existing market actors. Cash and vouchers used when the context is inappropriate can distort markets and may have negative effects such as inflation. Market monitoring is essential

to understand the impact of cash and vouchers on local economies and people.

3. *Cash and voucher delivery mechanisms:* Cash and vouchers can be delivered through local banks, shops, traders, local money transfer companies, remittance companies and post offices. They can be delivered physically or through technologies such as mobile banking and mobile phone networks. Banks are usually efficient and effective but may be less accessible to vulnerable people; if banks are accessible, perhaps through mobile banking, they can be a more secure option. The choice of delivery mechanism requires an assessment of options and consultation with recipients. Issues to consider are costs for recipients (bank charges, travel time and costs, time at collection points), costs for the organisation (charges and set-up costs of provider, staff time to set up and administer, and transport, security, education and training of recipients), efficiency and effectiveness (reliability, resilience, accountability, transparency, monitoring, flexibility, financial control, financial security and access by vulnerable people). An approach that may appear costly may still be the most appropriate transfer mechanism.

4. *Considering risks:* Common concerns on the risks of cash and voucher transfers include fears that cash and vouchers could contribute to price inflation (leaving disaster-affected people, and others, with less purchasing power), the use of cash and vouchers for anti-social purposes (e.g. alcohol and/or tobacco abuse) and differential access of women and men to cash compared with in-kind resources. Other concerns are that transporting cash may create security risks for implementing staff and for the affected population (see Protection Principle 1 on page 33) and that the attractiveness of cash may make it more difficult to target recipients and may increase the risks of corrupt diversion or seizure by armed groups. However, in-kind distributions also have risks (see Food security – food transfers standards 4–5 on pages 188–192). The risks for cash and vouchers can be minimised through good design, thorough risk analysis and good management. Decision-making should be through evidence-based consultation: unfounded fears should not influence programme planning.

5. *Setting the value of the cash or voucher transfer:* The value set for transfers is context-specific. Calculations should be in coordination with other agencies and based on the disaster-affected population's priorities and needs, prices for key goods expected to be purchased in local markets, other assistance that has been and/or will be given, additional related costs (e.g. travel assistance for people with restricted mobility), method, size and frequency of payments and timing of payment in relation to seasonality, and objectives of the programme and transfer (e.g. covering food needs based on the food basket or providing employment based on the daily labour rate).

Price fluctuations can reduce the success of cash and voucher transfers. Budget flexibility is essential to adjust the value of the transfer or add a commodity component, based on market monitoring.

6. **Choosing which type of cash or voucher transfer:** The appropriate type of transfer depends upon the programme objectives and local context. A combination of approaches may be appropriate, including with in-kind assistance and seasonal variations. Agencies should find out what disaster-affected populations consider the most appropriate form(s) of transfer through informed consultations (see Food security – livelihoods standard 2 on page 208).

7. **Targeting in cash and voucher transfer programmes:** The challenges can be as significant for in-kind commodities and services, but due to the attractiveness of cash and vouchers, particular attention is needed to minimise exclusion and inclusion errors. People can be reached either by direct targeting (to the disaster-affected households or population) or by indirect targeting (e.g. local traders or service providers). Insecure conditions may require an indirect targeting approach (see Protection Principle 1 on page 33). Gender affects decisions on the household member registered to receive cash or vouchers, as with in-kind transfers (see Food security – food transfers standard 5 on page 192). Coordination with stakeholders, including government welfare and social protection programmes providing cash transfers, is essential for targeting (as for in-kind transfers).

8. **Monitoring of cash and voucher transfers:** Baseline information is required, with monitoring before, during and after transfer programmes, taking into account the direct and indirect impacts of cash and vouchers in the market. Changes in the intervention should respond to the changes of the context and market situation. Monitoring should include prices of key goods, multiplier effects in local economies and price fluctuations. Key questions are: What are people buying with the cash and vouchers provided? Can people receive and spend cash safely? Are cash and vouchers being diverted? Do women influence how the cash or voucher is spent (see Core Standard 5 on page 68).

4.3.   Food security – livelihoods

The resilience of people's livelihoods and their vulnerability to food insecurity are largely determined by the resources (or assets) available to them and how these have been affected by a disaster. These resources include financial capital (such as cash, credit, savings) and also include physical (houses, machinery), natural (land, water), human (labour, skills), social (networks, norms) and political (influence, policy) capital. Key to those who produce food is whether they have access to land that can support production and whether they have the means to continue to farm. Key to those who need income to get their food is whether they have access to employment, markets and services. For people affected by disasters, the preservation, recovery and development of the resources necessary for their food security and future livelihoods should be a priority.

Prolonged political instability, insecurity and the threat of conflict may seriously restrict livelihood activities and access to markets. Households may have to abandon their plots and may lose assets, whether left behind, destroyed or taken by warring parties.

The three standards relate to primary production, income generation and employment, and access to markets, including goods and services.

Food security – livelihoods standard 1: Primary production

Primary production mechanisms are protected and supported.

Key actions (to be read in conjunction with the guidance notes)

- Base the interventions to support primary production on livelihoods assessment, context analysis and a demonstrated understanding of the viability of production systems, including access to and availability of necessary inputs, services and market demand (see guidance note 1).

- Introduce new technologies only where their implications for local production systems, cultural practices and the natural environment are understood and accepted by food producers and local consumers (see guidance note 2).

- Provide production inputs or cash to purchase a range of inputs in order to give producers flexibility in devising strategies and managing their production and reducing risks (see guidance note 3).

- Deliver inputs on time, ensure they are locally acceptable and conform to appropriate quality norms (see guidance notes 4–5).

- Introduce inputs and services with care, not to exacerbate vulnerability or increase risk, e.g. by increasing competition for scarce natural resources or by damaging existing social networks (see guidance note 6).

- Train food producers in better management practices where possible and appropriate (see guidance notes 1–2, 5–6).

◗ Purchase inputs and services locally whenever possible, unless this would adversely affect local producers, markets or consumers (see guidance note 7).

◗ Carry out regular monitoring to assess whether production inputs are used appropriately by beneficiaries (see guidance note 8).

Key indicators (to be read in conjunction with the guidance notes)

◗ All households with assessed needs have access to the necessary inputs to protect and restart primary production to the level pre-disaster, when justified, and in accordance with the agricultural calendar (see guidance notes 1–6).

◗ All targeted households are given cash or vouchers, where it is considered (or assessed) to be operationally viable, at market value of required inputs, giving households choices on livelihoods options (see guidance notes 3, 5 and 7).

Guidance notes

1. *Viability of primary production:* To be viable, food production strategies must have a reasonable chance of developing adequately and succeeding (see Livestock Emergency Guidelines and Standards (LEGS) in References and further reading). This may be influenced by a wide range of factors including:

   - access to sufficient natural resources (farmland, pasture, fodder, water, rivers, lakes, coastal waters, etc.). The ecological balance should not be endangered, e.g. by over-exploitation of marginal lands, over-fishing or pollution of water, especially in peri-urban areas
   - levels of skills and capacities, which may be limited where populations are seriously affected by disease or where education and training may be barred to some groups
   - labour availability in relation to existing patterns of production and the timing of key agricultural and aquaculture activities
   - availability and access to the inputs needed for agricultural and aquaculture production.

   The pre-disaster level of production may not have been a good one and attempting to return to it could contradict the 'do no harm' principle (see Protection Principle 1 on page 33).

2. *Technological development:* 'New' technologies may include improved crop varieties, livestock or fish-stock species, new tools, fertilisers or innovative management practices. As far as possible, food production activities should build on or strengthen existing patterns and/or be linked with

national development plans. New technologies should only be introduced after a disaster if they have previously been tested in the local area and are known to be adapted and acceptable to beneficiaries. When introduced, new technologies should be accompanied by appropriate community consultations, provision of information, training and other relevant support. Wherever possible this should be done in coordination with private and public extension providers and input suppliers to ensure ongoing support and accessibility to the technology in the future and, critically, commercial viability.

3. *Improving choice:* Interventions that offer producers greater choice include cash or credit in lieu of (or to complement) productive inputs, and seed and livestock fairs using vouchers that provide farmers with the opportunity to select seed or livestock of the varieties and species of their choice. Support to production should assess potential implications for nutrition, including access to nutrient-rich food through own production or through cash generated by this production. The provision of animal fodder during drought can provide a more direct human nutrition benefit to pastoralists than the provision of food transfers to people. The feasibility of transferring cash to households in order to provide access to production inputs should be based on availability of goods locally, access to markets and availability of a safe and affordable transfer mechanism.

4. *Timeliness and acceptability:* Examples of production inputs include seeds, tools, fertiliser, livestock, fishing equipment, hunting implements, loans and credit facilities, market information and transport facilities. An alternative to in-kind inputs is to provide cash or vouchers to enable people to purchase inputs of their choice. The provision of agricultural inputs and veterinary services must be timed to coincide with the relevant agricultural and animal husbandry seasons. For example, provision of seeds and tools must precede the planting season and emergency destocking of livestock during drought should take place before excess livestock mortality occurs, while restocking should start when recovery is well assured, e.g. following the next rains.

5. *Seeds:* Priority should be given to seed of crops and varieties that are already in local use, so that farmers can use their own criteria to establish quality. Crops on offer should be those of highest priority for the upcoming season. Specific varieties should be approved by farmers and local agricultural experts. Minimally, seeds should be adapted to the local agro-ecology and to farmers' own management conditions, be disease resistant and be chosen with consideration of future climate change scenarios such as floods or droughts and sea-level rise. Seeds originating from outside the region need to be adequately tested for quality and checked for appropriateness to local conditions. Farmers should be given access to a range of crops and

varieties in any seed-related intervention so that they themselves can strategise about what is best for their particular farming system. Hybrid seeds may be appropriate where farmers are familiar with them and have experience in growing them. This can only be determined through consultation with the population. When seeds are provided free of charge and farmers grow maize, farmers may prefer hybrid seeds to local varieties because these are otherwise costly to purchase. Government policies regarding hybrid seeds should also be complied with before distribution. Genetically modified (GMO) seeds should not be distributed unless they have been approved by the local authorities. In such cases, farmers should also be aware that the aid contains GMO seed.

6. **Impact on rural livelihoods:** Primary food production may not be viable if there is a shortage of vital natural resources (and may not be viable for the long term if they were on the decline before the disaster) or lack of access for certain populations (e.g. landless people). Promoting production that requires increased (or changed) access to locally available natural resources may heighten tensions within the local population, which in turn can restrict access to water and other essential needs. Care should be taken when providing resources, whether in-kind or cash, that these do not increase security risks for recipients or create conflict (see Food security – livelihoods standard 2 on page 208 and Food security – cash and voucher transfers standard 1 on page 200). Also, the free provision of inputs may disturb traditional mechanisms for social support and redistribution while pushing the private sector out of business and jeopardising future access to inputs.

7. **Local purchase of inputs:** Inputs and services for food production, such as veterinary services and seed, should be obtained through existing local legal and verifiable supply systems where possible. To support the local private sector, mechanisms such as cash or vouchers should be used, linking primary producers directly to suppliers. In designing such systems to enable local purchase, availability of appropriate inputs and suppliers' ability to increase supply should be considered, given the risk of inflation (e.g. raising prices of scarce items) and quality of inputs. Direct provision of imported inputs should only be undertaken when local alternatives are not feasible.

8. **Monitoring usage:** Indicators of the process and outputs from food production, processing and distribution may be estimated, e.g. area planted, quantity of seed planted per hectare, yield and number of livestock offspring. It is important to determine how producers use the inputs (i.e. verifying that seeds are indeed planted and that tools, fertilisers, nets and fishing gear are used as intended) or how cash is spent on inputs. The quality of the inputs should also be reviewed in terms of their performance, their acceptability and the preferences of producers. Important for evaluation is consideration of how the project has affected food available to the household, e.g. household

food stocks, the quantity and quality of food consumed or the amount of food traded or given away. Where the project aims to increase production of a specific food type, such as animal or fish products or protein-rich legumes, the households' use of these products should be investigated.

Food security – livelihoods standard 2: Income and employment

Where income generation and employment are feasible livelihood strategies, women and men have equal access to appropriate income-earning opportunities.

Key actions (to be read in conjunction with the guidance notes)

▶ Base the decisions on income-generation activities on a market assessment and on an adequate participatory analysis of the capabilities of households to engage in the activities (see guidance notes 1–2).

▶ Base the type of remuneration (cash, voucher, food or a combination of these) on sound analysis of local capacities, immediate needs, market systems and the disaster-affected population's preferences (see guidance note 3).

▶ Base the level of remuneration on needs, objectives for livelihoods restoration and local labour rates (see guidance note 4).

▶ Ensure procedures to provide a safe, secure working environment are in place (see guidance note 5).

▶ Take measures to avoid diversion and/or insecurity when involving large sums of cash (see guidance note 6).

Key indicators (to be read in conjunction with the guidance notes)

▶ All the targeted people generate incomes through their activities and contribute to meeting their basic and other livelihoods needs.

▶ Responses providing employment opportunities are equally available to women and men and do not negatively affect the local market or negatively impact on normal livelihood activities (see guidance note 7).

▶ Populations are kept aware of and understand remuneration as a contribution towards the food security of all household members equally (see guidance note 8).

Guidance notes

1. *Appropriateness of initiatives:* A market analysis is fundamental to justify and define activities. Existing tools to understand markets and economic

systems should be used (see markets section in References and further reading). There should be maximum use of local human resources in project design and the identification of appropriate activities. Alternatives for certain groups (such as pregnant women, persons with disabilities or older people) should be discussed within the targeted group. Where there are large numbers of displaced people (refugees or internally displaced persons), there should be consideration of opportunities to provide employment and skills to both displaced people and hosts. Locations for activities should consider the threat of attacks, risks to safety (such as mined areas) and environmentally unsuitable areas (e.g. land that is contaminated or polluted, prone to subsidence or flooding, or excessively steep) (see Protection Principles 1–3 on pages 33–38).

2. *Income transfers to households with limited capacities to participate:* While many households may be able to make use of employment and income-generation activities, the effect of disaster on some households may not allow them to take advantage of these opportunities or the period for receiving adequate returns may be too long for some. Safety-net measures such as unconditional cash and/or food transfers should be considered for such households, with a plan to either link up with existing social protection systems or advocate for new safety nets where needed.

3. *Type of remuneration:* Remuneration may be in cash or in food or a combination of these and should enable food insecure households to meet their needs. Rather than payment for community works, remuneration may take the form of an incentive to help people to undertake tasks of direct benefit to themselves. People's purchasing needs and the impact of giving either cash or food for other basic needs (such as school, access to health services and social obligations) should be considered. The type and level of remuneration should be decided case-by-case, taking account of the factors above, the availability of cash and food and possible impact on local labour markets.

4. *Payments:* There are no universally accepted guidelines for setting levels of remuneration, but where remuneration is in-kind and provided as an income transfer, the resale value (e.g. of food) on local markets must be considered. The net gain in income to individuals through participation in programme activities should be greater than if they had spent their time on other activities. This applies to food and cash for work activities and also credit, business start-ups, etc. Income-earning opportunities should enhance the range of income sources and not replace existing sources. Remuneration should not have a negative impact on local labour markets, e.g. by causing wage rate inflation, diverting labour from other activities or undermining essential public services.

5. *Risk in the work environment:* A high-risk working environment should be avoided by practical procedures for minimising risk or treating injuries, e.g.

briefings, protective clothing and first-aid kits, where necessary. This should include minimising the risk of HIV exposure. Practices for increasing safety in transit include securing safe access routes to work, ensuring routes are well lit, providing torches, using early warning systems (which may utilise bells, whistles, radios and other devices) and security norms, such as travelling in groups or avoiding travel after dark. Particular attention must be paid to women, girls and others at risk of sexual assault. Ensure that all participants are aware of emergency procedures and can access early warning systems (see Protection Principles 1 and 3 on pages 33–38).

6. **Risk of insecurity and diversion:** Handing out resources in the form of food or cash for work (e.g. loans or payments for work done) introduces security concerns for both programme staff and the recipients (see Food security – food transfers standard 5, guidance note 6 on page 195 and Food security – cash and voucher transfers standard 1, guidance note 4 on page 202).

7. **Caring responsibilities and livelihoods:** Participation in income-earning opportunities should not undermine childcare or other caring responsibilities as this could increase the risk of undernutrition and other health risks. Programmes may need to consider employing care-providers or providing care facilities. It may not be appropriate to introduce increased workloads into people's lives, especially women's. Programmes should not adversely affect access to other opportunities, such as other employment or education, or divert household resources from productive activities already in place. Participation in income generation should respect national laws for the minimum age for admission to employment, usually not less than the age of completion of compulsory schooling.

8. **Use of remuneration:** Fair remuneration means that the income generated contributes a significant proportion of the resources necessary for food security. Household management of cash or food transfers (including intra-household distribution and end uses) must be understood, because the way they are distributed can either exacerbate or diffuse existing tensions, affecting the food security of household members differently. Responses that generate income and employment often have multiple food security objectives, including community-level resources that affect food security. For example, repairing roads may improve access to markets and access to healthcare, while repairing or constructing water-harvesting and irrigation systems may improve productivity.

Food security – livelihoods standard 3: Access to markets

The disaster-affected population's safe access to market goods and services as producers, consumers and traders is protected and promoted.

Key actions (to be read in conjunction with the guidance notes)

▶ Protect and reinforce access to affordable operating markets for producers, consumers and traders (see guidance note 1).

▶ Base food security and livelihoods responses on a demonstrated understanding of whether local markets are functioning or are disrupted, as well as their potential for strengthening (see guidance note 2).

▶ Base advocacy for improvements and policy changes on the market analysis conducted before each intervention (see guidance note 3).

▶ Take steps to promote and support market access for vulnerable people (see guidance note 4).

▶ Control the adverse effects of responses, including food purchases and distribution, on local markets (see guidance note 5).

▶ Minimise the negative consequences of extreme seasonal or other abnormal price fluctuations on markets (see guidance note 6).

Key indicators (to be read in conjunction with the guidance notes)

▶ Interventions are designed to support the recovery of markets, either through direct intervention or through the promotion of local traders via cash and/or voucher programmes.

▶ All targeted populations have safe and full access to market goods, services and systems throughout the duration of the programme.

Guidance notes

1. ***Market demand and supply:*** Economic access to markets is influenced by purchasing power, market prices and availability. Affordability depends on the terms of trade between basic needs (food, essential agricultural inputs such as seeds, tools, healthcare, etc.) and income sources (cash crops, livestock, wages, etc.). Erosion of assets occurs when deterioration of trade forces people to sell assets (often at low prices) in order to buy basic needs (at inflated prices). Access to markets may also be influenced by the political

and security environment and by cultural or religious considerations, which restrict access by certain groups such as minorities.

2. *Market analysis:* Consideration should be given to access to functioning markets for all affected people, including vulnerable individuals. Responses that remunerate in cash, vouchers or food or provide inputs should be preceded by an appropriate level of market analysis for the commodity supplied. Local purchase of surpluses will support local producers but adverse risks also need to be identified. Imports are likely to reduce local prices (see Food security and nutrition assessment standard 1, guidance note 7 on page 152).

3. *Advocacy:* Markets operate in the wider national and global economies, which influence local market conditions. For example, governmental policies, including pricing and trade policies, influence access and availability. Although actions at this level are beyond the scope of disaster response, these factors should be analysed as there may be opportunities for a joint agency approach or to advocate for improvements with government and other organisations (see Protection Principle 3 on page 38).

4. *Vulnerable people:* Vulnerability analysis to identify the people who have restricted access to markets and livelihood opportunities should be carried out. Persons with disabilities, PLHIV, older people and women with caring responsibilities must be supported to access markets.

5. *Impact of interventions:* Local procurement of food, seeds or other commodities may cause local inflation to the disadvantage of consumers but to the benefit of local producers. Conversely, imported food may drive prices down and act as a disincentive to local food production, potentially increasing food insecurity. Provision of cash may have positive multiplier effects in local economies but could also cause local inflation for key goods. Those responsible for procurement should monitor these effects and take them into account. Food distribution could also affect the purchasing power of beneficiaries, as it is a form of income transfer. Some commodities are easier to sell for a good price than others, e.g. oil versus blended food. The 'purchasing power' associated with a given food or food basket will influence whether it is eaten or sold by the beneficiary household. An understanding of household sales and purchases is important in determining the wider impact of food distribution programmes.

6. *Abnormally extreme seasonal price fluctuations* may adversely affect poor agricultural producers, who have to sell their produce when prices are at their lowest (usually just after harvest) or livestock owners who are forced to sell during drought. Conversely, consumers who have little disposable income cannot afford to invest in food stocks, depending instead on small

but frequent purchases. Therefore, they are forced to buy even when prices are high (e.g. during drought). Examples of interventions which can minimise these effects include improved transport and storage systems, diversified food production and cash or food transfers at critical times.

Appendix 1

Food security and livelihoods assessment checklists

Food security assessments often broadly categorise the affected population into livelihood groupings, according to their sources of, and strategies for, obtaining income or food. This may also include a breakdown of the population according to wealth groups or strata. It is important to compare the prevailing situation with the history of food security pre-disaster. So-called 'average normal years' may be considered as a baseline. The specific roles and vulnerabilities of women and men, and the implications for household food security should be considered.

The following checklist questions cover the broad areas that are usually considered in a food security assessment.

1 Food security of livelihood groups

▶ Are there groups in the population who share the same livelihood strategies? How can these be categorised according to their main sources of food or income?

2 Food security pre-disaster (baseline)

▶ How did the different livelihood groups acquire food or income before the disaster? For an average year in the recent past, what were their sources of food and income?

▶ How did these different sources of food and income vary between seasons in a normal year? (Constructing a seasonal calendar may be useful.)

▶ Looking back over the past five or ten years, how has food security varied from year to year? (Constructing a timeline or history of good and bad years may be useful.)

▶ What kind of assets, savings or other reserves are owned by the different livelihood groups (e.g. food stocks, cash savings, livestock holdings, investments, credit, unclaimed debt, etc.)?

▶ Over a period of a week or a month, what do household expenditures include and what proportion is spent on each item?

▶ Who is responsible for management of cash in the household and on what is cash spent?

▶ How accessible is the nearest market for obtaining basic goods? (Consider distance, security, ease of mobility, availability of market information, transport, etc.)

▶ What is the availability and price of essential goods, including food?

▶ Prior to the disaster, what were the average terms of trade between essential sources of income and food, e.g. wages to food, livestock to food, etc.?

3 Food security during disaster

▶ How has the disaster affected the different sources of food and income for each of the livelihood groups identified?

▶ How has it affected the usual seasonal patterns of food security for the different groups?

▶ How has it affected access to markets, market availability and prices of essential goods?

▶ For different livelihood groups, what are the different coping strategies and what proportion of people are engaged in them?

▶ How has this changed as compared with the pre-disaster situation?

▶ Which group or population is most affected?

▶ What are the short- and medium-term effects of coping strategies on people's financial and other assets?

▶ For all livelihood groups, and all vulnerable people, what are the effects of coping strategies on their health, general well-being and dignity? Are there risks associated with coping strategies?

Appendix 2

Seed security assessment checklist

Below are sample questions for seed security assessments:

1. Pre-disaster (baseline)

▶ What are farmers' most important crops? What do they use them for – consumption, income or both? Are these crops grown each season? What lesser crops might become important in times of stress?

▶ How do farmers usually get seed or other planting material for these crops? (Consider all the channels.)

▶ What are the sowing parameters for each major crop? What is the average area planted? What are the seeding rates? What are the multiplication rates (ratios of seed or grain harvested to seed planted)?

▶ Are there important or preferred varieties of specific crops?

▶ Which production inputs are essential for particular crops or varieties?

▶ Who in the household is responsible for decision-making, managing crops and disposing of crop products at different stages of production and post-production?

2. After disaster

▶ Is a farming-related intervention feasible from the beneficiaries' point of view?

▶ Are farmers confident the situation is now stable and secure enough that they can successfully cultivate, harvest and sell or consume a crop?

▶ Do they have sufficient access to fields and other means of production (manure, implements, draught animals)?

▶ Are they prepared to re-engage in agriculture?

3. Assessing seed supply and demand: home stocks

▶ Are adequate amounts of home-produced seed available for sowing? This includes both seed from a farmer's own harvest and seed potentially available through social networks (e.g. neighbours).

▶ Is this a crop that farmers still want to plant? Is it adapted to local conditions? Is there still a demand for it?

▶ Are the varieties available through a farmer's own production still suitable for planting next season? Does the quality of the seed meet the farmer's normal standards?

4. Assessing seed supply and demand: local markets

▶ Are markets generally functioning despite the disaster (are market days being held, are farmers able to move, sell and buy freely)?

▶ Are current volumes of available seed or grain comparable to those under normal conditions at the same time during previous seasons?

▶ Are crops and varieties that farmers find suitable for growing found in the markets?

▶ Are current market prices of seed or grain comparable to the prices at the same time in previous seasons? If there is a price differential, is the magnitude likely to be a problem for farmers?

5. Assessing seed supply and demand: formal sector seed

▶ Are the crops and varieties on offer from the formal sector adapted to particular stress zones? Is there evidence farmers like them?

▶ Can the amounts of formal sector seed available meet any need for aid? If not, what proportion of farmers' needs could be covered?

Appendix 3

Nutrition assessment checklist

Below are sample questions for assessments examining the underlying causes of undernutrition, the level of nutrition risk and possibilities for response. The questions are based on the conceptual framework of the causes of undernutrition (see page 146). The information is likely to be available from a variety of sources and gathering it will require various assessment tools, including key informant interviews, observation and review of secondary data (see also Core Standards 1, 3–4 on pages 55–65).

Pre-emergency situation

What information already exists on the nature, scale and causes of undernutrition among the affected population (see Food security and nutrition assessment standard 2 on page 154)?

The current risk of undernutrition

1. The risk of undernutrition related to reduced food access – see Appendix 1: Food security and livelihoods assessment checklists.
2. The risk of undernutrition related to infant and young child feeding and care practices:
    - Is there a change in work and social patterns (e.g. due to migration, displacement or armed conflict) which means that roles and responsibilities in the household have changed?
    - Is there a change in the normal composition of households? Are there large numbers of separated children?
    - Has the normal care environment been disrupted (e.g. through displacement), affecting access to secondary caregivers, access to foods for children, access to water, etc.?
    - Are any infants not breastfed? Are there infants who are artificially fed?
    - Has there been any evidence or suspicion of a decline in infant feeding practices in the emergency, especially any fall in breastfeeding initiation or exclusive breastfeeding rates, any increase in artificial feeding rate and/or any increase in proportion of infants not breastfed?

- Are age-appropriate, nutritionally adequate, safe complementary foods and the means to prepare them hygienically accessible?
- Is there any evidence or suspicion of general distribution of breastmilk substitutes such as infant formula, other milk products, bottles and teats, either donated or purchased?
- In pastoral communities, have the herds been away from young children for long? Has access to milk changed from normal?
- Has HIV and AIDS affected caring practices at household level?

3. The risk of undernutrition related to poor public health (see Health chapter on page 287):
    - Are there any reports of disease outbreaks which may affect nutritional status, such as measles or acute diarrhoeal disease? Is there risk that these outbreaks will occur? (See Essential health services – control of communicable diseases standards 1–3 on pages 312–316.)
    - What is the estimated measles vaccination coverage of the affected population? (See Essential health services – child health standard 1 on page 321.)
    - Is Vitamin A routinely given with measles vaccination? What is the estimated Vitamin A supplementation coverage?
    - Are there any estimates of mortality rates (either crude or under-5)? What are they and what method has been used? (See Essential health services standard 1 on page 309.)
    - Is there, or will there be, a significant decline in ambient temperature which is likely to affect the prevalence of acute respiratory infection or the energy requirements of the affected population?
    - Is there a high prevalence of HIV?
    - Are people already vulnerable to undernutrition due to poverty or ill health?
    - Is there overcrowding or a risk of or high prevalence of TB?
    - Is there a high incidence of malaria?
    - Have people been in water or wet clothes or exposed to other harsh environmental conditions for long periods of time?

4. What formal and informal local structures are currently in place through which potential interventions could be channelled?
    - What is the capacity of the Ministry of Health, religious organisations, community support groups, breastfeeding support groups or NGOs with a long- or short-term presence in the area?
    - What nutrition interventions or community-based support were already in place and organised by local communities, individuals, NGOs, government organisations, UN agencies, religious organisations, etc.? What are the nutrition policies (past, ongoing and lapsed), the planned long-term nutrition responses and programmes that are being implemented or planned in response to the current situation?

Appendix 4

Measuring acute malnutrition

In major nutritional emergencies, it may be necessary to include infants aged less than 6 months, pregnant and breastfeeding women, older children, adolescents, adults or older people in nutrition assessments or nutritional programmes.

Surveys of age groups other than children aged 6–59 months should only be undertaken if:

▶ a thorough contextual analysis of the situation is undertaken, including an analysis of the causes of malnutrition. Only if the results of this analysis suggest that the nutritional status of young children does not reflect the nutritional status of the general population should a nutrition survey for another age group be considered

▶ technical expertise is available to ensure a high quality of data collection, adequate analysis and correct presentation and interpretation of results

▶ the resource and/or opportunity costs of including other age groups in a survey have been considered

▶ clear and well-documented objectives for the survey are formulated.

Infants under 6 months

While research is ongoing for this age group, the evidence base for assessment and management is currently limited. Most guidelines recommend the same anthropometric case definitions of acute infant malnutrition as for older children aged 6–59 months (except for mid upper arm circumference (MUAC) which is not presently recommended for infants <6 months). Admission criteria focus on current size rather than an assessment of growth. The switch from NCHS growth references to WHO 2006 growth standards results in more cases of infant <6 month wasting. The implications of this change should be considered and addressed. Potential issues include more infants presenting to feeding programmes or caregivers becoming concerned about the adequacy of exclusive breastfeeding. It is important to assess and consider:

- the infants longitudinal growth – is the rate of growth good despite body size being small (some infants may for example be 'catching up' following low birth weight)?
- infant feeding practices – is the infant exclusively breastfeeding?
- clinical status – does the infant have any medical complications or conditions which are treatable or which make him/her high risk?
- maternal factors – e.g. does the mother lack family support or is she depressed? Inpatient admission to therapeutic feeding programmes should be a priority for high risk infants.

Children 6–59 months

The table below shows the commonly used indicators of different grades of malnutrition among children aged 6–59 months. Weight for height (WFH) indices should be calculated using the WHO 2006 child growth standards. The WFH Z score (according to WHO standards) is the preferred indicator for reporting anthropometric survey results. MUAC is an independent criterion for acute malnutrition and is one of the best predictors of mortality. The prevalence of low MUAC is also investigated in surveys to predict case loads for supplementary feeding and therapeutic care programmes. The cut-offs commonly used are <11.5cm for severe acute malnutrition, and 11.5–<12.5cm for moderate acute malnutrition. It is also often used, with a higher cut-off, as part of a two-stage screening process. It should not be used alone in anthropometric surveys but can be used as sole admission criteria for feeding programmes.

	Global acute malnutrition	**Moderate acute malnutrition**	**Severe acute malnutrition**
Children 6.0–59.9 months	WFH <-2 Z score and/or MUAC <12.5cm and/or nutritional oedema	WFH -3 - <-2 Z score and/or MUAC 11.5-<12.5cm	WFH <-3 Z score and/or MUAC <11.5cm and/or nutritional oedema

Children aged 5–19 years

Use of the WHO 2007 growth standards is recommended to determine nutrition status in children aged 5–19 years. These growth reference data curves are a reconstruction of the 1977 NCHS/WHO reference and are closely aligned with the WHO child growth standards for children 6–59 months and the recommended cut-offs for adults. The use of MUAC in older children and adolescents, particularly in the context of HIV, may be considered. As this is a developing technical area, it is important to refer to latest guidance and technical updates.

Adults (20–59.9 years)

There is no agreed definition of acute malnutrition in adults, but evidence suggests that cut-offs for severe acute malnutrition could be lower than a body mass index (BMI) of 16 and lower than 18.5 for mild and moderate acute malnutrition. Surveys of adult malnutrition should aim to gather data on weight, height, sitting height and MUAC measurements. These data can be used to calculate BMI. BMI should be adjusted for Cormic index (the ratio of sitting height to standing height) only to make comparisons between populations. Such adjustment can substantially change the apparent prevalence of undernutrition in adults and may have important programmatic ramifications. MUAC measurements should always be taken. If immediate results are needed or resources are severely limited, surveys may be based on MUAC measurements alone.

Because the interpretation of anthropometric results is complicated by the lack of validated functional outcome data and benchmarks for determining the meaning of the result, such results must be interpreted along with detailed contextual information. Guidance on assessment can be found under References and further reading.

For screening individuals for nutritional care admission and discharge, criteria should include a combination of anthropometric indices, clinical signs (particularly weakness, recent weight loss) and social factors (access to food, presence of caregivers, shelter, etc.). Note that oedema in adults can be caused by a variety of reasons other than malnutrition, and clinicians should assess adult oedema to exclude other causes. Individual agencies should decide on the indicator to determine eligibility for care, taking into account the known shortcomings of BMI and the lack of information on MUAC and the programme implications of their use. As this is a developing technical area, it is important to refer to latest guidance and technical updates.

MUAC may be used as a screening tool for pregnant women, e.g. as a criterion for entry into a feeding programme. Given their additional nutritional needs, pregnant women may be at greater risk than other groups in the population. MUAC does not change significantly through pregnancy. MUAC <20.7cm (severe risk) and <23cm (moderate risk) have been shown to carry a risk of growth retardation of the foetus. Suggested cut-off points for risk vary by country and range from 21cm to 23cm. Less than 21cm has been suggested as an appropriate cut-off for selection of women at risk during emergencies.

Older people

There is currently no agreed definition of malnutrition in older people and yet this group may be at risk of malnutrition in emergencies. WHO suggests that the BMI thresholds for adults may be appropriate for older people aged 60–69 years and above. However, accuracy of measurement is problematic because of spinal curvature (stooping) and compression of the vertebrae. Arm span or demi-span can be used instead of height, but the multiplication factor to calculate height varies according to the population. Visual assessment is necessary. MUAC may be a useful tool for measuring malnutrition in older people but research on appropriate cut-offs is currently still in progress.

Persons with disabilities

No guidelines currently exist for the measurement of individuals with physical disabilities and therefore they are often excluded from anthropometric surveys. Visual assessment is necessary. MUAC measurements may be misleading in cases where upper arm muscle might build up to aid mobility. There are alternatives to standard measures of height, including length, arm span, demi-span or lower leg length. It is necessary to consult the latest research to determine the most appropriate way of measuring disabled individuals for whom standard weight, height and MUAC measurement is not appropriate.

Appendix 5

Measures of the public health significance of micronutrient deficiencies

Where clinical micronutrient deficiencies are detected, they should be urgently treated on an individual basis. Individual cases of clinical micronutrient deficiencies are also usually indicative of an underlying problem of micronutrient deficiency at the population level. Measurement and classification of micronutrient deficiencies at the population level is important for planning and monitoring interventions.

Biochemical tests have the advantage of providing objective measures of micronutrient status. However, the collection of biological samples for testing often presents logistical, staff training, cold chain and sometimes acceptability challenges. Biochemical measurements are also not always as clearly useful, i.e. as sensitive and specific, as might be imagined. There may also be variations according to the time of day the sample is collected and according to the season of the year, as with acute malnutrition. Good quality control is essential and should always be considered when selecting a laboratory for sample testing.

When assessing micronutrient status the possibility of excessive intakes as well as deficiency should be kept in mind. This is of particular concern when multiple, highly fortified products or supplements are used to deliver micronutrients to the affected population.

The table below shows classifications of the public health significance of selected micronutrient deficiencies using different indicators.

Micronutrient deficiency indicator	Recommended age group for prevalence surveys	Definition of a public health problem	
		Severity	Prevalence (%)
Vitamin A deficiency			
Night blindness (XN)	24–71 months	Mild	> 0 – < 1
		Moderate	≥1 – < 5
		Severe	≥ 5
Bitots spots (X1B)	6–71 months	Not specified	> 0.5
Corneal Xerosis/ulceration/ keratomalacia (X2, X3A, X3B)	6–71 months	Not specified	> 0.01
Corneal scars (XS)	6–71 months	Not specified	> 0.05
Serum retinol (≤ 0.7 µmol/L)	6–71 months	Mild	≥ 2 – < 10
		Moderate	≥10 – < 20
		Severe	≥ 20
Iodine deficiency			
Goitre (visible + palpable)	School-age children	Mild	5.0 – 19.9
		Moderate	20.0 – 29.9
		Severe	≥ 30.0
Median urinary iodine concentration (mg/l)	School-age children	Excessive intake	> 300[1]
		Adequate intake	100 – 199[1]
		Mild deficiency	50 – 99[1]
		Moderate deficiency	20 – 49[1]
		Severe deficiency	< 20[1]

Micronutrient deficiency indicator	Recommended age group for prevalence surveys	Definition of a public health problem	
		Severity	Prevalence (%)
Iron deficiency			
Anaemia (Non-pregnant women haemoglobin <12.0 g/dl; children 6–59 months <11.0 g/dl)	Women, children 6–59 months	Low	5 – 20
		Medium	20 – 40
		High	≥ 40
Beriberi[1]			
Clinical signs	Whole population	Mild	≥ 1 case & <1%
		Moderate	1 – 4
		Severe	≥ 5
Dietary intake (< 0.33 mg/1000 kcal)	Whole population	Mild	≥ 5
		Moderate	5 – 19
		Severe	20 – 49
Infant mortality	Infants 2–5 months	Mild	No increase in rates
		Moderate	Slight peak in rates
		Severe	Marked peak in rates
Pellagra[1]			
Clinical signs (dermatitis) in surveyed age group	Whole population or women >15 years	Mild	≥ 1 case & <1%
		Moderate	1 – 4
		Severe	≥ 5
Dietary intake of niacin equivalents <5 mg/day	Whole population or women >15 years	Mild	5 – 19
		Moderate	20 – 49
		Severe	≥ 50
Scurvy[1]			
Clinical signs	Whole population	Mild	≥ 1 case &< 1%
		Moderate	1 – 4
		Severe	≥ 5

1   For information about biochemical tests and public health thresholds consult the latest literature or seek specialist advice.

Appendix 6

Nutritional requirements

The following figures can be used for planning purposes in the initial stage of a disaster. The minimum nutrient requirements given in the table overleaf should be used to assess the adequacy of general rations targeting the population. Requirements are calculated based on an assumed demographic profile, assumptions about the ambient temperature and people's activity levels. They also take into account the additional needs of pregnant and breastfeeding women. The requirements are not intended for assessing the adequacy of supplementary or therapeutic care rations or for assessing rations targeted at particular groups of people, such as individuals suffering from TB or people living with HIV.

There are two important points to consider before using the requirements listed overleaf. Firstly, these average population minimum requirements for population groups incorporate the requirements of all age groups and both sexes. They are therefore not specific to any single age or sex group and should not be used as requirements for an individual. Secondly, nutritional requirements are based on a population profile.

Nutrient	Minimum population requirements[1]
Energy	2,100 kcals
Protein	53 g (10% of total energy)
Fat	40 g (17% of total energy)
Vitamin A	550 µg RAE*
Vitamin D	6.1 µg
Vitamin E	8.0 mg alpha-TE*
Vitamin K	48.2 µg
Vitamin B1 (Thiamin)	1.1 mg
Vitamin B2 (Riboflavin)	1.1 mg
Vitamin B3 (Niacin)	13.8 mg NE
Vitamin B6 (Pyidoxine)	1.2 mg
Vitamin B12 (Cobalamin)	2.2 µg
Folate	363 µg DFE*
Pantothenate	4.6 mg
Vitamin C	41.6 mg
Iron	32 mg
Iodine	138 µg
Zinc	12.4 mg
Copper	1.1 mg
Selenium	27.6 µg
Calcium	989 mg
Magnesium	201 mg

* Alpha-TE - alpha-tocopherol equivalents
  RAE - retinol activity equivalents
  DFE - dietary folate equivalents
1   Expressed as reference nutrient intakes (RNI) for all nutrients except energy and copper.

Reference: RNI from FAO/WHO (2004), Vitamin and Mineral Requirements in Human Nutrition. Second edition, were used for all vitamin and mineral requirement calculations except copper, as requirements for this mineral were not included in FAO/WHO (2004). Requirements for copper are taken from WHO (1996), Trace Elements in Human Nutrition and Health.

The following table gives an indicator of the average global population structure broken down by age. However, it is important to note that this is context-specific and can vary significantly. For example, in some rural communities, out-migration of middle generations has resulted in disproportionately high numbers of older people caring for children.

Group	% of population
0–6 months	1.32
7–11 months	0.95
1–3 years	6.58
4–6 years	6.41
7–9 years	6.37
10–18 years females	9.01
10–18 years males	9.52
19–50 females	17.42
51–65 females	4.72
19–65 males	27.90
65+ females	2.62
65+ males	2.18
Pregnant	2.40
Breastfeeding	2.60

Reference: United Nations (2003), World Population Prospects: The 2002 Revision, Interpolated Population by Sex, Single Years of Age and Single Calendar Years, 1950 to 2050.

The population energy requirements should be adjusted for the following factors:

- the demographic structure of the population, in particular the percentage of those under 5 years of age and the percentage of females
- mean adult weights and actual, usual or desirable body weights
- activity levels to maintain productive life – requirements will increase if activity levels exceed light (i.e. 1.6 x Basal Metabolic Rate)
- average ambient temperature and shelter and clothing capacities – requirements will increase if the mean ambient temperature is less than 20°C

- the nutritional and health status of the population – requirements will increase if the population is malnourished and has extra requirements for catch-up growth. HIV and AIDS prevalence may affect average population requirements (see Food security – food transfers standard 1 on page 180). Whether general rations should be adjusted to meet these needs will depend on contextual analysis and current international recommendations.

If it is not possible to gain this kind of information from assessments, the figures in the table above should be used as the minimum requirements.

References and further reading

Sources

Black et al (2008), Maternal and child undernutrition 1. Maternal and child undernutrition: global and regional exposures and health consequences. www.thelancet.com, series, 17 January.

CARE (2008), Coping Strategies Index: CSI Field Methods Manual.

Castleman, T, Seumo-Fasso, E and Cogill, B (2004 rev.), Food and Nutrition Implications of Antiretroviral Therapy in Resource Limited Settings. FANTA (Food and Nutrition Technical Assistance) technical note no. 7. Washington DC.

Coates, J, Swindale, A and Bilinsky, P (2007), Household Food Insecurity Access Scale (HFIAS) for Measurement of Food Access. Indicator Guide. Version 3. FANTA. Washington DC.

Committee on World Food Security (2004), Voluntary guidelines to support the progressive realization of the right to adequate food in the context of national food security. Rome.

IFE Core Group (2007), Operational Guidance on Infant and Young Child Feeding in Emergencies. www.ennonline.net/ife

Inter-Agency Network for Education in Emergencies (INEE) (2004), Minimum Standards for Education in Emergencies, Chronic Crises and Early Reconstruction (includes School Feeding in Emergencies). Geneva.

International Labour Office (ILO) (1973), Minimum Age Convention No. 138. www.ilo.org/ilolex/english/convdisp1.htm

LEGS (2009), Livestock Emergency Guidelines and Standards (LEGS). Practical Action Publishing, UK. www.livestock-emergency.net/userfiles/file/legs.pdf

Pejic, J (2001), The Right to Food in Situations of Armed Conflict: The Legal Framework. International Review of the Red Cross, vol. 83, no. 844, p. 1097. Geneva. www.icrc.org.

SMART (Standardised Monitoring and Assessments of Relief and Transition) Guidelines: SMART methodology version.

Swindale, A and Bilinsky, P (2006), Household Dietary Diversity Score (HDDS) for Measurement of Household Food Access: Indicator Guide. Version 2. FANTA. Washington DC.

The Right to Adequate Food (Article 11: 12/05/99. E/C 12/1999/5, CESCR General Comment 12. United National Economic and Social Council (1999). www.unhchr.ch

UNHCR, World Food Programme (WFP), University College London and IASC Nutrition Cluster (2006), NutVal 2006 version 2.2. www.nutval.net/2008/05/download-page.html

WFP (2006), Food Distribution Guidelines. Rome.

WHO (2009), Child Growth Standards and the identification of severe acute malnutrition in infants and children.

WHO (2007), Growth reference for school-aged children and adolescents. www.who.int/growthref/en/

WHO (1981), The International Code of Marketing of Breast-Milk Substitutes. The full code and subsequent relevant World Health Assembly resolutions: www.ibfan.org

Further reading

Assessment references

Initial assessment

IASC (2009), Multi-sectoral Initial Rapid Assessment (IRA) Tool. Global Health, Nutrition and WASH Clusters.

Food security assessment

CARE (2002), Household Livelihood Security Assessments: A Toolkit for Practitioners. USA.

FANTA-2 (2009), Alternative Sampling Designs for Emergency Settings: A Guide for Survey Planning, Data Collection and Analysis. Washington DC. www.fantaproject.org/publications/asg2009.shtml

FAO and WFP (2009), Crop and Food Security Assessment Missions (CFSAM) Guidelines. Rome.

Save the Children (2008), The Household Economy Approach: A guide for programme planners and policy-makers. London.

WFP (2009), Emergency Food Security Assessment Handbook (EFSA) – second edition. Rome.

WFP (2009), Comprehensive Food Security and Vulnerability Analysis (CFSVA) Guidelines. Rome.

Seed security assessment

Longley, C et al (2002), Do Farmers Need Relief Seed? A Methodology for Assessing Seed Systems. Disasters, 26, 343–355.

Sperling, L (2008), When disaster strikes: a guide to assessing seed system security. International Center for Tropical Agriculture. Cali, Colombia.

Livelihood assessment

Jaspers, S and Shoham, J (2002), A Critical Review of Approaches to Assessing and Monitoring Livelihoods in Situations of Chronic Conflict and Political Instability. ODI. London.

IASC (2009), Matrix on Agency Roles and Responsibilities for Ensuring a Coordinated, Multi-Sectoral Fuel Strategy in Humanitarian Settings. Version 1.1. Task Force on Safe Access to Firewood and Alternative Energy in Humanitarian Settings.

Markets

CARE (2008), Cash, Local Purchase, and/or Imported Food Aid?: Market Information and Food Insecurity Response Analysis.

Mike, A (2010), Emergency Market Mapping and Analysis (EMMA) toolkit. Practical action, Oxfam GB.

Food consumption

Food and Nutrition Technical Assistance Project (2006), Household Dietary Diversity Score (HDDS).

WFP (2008), Food Consumption Analysis: Calculation and Use of the Food Consumption Score in Food Security Analysis. Technical Guidance Sheet.Rome.

Participatory methodologies

ActionAid (2004), Participatory Vulnerability Analysis. London.

CARE (2009), Climate Vulnerability and Capacity Analysis handbook.

IFRC (2007), How to do a Vulnerability and Capacity Assessment (VCA), a step-by-step guide for Red Cross and Red Crescent Staff and Volunteers. Geneva.

Tearfund (2009), Climate change and Environmental Degradation Risk and Adaptation assessment CEDRA.

Nutrition and food security information systems

Famine Early Warning Systems Network (FEWS NET): www.fews.net

Food Insecurity and Vulnerability Information and Mapping Systems (FIVIMS): www.fivims.net/index.jsp

Integrated Food Security Phase Classification (2008), Technical Manual. Version 1.1.

Global Information and Early Warning System on Food and Agriculture, FAO: www.fao.org

Shoham, J, Watson, F and Dolan, C, The use of nutrition indicators in surveillance systems, Technical paper 2. ODI. London.

Anthropometric assessment

Centers for Disease Control and Prevention (CDC) and WFP (2005), A Manual: Measuring and Interpreting Malnutrition and Mortality. Rome.

Collins, S, Duffield, A and Myatt, M (2000), Adults: Assessment of Nutritional Status in Emergency-Affected Populations. Geneva.

UN ACC Sub Committee on Nutrition (2001), Assessment of Adult Undernutrition in Emergencies. Report of an SCN working group on emergencies special meeting in SCN News, 22, pp49–51. Geneva.

Save the Children UK (2004), Emergency nutrition assessment, and guidance for field workers. London

Young, H and Jaspars, S (2006), The meaning and measurement of acute malnutrition in emergencies. A primer for decision makers. London.

Micronutrient assessment

Gorstein, J et al (2007), Indicators and methods for cross sectional surveys of vitamin and mineral status of populations.

Seal, A and Prudhon, C (2007), Assessing micronutrient deficiencies in emergencies: Current practice and future directions. Geneva

IYCF assessment

CARE (2010), Infant and young child feeding practices. Collecting and Using Data: A Step-by-Step Guide. www.ennonline.net/resources

Infant and young child feeding

IFE Core Group (2009), Protecting infants in emergencies, Information for the media. www.ennonline.net/ife

IFE Core Group and collaborators (2009), IFE Module 1: Orientation package on IFE. www.ennonline.net/ife

IFE Core Group and collaborators (2007), Module 2 on Infant Feeding in Emergencies for health and nutrition workers in emergency situations. www.ennonline.net/ife

UNICEF and WHO (2003), Global Strategy for infant and young child feeding. Geneva.

UNHCR (2009), Guidance on Infant Feeding and HIV in the Context of Refugees and Displaced Populations. www.ennonline.net/ife

USAID, AED, FANTA, University of California DAVIS, International Food Policy Research Institute (IFPRI), UNICEF and WHO (2007), Indicators for assessing infant and young child feeding practices. Washington DC.

WHO (2010), HIV and infant feeding. Principles and recommendationsfor infant feeding inthe context of HIV and a summary of evidence. Geneva.

WHO (2004), Guiding Principles for feeding infants and young children during emergencies. Geneva.

Food security interventions

General

Barrett, C and Maxwell, D (2005), Food Aid After Fifty Years: Recasting Its Role. London.

IASC (2005), Guidelines for Gender-based Violence Interventions in Humanitarian Settings – Focusing on Prevention of and Response to Sexual Violence in Emergencies, Chapters 1–4, Action Sheet 6.1 Food Security and Nutrition.

Maxwell, D et al (2008), Emergency food security interventions. ODI, Good Practice Review #10. Relief and Rehabilitation Network, ODI. London.

UNHCR, UNICEF, WFP and WHO (2002), Food and Nutrition Needs in Emergencies. Geneva.

Targeting and food distribution

Jaspars, S and Young, H (1995), General Food Distribution in Emergencies: from Nutritional Needs to Political Priorities. Good Practice Review 3. Relief and Rehabilitation Network, ODI. London.

UNHCR (2003), UNHCR Handbook for Registration. Geneva.

WFP (2009), School Feeding Quality Standards. Rome.

WFP (2008), Food Assistance in the context of HIV: Ration Design Guide. Rome.

WFP (2006), Targeting in Emergencies. Rome.

Supply chain management and food quality and safety

CARE, Food Resource Management handbook.

Logistics Cluster (2010), Logistics Operational Guide. WFP. Rome.

United Nations Humanitarian Response Depot (2010), Catalogue and Standard Operating Procedures. www.unhrd.org

WFP (2010), Food Quality Control: http://foodquality.wfp.org

WFP (2003), Food Storage Manual. Natural Resources Institute and WFP. Chatham, UK and Rome.

World Vision International, World Vision Food Resource Manual. Second edition.

World Vision International, Food Monitors Manual.

Cash and vouchers interventions

Action contre la faim (2007), Implementing Cash-Based Interventions. A guide for aid workers. Paris.

Adams, L (2007), Learnings from cash responses to the tsunami: Final report, HPG background paper.

Cash Learning Partnership (2010), Delivering Money: Cash Transfer Mechanisms in Emergencies. Save the Children UK, Oxfam GB and British Red Cross, with support from ECHO. London.

Creti, P and Jaspars, S (2006), Cash Transfer Programming in Emergencies, Oxfam GB. London.

Harvey, P (2005), Cash and Vouchers in Emergencies, HPG background paper. ODI. London.

Seed interventions

Catholic Relief Services (CRS) (2002), Seed Vouchers and Fairs: A Manual for Seed-Based Agricultural Recovery in Africa. CRS, incollaboration with ODI and the International Crops Research Institute for the Semi-Arid Tropics.

Sperling, L and Remington, T, with Haugen JM (2006), Seed Aid for Seed Security: Advice for Practitioners, Practice Briefs 1-10. International Centre for Tropical Agriculture and CRS. Rome.

General emergency nutrition manuals

IASC (2008), A toolkit for addressing nutrition in emergency situations.

IASC Nutrition Cluster's Capacity Development Working Group (2006), Harmonised Training Package (HTP).

Prudhon, C (2002), Assessment and Treatment of Malnutrition in Emergency Situations. Paris.

UNHCR and WFP (2009), Guidelines for Selective Feeding the Management of Malnutrition in Emergencies.

UNHCR, UNICEF, WFP and WHO (2002), Food and Nutrition Needs in Emergencies. Geneva.

WFP (2001), Food and Nutrition Handbook. Rome.

WHO (2000), The Management of Nutrition in Major Emergencies. Geneva.

Vulnerable people

FANTA and WFP (2007), Food Assistance Programming in the Context of HIV.

FAO and WHO (2002), Living Well with HIV and AIDS. A Manual on Nutritional Care and Support for People Living with HIV and AIDS.

HelpAge International (2001), Addressing the Nutritional Needs of Older People in Emergency Situations in Africa: Ideas for Action. Nairobi.
www.helpage.org/publications

HelpAge and UNHCR (2007), Older people in disasters and humanitarian crisis.

IASC (2006), Women, Girls, Boys and Men: Different Needs – Equal Opportunities.

Winstock, A (1994), The Practical Management of Eating and Drinking Difficulties in Children. Winslow Press. Bicester, UK.

Management of acute malnutrition

ENN, CIHD and ACF (2010), MAMI Report. Technical Review: Current evidence, policies, practices & programme outcomes.

ENN, IFE Core Group and collaborators (2009), Integration of IYCF support into CMAM. www.ennonline.net/resources

FANTA-2 (2008), Training guide for community based management of acute malnutrition.

Navarro-Colorado, C, Mason, F and Shoham, J (2008), Measuring the effectiveness of SFP in emergencies.

Navarro-Colorado, C and Shoham, J (forthcoming), Supplementary feeding minimum reporting package.

VALID International (2006), Community Based Therapeutic Care (CTC): A Field Manual.

WHO (1999), Management of Severe Malnutrition: A Manual for Physicians and Other Senior Health Workers. Geneva.

WHO, WFP, UNSCN and UNICEF (2007), Community-Based Management of Severe Acute Malnutrition. A Joint Statement by the WHO, WFP, the United Nations System Standing Committee on Nutrition and UNICEF.

Micronutrient deficiencies

Seal, A and Prudhon, C (2007), Assessing micronutrient deficiencies in emergencies: Current practice and future directions.

UNICEF, UNU and WHO (2001), Iron Deficiency Anaemia: Assessment, Prevention and Control. A Guide for Programme Managers. Geneva.

WHO (2000), Pellagra and Its Prevention and Control in Major Emergencies. Geneva.

WHO (1999), Scurvy and Its Prevention and Control in Major Emergencies. Geneva.

WHO (1999),Thiamine Deficiency And Its Prevention And Control In Major Emergencies. Geneva.

WHO (1997), Vitamin A Supplements: A Guide to Their Use in the Treatment and Prevention of Vitamin A Deficiency and Xeropthalmia. Second Edition. Geneva.

WHO and UNICEF (2007), Guiding principles for the use of multiple vitamin and mineral preparations in emergencies.

Minimum Standards in Shelter, Settlement and Non-Food Items

How to use this chapter

This chapter is divided into two main sections:

Shelter and settlement

Non-food items: clothing, bedding and household items

Both sections provide general standards for use in any of several response scenarios for displaced and non-displaced populations, including temporary or transitional individual household shelter on original sites, or the return to repaired dwellings; temporary accommodation with host families; and/or temporary communal settlement comprising planned or self-settled camps, collective centres, transit or return centres.

The Protection Principles and Core Standards must be used consistently with this chapter.

Although primarily intended to inform humanitarian response to a disaster, the minimum standards may also be considered during disaster preparedness and the transition to recovery and recon-struction activities.

Each section contains the following:

- **Minimum standards:** These are qualitative in nature and specify the minimum levels to be attained in humanitarian response regarding the provision of shelter.

- **Key actions:** These are suggested activities and inputs to help meet the standards.

- **Key indicators:** These are 'signals' that show whether a standard has been attained. They provide a way of measuring and communicating the processes and results of key actions; they relate to the minimum standard, not to the key action.

- **Guidance notes:** These include specific points to consider when applying the minimum stan-dards, key actions and key indicators in different situations. They provide guidance on tackling practical difficulties, benchmarks or advice on priority issues. They may also include critical issues relating to the standards, actions or indicators, and describe dilemmas, controversies or gaps in current knowledge.

If required key actions and indicators cannot be met, the resulting adverse implications on the affected population should be appraised and appropriate mitigating actions taken.

A needs assessment checklist is provided to inform the application of the minimum standards in both defining and monitoring response activities, and a list of references and further reading, including a selection of practical 'how to' guidance resources, is also included.

Contents

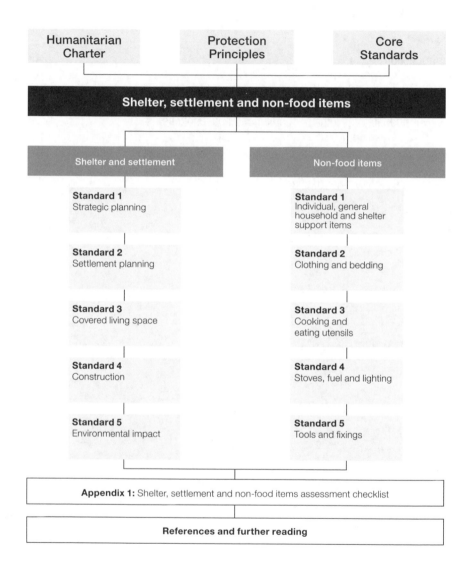

Humanitarian Charter	Protection Principles	Core Standards

Shelter, settlement and non-food items

Shelter and settlement	Non-food items
Standard 1 Strategic planning	**Standard 1** Individual, general household and shelter support items
Standard 2 Settlement planning	**Standard 2** Clothing and bedding
Standard 3 Covered living space	**Standard 3** Cooking and eating utensils
Standard 4 Construction	**Standard 4** Stoves, fuel and lighting
Standard 5 Environmental impact	**Standard 5** Tools and fixings

Appendix 1: Shelter, settlement and non-food items assessment checklist

References and further reading

Introduction

Links to the Humanitarian Charter and international law

The minimum standards for shelter, settlement and non-food items are a practical expression of the shared beliefs and commitments of humanitarian agencies and the common principles, rights and duties governing humanitarian action that are set out in the Humanitarian Charter. Founded on the principle of humanity, and reflected in international law, these principles include the right to life and dignity, the right to protection and security and the right to receive humanitarian assistance on the basis of need. A list of key legal and policy documents that inform the Humanitarian Charter is available for reference in Annex 1 (see page 356), with explanatory comments for humanitarian workers. In humanitarian action, shelter, settlement and associated non-food items are familiar terms that fall within the scope of the right to adequate housing, which is enshrined in human rights law.

Everyone has the right to adequate housing. This right is recognised in key international legal instruments (see References and further reading: International legal instruments). This includes the right to live in security, peace and dignity, with security of tenure, as well as protection from forced eviction and the right to restitution. These instruments define adequate housing as ensuring:

▶ sufficient space and protection from cold, damp, heat, rain, wind or other threats to health, including structural hazards and disease vectors

▶ the availability of services, facilities, materials and infrastructure

▶ affordability, habitability, accessibility, location and cultural appropriateness

▶ sustainable access to natural and common resources; safe drinking water; energy for cooking, heating and lighting; sanitation and washing facilities; means of food storage; refuse disposal; site drainage; and emergency services

▶ the appropriate siting of settlements and housing to provide safe access to healthcare services, schools, childcare centres and other social facilities and to livelihood opportunities

▶ that building materials and policies relating to housing construction appropriately enable the expression of cultural identity and diversity of housing.

The minimum standards in this chapter are not a complete expression of the right to adequate housing as defined by the relevant international legal instruments. Rather, the minimum standards reflect the **core** content of the right to adequate housing and contribute to the progressive realisation of this right.

The importance of shelter, settlement and non-food items in disasters

Shelter is a critical determinant for survival in the initial stages of a disaster. Beyond survival, shelter is necessary to provide security, personal safety and protection from the climate and to promote resistance to ill health and disease. It is also important for human dignity, to sustain family and community life and to enable affected populations to recover from the impact of disaster. Shelter and associated settlement and non-food item responses should support existing coping strategies and promote self-sufficiency and self-management by those affected by the disaster. Local skills and resources should be maximised where this does not result in adverse effects on the affected population or local economy. Any response should take into account known disaster risks and minimise the long-term adverse impact on the natural environment, while maximising opportunities for the affected population to maintain or establish livelihood support activities.

Thermal comfort, protection from the effects of the climate and personal safety and dignity are achieved by meeting a combination of needs at the level of the individuals themselves, the covered space they inhabit and the location in which their covered area is situated. Similarly, meeting these needs requires an appropriate combination of the means to prepare, cook and eat food; clothing and bedding; an adequate covered area or shelter; a means of space heating and ventilation as required; and access to essential services.

The shelter, settlement and non-food item needs of populations affected by a disaster are determined by the type and scale of the disaster and the extent to which the population is displaced. The response will also be informed by the ability and desire of displaced populations to return to the site of their original dwelling and to start the recovery process: where they are unable or unwilling to return, they will require temporary or transitional shelter and settlement solutions (see the diagram opposite). The local context of the disaster will inform the response, including whether the affected area is rural or urban; the local climatic and environmental conditions; the political and security situation; and the ability of the affected population to contribute to meeting their shelter needs.

Shelter and settlement options and response scenarios

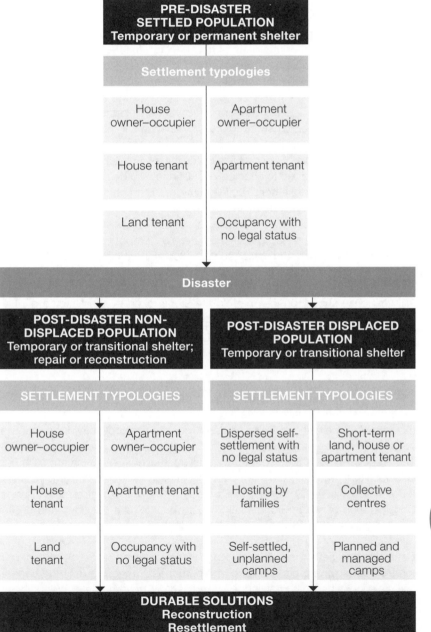

PRE-DISASTER SETTLED POPULATION
Temporary or permanent shelter

Settlement typologies

House owner–occupier	Apartment owner–occupier
House tenant	Apartment tenant
Land tenant	Occupancy with no legal status

Disaster

POST-DISASTER NON-DISPLACED POPULATION
Temporary or transitional shelter; repair or reconstruction

SETTLEMENT TYPOLOGIES

House owner–occupier	Apartment owner–occupier
House tenant	Apartment tenant
Land tenant	Occupancy with no legal status

POST-DISASTER DISPLACED POPULATION
Temporary or transitional shelter

SETTLEMENT TYPOLOGIES

Dispersed self-settlement with no legal status	Short-term land, house or apartment tenant
Hosting by families	Collective centres
Self-settled, unplanned camps	Planned and managed camps

DURABLE SOLUTIONS
Reconstruction
Resettlement
Reintegration

In extreme weather conditions, where shelter may be critical to survival or, as a result of displacement, the affected population may be unable to construct appropriate shelter, rapidly deployable shelter solutions, such as tents or similar, will be required or temporary accommodation provided in existing public buildings. Displaced populations may arrange shelter with host families, settle as individual households or in groups of households within existing settlements or may need to be temporarily accommodated in planned and managed camps or collective centres.

Affected populations should be supported where possible to repair or adapt existing dwellings or build new structures. Assistance can include the provision of appropriate construction materials, tools and fixings, cash or vouchers, technical guidance and training or a combination of these. Support or technical assistance should be provided to affected populations who do not have the capacity or expertise to undertake construction activities. The rights and needs of those who are secondarily affected by the disaster, such as neighbouring populations hosting those displaced by the disaster, must also be considered. Where public buildings, particularly schools, have been used as temporary communal accommodation, the planned and managed safe relocation of the sheltered population should be undertaken as soon as possible to allow for normal activities to resume.

Any response should be informed by the steps taken by the affected population to provide temporary or permanent shelter using their own capacities and resources. Shelter responses should enable affected populations to incrementally upgrade and/or make the transition from emergency to durable housing solutions.

The repair of damaged public buildings or the provision of temporary structures to serve as schools, healthcare centres and other communal facilities may also be required. The sheltering of livelihood assets such as livestock may be an essential complement to the provision of household shelter for some affected populations. The response should be informed by existing shelter and settlement risks and vulnerabilities regarding location, planning, design and construction, including those made worse by the disaster or due to the impact of climate change. Consideration of the environmental impact of settlement solutions and shelter construction is also critical to minimising the long-term impact of a disaster.

Better shelter, settlement and non-food items disaster response is achieved through better preparedness. Such preparedness is the result of the capacities, relationships and knowledge developed by governments, humanitarian agencies, local civil society organisations, communities and individuals to anticipate and respond effectively to the impact of likely, imminent or current hazards. Preparedness is informed by an analysis of risks and the use of early warning systems.

Links to other chapters

Many of the standards in the other chapters are relevant to this chapter. Progress in achieving standards in one area often influences and sometimes even determines progress in other areas. For an intervention to be effective, close coordination and collaboration is required with other sectors. For example, the complementary provision of an adequate water supply and sanitation facilities in areas where shelter assistance is being provided is necessary to ensure the health and dignity of the affected population. Similarly, the provision of adequate shelter contributes to the health and well-being of displaced populations, while essential cooking and eating utensils and fuel for cooking are required to enable food assistance to be utilised and nutritional needs met. Coordination with local authorities, other responding agencies and community-based and representative organisations is also necessary to ensure that needs are met, that efforts are not duplicated and that the quality of shelter, settlement and non-food item interventions is optimised.

Links to the Protection Principles and Core Standards

In order to meet the standards of this Handbook, all humanitarian agencies should be guided by the Protection Principles, even if they do not have a distinct protection mandate. The Principles are not 'absolute': circumstances may limit the extent to which agencies are able to fulfil them. Nevertheless, the Principles reflect universal humanitarian concerns which should guide action at all times.

The process by which an intervention is developed and implemented is critical to its effectiveness. The six Core Standards are essential process and personnel standards covering participation, initial assessment, response, targeting, monitoring, evaluation, aid worker performance, and supervision and support to personnel. They provide a single reference point for approaches that support all other standards in the Handbook. Each technical chapter, therefore, requires the companion use of the Core Standards to help attain its own standards. In particular, to ensure the appropriateness and quality of any response, the participation of disaster-affected people – including the groups and individuals most frequently at risk in disasters – should be maximised.

Vulnerabilities and capacities of disaster-affected populations

This section is designed to be read in conjunction with, and to reinforce, the Core Standards.

It is important to understand that to be young or old, a woman or a person with a disability or HIV does not, of itself, make a person vulnerable or at increased risk. Rather, it is the interplay of factors that does so: for example, someone who is over 70 years of age, lives alone and has poor health is likely to be more vulnerable than someone of a similar age and health status living within an extended family and with sufficient income. Similarly, a 3-year-old girl is much more vulnerable if she is unaccompanied than if she were living in the care of responsible parents.

As the shelter, settlement and non-food item standards and Key actions are implemented, a vulnerability and capacity analysis helps to ensure that a disaster response effort supports those who have a right to assistance in a non-discriminatory manner and who need it most. This requires a thorough understanding of the local context and of how a particular crisis impacts on particular groups of people in different ways due to their pre-existing vulnerabilities (e.g. being very poor or discriminated against), their exposure to various protection threats (e.g. gender-based violence including sexual exploitation), disease incidence or prevalence (e.g. HIV or tuberculosis) and possibilities of epidemics (e.g. measles or cholera). Disasters can make pre-existing inequalities worse. However, support for people's coping strategies, resilience and recovery capacities is essential. Their knowledge, skills and strategies need to be supported and their access to social, legal, financial and psychosocial support advocated for. The various physical, cultural, economic and social barriers they may face in accessing these services in an equitable manner also need to be addressed.

The following points highlight some of the key areas that will ensure that the rights and capacities of all vulnerable people are considered:

▶ Optimise people's participation, ensuring that all representative groups are included, especially those who are less visible (e.g. individuals who have communication or mobility difficulties, those living in institutions, stigmatised youth and other under- or unrepresented groups).

▶ Disaggregate data by sex and age (0–80+ years) during assessment – this is an important element in ensuring that the sector or area adequately considers the diversity of populations.

▶ Ensure that the right to information on entitlements is communicated in a way that is inclusive and accessible to all members of the community.

The minimum standards

1. Shelter and settlement

Non-displaced disaster-affected populations should be assisted on the site of their original homes with temporary or transitional household shelter, or with resources for the repair or construction of appropriate shelter. Individual household shelter for such populations can be temporary or permanent, subject to factors including the extent of the assistance provided, land-use rights or ownership, the availability of essential services and the opportunities for upgrading and expanding the shelter. Displaced populations who are unable to return to their original homes often prefer to stay with other family members or people with whom they share historical, religious or other ties, and should be assisted to do so. When such dispersed settlement is not possible, temporary communal settlement can be provided in planned or self-settled camps, along with temporary or transitional household shelter, or in suitable large public buildings used as collective centres.

Shelter and settlement standard 1: Strategic planning

Shelter and settlement strategies contribute to the security, safety, health and well-being of both displaced and non-displaced affected populations and promote recovery and reconstruction where possible.

Key actions (to be read in conjunction with the guidance notes)

▶ Assess and analyse the shelter and settlement needs of the affected population in consultation with the relevant authorities and the population themselves (see guidance note 1).

▶ Develop a shelter and settlement response plan (including early recovery where possible) in coordination with the relevant authorities, responding agencies and the affected population (see guidance note 1).

▶ Prioritise and support the return of affected households to their original dwellings or the site of their dwelling where possible (see guidance note 2).

▶ Assist those who are unable or unwilling to return to their original dwellings to be hosted by other households or to be accommodated within temporary communal settlements (see guidance notes 3–4).

▶ Ensure access to non-food items, shelter solutions (such as tents or shelter kits), construction materials, cash, technical assistance or information or a combination of these, as required (see guidance notes 5–6).

▶ Ensure dwellings or settlements are located at a safe distance from any actual or potential threats and that risks from existing hazards are minimised (see guidance note 7).

▶ Ensure that debris resulting from the disaster is removed from key locations including the sites of damaged or destroyed homes, temporary communal settlements, essential public buildings and access routes (see guidance note 8).

▶ Plan safe access to water and sanitation services, health facilities, schools and places for recreation and worship, and to land, markets or services used for the continuation or development of livelihood support activities (see guidance notes 9–10).

Key indicators (to be read in conjunction with the guidance notes)

▶ Shelter and settlement solutions to meet the essential needs of all the disaster-affected population are agreed with the population themselves and relevant authorities in coordination with all responding agencies (see guidance note 1).

▶ All temporary shelter and settlement solutions are safe and adequate and will remain so until more durable solutions are achieved (see guidance notes 2–10).

Guidance notes

1. *Assessment, consultation and coordination:* An initial needs assessment is essential to identify the shelter and settlement needs of the affected population, post-disaster risks, vulnerabilities and capacities, opportunities to address recovery from the outset and the need for more detailed assessment including environmental impact. The disaster-affected population (especially vulnerable people with specific needs), along with the relevant authorities, should be involved in any such assessment. Existing contingency plans should be used to inform response activities, in coordination with the relevant authorities, humanitarian and other agencies and the affected population using agreed coordination mechanisms. The availability of resources, the local context (including seasonal weather patterns), security and access to existing or new sites and land will inform response planning (see Core Standards 1–5 on pages 55–68, Non-food items standards 1–5 on pages 269–276 and Appendix 1: Shelter, settlement and non-food items assessment checklist).

2. **Return:** The opportunity to return to their own land and dwellings is a major goal for most disaster-affected populations. The repair of dwellings or the upgrading of shelter solutions determined by the population themselves supports communal coping strategies, retains established settlement patterns and enables the use of existing infrastructure (see Core Standard 1 on page 55). Return may be delayed or prevented and so require a period of temporary settlement elsewhere. Issues affecting return include the continuation of the disaster, such as ongoing flooding, landslides or earthquake aftershocks, and security concerns, such as occupation of property or land and the need for restitution, continuing violent conflict, ethnic or religious tension, fear of persecution or landmines and unexploded ordnance. The reconstruction of schools is also important to enable displaced populations to return. Return by female-headed households, those widowed or orphaned by the disaster or persons with disabilities may be inhibited by inadequate or discriminatory land and property legislation or customary procedures. Displaced populations who may not have the ability to undertake reconstruction activities may also be discouraged or prevented from returning.

3. **Hosting by families and communities:** Displaced populations who are unable to return to their original homes often prefer to stay with other family members or people with whom they share historical, religious or other ties (see Core Standard 1 on page 55). Assistance for such hosting may include support to expand or adapt an existing host family shelter and facilities to accommodate the displaced household, or the provision of an additional separate shelter adjacent to the host family. The resulting increase in population density should be assessed and the demand on social facilities, infrastructure provision and natural resources should be evaluated and mitigated.

4. **Temporary communal settlement:** Although they should not become a default response, temporary planned camps can be used to accommodate affected populations who are unable or unwilling to return to the site of their original dwelling and for whom hosting by other families is not an option. Such settlement solutions may be required in areas where security threats increase the risk to isolated populations or where access to essential services and resources such as water, food and locally sourced building materials is limited. Existing buildings used as collective centres can provide rapid temporary protection from the climate. Buildings used for such purposes may require adaptation or upgrading, for example the provision of internal subdivisions and ramps for those with mobility difficulties. In many countries, the use of pre-identified buildings for collective centres is the established response to known types of disaster, with associated management and service provision responsibilities. Although school buildings are often used to accommodate disaster-affected populations, alternative structures

should be identified to enable schooling to continue. The planning of temporary communal settlements should consider the implications on the personal safety, privacy and dignity of occupants and access to essential facilities. It is necessary to ensure that temporary communal settlements do not themselves become targets for attack, pose a security risk to the surrounding population or result in unsustainable demands on the surrounding natural environment.

5. **Types of shelter assistance:** Combinations of different types of assistance may be required to meet the shelter needs of affected populations. Basic assistance can include personal items, such as clothing and bedding, or general household items, such as stoves and fuel. Shelter support items can include tents, plastic sheeting and toolkits, building materials and temporary or transitional shelters using materials that can be reused as part of permanent shelters. Manual or specialist labour, either voluntary or contracted, may also be required, as well as technical guidance on appropriate building techniques. The use of cash or vouchers to promote the use of local supply chains and resources should be considered, subject to the functioning of the local economy. Cash can also be used to pay for rental accommodation. Information or advice distributed through public campaigns or local centres on how to access grants, materials or other forms of shelter support can complement commodity-based assistance.

6. **Transitional shelter:** An approach rather than a phase of response, the provision of transitional shelter responds to the fact that post-disaster shelter is often undertaken by the affected population themselves, and this self-management should be supported (see Core Standard 1 on page 55). Post-disaster shelter solutions that can be reused in part or in whole in more permanent structures, or relocated from temporary to permanent locations, can promote the transition by affected populations to more durable shelter. For non-displaced populations on the site of their original homes, transitional shelter can provide a basic starter home, to be upgraded, expanded or replaced over time as resources permit. For displaced populations, transitional shelter can provide appropriate shelter which can be disassembled and reused when the affected populations are able to return to the sites of their original homes or are resettled in new locations. Transitional shelter can also be provided to affected populations hosted by other households who can accommodate the erection of an adjacent or adjoining shelter. Any such structures can be removed and reused when the affected populations are able to return to their original sites or elsewhere.

7. **Risk, vulnerability and hazard assessments:** Undertake and regularly review a comprehensive risk and vulnerability assessment (see Core Standard 3 on page 61). Actual or potential security threats and the unique

risks and vulnerabilities due to age, gender, disability, social or economic status, the dependence of affected populations on natural environmental resources, and the relationships between affected populations and any host communities should be included in any such assessments (see Protection Principle 3 on page 38). Risks posed by natural hazards such as earthquakes, volcanic activity, landslides, flooding or high winds should inform the planning of shelter and settlement solutions. Settlement locations should not be prone to diseases or contamination or have significant vector risks. Potentially hazardous materials and goods can be deposited or exposed following natural disasters such as earthquakes, floods and typhoons. Mines and unexploded ordnance can be present due to previous or current conflicts. The stability of building structures in inhabited areas affected by the disaster should be assessed by technical specialists. For collective centres, the ability of existing building structures to accommodate any additional loading and the increased risk of the failure of building components such as floors, internal dividing walls, roofs, etc., should be assessed.

8. **Debris removal:** The removal of debris following a natural disaster or conflict is a priority to enable the provision of shelter and the establishment of appropriate settlement solutions. Debris management planning should be initiated immediately after the disaster to ensure debris can be recycled or identified for separation, collection and/or treatment (see Shelter and settlement standard 5 on page 265). Key issues include the presence of corpses requiring identification and appropriate handling, the retrieval of personal possessions, structurally dangerous locations and hazardous materials and ownership of salvageable materials for reuse or sale. The removal of debris may provide opportunities for cash for work programmes and/or require the use of major equipment and expertise to undertake. The use, management, ownership and environmental impact of disposal sites should be considered.

9. **Schools, health facilities and community infrastructure:** Access to essential services should be ensured, including schools, health facilities, safe play areas and communal meeting areas. Existing or repaired service infrastructure should be used, with additional temporary services or facilities as required. Where the repair or construction of public buildings is subject to the development of new settlement plans or other regulatory processes, temporary structures may be required to provide immediate, short-term facilities. Any such service provision using temporary or permanent structures should meet agreed standards (see WASH standard 1 on page 89, Health systems standard 1 on page 296 and INEE Minimum Standards for Education: Preparedness, Response, Recovery).

10. *Livelihood support:* The settling of disaster-affected populations should be informed by their pre-disaster economic activities and the opportunities within the post-disaster context (see Food security and nutrition assessment standards 1–2 on pages 150–154 and Core Standard 1 on page 55). Land availability and access for cultivation and grazing, and access to market areas and local services for particular economic activities should be considered.

Shelter and settlement standard 2: Settlement planning

The planning of return, host or temporary communal settlements enables the safe and secure use of accommodation and essential services by the affected population.

Key actions (to be read in conjunction with the guidance notes)

▶ Identify and use existing planning processes where possible, informed by agreed best practice, minimising settlement risk and vulnerabilities (see guidance note 1).

▶ Identify housing, land and property ownership and/or use rights for buildings or locations (see guidance note 2).

▶ Ensure safe access to all shelters and settlement locations and to essential services (see guidance notes 3–4).

▶ Use existing settlement patterns and topographical features to minimise adverse impact on the natural environment (see guidance note 5).

▶ Involve the affected population in the planning of temporary communal settlements by family, neighbourhood or village groups as appropriate (see guidance note 6).

▶ Ensure sufficient surface area and adequate fire separation in temporary planned and self-settled camps (see guidance notes 7–8).

▶ Minimise vector risks (see guidance note 9).

Key indicators (to be read in conjunction with the guidance notes)

▶ Through agreed planning processes, all shelter-assisted populations are consulted on and agree to the location of their shelter or covered area and access to essential services (see guidance note 1).

▶ All settlement plans demonstrate that risks and vulnerabilities in the use of shelters, covered areas and essential services have been identified and mitigated (see guidance notes 2–9).

Guidance notes

1. *Planning processes:* Local planning practices should be used and informed by the type of disaster or crisis, identified hazards and the impact on the affected population. Appropriate measures to minimise settlement risks and vulnerabilities should be used. Existing planning regulations should be complied with where required by the relevant authorities and where this does not impede the humanitarian imperative of meeting urgent shelter and settlement needs. The longer-term implications of planning decisions, particularly regarding sites for temporary communal settlement, should be identified.

2. *Housing, land and property ownership, rights and usage:* For both non-displaced and displaced populations, identify ownership of relevant land, housing or other buildings and the holders of formal or customary use rights. Such issues are often controversial, especially where records may not have been kept or where conflict may have affected possession. Multi-occupancy dwellings or buildings with mixed usage will involve common or shared ownership or occupancy rights. The identification of the land or property rights of vulnerable people should be sought and such people supported, in particular women, those widowed or orphaned by the disaster, persons with disabilities, tenants, social occupancy rights-holders and informal settlers. Clarify formal, informal or understood rights of ownership or inheritance, particularly following a disaster in which the holder of the rights or title may have died or been displaced. The provision of group tenure or similar to a number of households where no formal rights existed before the disaster can assist in the incremental establishment of such rights. The provision of shelter assistance may also be perceived or used as legitimising land title claims which could inhibit or prevent humanitarian action. The use of land for temporary communal settlements should consider existing use rights of the land or natural environmental resources by the host or neighbouring communities (see Shelter and settlement standard 5 on page 265).

3. *Essential services and facilities:* Disaster-affected populations returning to the site of their original homes, being hosted or accommodated in temporary communal settlements all require safe, secure and equitable access to essential services. These include, as appropriate, water, sanitary facilities, fuel for cooking or communal cooking facilities, healthcare, solid waste disposal, schools, social facilities, places of worship, meeting points, recreational areas, including child-friendly spaces and space for livestock accommodation (ensuring adequate separation of any such livestock from residential spaces). Sufficient space should be provided for culturally appropriate burials and associated rituals. The use of existing or repaired facilities should be maximised where this does not adversely affect neighbouring or host communities. Additional facilities or access points to

meet the needs of the target population, and in particular vulnerable people, should be provided. The social structure and gender roles of the affected population and the requirements of vulnerable people should be reflected in the service provision, for example ensuring services are within reasonable walking distance for individuals with mobility difficulties and the provision of safe breastfeeding areas in temporary communal settlements. Appropriate access to facilities for older people, those with physical disabilities and those who need frequent access should be ensured. Administrative offices, warehousing and staff accommodation and quarantine areas in temporary communal settlements should be provided as required (see WASH standard 1 on page 89 and Health systems standard 1 on page 296).

4. **Access:** Access to the settlement, the condition of local road infrastructure and proximity to transport hubs for the supply of relief assistance should be assessed, taking into account seasonal constraints, hazards and security risks. For temporary communal settlements, the site itself and any primary storage and food distribution points should be accessible by heavy trucks from an all-weather road. Other facilities should be accessible by light vehicles. Roads and pathways within settlements should provide safe, secure and all-weather access to individual dwellings and communal facilities including schools and healthcare facilities. Artificial lighting should be provided as required. Within temporary communal settlements or collective centres, access and escape routes should avoid creating isolated or screened areas that could pose a threat to the personal safety of users. Steps or changes of level close to exits in collective centres should be avoided and handrails for any stairways and ramps should be provided. For occupants with mobility difficulties, space on the ground floor should be provided, close to exits or along access routes without changes of level. The occupants of buildings used as collective centres should be within an agreed reasonable distance of a minimum of two exits, providing alternative escape routes, and these exits should be clearly visible.

5. **Site selection and drainage:** Surface water drainage and the risks of ponding or flooding should be assessed when selecting sites and planning temporary communal settlements. The site gradient should not exceed 5 per cent, unless extensive drainage and erosion control measures are taken, or be less than 1 per cent to provide for adequate drainage. Drainage channels may still be required to minimise flooding or ponding. The lowest point of the site should be not less than three metres above the estimated maximum level of the water table. The ground conditions should be suitable for excavating toilet pits and should inform the locations of toilets and other facilities (see Excreta disposal standards 1–2 on pages 105–107 and Drainage standard 1 on page 121).

6. **Site planning for temporary communal settlements:** Space allocation within collective centres and household plots within temporary planned camps should be informed by existing social practices and use of shared resources, including water and sanitation facilities, communal cooking, food distribution, etc. Neighbourhood planning should support existing social networks, contribute to security and enable self-management by the affected population. The plot layout in temporary planned camps should maintain the privacy and dignity of separate households by ensuring that each household shelter opens onto common space or a screened area for the use of the household instead of being opposite the entrance to another shelter. Safe, integrated living areas for displaced populations that include a significant number of single adults or unaccompanied children should be provided. For dispersed settlements, the principles of neighbourhood planning should also apply, e.g. groups of households return to a defined geographical area or identify host families in close proximity to one another (see Protection Principle 1 on page 33).

7. **Surface area of temporary planned or self-settled camps:** For camp-type settlements, a minimum usable surface area of 45 square metres for each person including household plots should be provided. The area should have the necessary space for roads and footpaths, external household cooking areas or communal cooking areas, educational facilities and recreational areas, sanitation, firebreaks, administration, water storage, distribution areas, markets, storage and limited kitchen gardens for individual households. Where communal services can be provided by existing or additional facilities outside of the planned area of the settlement, the minimum usable surface area should be 30m² for each person. Area planning should also consider changes in the population. If the minimum surface area cannot be provided, the consequences of higher-density occupation should be mitigated, for example through ensuring adequate separation and privacy between individual households, space for the required facilities, etc.

8. **Fire safety:** Assess fire risks to inform the site planning of temporary communal settlements and the grouping of individual household shelters. Mitigating actions should include the provision of a 30-metre firebreak between every 300 metres of built-up area, and a minimum of 2 metres (but preferably twice the overall height of any structure) between individual buildings or shelters to prevent collapsing structures from touching adjacent buildings. Preferred cooking practices and the use of stoves or heaters should also inform the overall site planning and the safe separation of household shelters (see Non-food items standard 4 on page 274).

9. **Vector risks:** Low-lying areas, debris resulting from the disaster, vacant buildings and excavations, such as those resulting from the use of local

earth for construction, can provide breeding grounds for pests which could pose health risks to nearby populations. For temporary communal settlements, appropriate site selection and the mitigation of vector risks are key to reducing the impact of vector-borne diseases on affected populations (see Vector control standards 1–3 on page 111–116).

Shelter and settlement standard 3: Covered living space

People have sufficient covered living space providing thermal comfort, fresh air and protection from the climate ensuring their privacy, safety and health and enabling essential household and livelihood activities to be undertaken.

Key actions (to be read in conjunction with the guidance notes)

▶ Ensure that each affected household has adequate covered living space (see guidance notes 1–2).

▶ Enable safe separation and privacy as required between the sexes, between different age groups and between separate families within a given household as required (see guidance note 3).

▶ Ensure that essential household and livelihood activities can be carried out within the covered living space or adjacent area (see guidance note 4).

▶ Promote the use of shelter solutions and materials that are familiar to the disaster-affected population and, where possible, culturally and socially acceptable and environmentally sustainable (see guidance notes 5–6).

▶ Assess the specific climatic conditions for all seasons to provide optimal thermal comfort, ventilation and protection (see guidance notes 7–10).

Key indicators (to be read in conjunction with the guidance notes)

▶ All affected individuals have an initial minimum covered floor area of 3.5m² per person (see guidance notes 1–2).

▶ All shelter solutions and materials meet agreed technical and performance standards and are culturally acceptable (see guidance notes 3–10).

Guidance notes

1. **Climate and context:** In cold climates, household activities typically take place within the covered area and affected populations may spend substantial time inside to ensure adequate thermal comfort. In urban settings,

household activities typically occur within the covered area as there is usually less adjacent external space that can be used. A covered floor area in excess of 3.5m^2 per person will often be required to meet these considerations. The floor-to-ceiling height is also a key factor, with greater height being preferable in hot and humid climates to aid air circulation, while a lower height is preferable in cold climates to minimise the internal volume that requires heating. The internal floor-to-ceiling height should be a minimum of two metres at the highest point. In warmer climates, adjacent shaded external space can be used for food preparation and cooking. Shelter solutions may have to accommodate a range of climatic extremes from cold nights and winters to hot days and summers. Where materials for a complete shelter cannot be provided, roofing materials to provide the minimum covered area should be prioritised. The resulting enclosure may not provide the necessary protection from the climate nor security, privacy and dignity, so steps should be taken to meet these needs as soon as possible (see guidance note 2).

2. **Duration:** In the immediate aftermath of a disaster, particularly in extreme climatic conditions where shelter materials are not readily available, a covered area of less than 3.5m^2 per person may be appropriate to save life and to provide adequate short-term shelter. In such instances, the covered area should reach 3.5m^2 per person as soon as possible to minimise adverse impact on the health and well-being of the people accommodated. If 3.5m^2 per person cannot be achieved, or is in excess of the typical space used by the affected or neighbouring population, the impact on dignity, health and privacy of a reduced covered area should be considered. Any decision to provide less than 3.5m^2 per person should be highlighted, along with actions to mitigate adverse effects on the affected population. Temporary or transitional shelter solutions may be required to provide adequate shelter for an extended duration, through different seasonal climates and potentially for several years. Response plans agreed with local authorities or others should ensure that temporary or transitional shelters are not allowed to become default permanent housing.

3. **Cultural practices, safety and privacy:** Existing local practices in the use of covered living space, for example sleeping arrangements and the accommodation of extended family members, should inform the covered area required. Consultation should include members of vulnerable groups and those caring for such individuals. Opportunities for internal subdivision within individual household shelters should be provided. In collective accommodation, the grouping of related families, well-planned access routes through the covered area and materials to screen personal and household space can aid the provision of adequate personal privacy and

safety. The psychosocial benefits of ensuring adequate space provision and privacy while minimising overcrowding should be maximised in both individual household shelters and temporary collective accommodation (see Protection Principle 1 on page 33).

4. **Household and livelihood activities:** The covered area should provide space for the following activities: sleeping, washing and dressing; care of infants, children and the ill or infirm; storage of food, water, household possessions and other key assets; cooking and eating indoors when required; and the common gathering of the household members. The planning of the covered area, in particular the location of openings and subdivisions, should maximise the use of the internal space and any adjacent external area.

5. **Shelter solutions, materials and construction:** Defined shelter solutions such as family tents, shelter kits, packages of materials or prefabricated buildings should be provided where local post-disaster shelter options are not readily available, are inadequate or cannot be sustainably supported by the local natural environment. Where reinforced plastic sheeting is provided as a relief item for emergency shelter, it should be complemented with rope, tools, fixings and supporting materials such as timber poles or locally procured framing elements. Any such materials or defined shelter solutions should meet agreed national and international specifications and standards and be acceptable to the affected population. When only part of the materials for a basic shelter are provided (e.g. plastic sheeting), assess and mitigate any potential adverse impact on the local economy or natural environment of the sourcing of other materials needed (e.g. timber poles for framing). The technical and financial ability of the affected population to maintain and repair their shelter should also inform the specification of materials and technologies (see Non-food items standard 5 on page 276). Regular monitoring should be undertaken to ensure that the performance of shelter solutions remains adequate over time.

6. **Participatory design:** All members of each affected household should be involved to the maximum extent possible in determining the type of shelter assistance to be provided. The opinions of those groups or individuals who typically have to spend more time within the covered living space and those with specific accessibility needs should be prioritised. This should be informed by assessments of existing typical housing. Make households aware of the disadvantages as well as advantages of unfamiliar 'modern' forms of construction and materials which may be seen as improving the social status of such households (see Core Standard 1 on page 55).

7. **In warm, humid climates:** Shelters should be oriented and designed to maximise ventilation and minimise entry of direct sunlight. The roof should have a reasonable slope for rainwater drainage with large overhangs except

in locations vulnerable to high winds. The construction of the shelter should be lightweight, as low thermal capacity is required. Adequate surface water drainage should be ensured around the shelter together with the use of raised floors to minimise the risk of water entering the covered area.

8. *In hot, dry climates:* Construction should be heavyweight to ensure high thermal capacity, allowing changes in night and day temperatures to alternately cool and heat the interior, or lightweight with adequate insulation. Care should be taken in the structural design of heavyweight construction in areas with seismic risks. If only plastic sheeting or tents are available, a double-skinned roof should be provided with ventilation between the layers to reduce radiant heat gain. Door and window openings positioned away from the direction of the prevailing wind will minimise heating by hot winds and heat radiation from the surrounding ground. Flooring that meets the external walling without gaps should be provided to minimise dust and vector penetration.

9. *In cold climates:* Heavyweight construction with high thermal capacity is required for shelters that are occupied throughout the day. Lightweight construction with low thermal capacity and substantial insulation is more appropriate for shelters that are occupied only at night. Minimise air flow, particularly around door and window openings, to ensure personal comfort while also providing adequate ventilation for space heaters or cooking stoves. Stoves or other forms of space heaters are essential and must be appropriate to the shelter. Assess and mitigate potential fire risks from the use of stoves and heaters (see Non-food items standard 4 on page 274). Surface-water drainage should be provided around the shelter and raised floors should be used to minimise the risk of water due to rain or snow melt from entering the covered area. The loss of body heat through the floor should be minimised by ensuring that the floor is insulated and through the use of insulated sleeping mats, mattresses or raised beds (see Non-food items standard 2 on page 271).

10. *Ventilation and vector control:* Adequate ventilation should be provided within individual household shelters and public buildings such as schools and healthcare facilities to maintain a healthy internal environment, minimise the effect of smoke from indoor household stoves and resulting respiratory infections and eye problems and limit the risk of transmission of diseases such as TB spread by droplet infection. Local building practices, the patterns of shelter use by displaced people and material selection should inform vector control measures (see Essential health services – control of communicable diseases standard 1 on page 312 and Vector control standards 1–3 on pages 111–116).

Shelter and settlement standard 4: Construction

Local safe building practices, materials, expertise and capacities are used where appropriate, maximising the involvement of the affected population and local livelihood opportunities.

Key actions (to be read in conjunction with the guidance notes)

▶ Involve the affected population, local building professionals and the relevant authorities in agreeing appropriate safe building practices, materials and expertise which maximise local livelihood opportunities (see guidance notes 1–3).

▶ Ensure access to additional support or resources to disaster-affected people who do not have the capacity, ability or opportunity to undertake construction-related activities (see guidance notes 1–3).

▶ Minimise structural risks and vulnerabilities through appropriate construction and material specifications (see guidance notes 4–5).

▶ Meet agreed standards for materials and the quality of work (see guidance notes 5–6).

▶ Manage the provision of materials, labour, technical assistance and regulatory approval through appropriate bidding, procurement and construction administration practices (see guidance note 7).

▶ Enable the maintenance and upgrading of individual household shelters using locally available tools and resources (see guidance note 8).

Key indicators (to be read in conjunction with the guidance notes)

▶ All construction is in accordance with agreed safe building practices and standards (see guidance notes 2–7).

▶ Construction activities demonstrate the involvement of the affected population and the maximising of local livelihood opportunities (see guidance notes 1–2, 8).

Guidance notes

1. *Participation of affected populations:* Participation by the affected population in shelter and settlement activities should be informed by existing practices through which housing and settlements are planned, constructed and maintained. Skills training programmes and apprenticeship schemes

can maximise opportunities for participation during construction, particularly for individuals lacking the required building skills or experience. Women of all ages should be encouraged to participate in shelter and construction-related activities and training. Contributions from those less able to undertake physical tasks or those requiring specialist technical expertise can include site monitoring and inventory control, the provision of childcare, temporary accommodation or the preparation of food for those engaged in construction works and administrative support. The other demands on the time and labour resources of the affected population should be considered. The provision of assistance from volunteer community labour teams or contracted labour can complement the involvement of individual households. Such assistance is essential to support female-headed households, as women may be at particular risk from sexual exploitation in seeking assistance for the construction of their shelter (see Core Standard 1 on page 55, Protection Principle 2 on page 36 and Non-food items standard 5 on page 276). Persons with mobility difficulties, older people and others unable to undertake construction activities may also need assistance.

2. ***Technical expertise and experience:*** Appropriate technical design, construction and management expertise should complement the skills and understanding of the affected population and provide experience of established technical and regulatory processes (see Core Standard 6 on page 71). In locations vulnerable to seasonal or cyclical disasters, the involvement of technical specialists who have previous experiences of appropriate, local solutions or agreed best practices can inform the design and construction process.

3. ***Sourcing of materials and labour:*** The rapid provision of shelter solutions or materials and tools, either separately or in the form of a predefined kit, can enable the affected population to erect or construct shelters themselves. Where possible, local livelihoods should be supported through the local procurement of building materials, specialist building skills and manual labour informed by rapid market assessments and analyses. If the local sourcing of materials is likely to have a significant adverse impact on the local economy or the natural environment, the following may be required: the use of multiple sources; alternative materials or production processes; materials sourced regionally or internationally; or proprietary shelter systems (see Shelter and settlement standard 5 on page 265). The reuse of materials salvaged from damaged buildings, having identified the rights to such material, should be promoted.

4. ***Disaster prevention and risk reduction:*** Construction resilience should be consistent with known climatic conditions and natural hazards and should consider adaptations to address the local impact of climate change.

Changes to building standards or building practices as a result of the disaster should be applied in consultation with the disaster-affected population and the relevant authorities.

5. **Safe public building design and construction:** Temporary and permanent public buildings such as schools and healthcare facilities should be constructed or repaired to be disaster-resilient and to ensure safety and access for all. Such facilities should comply with sector-specific construction standards and approval procedures, including accessibility requirements for those with mobility, visual or communication difficulties. The repair or construction of such buildings should be undertaken in consultation with the appropriate authorities and informed by an agreed service infrastructure and affordable maintenance strategy (see INEE Minimum Standards in Education: Preparedness, Response, Recovery).

6. **Construction standards:** Standards and guidelines on construction should be agreed with the relevant authorities to ensure that key safety and performance requirements are met. Where applicable local or national building codes have not been customarily adhered to or enforced, incremental compliance should be agreed, reflecting local housing culture, climatic conditions, resources, building and maintenance capacities, accessibility and affordability.

7. **Procurement and construction management:** A construction schedule should be developed to plan activities. The schedule should include key milestones such as target completion dates, the relocation of displaced populations to specific shelter and settlement solutions and the onset of seasonal weather patterns. A responsive, efficient and accountable supply chain and construction management system for materials, labour and site supervision should also be established. This should include sourcing, procurement, transportation, handling and administration, from point of origin through to the respective sites as required (see Food security – food transfers standard 4 on page 188).

8. **Upgrading and maintenance:** As initial shelter responses typically provide only a minimum level of enclosed space and material assistance, affected populations will need to seek alternative means of increasing the extent or quality of the enclosed space provided. The form of construction and the materials used should enable individual households to maintain and incrementally adapt or upgrade the shelter to meet their longer-term needs using locally available tools and materials (see Non-food items standard 5 on page 276).

> **Shelter and settlement standard 5: Environmental impact**
>
> Shelter and settlement solutions and the material sourcing and construction techniques used minimise adverse impact on the local natural environment.

Key actions (to be read in conjunction with the guidance notes)

▶ Assess and analyse the adverse impact of the disaster on the local natural environment and environmental risks and vulnerabilities (see guidance note 1).

▶ Consider the extent of available local natural resources when planning the temporary or permanent settling of the affected population (see guidance notes 1–3).

▶ Manage local natural environmental resources to meet the ongoing and future needs of disaster-affected populations (see guidance notes 1–3).

▶ Minimise the adverse impact on local natural environmental resources which can result from the production and supply of construction materials and the building process (see guidance notes 3–4).

▶ Retain trees and other vegetation where possible to increase water retention, minimise soil erosion and provide shade (see guidance note 5).

▶ Restore the location of temporary communal settlements to their original condition once they are no longer needed, unless agreed otherwise (see guidance note 6).

Key indicators (to be read in conjunction with the guidance notes)

▶ The planning of all return, host or temporary communal settlements demonstrate that adverse impact on the natural environment has been minimised and/or mitigated (see guidance notes 1–6).

▶ The construction processes and sourcing of materials for all shelter solutions demonstrate that adverse impact on the local natural environment has been minimised and/or mitigated (see guidance note 4).

Guidance notes

1. *Environmental assessment:* The impact of a disaster on the natural environment should be assessed to inform the response and mitigating activities required. Many natural disasters, for example landslides, are often a direct

result of the mismanagement of natural environmental resources. Alternatively, they may be due to existing environmental risks or vulnerabilities, such as seasonal flooding in low-lying areas or the lack of natural environmental resources that can be safely harvested. An understanding of these risks is essential to inform settlement planning and to ensure that known vulnerabilities including the impact of climate change are addressed as part of the response.

2. *Sustainability and the management of environmental resources:* Where the environmental resources required to support a substantial increase in human habitation are limited, any such unsustainable demand on the natural environment should be mitigated. Where such natural resources are available, temporary communal settlements should be managed to minimise environmental damage. Sustainable external supplies of fuel and options for livestock grazing, agricultural production and other natural resource-dependent livelihood support activities should be provided and managed. Fewer but larger managed settlements may be more environmentally sustainable than a larger number of smaller, dispersed settlements that are not as easily managed or monitored. The impact on the natural environmental resource needs of populations hosting those affected by the disaster or settled close to the affected area should be considered.

3. *Mitigating long-term environmental impact:* The management of natural environmental resources should be considered at all planning levels. Where the need to provide shelter for affected populations has a significant adverse impact on the natural environment through the depletion of local environmental resources, the long-term effects should be minimised through complementary environmental management and rehabilitation activities. Consultation with appropriate environmental agencies is recommended.

4. *Sourcing of construction materials:* The environmental impact of sourcing natural environmental resources should be assessed, such as water, construction timber, sand, soil and grasses, as well as fuel for the firing of bricks and roof tiles. Identify customary users, extraction and regeneration rates and the ownership or control of these resources. Alternative or complementary sources of supply may support the local economy and reduce any long-term adverse impact on the local natural environment. The use of multiple sources and the reuse of salvaged materials, alternative materials and production processes (such as the use of stabilised earth blocks) should be promoted. This should be combined with mitigation practices, such as complementary replanting.

5. *Erosion:* Shelter and settlement solutions should be planned to retain trees and other vegetation to stabilise the soil and to maximise the opportunities for shade and protection from the climate. Natural contours should be used

for such elements as roads, pathways and drainage networks in order to minimise erosion and flooding. Where this cannot be achieved, any likely erosion should be contained through the provision of excavated drainage channels, piped drainage runs under roadways or planted earth banks to minimise water run-off (see Drainage standard 1 on page 121).

6. *Handover:* The natural regeneration of the environment should be enhanced in and around temporary communal settlements through appropriate environmental rehabilitation measures. The eventual discontinuation of any such settlements should be managed to ensure the satisfactory removal of all material or waste that cannot be reused or that could have an adverse effect on the natural environment.

2. Non-food items: clothing, bedding and household items

Clothing, blankets and bedding materials meet the most personal human needs for shelter from the climate and for the maintenance of health, privacy and dignity. Access to basic goods and supplies is required to enable affected populations to prepare and consume food, provide thermal comfort, meet personal hygiene needs and build, maintain or repair shelters (see Hygiene promotion standard 2 on page 94 and Water supply standard 1 on page 97).

All affected populations – whether they are able to return to the site of their orginial homes, are hosted by other families or are accommodated in temporary communal settlements – will have individual and household non-food item needs that must be assessed and met as appropriate. Populations secondarily affected by disasters, in particular host families, may also require non-food item assistance to meet the additional burden of hosting or the impact of the disaster on the local economy and access to such items.

Although the distribution of non-food items is a common response activity, the provision of cash or vouchers to access such non-food items where local markets are still functioning should be considered (see Food security – cash and voucher transfers standard 1 on page 200).

Items for individual or household use typically do not require additional information or instruction on how they are to be used. However, items to support shelter repair or construction, for example building materials, fixings and tools, will usually require additional technical guidance in the safe and effective use of such items. Similarly, items to meet personal hygiene needs should be supported by appropriate hygiene promotion activities (see Hygiene promotion standards 1–2 on pages 91–94).

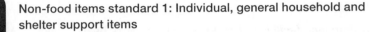

Non-food items standard 1: Individual, general household and shelter support items

The affected population has sufficient individual, general household and shelter support items to ensure their health, dignity, safety and well-being.

Key actions (to be read in conjunction with the guidance notes)

▶ Assess the separate needs of the affected population for non-food items (see guidance notes 1–2 and Water supply standard 3 on page 103).

▶ Identify which non-food items can be sourced locally or obtained by the affected population themselves through the provision of cash or voucher assistance (see guidance note 3).

▶ Consider the appropriateness of all non-food items within a given package (see guidance note 4).

▶ Plan for orderly, transparent and equitable distributions of all non-food items (see guidance note 5).

▶ Provide instruction, technical guidance or promotion in the use of shelter support items as required (see guidance note 6).

▶ Plan to replenish non-food items for populations displaced for an extended period of time (see guidance note 7).

Key indicator (to be read in conjunction with the guidance notes)

▶ The assessed non-food item needs of the entire disaster-affected population have been met (see guidance notes 1–7).

Guidance notes

1. ***Needs assessment:*** The separate needs for personal items, such as clothing and personal hygiene, general household items, such as food storage and preparation, and items to support the meeting of shelter needs, such as plastic sheeting, rope, tools or basic building materials, should be assessed. A distinction should be made between individual and communal needs, in particular for cooking and fuel. Non-food item needs that can be met using familiar, locally sourced products should be identified. The need for boxes, bags or similar containers for the storage and transportation of personal and household goods for displaced populations and those in transit should be considered for inclusion as part of any non-food item assistance. The provision of non-food items should be part of an overall disaster response plan (see

269

Core Standards 1–3 on pages 55–61 and Shelter and settlement standard 1 on page 249).

2. **Communal facilities:** Non-food items should be provided to support personal hygiene, health, food preparation and cooking, etc., as appropriate for schools and other communal facilities. Access should be made available to recreation and learning materials. Links should be established between the health and education sectors to ensure public health and hygiene messages support the appropriate use of non-food items (see Hygiene promotion standards 1–2 on pages 91–94 and INEE Minimum Standards in Education: Preparedness, Response, Recovery).

3. **Sourcing non-food items:** Disasters affect the local economy and supply chains, often necessitating the external sourcing of non-food items and the direct distribution to individuals, households or communities. A rapid market analysis as part of the initial needs assessment can determine whether familiar non-food items can be sourced locally or in neighbouring, non-affected areas. Where the local economy is still functioning, or can be supported through specific assistance in sourcing or supply chain management, the provision of cash and/or vouchers can enable affected populations to manage their own relief item needs (see Food security – cash and vouchers standard 1 on page 200). Any such assistance should be planned to ensure that vulnerable people are not disadvantaged and that relief needs are met.

4. **Relief packages:** Non-food items are often packaged and pre-positioned in warehouses based on standard specifications and contents. The quantity and specification of non-food items in a household package should be considered with reference to the number of people in a typical household, their age, sex and the presence of people with specific needs, as well as the items' cultural acceptability.

5. **Distribution:** Efficient and equitable distribution methods should be planned in consultation with the affected population. The population should be informed of any such distributions and any registration or assessment process required to participate. Formal registration or the allocation of tokens should be undertaken. Ensure that vulnerable individuals or households are not omitted from distribution lists and can access both the information and the distribution itself. A grievance process should be established to address any concerns arising during registration or distribution. Relevant local authorities should be consulted on which distribution locations are most suitable for safe access and receipt of the non-food items, as well as for safe return of recipients. The walking distances involved, the terrain and the practicalities and cost implications of transporting larger goods such as shelter support items should be considered. The monitoring of distributions and the use of the provided non-food items should be undertaken to assess the adequacy

and appropriateness of both the distribution process and the non-food items themselves (see Food security – food transfers standard 5 on page 192).

6. **Promotion, instruction and technical guidance:** Individual and general household items should be familiar to the disaster-affected population for use without additional guidance. However, technical guidance and instruction should be provided as appropriate to complement the provision of shelter support items such as construction materials, tools and fixings (see Non-food items standard 5 on page 276). Packaging can carry simple diagrams illustrating how the items can be used safely to repair or construct safe and adequate shelter. The disaster-affected population and local construction specialists should be involved in on-site awareness-raising activities (for example, the repair or erection of demonstration shelters) in order to better understand the construction techniques required. Any weaknesses in pre-disaster shelter and settlement design and construction that may have contributed to the damage or destruction of homes, and local examples of good practice that withstood the disaster, should be highlighted to those involved in construction activities.

7. **Replenishment:** The planning of relief distributions should consider the rate of consumption, the resulting duration of use and the ability of the affected population to replenish such items.

Non-food items standard 2: Clothing and bedding

The disaster-affected population has sufficient clothing, blankets and bedding to ensure their personal comfort, dignity, health and well-being.

Key actions (to be read in conjunction with the guidance notes)

▶ Identify the separate clothing needs of women, girls, men and boys of all ages including infants and vulnerable or marginalised individuals and ensure access to required items in the correct sizes and appropriate to the culture, season and climate (see guidance notes 1–5).

▶ Identify the blanket and bedding needs of the affected population and ensure access to blankets and bedding as required to provide sufficient thermal comfort and to enable appropriate sleeping arrangements (see guidance notes 2–5).

▶ Assess the need for insecticide-treated bed nets and provide as required (see Vector control standards 1–3 on pages 111–116).

Key indicators (to be read in conjunction with the guidance notes)

▶ All women, girls, men and boys have at least two full sets of clothing in the correct size that are appropriate to the culture, season and climate (see guidance notes 1–5).

▶ All affected people have a combination of blankets, bedding, sleeping mats or mattresses and insecticide-treated bed nets where required to ensure sufficient thermal comfort and enable appropriate sleeping arrangements (see guidance notes 2–5 and Vector control standards 1–3 on pages 111–116).

Guidance notes

1. *Changes of clothing:* All affected people should have access to sufficient changes of clothing to ensure their thermal comfort, dignity, health and well-being. This will require at least two sets of essential items, particularly underclothes, to enable laundering.

2. *Appropriateness:* Clothing (including footwear as required) should be appropriate to climatic conditions and cultural practices and sized according to need. Infants and children up to 2 years of age should also have a blanket in addition to appropriate clothing. Bedding materials should reflect cultural practices and be sufficient in quantity to enable separate sleeping arrangements as required.

3. *Thermal performance:* The insulating properties of clothing and bedding should be considered, as well as the effect of wet or damp climatic conditions on the thermal performance of such items. A combination of clothing and bedding items should be considered to ensure the required level of thermal comfort is met. Using insulated sleeping mats or mattresses to combat heat loss through the ground may be more effective than providing additional blankets.

4. *Durability:* Clothing and bedding should be sufficiently durable to accommodate typical wear and prolonged usage.

5. *Specific needs:* Those individuals most at risk should have additional clothing and bedding to meet their needs. This includes people with incontinence problems, people with chronic illness, pregnant and lactating women, older people and individuals with impaired mobility. Infants, children, those with restricted mobility and older people are more prone to heat loss and hence may require additional clothing, blankets, etc., to maintain appropriate levels of thermal comfort. Given their lack of mobility, older people and the ill or infirm will require particular attention, such as the provision of mattresses or raised beds.

Non-food items standard 3: Cooking and eating utensils

The disaster-affected population has access to culturally appropriate items for preparing and storing food, and for cooking, eating and drinking.

Key action (to be read in conjunction with the guidance notes)

▶ Identify the needs of the affected population for preparing and storing food, and for cooking, eating and drinking, and enable access to culturally appropriate items as required (see guidance notes 1–2).

Key indicators (to be read in conjunction with the guidance notes)

▶ Each household or group of four to five individuals has access to two family-sized cooking pots with handles and lids, a basin for food preparation or serving, a kitchen knife and two serving spoons (see guidance notes 1–2).

▶ All disaster-affected people have access to a dished plate, a spoon or other eating utensils and a mug or drinking vessel (see guidance notes 1–2).

Guidance notes

1. *Appropriateness:* The choice of cooking items and eating utensils should be culturally appropriate and should enable safe practices to be followed. Women or those typically overseeing the preparation of food should be consulted when specifying items. The quantities of cooking items should be informed by cultural practices such as those requiring separate cooking arrangements for different family groups within a household or the separation of particular foods during preparation. The type and size of cooking and eating utensils should be suitable for older people, persons with disabilities and children.

2. *Materials:* All plastic items (buckets, bowls, jerrycans, water storage containers, etc.) should be made of food-grade plastic. All metallic goods (cutlery, bowls, plates and mugs, etc.), should be stainless steel or enamelled.

> ## Non-food items standard 4: Stoves, fuel and lighting
>
> The disaster-affected population has access to a safe, fuel-efficient stove and an accessible supply of fuel or domestic energy, or to communal cooking facilities. Each household also has access to appropriate means of providing sustainable artificial lighting to ensure personal safety.

Key actions (to be read in conjunction with the guidance notes)

▶ Identify and meet household cooking and space heating needs by ensuring access to safe, fuel-efficient stoves, an accessible supply of fuel or domestic energy or communal cooking facilities (see guidance note 1).

▶ Ensure that stoves can be safely used and fire risks are minimised (see guidance notes 2–3).

▶ Identify and prioritise environmentally and economically sustainable sources of fuel or domestic energy (see guidance note 4).

▶ Ensure that fuel is sourced and stored in a safe and secure manner (see guidance note 5).

▶ Identify and meet household needs for sustainable means of providing artificial lighting and access to matches or a suitable alternative means of igniting fuel or candles, etc. (see guidance note 6).

Key indicators (to be read in conjunction with the guidance notes)

▶ Fuel-efficient stoves with the required supply of fuel or domestic energy are used by the affected population (see guidance notes 1–3).

▶ No incidents are reported of harm to people in the routine use of stoves and the sourcing and storage of fuel (see guidance notes 4–5).

▶ The disaster-affected population has access to a safe and sustainable means of providing artificial lighting and access to matches or a suitable alternative means of igniting fuel or candles, etc. (see guidance note 6).

Guidance notes

1. *Stoves:* The specification of stoves is informed by existing local practices. Energy-efficient cooking practices should be promoted, including the use of fuel-efficient stoves, firewood preparation, fire management, food preparation, shared cooking, etc. In communal accommodation, common

or centralised cooking facilities are preferable to the provision of individual household stoves, to minimise fire risks and indoor smoke pollution (see Food security – food transfers standard 2 on page 184).

2. **Ventilation:** Flues should be fitted to stoves in enclosed areas to vent exhaust gases or smoke to the exterior in a safe manner. Weather-protected openings should be used to ensure adequate ventilation and to minimise the risk of respiratory problems.

3. **Fire safety:** Safe separation should be ensured between the stove and the elements of the shelter. Internal stoves should be placed on a non-flammable base with a non-flammable sleeve around the flue where it passes through the structure of the shelter to the exterior. Stoves should be located away from entrances and placed to enable safe access during use.

4. **Sustainable sources of fuel:** Sources of fuel should be managed, particularly where host or neighbouring communities also rely upon them. Resources should be replenished to ensure sustainability of supply, e.g. establishing firewood tree plantations to reduce or eliminate firewood extraction from existing forests. The use of non-traditional fuel sources should be supported, for example briquettes produced from sawdust and other organic matter, where this is acceptable to the affected populations.

5. **Collecting and storing fuel:** The disaster-affected population, in particular women and girls, should be consulted about the location and means of collecting fuel for cooking and heating to address issues of personal safety. The demands of collecting fuel on particularly vulnerable people, such as female-headed households, those caring for chronically ill individuals or persons with mobility or access difficulties, should be addressed. The use of less labour-intensive fuels should be promoted, including fuel-efficient stoves and accessible fuel sources. Fuel should be stored at a safe distance from the stove itself, and any liquid fuel such as kerosene should be kept out of the reach of children and infants.

6. **Artificial lighting:** Lanterns or candles can provide familiar and readily sourced lighting, although the fire risk of using such items should be assesed. Provide other types of artificial lighting to contribute to personal safety in and around settlements where general illumination is not available. The use of energy-efficient artificial lighting should be considered, such as light-emitting diodes (LEDs), and the provision of solar panels to generate localised electrical energy.

> ### Non-food items standard 5: Tools and fixings
>
> The affected population, when responsible for the construction or maintenance of their shelter or for debris removal, has access to the necessary tools, fixings and complementary training.

Key actions (to be read in conjunction with the guidance notes)

▶ Identify and meet the tools and fixings needs of populations responsible for the safe construction of part or all of their shelters or communal facilities, for the carrying-out of essential maintenance or for debris removal (see guidance notes 1–2).

▶ Ensure that adequate mechanisms for the use, maintenance and safekeeping of tools and fixings, where they are provided for communal or shared use, are agreed and commonly understood (see guidance notes 1–2).

▶ Provide training or guidance where necessary in the use of the tools and in construction, maintenance or debris removal (see guidance note 3).

Key indicators (to be read in conjunction with the guidance notes)

▶ All households or community groups have access to tools and equipment to safely undertake construction, maintenance or debris removal tasks where required (see guidance notes 1–2).

▶ All households or community groups have access to training and awareness-raising in the safe use of tools and fixings provided (see guidance note 3).

Guidance notes

1. *Typical tool sets:* Tools and fixings provided should be familiar and appropriate to the context. Fixings, such as nails of different sizes, galvanised wire and rope, and items to help setting-out and measuring, should be considered. Communal tools should be provided where such tools are for use on public buildings and are only required for a limited period of time, or where such resources are limited. Any such shared use, maintenance and safekeeping should be agreed before distribution.

2. *Livelihood activities:* Where possible, the tools provided should also be appropriate for livelihood support activities. Tool use should be monitored to avoid negative impacts on the environment (such as unauthorised

or unsustainable harvesting of natural resources, etc.) and any shared or communal use of such tools.

3. ***Training and technical assistance:*** Training or awareness-raising should be available in the safe use and simple maintenance of tools and in planned activities. Assistance from extended family members, neighbours or contracted labour to undertake the designated construction or maintenance tasks should be provided to female-headed households and other identified vulnerable people (see Shelter and settlements standard 4, guidance note 1 on page 262).

Appendix 1

Shelter, settlement and non-food items assessment checklist

This list of questions serves as a guide and checklist to ensure that appropriate information is obtained to inform post-disaster shelter and settlement response. The list of questions is not mandatory, and should be used and adapted as appropriate. It is assumed that information on the underlying causes of the disaster, the security situation, the basic demographics of the displaced and any host population and the key people to consult and contact, is separately obtained (see Core Standard 3 on page 61).

1 Shelter and settlement

Assessment and coordination

▶ Has an agreed coordination mechanism been established by the relevant authorities and agencies?

▶ What baseline data are available on the affected population and what are the known hazards and shelter and settlement risks and vulnerabilities?

▶ Is there a contingency plan to inform the response?

▶ What initial assessment information is already available?

▶ Is an inter-agency and/or multisectoral assessment planned and does this include shelter, settlement and non-food items?

Demographics

▶ How many people comprise a typical household?

▶ How many people, disaggregated by sex and age, within the disaster-affected population comprise individuals who do not form typical households (such as unaccompanied children) or particular minority groups with household sizes that are not typical?

- How many affected households lack adequate shelter and where are these households?

- How many people, disaggregated by sex and age, who are not members of individual households are without any or with inadequate shelter and where are these households?

- How many affected households who lack adequate shelter have not been displaced and can be assisted at the site of their original homes?

- How many affected households who lack adequate shelter have been displaced and will require shelter assistance with host families or within temporary communal settlements?

- How many people, disaggregated by sex and age, lack access to communal facilities such as schools, health clinics and community centres?

Risks

- What is the immediate risk to life of the lack of adequate shelter, and how many people are at risk?

- What are the potential further risks to lives, health and security of the affected population as a result of the ongoing effects of the disaster or other known hazards on the provision of shelter?

- What are the particular risks for vulnerable people, including women, children, unaccompanied minors, persons with disabilities or chronic illnesses, due to the lack of adequate shelter and why?

- What is the impact on any host populations of the presence of displaced populations?

- What are the potential risks for conflict or discrimination among or between groups within the affected population?

Resources and constraints

- What are the material, financial and human resources of the affected populations to meet some or all of their urgent shelter needs?

- What are the issues regarding land availability, ownership and usage to meet urgent shelter needs, including temporary communal settlements where required?

- What are the issues facing potential host populations in accommodating displaced populations within their own dwellings or on adjacent land?

▶ What are the opportunities and constraints of utilising existing, available and unaffected buildings or structures to accommodate displaced populations temporarily?

▶ What is the topographical and local environmental suitability of using accessible vacant land to accommodate temporary settlements?

▶ What are the requirements and constraints of local authority regulations in developing shelter solutions?

Materials, design and construction

▶ What initial shelter solutions or materials have been provided to date by the affected populations or other actors?

▶ What existing materials can be salvaged from the damaged site for use in the reconstruction of shelters?

▶ What are the typical building practices of the affected population and what are the different materials that are used to provide the structural frame and roof, and external wall enclosures?

▶ What alternative design or materials solutions are potentially available and familiar or acceptable to the affected population?

▶ What design features are required to ensure safe and ready access to and use of shelter solutions by all members of the affected population, in particular those with mobility difficulties?

▶ How can the potential shelter solutions identified minimise future risks and vulnerabilities?

▶ How are shelters typically built and by whom?

▶ How are construction materials typically obtained and by whom?

▶ How can women, youths, persons with disabilities and older people be trained or assisted to participate in the building of their own shelters and what are the constraints?

▶ Will additional assistance, through the provision of voluntary or contracted labour or technical assistance, be required to support individuals or households lacking the capacity or opportunity to build?

Household and livelihood activities

▶ What household and livelihood support activities typically take place in or adjacent to the shelters of the affected population and how does the resulting space provision and design reflect these activities?

▶ What legal and environmentally sustainable livelihood support opportunities can be provided through the sourcing of materials and the construction of shelter and settlement solutions?

Essential services and communal facilities

▶ What is the current availability of water for drinking and personal hygiene and what are the possibilities and constraints in meeting the anticipated sanitation needs?

▶ What is the current provision of social facilities (health clinics, schools, places of worship, etc.) and what are the constraints and opportunities of accessing these facilities?

▶ If communal buildings, particularly schools, are being used for shelter by displaced populations, what are the process and timeline for returning them to the intended use?

Host community and environmental impact

▶ What are the issues of concern for the host community?

▶ What are the organisational and physical planning issues of accommodating the displaced populations within the host community or within temporary settlements?

▶ What are the local environmental concerns regarding the local sourcing of construction materials?

▶ What are the local environmental concerns regarding the needs of the displaced population for fuel, sanitation, waste disposal, grazing for animals, if appropriate, etc.?

2 Non-food items

Non-food item needs

▶ What are the critical non-food items required by the affected population?

▶ Can any of the required non-food items be obtained locally?

▶ Is the use of cash or vouchers possible?

▶ Will technical assistance be required to complement the provision of shelter support items?

Clothing and bedding

▶ What type of clothing, blankets and bedding are typically used by women, men, children and infants, pregnant and lactating women and older people, and what are the particular social and cultural considerations?

▶ How many women and men of all ages, children and infants have inadequate or insufficient clothing, blankets or bedding to provide protection from the adverse effects of the climate and to maintain their health, dignity and well-being?

▶ What are the potential risks to the lives, health and personal safety of the affected population through the need for adequate clothing, blankets or bedding?

▶ What vector-control measures, particularly the provision of mosquito nets, are required to ensure the health and well-being of households?

Cooking and eating, stoves and fuel

▶ What cooking and eating utensils did a typical household have access to before the disaster?

▶ How many households do not have access to sufficient cooking and eating utensils?

▶ How did affected populations typically cook and heat their dwellings before the disaster and where did the cooking take place?

▶ What fuel was typically used for cooking and heating before the disaster and where was this obtained?

▶ How many households do not have access to a stove for cooking and heating, and why?

▶ How many households do not have access to adequate supplies of fuel for cooking and heating?

▶ What are the opportunities and constraints, in particular the natural environmental concerns, of sourcing adequate supplies of fuel for the disaster-affected and neighbouring populations?

▶ What is the impact on the disaster-affected population, and in particular women of all ages, of sourcing adequate supplies of fuel?

▶ What cultural issues regarding cooking and eating should be taken into account?

Tools and equipment

▶ What basic tools to repair, construct or maintain a shelter do the households have access to?

▶ What livelihood support activities can also utilise the basic tools for construction, maintenance and debris removal?

▶ What training or awareness-raising activities are required to enable the safe use of tools?

References and further reading

International legal instruments

The Right to Adequate Housing (Article 11 (1) Covenant on Economic, Social and Cultural Rights), CECSR General Comment 4, 12 December 1991. Committee on Economic, Social and Cultural Rights.

Convention on the Elimination of All Forms of Discrimination Against Women (1981); Article 14(2)(h).

Convention on the Rights of the Child (1990); Article 27(3).

International Convention on the Elimination of All Forms of Racial Discrimination (1969); Article 5(e)(iii).

International Convention Relating to the Status of Refugees (1954); Article 21.

Universal Declaration of Human Rights (1948); Article 25.

General

Corsellis, T and Vitale, A (2005), Transitional Settlement: Displaced Populations. Oxfam. Oxford.

Davis, J and Lambert, R (2002), Engineering in Emergencies: A Practical Guide for Relief Workers. RedR/IT Publications. London.

Inter-Agency Network for Education in Emergencies (INEE) (2010), Minimum Standards for Education: Preparedness, Response, Recovery. New York. www. ineesite.org

Inter-Agency Standing Committee (IASC) (2008), Shelter Projects 2008. IASC Emergency Shelter Cluster. Geneva.

International Federation of Red Cross and Red Crescent Societies (IFRC) (2010), Owner-Driven Housing Reconstruction Guidelines. Geneva.

IFRC and United Nations Human Settlements Programme (UN-Habitat) (2010), Shelter Projects 2009. IFRC. Geneva.

OCHA (2010), Shelter after disaster: strategies for transitional settlement and reconstruction. Geneva.

ProVention Consortium (2007), Tools for Mainstreaming Disaster Risk Reduction: Construction Design, Building Standards and Site Selection, Guidance Note 12. Geneva.

United Nations Disaster Relief Organization (UNDRO) (1982), Shelter After Disaster: Guidelines for Assistance. Geneva.

UNHCR (2007), Handbook for Emergencies. Third Edition. Geneva.

United Nations Office for the Coordination of Humanitarian Affairs (OCHA), UN Refugee Agency (UNHCR), Office of the UN High Commissioner for Human Rights (OHCHR), Food and Agriculture Organization of the UN (FAO), Norwegian Refugee Council (NRC) (2006), Handbook on the Implementation of the UN Principles on Housing and Property Restitution Rights for Refugees and Displaced Persons (The 'Pinheiro Principles').

World Bank (2010), Handbook for Post-Disaster Housing and Community Reconstruction. Washington DC.

Temporary communal settlement

CCCM Cluster (2010), Collective Centre Guidelines. UNHCR and International Organization for Migration. Geneva.

NRC (2008), Camp Management Toolkit. Oslo.

Environment

Kelly, C (2005), Guidelines for Rapid Environmental Impact Assessment in Disasters. Benfield Hazard Research Center, University College London and CARE International. London.

Kelly, C (2005), Checklist-Based Guide to Identifying Critical Environmental Considerations in Emergency Shelter Site Selection, Construction, Management and Decommissioning. ProAct Network and CARE International.

UNHCR (2002), Environmental Considerations in the Life Cycle of Refugee Camps. Geneva.

WWF and American Red Cross (2010), Green Recovery and Reconstruction Toolkit for Humanitarian Aid. Washington DC. www.worldwildlife.org/what/partners/humanitarian/green-recovery-and-reconstruction-toolkit.html

Cash, vouchers and market assessments

Albu, M (2010), The Emergency Market Mapping and Analysis Toolkit. Practical Action Publishing. Rugby, UK.

Creti, P and Jaspars, S (2006), Cash Transfer Programming in Emergencies. Oxfam. Oxford

International Committee of the Red Cross (ICRC) and IFRC (2007), Guidelines for cash transfer programming. Geneva.

Disabilities

Handicap International, Disability Checklist for Emergency Response. www.handicap-international.de/fileadmin/redaktion/pdf/disability_checklist_booklet_01.pdf

Gender

IASC (2006), Women, Girls, Boys and Men: Different Needs – Equal Opportunities: The Gender Handbook in Humanitarian Action. Geneva.

Psychosocial support

IASC (2007), Guidelines on Mental Health and Psychosocial Support in Emergency Settings. Geneva.

Schools and public buildings

UN International Strategy for Disaster Reduction, INEE, World Bank (2009), Guidance Notes on Safer School Construction.

Non-food items and emergency items

IASC Emergency Shelter Cluster (2007), Selecting NFIs for Shelter. Geneva.

IASC Task Force on Safe Access to Firewood and Alternative Energy in humanitarian settings (2009), Decision Tree Diagrams on Factors Affecting Choice of Fuel Strategy in Humanitarian Settings. Geneva.

ICRC and IFRC (2009), Emergency Items Catalogue. Third Edition. Geneva.

IFRC and Oxfam International (2007), Plastic Sheeting: a guide to the specification and use of plastic sheeting in humanitarian relief. Oxford.

Inter-Agency Procurement Services Offices (2000), Emergency Relief Items: Compendium of Generic Specifications. Vols 1 and 2. United Nations Development Programme. New York.

OCHA (2004), Tents: A Guide to the Use and Logistics of Family Tents in Humanitarian Relief. Geneva.

Minimum Standards in Health Action

How to use this chapter

This chapter is divided into two main sections:

> Health systems
>
> Essential health services

A health systems approach to the design, implementation, monitoring and evaluation of health services is adopted as a framework for organising health services during disaster response. This is the best approach to ensure that priority health needs are identified and met in an efficient and effective manner. Principles such as supporting national and local health systems, coordination and standardisation of tools and approaches are stressed throughout.

The Protection Principles and Core Standards must be used consistently with this chapter.

Although primarily intended to inform humanitarian response to a disaster, the minimum standards may also be considered during disaster preparedness.

Each section contains the following:

- **Minimum standards:** These are qualitative in nature and specify the minimum levels to be attained in disaster response regarding the provision of health services.

- **Key actions:** These are suggested activities and inputs to help meet the standards.

- **Key indicators:** These are 'signals' that show whether a standard has been attained. They provide a way of measuring and communicating the processes and results of key actions; they relate to the minimum standard, not to the key action.

- **Guidance notes:** These include specific points to consider when applying the minimum standards, key actions and key indicators in different situations. They provide guidance on tackling practical difficulties, benchmarks or advice on priority issues. They may also include critical issues relating to the standards, actions or indicators, and describe dilemmas, controversies or gaps in current knowledge.

If the required key actions and indicators cannot be met, the resulting adverse implications on the affected population should be appraised and appropriate mitigating actions taken.

Appendices at the end of the chapter include a checklist for health service assessments, sample surveillance reporting forms and formulas for calculating key health indicators. A references and further reading section is also provided.

Contents

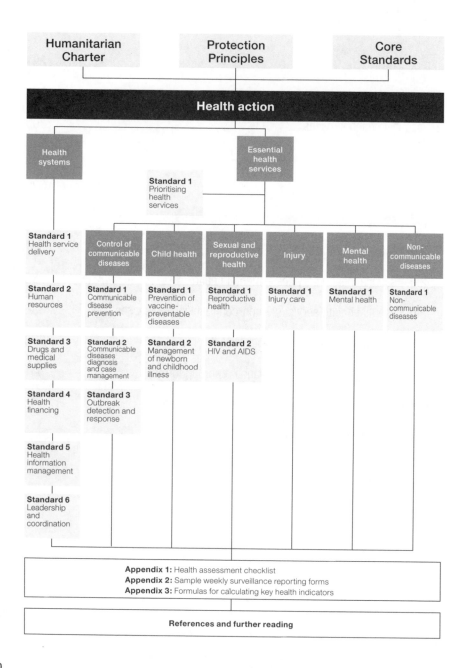

Introduction

Links to the Humanitarian Charter and international law

The minimum standards in health action are a practical expression of the shared beliefs and commitments of humanitarian agencies and the common principles, rights and duties governing humanitarian action that are set out in the Humanitarian Charter. Founded on the principle of humanity, and reflected in international law, these principles include the right to life with dignity, the right to protection and security, and the right to receive humanitarian assistance on the basis of need. A list of key legal and policy documents that inform the Humanitarian Charter is available for reference in Annex 1 (see page 356), with explanatory comments for humanitarian workers.

Although states are the main duty-bearers with respect to the rights set out above, humanitarian agencies have a responsibility to work with disaster-affected populations in a way that is consistent with these rights. From these general rights flow a number of more specific entitlements. These include the rights to participation, information and non-discrimination, as well the specific rights to water, food, shelter and health that underpin these and the minimum standards in this Handbook.

Everyone has the right to health, as enshrined in a number of international legal instruments. The right to health can be assured only if the population is protected, if the professionals responsible for the health system are well trained and committed to universal ethical principles and professional standards, if the system in which they work is designed to meet minimum standards of need, and if the state is willing and able to establish and secure these conditions of safety and stability. In times of armed conflict, civilian hospitals and medical facilities may in no circumstances be the object of attack, and health and medical staff have the right to be protected. The carrying-out of acts or activities that jeopardise the neutrality of health facilities, such as carrying arms, is prohibited.

The minimum standards in this chapter are not a full expression of the right to health. However, the Sphere standards reflect the core content of the right to health, especially during emergencies, and contribute to the progressive realisation of this right globally.

The importance of health action in disasters

Access to healthcare is a critical determinant for survival in the initial stages of disaster. Disasters almost always have significant impacts on the public health and well-being of affected populations. The public health impacts may be described as direct (e.g. death from violence and injury) or indirect (e.g. increased rates of infectious diseases and/or malnutrition). These indirect health impacts are usually related to factors such as inadequate quantity and quality of water, breakdowns in sanitation, disruption of or reduced access to health services and deterioration of food security. Lack of security, movement constraints, population displacement and worsened living conditions (overcrowding and inadequate shelter) can also pose public health threats. Climate change is potentially increasing vulnerability and risk.

The primary goals of humanitarian response to humanitarian crises are to prevent and reduce excess mortality and morbidity. The main aim is to maintain the crude mortality rate (CMR) and under-5 mortality rate (U5MR) at, or reduce to, less than double the baseline rate documented for the population prior to the disaster (see table on baseline reference mortality data by region on page 311). Different types of disaster are associated with differing scales and patterns of mortality and morbidity (see table on public health impact of selected disasters opposite), and the health needs of an affected population will therefore vary according to the type and extent of the disaster.

The contribution from the health sector is to provide essential health services, including preventive and promotive interventions that are effective in reducing health risks. Essential health services are priority health interventions that are effective in addressing the major causes of excess mortality and morbidity. The implementation of essential health services must be supported by actions to strengthen the health system. The way health interventions are planned, organised and delivered in response to a disaster can either enhance or undermine the existing health systems and their future recovery and development.

An analysis of the existing health system is needed to determine the system's level of performance and to identify the major constraints to the delivery of, and access to, health services. In the early stages of a disaster, information may be incomplete and important public health decisions may have to be made without all of the relevant data being available. A multi-sectoral assessment should be conducted as soon as possible (see Core Standard 3 on page 61).

Better response is achieved through better preparedness. Preparedness is based on an analysis of risks and is well linked to early warning systems. Preparedness includes contingency planning, stockpiling of equipment and supplies, establishment and/or maintenance of emergency services and stand-by arrangements, communications, information management and coordination arrangements, personnel training, community-level planning, drills and exercises. The enforcement of building codes can dramatically reduce the number of deaths and serious injuries associated with earthquakes and/or ensure that health facilities remain functional after disasters.

Public health impact of selected disasters

NB: Even for specific types of disaster, the patterns of morbidity and mortality vary significantly from context to context.

Effect	Complex emergencies	Earthquakes	High winds (without flooding)	Floods	Flash floods/ tsunamis
Deaths	Many	Many	Few	Few	Many
Severe injuries	Varies	Many	Moderate	Few	Few
Increased risk of communicable diseases	High	Varies*	Small	Varies*	Varies*
Food scarcity	Common	Rare	Rare	Varies	Common
Major population displacements	Common	Rare (may occur in heavily damaged urban areas)	Rare (may occur in heavily damaged urban areas)	Common	Varies

* Depends on post-disaster displacement and living conditions of the population
Source: Adapted from Pan American Health Organization, 2000

Links to other chapters

Because of the impacts of the different determinants of health on health status, many of the standards in the other chapters are relevant to this chapter. Progress in achieving standards in one area often influences and even determines progress in other areas. For a disaster response to be effective, close coordination and collaboration are required with other sectors. Coordination with local authorities, other responding agencies and community-based organisations is also necessary to ensure that needs are met, that efforts are not duplicated and that the use of resources is optimised and the quality of health services is adequate. Reference to specific standards or guidance notes in other technical chapters is made where relevant. Reference is also made to companion and complementary standards.

Links to the Protection Principles and Core Standards

In order to meet the standards of this Handbook, all humanitarian agencies should be guided by the Protection Principles, even if they do not have a distinct protection mandate or specialist capacity in protection. The Principles are not 'absolute': it is recognised that circumstances may limit the extent to which agencies are able to fulfil them. Nevertheless, the Principles reflect universal humanitarian concerns which should guide action at all times.

The Core Standards are essential process and personnel standards shared by all sectors. The six Core Standards cover participation, initial assessment, response, targeting, monitoring, evaluation, aid worker performance, and supervision and support to personnel. They provide a single reference point for approaches that underpin all other standards in the Handbook. Each technical chapter, therefore, requires the companion use of the Core Standards to help attain its own standards. In particular, to ensure the appropriateness and quality of any response, the participation of disaster-affected people – including the groups and individuals most frequently at risk in disasters – should be maximised.

Vulnerabilities and capacities of disaster-affected populations

This section is designed to be read in conjunction with, and to reinforce, the Core Standards.

It is important to understand that to be young or old, a woman, or a person with a disability or HIV, does not, of itself, make a person vulnerable or at increased risk. Rather it is the interplay of factors that does so: for example, someone who is over 70 years of age, lives alone and has poor health is likely to be more vulnerable than someone of a similar age and health status living within an extended family and with sufficient income. Similarly, a 3-year-old girl is much more vulnerable if she is unaccompanied than if she were living in the care of responsible parents.

As the health action standards and key actions are implemented, a vulnerability and capacity analysis helps to ensure that a disaster response effort supports those who have a right to assistance in a non-discriminatory manner and who need it most. This requires a thorough understanding of the local context and of how a particular disaster impacts on particular groups of people in different ways due to their pre-existing vulnerabilities (e.g. being very poor or discriminated against), their exposure to various protection threats (e.g. gender-based violence including sexual exploitation), disease incidence or prevalence (e.g. HIV or tuberculosis) and possibilities of epidemics (e.g. measles or cholera). Disasters can make pre-existing inequalities worse. However, support for people's coping strategies, resilience and recovery capacities is essential. Their knowledge, skills and strategies need to be supported and their access to social, legal, financial and psychosocial support advocated for. The various physical, cultural, economic and social barriers they may face in accessing these services in an equitable manner also need to be addressed.

The following highlight some of the key areas that will ensure that the rights and capacities of all vulnerable people are considered:

▶ Optimise people's participation, ensuring that all representative groups are included, especially those who are less visible (e.g. persons who have communication or mobility difficulties, those living in institutions, stigmatised youth and other under- or unrepresented groups).

▶ Disaggregate data by sex and age (0–80+ years) during assessment as an important element in ensuring that the health sector adequately considers the diversity of populations.

▶ Ensure that the right to information on entitlements is communicated in a way that is inclusive and accessible to all members of the population.

The minimum standards

1. Health systems

The World Health Organization (WHO) defines health systems as: "all the organizations, institutions and resources that are devoted to producing health actions". It includes the full range of players engaged in the provision, financing and management of health services, efforts to influence determinants of health as well as providing direct health services, and encompassing all levels: central, regional, district, community and household.

The health system standards of Sphere are organised according to the WHO health system framework, consisting of six building blocks: leadership, human resources, drugs and medical supplies, health financing, health information management and service delivery. There are many interconnections and interactions between each of these functions and an action affecting one component can affect the others. These health system building blocks are the functions that are required to deliver essential health services. Health interventions during disaster response should be designed and implemented in a way that contributes to strengthening health systems.

Health systems standard 1: Health service delivery

People have equal access to effective, safe and quality health services that are standardised and follow accepted protocols and guidelines.

Key actions (to be read in conjunction with the guidance notes)

▶ Provide health services at the appropriate level of the health system. Levels include household and community, clinic or health post, health centre and hospital (see guidance note 1).

▶ Adapt or establish standardised case management protocols for the most common diseases, taking account of national standards and guidelines (see guidance note 2).

▶ Establish or strengthen a standardised referral system and ensure it is utilised by all agencies (see guidance note 1).

▶ Establish or strengthen a standardised system of triage at all health facilities to ensure those with emergency signs receive immediate treatment.

▶ Initiate health education and promotion at community and health facility levels (see guidance note 3).

▶ Establish and follow safe and rational use of blood supply and blood products (see guidance note 5).

▶ Ensure that laboratory services are available and used when indicated (see guidance note 6).

▶ Avoid the establishment of alternative or parallel health services, including mobile clinics and field hospitals (see guidance notes 7–8).

▶ Design health services in a manner that ensures patients' rights to privacy, confidentiality and informed consent (see guidance note 9).

▶ Implement appropriate waste management procedures, safety measures and infection control methods in health facilities (see guidance notes 10–11 and Solid waste management standard 1 on page 117).

▶ Dispose of dead bodies in a manner that is dignified, culturally appropriate and based on good public health practice (see guidance note 12 and Solid waste management standard 1, guidance note 8 on page 120).

Key indicators (to be read in conjunction with the guidance notes)

▶ There are an adequate number of health facilities to meet the essential health needs of all the disaster-affected population:

- one basic health unit/10,000 population (basic health units are primary healthcare facilities where general health services are offered)
- one health centre/50,000 people
- one district or rural hospital/250,000 people
- >10 inpatient and maternity beds/10,000 people
(see guidance note 1).

▶ Utilisation rates at health facilities are 2–4 new consultations/person/year among the disaster-affected population and >1 new consultations/person/year among rural and dispersed populations (see guidance note 4 and Appendix 3: Formulas for calculating key health indicators).

Guidance notes

1. ***Level of care:*** Health facilities are categorised by level of care according to their size and the services provided. The number and location of health facilities required can vary from context to context.

Health systems must also develop a process for continuity of care. This is best achieved by establishing an effective referral system, especially for life-saving interventions. The referral system should function 24 hours a day, seven days a week.

2. **National standards and guidelines:** In general, agencies should adhere to the health standards and guidelines of the country where the disaster response is being implemented, including treatment protocols and essential medicines lists. When they are outdated or do not reflect evidence-based practice, international standards should be used as reference and the lead agency for the health sector should support the Ministry of Health (MOH) to update them.

3. **Health promotion:** An active programme of community health promotion should be initiated in consultation with local health authorities and community representatives, ensuring a balanced representation of women and men. The programme should provide information on the major health problems, health risks, the availability and location of health services and behaviours that protect and promote good health, and address and discourage harmful practices. Public health messages and materials should utilise appropriate language and media, be culturally sensitive and easy to understand. Schools and child-friendly spaces are important venues for spreading information and reaching out to children and parents (see INEE Minimum Standards for Education – access and learning environment standard 3).

4. **Utilisation rate of health services:** There is no minimum threshold figure for the use of health services, as this will vary from context to context. Among stable rural and dispersed populations, utilisation rates should be at least 1 new consultation/person/year. Among disaster-affected populations, an average of 2–4 new consultations/person/year may be expected. If the rate is lower than expected, it may indicate inadequate access to health services. If the rate is higher, it may suggest over-utilisation due to a specific public health problem or under-estimation of the target population. In analysing utilisation rates, consideration should ideally also be given to utilisation by sex, age, ethnic origin and disability (see Appendix 3: Formulas for calculating key health indicators).

5. **Safe blood transfusion:** Efforts should be coordinated with the national blood transfusion service (BTS), if one exists. Collection of blood should only be from voluntary non-remunerated blood donors. Good laboratory practice should be established, including screening for transfusion-transmissible infections, blood grouping, compatibility testing, blood component production and the storage and transportation of blood products. Unnecessary transfusions can be reduced through the effective clinical use of blood, including the use of alternatives to transfusion (crystalloids and colloids), wherever possible. Appropriate clinical staff should be trained to ensure the provision of safe blood and its effective clinical use.

6. **Laboratory services:** The most common communicable diseases can be diagnosed clinically (e.g. diarrhoea, acute respiratory infections) or with the assistance of rapid diagnostic tests or microscopy (e.g. malaria). Laboratory testing is most useful for confirming the cause of a suspected outbreak, testing for culture and antibiotic sensitivity to assist case management decisions (e.g. dysentery) and selecting vaccines where mass immunisation may be indicated (e.g. meningococcal meningitis). For certain non-communicable diseases, such as diabetes, laboratory testing is essential for diagnosis and treatment.

7. **Mobile clinics:** During some disasters, it may be necessary to operate mobile clinics in order to meet the needs of isolated or mobile populations who have limited access to healthcare. Mobile clinics have also been proven crucial in increasing access to treatment in outbreaks where a large number of cases are expected, such as malaria outbreaks. Mobile clinics should be introduced only after consultation with the lead agency for the health sector and with local authorities (see Health systems standard 6 on page 307).

8. **Field hospitals:** Occasionally, field hospitals may be the only way to provide healthcare when existing hospitals are severely damaged or destroyed. However, it is usually more effective to provide resources to existing hospitals so that they can start working again or cope with the extra load. It may be appropriate to deploy a field hospital for the immediate care of traumatic injuries (first 48 hours), secondary care of traumatic injuries and routine surgical and obstetrical emergencies (days 3–15) or as a temporary facility to substitute for a damaged local hospital until it is reconstructed. Because field hospitals are highly visible, there is often substantial political pressure from donor governments to deploy them. However, it is important to make the decision to deploy field hospitals based solely on need and value added.

9. **Patients' rights:** Health facilities and services should be designed in a manner that ensures privacy and confidentiality. Informed consent should be sought from patients (or their guardians if they are not competent to do so), prior to medical or surgical procedures. Health staff should understand that patients have a right to know what each procedure involves, as well as its expected benefits, potential risks, costs and duration.

10. **Infection control in healthcare settings and patient safety:** For an effective response during disasters, continuing infection prevention and control (IPC) programmes should be enforced at both national and peripheral levels, and at the various healthcare facility levels. Such an IPC programme at a healthcare facility should include:

    - defined IPC policies (e.g. routine and additional infection control measures to address potential threats)

- qualified, dedicated technical staff (IPC team) to run infection control programme with a defined scope, function and responsibility
- early warning surveillance system for detection of communicable disease outbreaks
- defined budget for activities (e.g. training of staff) and supplies in response to an emergency
- reinforced standard precautions and additional specific precautions defined for an epidemic disease
- administrative controls (e.g. isolation policies) and environmental and engineering controls (e.g. improving environmental ventilation)
- personal protective equipment used
- IPC practices monitored and recommendations reviewed regularly.

11. **Healthcare waste:** Hazardous waste generated in healthcare facilities can be segregated into infectious non-sharp waste, sharps and non-infectious common wastes. Poor management of healthcare waste potentially exposes health staff, cleaners, waste handlers, patients and others in the community to infections such as HIV and hepatitis B and C. Proper separation at the point of origin of the waste through to final category specific disposal procedures must be implemented in order to minimise the risk of infection. The personnel assigned to handle healthcare waste should be properly trained and should wear protective equipment (gloves and boots are minimum requirements). Treatment should be done according to the type of waste: for example, infectious non-sharp waste as well as sharps should be either disposed of in protected pits or incinerated.

12. **Handling the remains of the dead:** When disasters result in high mortality, the management of a large number of dead bodies will be required. Burial of large numbers of human remains in mass graves is often based on the false belief that they represent a health risk if not buried or burned immediately. In only a few special cases (e.g. deaths resulting from cholera or haemorrhagic fevers) do human remains pose health risks and require specific precautions.Bodies should not be disposed of unceremoniously in mass graves. People should have the opportunity to identify their family members and to conduct culturally appropriate funerals. Mass burial may be a barrier to obtaining death certificates necessary for making legal claims. When those being buried are victims of violence, forensic issues should be considered (see Shelter and settlement standard 2, guidance note 3 on page 255).

Health systems standard 2: Human resources

Health services are provided by trained and competent health work-forces who have an adequate mix of knowledge and skills to meet the health needs of the population.

Key actions (to be read in conjunction with the guidance notes)

▶ Review staffing levels and capacity as a key component of the baseline health assessment.

▶ Address imbalances in the number of staff, their mix of skills and gender and/or ethnic ratios where possible (see guidance note 1).

▶ Support local health workers and integrate them fully into health services, taking account of their competence (see guidance note 1).

▶ Ensure adequate ancillary workers for support functions in each health facility.

▶ Train clinical staff in the use of clinical protocols and guidelines (see guidance note 2).

▶ Provide supportive supervision to staff on a regular basis to ensure their compliance with standards and guidelines, including provision of feedback.

▶ Standardise training programmes and prioritise them according to key health needs and competence gaps.

▶ Ensure fair and reliable remuneration for all health workers, agreed between all agencies and in collaboration with the national health authorities.

▶ Ensure a safe working environment, including basic hygiene and protection for all health workers.

Key indicators (to be read in conjunction with the guidance notes)

▶ There are at least 22 qualified health workers (medical doctors, nurses and midwifes)/10,000 population (see guidance note 1):

  - at least one medical doctor/50,000 population
  - at least one qualified nurse/10,000 population
  - at least one midwife/10,000 population.

▶ There is at least one Community Health Worker (CHW)/1,000 population, one supervisor/10 home visitors and one senior supervisor.

▶ Clinicians are not required to consult more than 50 patients a day consistently. If this threshold is regularly exceeded, additional clinical staff are recruited (see guidance note 1 and Appendix 3: Formulas for calculating key health indicators).

Guidance notes

1. **Staffing levels:** The health workforce includes a wide range of health workers including medical doctors, nurses, midwives, clinical officers or physician assistants, lab technicians, pharmacists, CHWs, etc., as well as management and support staff. There is no consensus about an optimal level of health workers for a population and this can vary from context to context. However, there is correlation between the availability of health workers and coverage of health interventions. For example, the presence of just one female health worker or one representative of a marginalised ethnic group on a staff may significantly increase the access of women or people from minority groups to health services. Imbalance in staffing must be addressed through the redeployment and/or recruitment of health workers to areas where there are critical gaps in relation to health needs (see Core Standard 6 on page 71).

2. **Training and supervision of staff:** Health workers should have the proper training, skills and supervisory support for their level of responsibility. Agencies have an obligation to train and supervise staff to ensure that their knowledge is up-to-date. Training and supervision will be high priorities especially where staff have not received continuing education or where new protocols are introduced. As far as possible, training programmes should be standardised and prioritised according to key health needs and competence gaps identified through supervision. Records should be maintained of who has been trained in what by whom, when and where. These should be shared with the human resources section of the local health authorities (see Core Standard 6 on page 71).

Health systems standard 3: Drugs and medical supplies

People have access to a consistent supply of essential medicines and consumables.

Key actions (to be read in conjunction with the guidance notes)

▶ Review the existing lists of essential medicines of the disaster-affected country early in the response to determine their appropriateness (see guidance note 1).

▶ Establish and endorse a standardised essential medicines and medical equipment list that contains items appropriate for the health needs and the competence level of health workers (see guidance notes 1–2).

▶ Establish or adapt an effective medicines management system (see guidance note 3).

▶ Ensure essential medicines for the treatment of common illnesses are available.

▶ Accept donations of medicine only if they follow internationally recognised guidelines. Do not use donations that do not follow these guidelines and dispose of them safely.

Key indicator (to be read in conjunction with the guidance notes)

▶ No health facility is out of stock of selected essential medicines and tracer products for more than one week (see guidance note 4).

Guidance notes

1. **Essential medicines list:** Most countries have an established essential medicines list. This document should be reviewed, when necessary, in consultation with the lead health authority early in the disaster response to determine its appropriateness. Occasionally, alterations to essential medicines lists may be necessary, e.g. if there is evidence of resistance to recommended antimicrobials. If an updated list does not already exist, guidelines established by WHO should be followed, e.g. the WHO Model Lists of Essential Medicines. The use of standard pre-packaged kits should be limited to the early phases of a disaster.

2. **Medical equipment:** Care should be taken in defining a list of the necessary equipment available at different healthcare levels. This should also be linked to the required competency of the staff.

3. **Drug management:** Health agencies need to establish an effective system of drug management. The goal of such a system is to ensure the efficient, cost-effective and rational use of quality medicines, storage and correct disposal of expired medicines. This system should be based on the four key elements of the medicines management cycle: selection, procurement, distribution and use.

4. **Tracer products:** These include a list of essential or key medicines that are selected to regularly evaluate the functioning of the drug management system. The items to be selected as tracer products should be relevant to local public health priorities and should be available at all times at the health facilities. Examples include amoxicillin and paracetamol.

Health systems standard 4: Health financing

People have access to free primary healthcare services for the duration of the disaster.

Key actions (to be read in conjunction with the guidance notes)

▶ Identify and mobilise financial resources for providing free health services at the point of delivery to the affected population for the duration of the disaster (see guidance note 1).

▶ Where user fees are charged through the government system, make arrangements for their abolition or temporary suspension for the duration of the disaster response (see guidance note 2).

▶ Provide financial and technical support to the health system to cover any financial gaps created by the abolition and/or suspension of user fees and to cope with the increased demand for health services (see guidance note 1).

Key indicator (to be read in conjunction with the guidance notes)

▶ Primary healthcare services are provided to the disaster-affected population free of charge at all government and non-governmental organisation facilities for the duration of the disaster response.

Guidance notes

1. **Health financing:** The cost of providing essential health services varies according to the context. Such a context includes the existing health system, the population affected by the disaster and the specific health needs determined by the disaster. According to the WHO Commission on Macroeconomics and Health, providing a minimum package of essential health services would require expenditure of at least US$ 40/person/year in low-income countries (2008 figures). Providing health services in disaster settings is likely to incur higher costs than in stable settings.

2. **User fees** refer to direct payments by beneficiaries at the point of service delivery. User fees impede access to healthcare and result in poor and vulnerable people not always seeking appropriate healthcare when it is needed. A basic humanitarian principle is that services and goods provided by aid agencies should be free of charge to recipients. In contexts where this is not possible, providing members of the affected population with cash and/or vouchers can be considered to enable access to health services (see Food security – cash and voucher transfers standard 1 on page 200). Removal of

user fees must be accompanied by other measures to support the health system to compensate for the revenue forgone and increase use (e.g. paying incentives to health staff, providing additional supplies of medicine). The accessibility and quality of services must be monitored after the removal of user fees.

Health systems standard 5: Health information management

The design and delivery of health services are guided by the collection, analysis, interpretation and utilisation of relevant public health data.

Key actions (to be read in conjunction with the guidance notes)

▶ Decide on the use of the existing health information system (HIS), its adaptation or the use of alternative HIS (see guidance note 1).

▶ When relevant, conduct assessments and surveys to collect information that is not available from the HIS and is critical for deciding on priority health services (see guidance note 2).

▶ Develop and/or utilise standardised case definitions for all reportable diseases and health conditions and ensure they are used by all agencies.

▶ Design surveillance and early warning (EWARN) systems for detection of outbreaks as a component of the HIS and build upon existing HIS whenever possible (see Essential health services – control of communicable diseases standard 3 on page 316 and Appendix 2: Sample weekly surveillance reporting forms).

▶ Identify and report priority diseases and health conditions through the HIS.

▶ All responding agencies agree upon and use a common figure, such as population (see guidance note 3).

▶ Health facilities and agencies submit surveillance and other HIS data to the lead agency on a regular basis. The frequency of these reports will vary according to the context and to the type of data, e.g. daily, weekly, monthly.

▶ Use supplementary data consistently from other relevant sources, such as surveys, to interpret surveillance data and to guide decision-making (see guidance note 2).

▶ Take adequate precautions for the protection of data to guarantee the rights and safety of individuals and/or populations (see guidance note 4).

ndicators (to be read in conjunction with the guidance notes)

All health facilities and agencies regularly provide a HIS report within 48 hours of the end of the reporting period to the lead agency.

▶ All health facilities and agencies report cases of epidemic-prone diseases within 24 hours of onset of illness (see Essential health services – control of communicable diseases standard 3 on page 316).

▶ The lead agency produces a regular overall health information report, including analysis and interpretation of epidemiological data, as well as a report on the coverage and utilisation of the health services.

Guidance notes

1. *Health information system:* A surveillance system should build upon the existing HIS whenever possible. In some disasters, a new or parallel HIS may be required. This is determined by an assessment of the performance and adequacy of the existing HIS and the information needs for the current disaster. During the disaster response, health data should include, but not be limited to, the following:

   - deaths recorded by health facilities including under-5 deaths
   - proportional mortality
   - cause-specific mortality
   - incidence rates for most common morbidities
   - proportional morbidity
   - health facility utilisation rate
   - number of consultations/clinician/day.

2. *Sources of data:* The interpretation and use of health facility data need to take into account the source of the information and its limitations. The use of supplemental data for decision-making is essential in a comprehensive HIS, for example estimates of prevalence of diseases or information on health-seeking behaviour. Other sources of data that may improve the analysis include population-based surveys, laboratory reports and quality of service measurements. Surveys and assessment must follow internationally recog-nised quality criteria and use standardised tools and protocols and, where possible, be submitted to a peer-review process.

3. *Disaggregation of data:* Data should be disaggregated by sex, age, vulner-ability of particular individuals, affected and host populations, and context (e.g. camp versus non-camp situation) as far as is practical to guide decision-making. Detailed disaggregation may be difficult during the early stages of an emergency. However, mortality and morbidity data should at least be disag-gregated for children under 5 years old. As time and conditions allow, more

detailed disaggregation should be sought to help detect potential inequalities and vulnerable people (see Core Standard 3 on page 61).

4. **Confidentiality:** Adequate precautions should be taken to protect the safety of the individual, as well as the data itself. Staff members should never share patient information with anyone not directly involved in the patient's care without the patient's permission. Special consideration should be given to persons with intellectual, mental or sensory impairment, which may compromise their ability to give informed consent. Data that relate to injury caused by torture or other human rights violations including sexual assault must be treated with the utmost care. Consideration may be given to passing on this information to appropriate actors or institutions if the individual gives their informed consent (see Health systems standard 1 on page 296 and Protection Principle 1, guidance notes 7–12 on page 35).

See Appendix 2 for sample mortality, EWARN and morbidity monitoring forms. See Appendix 3 for formulas for calculating key health indicators.

Health systems standard 6: Leadership and coordination

People have access to health services that are coordinated across agencies and sectors to achieve maximum impact.

Key actions (to be read in conjunction with the guidance notes)

▶ Ensure that representatives of the Ministry of Health lead or at the very least are closely involved in the health sector coordination, whenever possible.

▶ When the MOH lacks the necessary capacity or willingness to provide leadership in the response, an alternate agency with the requisite capacity must be identified to take the lead in health sector coordination (see guidance notes 1–2).

▶ Hold regular health coordination meetings for local and external partners at central, sub-national and field levels within the health sector, and between health and other sectors and appropriate cross-cutting theme groups (see guidance note 3 and Core Standard 2 on page 58).

▶ Clarify and document the specific responsibilities and capacities of each health agency to ensure optimal coverage of the population (see guidance note 1).

▶ Establish working groups within the health coordination mechanism whenever a particular situation may require it (e.g. outbreak preparedness and response, reproductive health).

▶ Regularly produce and disseminate updates and health sector bulletins.

Key indicator (to be read in conjunction with the guidance notes)

▶ The lead agency has developed a health sector response strategy document to prioritise interventions and define the role of the lead and partner agencies at the onset of emergency response (see guidance note 2).

Guidance notes

1. ***Lead health agency:*** The Ministry of Health should be the lead health agency and be responsible for leading the health sector response. In some situations, the MOH may lack capacity or willingness to assume the leadership role in an effective and impartial manner. In this situation, WHO, as a lead agency for the global health cluster, will generally take on this responsibility. On occasion, when both the MOH and WHO lack capacity, another agency may be required to coordinate activities. The lead health agency should ensure that responding health agencies coordinate with local health authorities and that they support the capacities of local health systems (see Core Standard 2 on page 58).

2. ***Health sector strategy:*** An important responsibility of the lead health agency is to develop an overall strategy for the emergency response within the health sector. Ideally, a document should be produced that specifies health sector priorities and objectives and outlines the strategies for achieving them. This document should be developed after consultation with relevant agencies and community representatives ensuring as inclusive a process as possible.

3. ***Coordination meetings*** should be action-oriented and provide a forum in which information is shared, priorities are identified and monitored, common health strategies are developed and adapted, specific tasks are allocated and standardised protocols and interventions are agreed upon. They should be used to ensure that all health partners use common denominators and other relevant figures, tools, guidelines and standards, whenever possible. Meetings should be held more frequently at the beginning of the disaster.

2. Essential health services

Essential health services are preventive and curative health services that are appropriate to address the health needs of populations affected by disasters. They include interventions that are most effective in preventing and reducing excess morbidity and mortality from communicable and non-communicable diseases, the consequences of conflict and mass casualty events. During disasters, death rates can be extremely high and identification of the major causes of morbidity and mortality is important for the design of appropriate essential health services. This part of the health chapter outlines the essential health service standards categorised under six sections: control of communicable diseases; child health; sexual and reproductive health; injury; mental health; and non-communicable diseases.

Essential health services standard 1: Prioritising health services

People have access to health services that are prioritised to address the main causes of excess mortality and morbidity.

Key actions (to be read in conjunction with the guidance notes)

▶ Collect and analyse data on health problems and risks with the aim of targeting the major causes of excess mortality and morbidity, in coordination with local health authorities (see Core Standard 3 on page 61).

▶ Identify vulnerable people (e.g. women, children, older people, persons with disabilities, etc.) who may be at particular risk (see Protection Principle 2 on page 36).

▶ Prioritise and implement health services that are appropriate, feasible and effective to reduce excess morbidity and mortality, in coordination with local health authorities (see guidance note 1).

▶ Identify barriers that impede access to prioritised health services and establish practical solutions to address them (see guidance note 2).

▶ Implement priority health services in coordination with all other sectors and/or clusters and cross-cutting themes (see Core Standard 2 on page 58).

indicators (to be read in conjunction with the guidance notes)

▶ The crude mortality rate (CMR) is maintained at, or reduced to, less than double the baseline rate documented for the population prior to the disaster (see guidance note 3).

▶ The under-5 mortality rate (U5MR) is maintained at, or reduced to, less than double the baseline rate documented for the population prior to the disaster (see guidance note 3).

Guidance notes

1. **Priority health services** are essential health services that are effective in addressing the major causes of excess mortality and morbidity. They vary according to the context, including the type of disaster and its impact. As far as possible, priority health services should be based on the principle of evidence-based practice and have a demonstrated public health benefit. Once mortality rates have declined to near-baseline levels, a more comprehensive range of health services can be introduced over time (see Core Standard 4 on page 65).

2. **Access to health services** should be based on the principles of equity and impartiality, ensuring equal access according to need without any discrimination. In practice, the location and staffing of health services should be organised to ensure optimal access and coverage. The particular needs of vulnerable people should be addressed when designing health services. Barriers to access may be physical, financial, behavioural and/or cultural, as well as communication barriers. Identifying and overcoming such barriers to the access of prioritised health services are essential (see Core Standard 3 on page 61 and Protection Principle 2 on page 36).

3. **Crude mortality rate and under-5 mortality rate:** The CMR is the most useful health indicator to monitor and evaluate the severity of an emergency situation. A doubling or more of the baseline CMR indicates a significant public health emergency, requiring immediate response. When the baseline rate is unknown or of doubtful validity, agencies should aim to maintain the CMR at least below 1.0/10,000/day.

   The U5MR is a more sensitive indicator than CMR. When the baseline rate is unknown or of doubtful validity, agencies should aim to maintain the U5MR at least below 2.0/10,000/day (see Appendix 3: Formulas for calculating key health indicators).

Baseline reference mortality data by region

Region	CMR (deaths/ 10,000/ day)	CMR emergency threshold	U5MR (deaths/ 10,000/ day)	U5MR emergency threshold
Sub-Saharan Africa	0.41	0.8	1.07	2.1
Middle East and North Africa	0.16	0.3	0.27	0.5
South Asia	0.22	0.4	0.46	0.9
East Asia and Pacific	0.19	0.4	0.15	0.3
Latin America and Caribbean	0.16	0.3	0.15	0.3
Central and Eastern European region/CIS* and Baltic States	0.33	0.7	0.14	0.3
Industrialised countries	0.25	0.5	0.03	0.1
Developing countries	0.22	0.4	0.44	0.9
Least developed countries	0.33	0.7	0.82	1.7
World	0.25	0.5	0.40	0.8

* Commonwealth of Independent States
Source: UNICEF, State of the World's Children 2009 (data from 2007)

2.1. Essential health services – control of communicable diseases

Morbidity and mortality due to communicable diseases tend to increase with disasters. In many conflict-affected settings, between 60 per cent and 90 per cent of deaths have been attributed to four major infectious causes: acute respiratory infections, diarrhoea, measles and malaria where endemic. Acute malnutrition exacerbates these diseases, especially in children under 5 years of age. Outbreaks of communicable diseases are far less commonly associated with acute-onset natural disasters. When outbreaks occur, they are generally associated with risk factors such as population displacement, overcrowding, inadequate shelter, insufficient and unsafe water and inadequate sanitation.

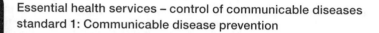

Essential health services – control of communicable diseases standard 1: Communicable disease prevention

People have access to information and services that are designed to prevent the communicable diseases that contribute most significantly to excess morbidity and mortality.

Key actions (to be read in conjunction with the guidance notes)

▶ Develop and implement general prevention measures in coordination with relevant sectors (see guidance note 1).

▶ Implement appropriate vector control methods for malaria, dengue and other vector-borne diseases depending on local epidemiology (see guidance notes 2–3).

▶ Implement disease-specific prevention measures, e.g. mass vaccination against measles as indicated (see Essential health services – child health standard 1 on page 321).

Key indicator (to be read in conjunction with the guidance notes)

▶ Incidence of major communicable diseases relevant to the context are stable (not increasing).

Guidance notes

1. *General prevention measures:* This includes good site planning, provision of clean water and proper sanitation, access to hygiene facilities, vaccination against specific diseases, sufficient and safe food supply, personal protection and vector control, and community health education and social mobilisation. Most of these intervention should be developed in coordination with other sectors, including:

   - shelter – adequate numbers of shelters and sufficient space between them, adequately ventilated, insect-proofed and sited away from standing water, close enough to water and sanitation facilities (see Shelter and settlement standards 1–3 on pages 249–258 and Non-food items standard 2 on page 271)
   - water, sanitation, hygiene – sufficient quantities of safe water and adequate sanitation facilities and hygiene promotion (see Hygiene promotion standards 1–2 on pages 91–94, Water supply standards 1–3 on pages 97–103 and Excreta disposal standards 1–2 on pages 105–107)

- environmental sanitation and safe waste management and vector control (see guidance notes 2–3, Shelter and settlement standard 4 on page 262, Vector control standards 1–3 on pages 111–116, Solid waste management standard 1 on page 117 and Drainage standard 1 on page 121)
- food security, nutrition and food assistance – access to adequate food and management of malnutrition (see Infant and young child feeding standards 1–2 on pages 159–160, Management of acute malnutrition and micronutrient deficiencies standards 1–3 on pages 165–173 and Food security standard 1 on page 176)
- health education and social mobilisation – develop messages to ensure the effective implementation of the above preventive measures.

2. *Malaria prevention:* Implement malaria prevention methods according to the risk of infection, the phase of the emergency and mobility of the population, the type of shelters and behaviour of the local vector in a malaria-endemic region. Vector control measures such as indoor residual spraying (IRS) with an effective insecticide and the distribution of long-lasting insecticide-treated nets (LLINs) should be guided by entomological assessments and expertise. To be effective as a community control measure, IRS requires coverage of at least 80 per cent of dwellings. LLINs provide long-term personal protection and are the standard net of choice. Distributions of untreated nets are not recommended (see Non-food items standard 2 on page 271 and Vector control standards 1–3 on pages 111–116).

Prioritisation for LLIN distribution to risk groups depends on the phase of the disaster and level of malaria transmission. In the early phase of disasters in areas of high to moderate malaria transmission, hospital patients, severely malnourished people and members of their households, pregnant women and children under 2 years of age should be prioritised. The next priority is those enrolled in supplementary feeding programmes, children under 5 years of age and households of pregnant women and children under 2 years of age. Eventually, the entire population at risk would require protection with LLINs. In the early phase of disasters in low transmission areas, LLINs should be used in clinical settings (for example, residential therapeutic feeding centres and hospitals).

3. *Dengue prevention:* Vector (larval and adult) control is the main method of dengue prevention. Dengue vector control should be guided by surveillance data on the distribution of human cases and vector density. The most productive breeding sites, which vary from place to place, need to be targeted. In urban areas, *Aedes* mosquitoes breed in water storage containers and other artificial water accumulation sites (plastic cups, used tyres, broken bottles, flower pots, etc.). Periodic draining and removal of containers is the most effective way of reducing the number of breeding grounds. Water stored

in houses should be covered at all times and the containers cleaned and scrubbed weekly. The disaster-affected population should be provided with proper water storage containers with lids. Treatment of containers with an approved larvicide is also effective in eliminating larvae. Spraying with insecticide is effective in reducing the number of adult mosquitoes. Personal protection measures should also be promoted (see Non-food items standard 2 on page 271 and Vector control standards 1–3 on pages 111–116).

Essential health services – control of communicable diseases standard 2: Communicable disease diagnosis and case management

People have access to effective diagnosis and treatment for those infectious diseases that contribute most significantly to preventable excess morbidity and mortality.

Key actions (to be read in conjunction with the guidance notes)

▶ Develop public health education messages to encourage people to seek care early for fever, cough, diarrhoea, etc.

▶ Provide healthcare at all first-level health facilities based upon standard case management protocol, or the Integrated Management of Childhood Illnesses (IMCI) and Integrated Management of Adult Illness (IMAI) where implemented and referral care for management of severe illness (see guidance note 1).

▶ Implement triage, diagnostic and case management protocols for early treatment of conditions such as pneumonia, malaria, diarrhoea, measles, meningitis, malnutrition and dengue and train staff on treatment protocols (see guidance notes 2–3 and Essential health services – child health standard 2 on page 323).

▶ Introduce tuberculosis control programmes only after recognised criteria are met (see guidance note 4).

Key indicator (to be read in conjunction with the guidance notes)

▶ Standardised case management protocols for the diagnosis and treatment of common infectious diseases are readily available and consistently used (see guidance notes 1–3 and Health systems standard 1 on page 296).

Guidance notes

1. *Integrated Management of Childhood Illnesses and Integrated Management of Adult Illness:* Mortality from communicable diseases can be reduced by early and accurate diagnosis and appropriate treatment. Use of IMCI and IMAI where implemented, or other national diagnostic algorithms, are important to triage and classify disease according to type and severity and to aid the administering of appropriate treatments. Danger signs are indications for referral to an inpatient facility. Standard case management protocols allow for appropriate diagnosis and rational drug use (see also Essential health services – child health standard 2 on page 323).

2. *Pneumonia:* The key to reducing mortality from pneumonia is prompt administration of oral antibiotics, such as amoxicillin, according to national protocols. Severe pneumonia will require hospitalisation and parenteral therapy.

3. *Malaria:* Access to prompt and effective treatment is key for successful malaria control. In malaria-endemic regions, establish a protocol for early (less than 24 hours) diagnosis of fever and treatment with highly effective first-line drugs. Artemisinin-based combination therapies (ACTs) are the norm for treatment of falciparum malaria. Drug choice should be determined in consultation with the lead health agency and the national malaria control programme. Consider drug quality when sourcing supplies. Malaria should preferably be diagnosed by laboratory test (rapid diagnostic test, microscopy) before treatment is started. However, treatment of clinical malaria should not be delayed if laboratory diagnosis is unavailable.

4. *Tuberculosis (TB) control:* Poorly implemented TB control programmes can potentially do more harm than good, by prolonging infectivity and by contributing to the spread of multidrug-resistant bacilli. While the management of individual patients with TB may be possible during disasters, a comprehensive programme of TB control should only be implemented if recognised criteria are met. These criteria include commitment and resources of agency, an assured stability of the population for at least 12–15 months and that a good quality programme can be delivered. When implemented, TB control programmes should be integrated with the national country programme and follow the Directly-Observed Therapy, Short-course strategy.

   In the acute phase of an emergency, the potential interruption of all treatments for all chronic diseases including TB and loss of patient follow-up are likely to be a significant problem. Strong collaboration must be established between the emergency health workers and the established national TB programme services. This will help ensure that people who were already on treatment prior to the disaster continue with their treatment (see Essential health services – non-communicable diseases standard 1 on page 336).

Essential health services – control of communicable diseases standard 3: Outbreak detection and response

Outbreaks are prepared for, detected, investigated and controlled in a timely and effective manner.

Key actions (to be read in conjunction with the guidance notes)

Detection

▶ Establish a disease EWARN (early warning) surveillance and response system based on a comprehensive risk assessment of communicable diseases, as part of the broader health information system (see guidance note 1 and Health systems standard 5 on page 305).

▶ Train healthcare staff and Community Health Workers to detect and report potential outbreaks.

▶ Provide populations with simple information on symptoms of epidemic-prone diseases and where to go for help.

Preparedness

▶ Prepare an outbreak investigation and response plan (see guidance note 2).

▶ Ensure that protocols for the investigation and control of common outbreaks, including relevant treatment protocols, are available and distributed to relevant staff.

▶ Ensure that reserve stocks of essential material are available for priority diseases or can be procured rapidly from a pre-identified source (see guidance note 3).

▶ Identify sites for isolation and treatment of infectious patients in advance, e.g. cholera treatment centres.

▶ Identify a laboratory, whether locally, regionally, nationally or in another country, that can provide confirmation of outbreaks (see guidance note 4).

▶ Ensure that sampling materials and transport media are available on-site for the infectious agents most likely to cause a sudden outbreak (see guidance note 5).

Control

▶ Describe the outbreak according to time, place and person, leading to the identification of high-risk individuals and adapted control measures (see guidance notes 6–8).

▶ Implement appropriate control measures that are specific to the disease and context (see guidance note 9).

Key indicators (to be read in conjunction with the guidance notes)

▶ A written outbreak investigation and response plan is available or developed at the beginning of disaster response.

▶ Health agencies report suspected outbreaks to the next appropriate level within the health system within 24 hours of detection.

▶ The lead health agency initiates investigation of reported cases of epidemic-prone diseases within 48 hours of notification.

▶ Case fatality rates (CFRs) are maintained below acceptable levels:

- cholera – 1 per cent or lower
- Shigella dysentery – 1 per cent or lower
- typhoid – 1 per cent or lower
- meningococcal meningitis – varies, 5–15 per cent
- malaria – varies, aim for <5 per cent in severely ill malaria patients
- measles – varies, 2–21 per cent reported in conflict-affected settings, aim for <5 per cent (see guidance note 10).

Guidance notes

1. ***Early warning system for outbreak detection:*** The key elements of such a system will include:

   - a network of implementing partners
   - implementation at all health facilities and at community level if possible
   - a comprehensive risk assessment of all potential epidemic-prone diseases
   - identification, based on risk assessment, of a small number of priority conditions (10–12) for weekly surveillance and a select number of diseases for immediate 'alert' reporting (see Appendix 2: Sample weekly surveillance reporting forms)
   - clear case definitions for each disease or condition on the standard surveillance form
   - alert thresholds defined for each priority disease or condition to initiate investigation

- communications to ensure rapid notification of formal or informal alerts (rumours, media reports, etc.) to relevant health authorities
- a system for recording and responding to immediate alerts
- data reporting, entry into standard database and analysis on a weekly basis
- feedback of weekly surveillance and immediate alert information to all partners
- regular supervision to ensure data quality as well as timeliness and completeness of reporting
- standard case investigation protocols and forms
- standard procedures for information-sharing and initiation of outbreak response.

2. **Outbreak investigation and control plan:** This must be prepared with full participation of all stakeholders. The following issues should be addressed:

- the criteria under which an outbreak control team is to be convened
- the composition of the outbreak control team
- the specific roles and responsibilities of organisations and positions in the team
- the arrangements for consulting and information-sharing at local and national levels
- the resources and facilities available to investigate and respond to outbreaks
- the list of essential medicines, supplies and diagnostics needed.

3. **Reserve stocks:** On-site reserves should include material to use in response to likely outbreaks. A pre-packaged diarrhoeal disease or cholera kit may be needed in some circumstances. It may not be practical to keep some stocks on-site, such as meningococcal vaccine. For these items, procedures for prompt procurement, shipment and storage should be determined in advance so that they can be rapidly obtained.

4. **Reference laboratories:** Laboratory testing is useful for confirming the diagnosis during a suspected outbreak for which mass immunisation may be indicated (e.g. meningococcal meningitis) or where culture and antibiotic sensitivity testing may influence case management decisions (e.g. shigellosis). A reference laboratory should also be identified either regionally or internationally that can assist with more sophisticated testing, e.g. serological diagnosis of measles, yellow fever, dengue fever and viral haemorrhagic fevers.

5. **Transport media and rapid tests:** Sampling materials (e.g. rectal swabs) and transport media (e.g. Cary-Blair media for cholera, *Shigella*, *E. coli* and *Salmonella*) and cold chain material for transport should be available on-site or readily accessible. In addition, several rapid tests are available that can be

useful in screening for communicable diseases in the field, including malaria and meningitis.

6. **Outbreak investigation:** The ten key steps in outbreak investigation are:

1. establish the existence of an outbreak
2. confirm the diagnosis
3. define a case
4. count cases
5. perform descriptive epidemiology (time, person, place)
6. determine who is at risk
7. develop hypotheses explaining exposure and disease
8. evaluate hypotheses
9. communicate findings
10. implement control measures.

These steps do not need to be implemented in any strict order and control measures should be implemented as soon as possible.

7. **Confirmation of the existence of an outbreak:** It is not always straightforward to determine whether an outbreak is present, and clear definitions of outbreak thresholds do not exist for all diseases. Nevertheless, thresholds exist for the diseases listed below:

- diseases for which a single case may indicate an outbreak: cholera, measles, yellow fever, viral haemorrhagic fevers
- diseases for which an outbreak should be suspected when cases of, or deaths due to, the disease exceed the number expected for the location or are double the previous weekly averages; shigellosis – in non-endemic regions and in refugee camps, a single case of shigellosis should raise concern about a potential outbreak
- malaria – definitions are situation-specific; an increase in the number of cases above what is expected for the time of year among a defined population in a defined area may indicate an outbreak. Without historic data, warning signals include a considerable increase in the proportion of fever cases that are confirmed as malaria in the past two weeks and an increasing trend of case fatality rates over past weeks
- meningococcal meningitis – in the meningitis belt, for populations above 30,000, 15 cases/100,000 persons/week; however, with high outbreak risk (i.e. no outbreak for 3+ years and vaccination coverage <80 per cent), this threshold is reduced to 10 cases/100,000 persons/week. In populations of less than 30,000, five cases in one week or a doubling of cases over a three-week period confirms an outbreak. In a camp, two confirmed cases in one week indicate an outbreak

- dengue – increase in fever cases in the past two weeks that show increased IgG levels (based on paired testing of consecutive sera-samples) of a febrile patient with 3–5 days illness and decreasing platelet count (<20,000).

8. **Outbreak response:** Key components of outbreak response are coordination, case management, surveillance and epidemiology, laboratory, specific preventive measures such as water and sanitation improvement depending on disease, risk communication, social mobilisation, media relations and information management, logistics and security.

9. **Control measures:** Control measures must be specifically developed to halt transmission of the agent causing the outbreak. Often, existing knowledge about the agent can guide the design of appropriate control measures in specific situations. In general, response activities include controlling the source and/or preventing exposure (e.g. through improved water source to prevent cholera), interrupting transmission and/or preventing infection (e.g. through mass vaccination to prevent measles or use of LLINs to prevent malaria) and modifying host defences (e.g. through prompt diagnosis and treatment or through chemoprophylaxis) (see Health systems standard 5 on page 305, Water supply standards 1–2 on pages 97–100, Hygiene promotion standards 1–2 on pages 91–94 and Vector control standards 1–3 on pages 111–116).

10. **Case fatality rates:** The acceptable CFRs for communicable diseases vary according to the general context, accessibility to health services and the quality and rapidity of case management. In general, aim to reduce CFRs to as low as possible. If CFRs exceed the minimum expected levels, an immediate evaluation of control measures should be undertaken and corrective steps followed to ensure CFRs are maintained at acceptable levels.

2.2. Essential health services – child health

During emergencies, children are especially vulnerable to increased rates of morbidity and mortality. Addressing their specific health needs requires child-focused interventions. Child health interventions must include those that address the major causes of excess morbidity and mortality, including acute respiratory infections, diarrhoea, measles, malnutrition and neonatal causes.

Essential health services – child health standard 1: Prevention of vaccine-preventable diseases

Children aged 6 months to 15 years have immunity against measles and access to routine Expanded Programme on Immunization (EPI) services once the situation is stabilised.

Key actions (to be read in conjunction with the guidance notes)

▶ Make an estimation of measles vaccination coverage of children aged 9 months to 15 years at the outset of the disaster response, to determine the risk of outbreaks (see guidance note 1).

▶ When measles vaccination coverage is <90 per cent or unknown, conduct a mass measles vaccination campaign for children aged 6 months to 15 years, including the administration of Vitamin A to children aged 6–59 months (see guidance notes 1–2).

▶ Ensure that all infants vaccinated between 6–9 months of age receive another dose of measles vaccine upon reaching 9 months (see guidance note 3).

▶ For mobile or displaced populations, establish an ongoing system to ensure that at least 95 per cent of newcomers to a camp or community aged between 6 months and 15 years receive vaccination against measles.

▶ Re-establish the EPI as soon as conditions permit to routinely immunise children against measles and other vaccine-preventable diseases included in the national schedule (see guidance note 4).

Key indicators (to be read in conjunction with the guidance notes)

▶ Upon completion of measles vaccination campaign:
- at least 95 per cent of children aged 6 months to 15 years have received measles vaccination
- at least 95 per cent of children aged 6–59 months have received an appropriate dose of Vitamin A.

▶ Once routine EPI services have been re-established, at least 90 per cent of children aged 12 months have had three doses of DPT (diphtheria, pertussis and tetanus), which is the proxy indicator for fully immunised children.

Guidance notes

1. **Measles vaccination coverage:** Determine measles vaccination coverage in the affected population through review of immunisation coverage data. Based on this review, determine if routine measles immunisation coverage has been ≥90 per cent for the preceding five years and/or if a measles vaccination campaign conducted in the preceding 12 months has reached ≥90 per cent of children aged 9 months to 5 years. If measles vaccination coverage is <90 per cent, unknown or doubts remain regarding the coverage estimates, the campaign should be carried out on the assumption that the coverage is inadequate to prevent outbreaks.

2. **Age ranges for measles vaccination:** Some older children may have escaped both previous measles vaccination campaigns and measles disease. These children remain at risk of measles and can serve as a source of infection for infants and young children who are at higher risk of dying from the disease. This is the reason for the recommendation to vaccinate up to the age of 15 years. In resource-poor settings, it may not be possible to vaccinate all children aged 6 months to 15 years. In these settings, priority should be given to children aged 6–59 months. All children in the target age group should be immunised against measles regardless of their previous immunisation status.

3. **Repeat measles vaccination for children aged 6–9 months:** All children aged 6–9 months who received the measles vaccine should receive an additional dose of measles vaccine upon reaching 9 months of age, with at least one month between the two doses.

4. **Re-establishment of the national EPI programme:** At the same time as the preparation of the mass vaccination campaign against measles, plans should begin to re-establish the EPI programme in coordination with national authorities. The prompt re-establishment of EPI vaccination not only protects children directly against diseases such as measles, diphtheria and pertussis, but has the added value of reducing the risk of respiratory infections.

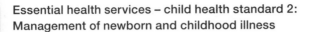

**Essential health services – child health standard 2:
Management of newborn and childhood illness**

Children have access to priority health services that are designed
to address the major causes of newborn and childhood morbidity
and mortality.

Key actions (to be read in conjunction with the guidance notes)

▶ Design health education messages to encourage the affected population to
seek early care for any illness (fever, cough, diarrhea, etc.) in the newborn. In
the design of health education messages, consider children who do not have
an adult caring for them (see Health systems standard 1, guidance note 3 on
page 298).

▶ Provide essential newborn care to all newborns according to Integrated
Management of Pregnancy and Childbirth (IMPAC) guidelines where possible
(see guidance note 1).

▶ Provide healthcare to children at first-level health facilities using national
protocol, or the IMCI guidelines where implemented, and hospital care for
severely ill children (see guidance note 2).

▶ Establish a standardised system of emergency assessment and triage at all
health facilities providing care to sick children to ensure those with emergency signs receive immediate treatment (see guidance note 3).

▶ Ensure that children attending health services are screened for their nutritional
status and referred to nutritional services (see Management of acute malnutrition and micronutrient deficiencies standards 1–3 on pages 165–173).

▶ Establish an appropriate case management protocol for the treatment of
diphtheria and pertussis in situations where the risk of outbreaks of these
diseases is high (see guidance note 6).

▶ Make available essential medicines for treatment of common childhood
illnesses in the appropriate dosages and formulations.

Key indicators (to be read in conjunction with the guidance notes)

▶ All children under 5 years old presenting with malaria have received effective anti-
malarial treatment within 24 hours of onset of their symptoms (see Essential health
services – control of communicable diseases standard 2 on page 314).

▶ All children under 5 years of age presenting with diarrhoea have received both
oral rehydration salts (ORS) and zinc supplementation (see guidance note 3).

323

> All children under 5 years of age presenting with pneumonia have received appropriate antibiotics (see guidance note 5).

Guidance notes

1. *Care of the newborn:* All newborns should ideally receive skilled care at birth (preferably in a health facility), be kept warm and receive early and exclusive breastfeeding. All newborns should be assessed for any problems, particularly feeding difficulties. All sick newborns should be assessed for possible sepsis and local infections.

2. *Integrated Management of Childhood Illness (IMCI):* IMCI is an integrated approach to child health that focuses on the care of children under 5 at primary-care level. Where IMCI has been developed in a country, and clinical guidelines adapted, these guidelines should preferably be incorporated into the standardised protocols, and health professionals trained appropriately.

3. *Triage:* IMCI and referral care guidelines can be enhanced when used in combination with rapid triage and treatment. Triage is the sorting of patients into priority groups according to their medical need, the resources available and their chances of survival. Clinical staff involved in the care of sick children should be trained using Emergency Triage, Assessment and Treatment (ETAT) guidelines to conduct rapid assessments.

4. *Management of diarrhoea:* Children with diarrhoea must be treated with low osmolality ORS and receive zinc supplementation. Low osmolality ORS shortens the duration of the diarrhoeal episode and reduces the need for intravenous fluid.

5. *Management of pneumonia:* Children with a cough should be assessed for fast and/or difficult breathing and chest indrawing. Those with fast and/or difficult breathing should receive an appropriate oral antibiotic; those with chest indrawing should be referred to hospital.

6. *Pertussis or diphtheria outbreaks:* Pertussis outbreaks are common in settings of population displacement. A vaccination campaign in response to a pertussis outbreak is usually avoided due to concerns about adverse events among older recipients of whole-cell DPT vaccine. However an outbreak can be used to address routine immunisation gaps. Case management includes antibiotic treatment of cases and early prophylactic treatment of contacts in households where there is an infant or a pregnant woman. Diphtheria outbreaks are less common but always a threat in populations with low diphtheria immunity in crowded settings. Mass vaccination campaigns with three separate doses of vaccine have been conducted in camp settings in response to diphtheria outbreaks. Case management includes the administration of both antitoxin and antibiotics.

2.3. Essential health services – sexual and reproductive health

All individuals, including those living in disaster-affected areas, have the right to reproductive health (RH). To exercise this right, affected populations must have access to comprehensive RH information and services to make free and informed choices. Quality RH services must be based on the needs of the affected population. They must respect the religious beliefs, ethical values and cultural backgrounds of the community, while conforming to universally recognised international human rights standards.

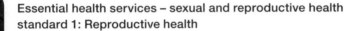

> **Essential health services – sexual and reproductive health standard 1: Reproductive health**
>
> People have access to the priority reproductive health services of the Minimum Initial Service Package (MISP) at the onset of an emergency and comprehensive RH as the situation stabilises.

Key actions (to be read in conjunction with the guidance notes)

▶ Identify a lead RH agency within the health sector or cluster to facilitate the coordination and implementation of the MISP and ensure that an RH officer (nominated by lead RH agency) is in place and functioning within the health sector or cluster (see guidance note 1).

▶ Implement measures to reduce the risk of sexual violence, in coordination with other relevant sectors or clusters (see guidance note 3).

▶ Ensure services for clinical management of sexual violence, including access to mental health and psychosocial support and legal assistance (see guidance note 3 and Protection Principle 2, guidance note 7 on page 37).

▶ Establish the minimum set of HIV prevention, treatment, care and support services to reduce the transmission of HIV (see Essential health services – sexual and reproductive health standard 2 on page 328).

▶ Ensure that emergency obstetric and newborn care services are made available and accessible including:

  - at health centres – skilled birth attendants and supplies for normal births and basic management of emergency obstetric and newborn complications; basic emergency obstetric care (BEmOC) and newborn care

- at referral hospitals – skilled medical staff and supplies for comprehensive management of obstetric and newborn complications; comprehensive emergency obstetric care (CEmOC) and newborn care
- a communication and transportation system to manage obstetric and newborn emergencies is established and functioning 24 hours a day, seven days a week from the community to the health centre and between the health centre and referral hospital
(see guidance note 4).

▶ Provide clean delivery kits to visibly pregnant women and birth attendants for clean home deliveries when access to a skilled health provider and health facility is not possible (see guidance note 4).

▶ Inform populations about the benefits and availability of clinical services for survivors of sexual violence and the emergency referral system for complications of pregnancy and childbirth (see guidance notes 3–4).

▶ Ensure that common contraceptive methods are available to meet demand (see guidance note 2).

▶ Plan to implement comprehensive RH services, integrated into primary healthcare, as soon as possible (see guidance note 1).

Key indicators (to be read in conjunction with the guidance notes)

▶ All health facilities have trained staff, sufficient supplies and equipment for clinical management of rape survivor services based on national or WHO protocols.

▶ All pregnant women in their third trimester have received clean delivery kits.

▶ There are at least four health facilities with BEmOC and newborn care/ 500,000 population.

▶ There is at least one health facility with CEmOC and newborn care/ 500,000 population.

▶ The proportion of deliveries by caesarean section is not less than 5 per cent or more than 15 per cent (see guidance note 4).

Guidance notes

1. *Minimum Initial Service Package:* The MISP defines those services that are most important for preventing RH-related morbidity and mortality among women, men and adolescents in disaster settings. It comprises a coordinated set of priority RH services that must be implemented simultaneously to prevent and manage the consequences of sexual violence, reduce the transmission of HIV, prevent excess maternal and newborn morbidity and mortality,

and begin planning for comprehensive RH services as soon as the situation stabilises. Planning for the integration of good-quality comprehensive RH activities into primary healthcare at the onset of an emergency is essential to ensuring a continuum of care. Comprehensive RH care involves upgrading existing services, adding missing services and enhancing service quality.

2. **RH supplies:** Supplies for the MISP must be ordered, distributed and stored to avoid delay in getting these essential products to the population. The Interagency Emergency Health Kit includes a limited quantity of medicines for patient post-exposure prophylaxis, magnesium sulphate and instruments and medicines for midwifery care, but not all supplies required for the MISP. The Interagency Reproductive Health Kits, developed by the Interagency Working Group on RH in crises, contain medicines and supplies for a three-month period.

3. **Sexual violence:** All actors in disaster response must be aware of the risk of sexual violence including sexual exploitation and abuse by humanitarians, and must work to prevent and respond to it. Aggregate information on reported incidents must be safely and ethically compiled and shared to inform prevention and response efforts. Incidence of sexual violence should be monitored. Measures for assisting survivors must be in place in all primary-level health facilities and include skilled staff to provide clinical management that encompasses emergency contraception, post-exposure prophylaxis to prevent HIV, presumptive treatment of sexually transmitted infections (STIs), wound care, tetanus prevention and hepatitis B prevention. The use of emergency contraception is a personal choice that can only be made by the women themselves. Women should be offered unbiased counselling so as to reach an informed decision. Survivors of sexual violence should be supported to seek and be referred for clinical care and have access to mental health and psychosocial support.

At the survivor's request, protection staff should provide protection and legal support. All examination and treatment should be done only with informed consent of the survivor. Confidentiality is essential at all stages (see Health systems standard 5, guidance note 4 on page 307 and Protection Principle 1, guidance notes 7–12 on page 35).

4. **Emergency obstetric and newborn care:** Approximately 4 per cent of the disaster-affected population will be pregnant women. Approximately 15 per cent of all pregnant women will experience an unpredictable obstetric complication during pregnancy or at the time of delivery that will require emergency obstetric care and 5–15 per cent of all deliveries will require surgery, such as caesarean section. In order to prevent maternal and newborn mortality and morbidity resulting from complications, skilled birth attendance at all births, BEmOC and neonatal resuscitation should be avail-

able at all primary healthcare facilities. BEmOC functions include parenteral antibiotics, parenteral uterotonic drugs (oxytocin), parenteral anticonvulsant drugs (magnesium sulfate), manual removal of retained products of conception using appropriate technology, manual removal of placenta, assisted vaginal delivery (vacuum or forceps delivery) and maternal and newborn resuscitation. CEmOC functions include all of the interventions in BEmOC as well as surgery under general anaesthesia (caesarean delivery, laparotomy) and rational and safe blood transfusion.

The referral system should ensure that women or newborns are referred and have the means to travel to and from a primary healthcare facility with BEmOC and newborn care, and to a hospital with CEmOC and newborn care services.

Essential health services – sexual and reproductive health standard 2: HIV and AIDS

People have access to the minimum set of HIV prevention, treatment, care and support services during disasters.

Key actions (to be read in conjunction with the guidance notes)

▶ Establish standard precautions and safe procedures for waste disposal within all healthcare settings (see guidance note 2 and Health systems standard 1, guidance notes 10–11 on pages 299–300).

▶ Establish and follow safe blood supply and rational use of blood transfusion (see guidance note 2 and Health systems standard 1, guidance note 5 on page 298).

▶ Establish access to good-quality free male and female condoms, including information on proper condom use.

▶ Ensure that health facilities provide syndromic management to all patients presenting with symptoms of a sexually transmitted infection.

▶ Ensure that post-exposure prophylaxis (PEP) services are provided to individuals within 72 hours of the incident of potential exposure to HIV (see guidance note 3).

▶ Provide information in accessible formats and education on HIV prevention to both the general public and high-risk groups (e.g. sex workers).

▶ Ensure prevention of mother-to-child transmission (PMTCT) of HIV by ensuring access to contraceptives, clean and safe child deliveries (including emergency obstetric care) and provision of anti-retroviral (ARV) drugs (see guidance note 4).

▶ Provide treatment, care and support for infants born from mothers known to be HIV positive, including guidance and counselling on infant feeding (see Infant and young child feeding standard 2 on page 160).

▶ Ensure that people living with HIV (PLHIV) receive healthcare including co-trimoxazole prophylaxis for HIV-related infections.

▶ Ensure that people who were previously on anti-retroviral therapy (ART) continue to receive treatment (see guidance note 4).

▶ Establish links between HIV and tuberculosis programmes where they exist.

▶ Ensure that people at higher risk of exposure to HIV have access to HIV prevention interventions for sexual transmission of HIV and access to clean injecting equipment for known injecting drug users where these services already exist.

▶ Initiate plans to broaden the range of HIV control services in the post-disaster phase (see guidance note 1).

Key indicators (to be read in conjunction with the guidance notes)

▶ People most at risk of exposure to HIV are targeted with a HIV prevention programme.

▶ Pregnant women known to be HIV positive have received ARV drugs for PMTCT.

▶ 100 per cent of transfused blood is screened for transfusion-transmissible infections including HIV.

▶ Individuals potentially exposed to HIV (occupational exposure in healthcare settings and non-occupational exposure) have received PEP within 72 hours of an incident.

▶ All primary healthcare facilities have antimicrobials to provide syndromic management to patients presenting with symptoms of an STI.

Guidance notes

1. *HIV control:* The minimum set of HIV prevention, treatment, care and support described in the key actions for this standard is comprised of actions that the health sector must take to prevent HIV transmission and to provide care and support to PLHIV. They should be implemented during the early stages of any disaster response.

2. **Prevention of HIV transmission in healthcare settings:** The prevention of transmission of HIV in healthcare settings (e.g. hospitals, healthcare clinics, vaccination campaigns) is a priority during the early stages of disaster response. Essential actions are ensuring the application of standard precautions, establishing safe and rational blood transfusion practices and the correct disposal of healthcare waste (see Health systems standard 1, guidance notes 5, 10–11 on pages 298–300).

3. **Post-exposure prophylaxis:** PEP to prevent HIV infection includes counselling, HIV exposure risk assessment, informed consent, assessment of the source and provision of ARV medicines. However, PEP should not be provided to a person who is known to be HIV positive; counselling and testing should never be mandatory nor should the provision of PEP be delayed while waiting for the test results.

4. **Anti-retroviral drugs:** The provision of ARV for PMTCT, PEP and long-term ART in disaster situations is feasible. Continuation of ART for those already on treatment prior to the disaster must be considered a priority during disaster response. Pregnant women already taking ART should continue taking ARV without interruption. Pregnant women known to be HIV positive should receive ARV for PMTCT according to the national protocol where possible.

Note
Caritas Internationalis and its Members do not promote the use of, or distribute any form of, artificial birth control.

2.4. Essential health services – injury

Injury is usually the major cause of excess mortality and morbidity following acute-onset natural disasters such as earthquakes. Many acute-onset natural disasters are mass casualty events, meaning more people are made patients than the locally available resources can manage using routine procedures. Injury due to physical violence is also associated with complex emergencies. During armed conflict for example, most trauma-related deaths occur in insecure regions away from health facilities and therefore cannot usually be prevented by medical care. Interventions that aim to protect the civilian population are required to prevent these deaths (see Protection Principle 3, guidance notes 1–5 on pages 38–39).

Essential health services – injury standard 1: Injury care

People have access to effective injury care during disasters to prevent avoidable morbidity, mortality and disability.

Key actions (to be read in conjunction with the guidance notes)

▶ Ensure that local health workers and those coordinating the health-sector response are familiar with mass casualty management (see guidance note 1).

▶ In mass casualty events, establish a standardised system of triage with clear guidance on assessment, prioritisation, basic resuscitation and referral (see guidance note 1).

▶ Ensure essential principles and skills for provision of first aid and basic resuscitation are widely understood by health workers (see guidance note 2).

▶ Ensure that local health workers are familiar with core principles of wound management (see guidance note 3).

▶ Provide a tetanus vaccine that contains toxoid to those with dirty wounds and to those involved in rescue or clean-up operations (see guidance note 4).

▶ Establish standardised protocols for the referral of injured patients for advanced care, including surgery and post-operative care (see guidance note 5).

▶ Ensure that definitive trauma and surgical services and post-trauma and post-surgical rehabilitation are established only by agencies with appropriate expertise and resources (see guidance note 5).

▶ Ensure standard assistive devices and mobility aids (e.g. wheelchairs, crutches) are available for injured patients and persons with disabilities as soon as practical and that these aids can be repaired locally (see guidance note 6).

Key indicator (to be read in conjunction with the guidance notes)

▶ All health facilities have trained staff and systems for the management of multiple casualties.

Guidance notes

1. **Triage:** Triage is the process of categorising patients according to the severity of their injuries or illness, and prioritising treatment according to the availability of resources and the patients' chances of survival. In mass casualty events, those with severe, life-threatening injuries may receive a lower priority than those with more survivable injuries. There is no standardised system of triage and several are in use throughout the world. The most common classification uses the four-colour code system: red signals high priority, yellow for medium priority, green is used for ambulatory patients and black for deceased.

2. **First aid and basic medical care:** Critical procedures include restoring and maintaining breathing which may require clearing and protecting the airway, along with controlling bleeding and administering intravenous fluids when required. These procedures may help to stabilise individuals with life-threatening injuries before transfer to a referral centre and greatly increase their chances of survival, even for severe injuries. Other non-operative procedures are equally vital, such as cleaning and dressing wounds and administering antibiotics and tetanus prophylaxis.

3. **Wound management:** In most disasters, many patients will present for care more than six hours after injury. Delayed presentation greatly increases the risk of wound infection and preventable excess mortality. It is, therefore, critical that local healthcare workers are familiarised with appropriate principles and protocols to prevent and manage wound infection, which include delayed primary closure and wound toilet and surgical removal of foreign material and dead tissue.

4. **Tetanus:** In sudden-onset natural disasters where there are usually a large number of injuries and trauma cases, risk of tetanus can be relatively high. While mass tetanus immunisation is not recommended, tetanus toxoid-containing vaccine (DT or Td – diphtheria and tetanus vaccines – or DPT, depending on age and vaccination history) is recommended for those with dirty wounds and for those involved in rescue or clean-up operations that put them at risk. Individuals with dirty wounds who have not previously been

vaccinated against tetanus should receive a dose of tetanus immune globulin (TIG), if available.

5. **Trauma and surgical care:** Trauma surgical care and war surgery save lives and long-term disability and require specific training and resources that few agencies possess. Inappropriate or inadequate surgery may do more harm than doing nothing. Moreover, surgery provided without any immediate rehabilitation can result in a complete failure in restoring functional capacities of the patient. Only organisations and professionals with the relevant expertise should, therefore, establish these services that save lives and prevent disability.

6. **Post-operative rehabilitation for trauma-related injury:** Early rehabilitation can greatly increase survival and enhance the quality of life for injured survivors. Patients requiring assistive devices (such as prostheses and mobility devices) will also need physical rehabilitation. Where available, partnership with community-based rehabilitation programmes can optimise the post-operative care and rehabilitation for injured survivors.

2.5. Essential health services – mental health

Mental health and psychosocial problems occur in all humanitarian settings. The horrors, losses, uncertainties and numerous other stressors associated with conflict and other disasters place people at increased risk of diverse social, behavioural, psychological and psychiatric problems. Mental health and psychosocial support involves multi-sectoral supports (see the 'intervention pyramid' diagram below). These supports require coordinated implementation e.g. through a cross-cluster or cross-sectoral working group. The mental health standard below focuses on actions by health actors. Readers should also consult Core Standard 1 on page 55 and Protection Principle 3 on page 38.

> **Essential health services – mental health standard 1: Mental health**
>
> People have access to health services that prevent or reduce mental health problems and associated impaired functioning.

Key actions (to be read in conjunction with the guidance notes)

▶ Ensure interventions are developed on the basis of identified needs and resources.

▶ Enable community members including marginalised people to strengthen community self-help and social support (see guidance note 1).

▶ Ensure that community workers including volunteers and staff at health services offer psychological first aid to people in acute distress after exposure to extreme stressors (see guidance note 2)

▶ Ensure that there is at least one staff member at every health facility who manages diverse, severe mental health problems in adults and children (see guidance note 3).

▶ Address the safety, basic needs and rights of people with mental health problems in institutions (see guidance note 4).

▶ Minimise harm related to alcohol and drugs.

▶ As part of early recovery, initiate plans to develop a sustainable community mental health system (see guidance note 5).

Key indicator (to be read in conjunction with the guidance notes)

▶ All health facilities have trained staff and systems for the management of mental health problems.

Guidance notes

1. *Community self-help and social support:* Community self-help and social support form a key element of overall mental health and psychosocial multi-sectoral supports (see diagram below) (see Core Standard 1 on page 55 and Protection Principle 4, guidance notes 9-13 on page 43 and Protection Principle 3, guidance note 15 on page 40). Health agencies often employ or engage community workers and volunteers who can enable community members, including marginalised people, to increase self-help and social support.

Intervention pyramid

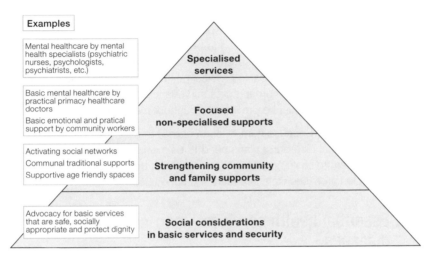

Examples

Mental healthcare by mental health specialists (psychiatric nurses, psychologists, psychiatrists, etc.)

Specialised services

Basic mental healthcare by practical primacy healthcare doctors

Basic emotional and pratical support by community workers

Focused non-specialised supports

Activating social networks

Communal traditional supports

Supportive age friendly spaces

Strengthening community and family supports

Advocacy for basic services that are safe, socially appropriate and protect dignity

Social considerations in basic services and security

Source: Interagency Steering Committee Reference Group on Mental Health and Psychosocial Support, 2010

2. ***Psychological first aid:*** Acute anxiety after exposure to extreme stressors (e.g. traumatic events) is best managed following the principles of psychological first aid, which is often mistakenly seen as a clinical intervention. Rather, it is a description of a humane, supportive response to a fellow human being who is suffering and who may need support. It entails basic, non-intrusive pragmatic care with a focus on listening but not forcing talk, assessing needs and concerns, ensuring that basic needs are met, encouraging social support from significant others and protecting from further harm. Psychological debriefing (i.e. the promotion of ventilation by encouraging the person to briefly but systematically recount perceptions, thoughts and emotional reactions experienced during a recent, stressful event) is at best ineffective and should not be applied. Similarly, benzodiazepines should be avoided in the management of acute distress because they may interfere with natural recovery.

3. ***Basic mental healthcare:*** People's mental health problems may be emergency-induced, pre-existing or both. People with severe mental health problems should have access to a network of community-based social supports as well as clinical care through available health services (e.g. general hospitals, primary care clinics, etc.). Organising basic clinical mental healthcare usually involves either organising rapid training and supervision of general health staff or adding a mental health professional to the health clinic. Essential psychotropics and anti-epileptics need to be available. Individuals

who have been receiving mental health treatment before the crisis need to have access to continued treatment.

4. **People in institutions:** Mental hospitals and residential homes for people with severe mental problems need to be visited regularly, especially early in the crisis, because the risk of severe neglect or abuse of people in institutions is extremely high. Safety, basic physical needs (water, food, shelter, sanitation and medical care), human rights surveillance and basic psychiatric and psychosocial care must be provided throughout the crisis.

5. **Early recovery:** Because humanitarian crises increase the rates of a broad range of mental disorders, plans need to be initiated to develop the mental health system to scale up effective mental health treatment coverage across the affected area (see Core Standard 4 on page 65).

2.6. Essential health services – non-communicable diseases

Population ageing and increase in life expectancy have shifted disease profiles from infectious to non-communicable diseases (NCDs) in many countries including low- and middle-income countries. As a result, NCDs are growing in importance as a major public health issue in disaster settings. Increases in health problems due to the exacerbation of existing chronic health conditions have become a common feature of many disasters.

Essential health services – non-communicable diseases standard 1: Non-communicable diseases

People have access to essential therapies to reduce morbidity and mortality due to acute complications or exacerbation of their chronic health condition.

Key actions (to be read in conjunction with the guidance note)

▶ Assess and document the prevalence of NCDs and share the data with agencies responding to the disaster (see guidance note 1).

▶ Ensure identification of individuals with NCDs who were receiving treatment before the emergency and ensure that they continue to do so. Avoid sudden discontinuation of treatment.

▶ Ensure that people with acute complications and exacerbations of NCDs that pose a threat to their life (e.g. heart diseases, severe hypertension) and individuals in pain (e.g. pain due to advanced cancer) receive treatment.

▶ In situations where treatments for NCDs are unavailable, establish clear standard operating procedures for referral.

▶ Ensure that essential diagnostic equipment, core laboratory tests and medication for the routine, ongoing management of NCDs are available through the primary healthcare system. This medication must be specified on the essential medicines list.

▶ Ensure that assistive devices (e.g. walking aids) are available for people with mobility or communication difficulties.

Key indicators (to be read in conjunction with the guidance note)

▶ All primary healthcare facilities have clear standard operating procedures for referrals of patients with NCDs to secondary and tertiary care facilities.

▶ All primary healthcare facilities have adequate medication for continuation of treatment to individuals with NCDs who were receiving treatment before the emergency.

Guidance note

1. **Non-communicable diseases** include heart disease, stroke, hypertension, chronic renal failure, bronchial asthma, dialysis-dependent chronic renal failure, insulin-dependent diabetes and epilepsy. During emergencies, individuals with chronic medical conditions are particularly vulnerable to exacerbations of their condition or to complications such as secondary infections and are at risk when treatment is interrupted. Clinical stabilisation and maintenance of therapy should be the mainstay of the health-sector response in humanitarian settings.

   People with NCDs need long-term medication and follow-up. The routine, ongoing management of NCDs should be available through the primary healthcare system, using medications from the essential medicines list. But it is generally not recommended to introduce new therapeutic regimens or programmes for the management of chronic health conditions during the relief effort especially if the regimen or programme is unlikely to be continued after the emergency phase.

Appendix 1

Health assessment checklist

Preparation

▶ Obtain available information on the disaster-affected population.

▶ Obtain available maps and aerial photographs.

▶ Obtain demographic and health data.

Security and access

▶ Determine the existence of the ongoing natural or human-generated hazards.

▶ Determine the overall security situation, including the presence of armed forces.

▶ Determine the access that humanitarian agencies have to the disaster-affected population.

Demographics and social structure

▶ Determine the total size of the disaster-affected population; age and sex breakdown of the population.

▶ Identify groups at increased risk, e.g. women, children, older people, persons with disabilities.

▶ Determine the average household size and estimates of the number of female- and child-headed households.

▶ Determine the existing social structure, including positions of authority and/ or influence.

Background health information

▶ Identify pre-existing health problems in the disaster-affected area prior to the disaster.

▶ Identify pre-existing health problems in the country of origin in refugees (area of origin for internally displaced persons).

▶ Identify existing risks to health, e.g. potential epidemic diseases.

▶ Identify previous sources of healthcare.

▶ Analyse the performance of health system functions.

Mortality rates

▶ Calculate the crude mortality rate.

▶ Calculate the age-specific mortality rates (e.g. under-5 mortality rate).

▶ Calculate cause-specific mortality rates.

▶ Calculate proportional mortality rate.

Morbidity rates

▶ Determine incidence rates of major diseases that have public health importance.

▶ Determine age- and sex-specific incidence rates of major diseases where possible.

Available resources

▶ Determine the capacity of the Ministry of Health of the country affected by the disaster.

▶ Determine the status of national health facilities, including total number by type of care provided, physical status and access.

▶ Determine the numbers and skills of available health staff.

▶ Determine the available health budgets and financing mechanism.

▶ Determine the capacity and functional status of existing public health programmes, e.g. Extended Programme on Immunization.

▶ Determine the availability of standardised protocols, essential medicines, supplies and logistics systems.

▶ Determine the status of existing referral systems.

▶ Determine the level of environmental health in healthcare facilities.

▶ Determine the status of the existing health information system.

Data from other relevant sectors

▶ Nutritional status

▶ Food and food security

▶ Environmental conditions

▶ Shelter – quality of shelter

▶ Education – health and hygiene education

Appendix 2

Sample weekly surveillance reporting forms

Mortality surveillance form 1*

Site: . . . .

Date from Monday: . . . . To Sunday: . . . .

Total population at beginning of this week: . . . .

Births this week: . . . . Deaths this week: . . . .

Arrivals this week (if applicable): . . . . Departures this week: . . . .

Total population at end of week: . . . . Total under 5 years population: . . . .

	0-4 yrs		5+ yrs		Total
	male	female	male	female	
Immediate cause					
Acute lower respiratory infection					
Cholera (suspected)					
Diarrhoea – bloody					
Diarrhoea – watery					
Injury – non-accidental					
Malaria					
Maternal death – direct					
Measles					
Meningitis (suspected)					
Neonatal (0–28 days)					
Other					
Unknown					
Total by age and sex					
Underlying cause					
AIDS (suspected)					
Malnutrition					
Maternal death – indirect					
Non-communicable diseases (specifiy)					
Other					
Total by age and sex					

* This form is used when there are many deaths and therefore more detailed information on individual deaths cannot
be collected due to time limitations.
- Other causes of mortality can be added according to context and epidemiological pattern.
- Age can be further disaggregated (0–11 mths, 1–4 yrs, 5–14 yrs, 15–49 yrs, 50–59 yrs, 60–69 yrs, 70–79 yrs,
80+ yrs) as feasible.
- Deaths should not be reported solely from health facilities, but should include reports from site and religious
leaders, community workers, women's groups and referral hospitals.
- Whenever possible, case definitions should be put on back of form.

Mortality surveillance form 2*

Site: . . . .

Date from Monday: . . . . To Sunday: . . . .

Total population at beginning of this week: . . . .

Births this week: . . . . Deaths this week: . . . .

Arrivals this week (if applicable): . . . . Departures this week: . . . .

Total population at end of week: . . . . Total under 5 years population: . . . .

No	Sex (m, f)	Age (days=d, mths=m, yrs=y)	Direct cause of death													Underlying causes				Date (dd/mm/yy)	Location in site (e.g. block no.)	Died in hospital or at home
			Acute lower respiratory infection	Cholera (suspected)	Diarrhoea – bloody	Diarrhoea – watery	Injury – non-accidental	Malaria	Maternal death – direct	Measles	Meningitis (suspected)	Neonatal (0–28 days)	Non-communicable dis. (specify)	Other (specify)	Unknown	AIDS (suspected)	Malnutrition	Maternal death – indirect	Other (specify)			
1																						
2																						
3																						
4																						
5																						
6																						
7																						
8																						

* This form is used when there is enough time to record data on individual deaths; it allows analysis by age, outbreak investigation by location and facility utilisation rates.
- Frequency of reporting (i.e. daily or weekly) depends upon the number of deaths.
- Other causes of death can be added as fits the situation.
- Deaths should not be reported solely from site health facilities, but should include reports from site and religious leaders, community workers, women's groups and referral hospitals.
- Whenever possible, case definitions should be put on back of form.

Sample weekly EWARN reporting form*

* This form is used in the acute phase of the emergency when the risk of epidemic-prone diseases is high

Date from Monday: . . . . To Sunday: . . . .

Town/Village/Settlement/Camp: . . . .

Province: . . . . District: . . . . Subdistrict: . . . .

Site name: . . . • Inpatient   • Outpatient   • Health centre   • Mobile clinic

Supporting agency(ies): . . . . Reporting officer & contact number: . . . .

Total population: . . . . Total under 5 years population: . . . .

A. WEEKLY AGGREGATE DATA

New cases of:	MORBIDITY		MORTALITY		Total
	< 5 years	5 years & over	< 5 years	5 years & over	
TOTAL ADMISSIONS					
TOTAL DEATHS					
Acute respiratory infection					
Acute watery diarrhoea					
Acute bloody diarrhoea					
Malaria – suspected/confirmed					
Measles					
Meningitis – suspected					
Acute haemorrhagic fever syndrome					
Acute jaundice syndrome					
Acute flaccid paralysis (AFP)					
Tetanus					
Other fever > 38.5°C					
Injuries/wounds					
Others					
Total					

- More than one diagnosis is possible; the most important should be recorded. Each case should be counted only once.
- Include only those cases that were seen (or deaths that occurred) during the surveillance week.
- Write "0" (zero) if you had no case or death during the week for one of the syndrome listed in the form.
- Deaths should be reported only in the mortality section, NOT in the morbidity section.
- Case definitions for each condition under surveillance should be written on the back on this form.
- Causes of morbidity can be added or subtracted according to the epidemiology and risk assessment of disease.
- The purpose of EWARN surveillance is the early detection of epidemic-prone diseases.
- Data on conditions such as malnutrition should be obtained through surveys (prevalence) rather than surveillance (incidence).

B. OUTBREAK ALERT

At any time you suspect any of the following diseases, please SMS or phone . . . .
or email . . . . with maximum information on time, place and number of cases and deaths:

cholera, shigellosis, measles, polio, typhoid, tetanus, hepatitis A or E, dengue, meningitis, diphtheria, pertussis, haemorrhagic fever

(this list of diseases will vary depending on the disease epidemiology of the country).

Sample routine morbidity surveillance reporting form*

* Morbidity surveillance can be expanded from EWARN after the acute phase to include other diseases and monitoring of other indicators as appropriate

Site: . . . .

Date from Monday: . . . . To Sunday: . . . .

Total population at beginning of this week/month: . . . .

Births this week/month: . . . . Deaths this week/month: . . . .

Arrivals this week/month (if applicable): . . . .

Departures this week/month: . . . .

Total population at end of week/month: . . . . Total under 5 years population: . . . .

Morbidity	Under 5 years (new cases)#			5 years and over (new cases)			Total	Repeat cases
Diagnosis*	Male	Female	Total	Male	Female	Total	new cases	Total
Acute respiratory infection**								
Acute watery diarrhoea								
Acute bloody diarrhoea								
Malaria – suspected/confirmed								
Measles								
Meningitis – suspected								
Acute haemorrhagic fever syndrome								
Acute jaundice syndrome								
Acute flaccid paralysis (AFP)								
Tetanus								
Other fever > 38.5°C								
AIDS – suspected ***								
Eye diseases								
Malnutrition ****								
Injuries – accidental								
Injuries – non-accidental								
Sexually transmitted infections								
Genital ulcer disease								
Male urethral discharge								
Vaginal discharge								
Lower abdominal pain								
Skin diseases								
Non-communicable diseases (e.g. diabetes)								
Worms								
Others								
Unknown								
Total								

* More than one diagnosis is possible; causes of morbidity can be added or subtracted according to context and epidemiological pattern.

** Acute respiratory tract infections: in some countries, this category may be divided into upper and lower tract infections.

*** HIV and AIDS prevalence is best assessed through surveys.

**** Malnutrition prevalence is best assessed through rapid surveys (MUAC or weight/height screening) as surveillance only reveals those who come to seek care.

\# Ages can be further disaggregated as feasible.

OUTBREAK ALERT

At any time you suspect any of the following diseases, please SMS or phone ....
or email.................with maximum information on time, place and number of cases and deaths:
cholera, dysentery/shigellosis, measles, AFP, typhoid, tetanus, hepatitis, dengue, meningitis,
diphtheria, pertussis, haemorrhagic fever.

Visits to health facility	Under 5 years			5 years and over			Total	
	Male	Female	Total	Male	Female	Total	Male	Female
Total visits								

Utilisation rate: Number of visits per person per year to health facility = total number of visits
in 1 week / total population x 52 weeks
- Ages can be further disaggregated (0–11 mths, 1–4 yrs, 5–14 yrs, 15–49 yrs, 50–59 yrs, 60+ yrs)
  as feasible.
Number of consulations per clinician: Number of total visits (new and repeat) / FTE clinician in health
facility/number of days health facility functioning per week.

Appendix 3

Formulas for calculating key health indicators

Crude mortality rate (CMR)

Definition: The rate of death in the entire population, including both women and men, and all ages.

Formula:

$$\frac{\text{Total number of deaths during time period}}{\text{Mid-period population at risk x Number of days in time period}} \times 10{,}000 \text{ persons} = \text{Deaths/ } 10{,}000 \text{ persons/ day}$$

Under-5 mortality rate (U5MR)

Definition: The rate of death among children below 5 years of age in the population.

Formula:

$$\frac{\text{Total number of deaths in children <5 years during time period}}{\text{Total number of children <5 years x Number of days in time period}} \times 10{,}000 \text{ persons} = \text{Deaths/ } 10{,}000 \text{ children under 5 years/ day}$$

Incidence rate

Definition: The number of new cases of a disease that occur during a specified period of time in a population at risk of developing the disease.

Formula:

$$\frac{\text{Number of new cases due to specific disease in time period}}{\text{Population at risk of developing disease x Number of months in time period}} \times 1{,}000 \text{ persons} = \text{New cases due to specific disease/ } 1{,}000 \text{ persons/ month}$$

Case fatality rate (CFR)

Definition: The number of people who die of a disease divided by the number of people who have the disease.

Formula:

$$\frac{\text{Number of people dying from disease during time period}}{\text{People who have the disease during time period}} \times 100 = x\%$$

Health facility utilisation rate

Definition: The number of outpatient visits per person per year. Whenever possible, a distinction should be drawn between new and old visits, and **new** visits should be used to calculate this rate. However, it is often difficult to differentiate between new and old visits, so they are frequently combined as total visits during a disaster.

Formula:

$$\frac{\text{Total number of visits in one week}}{\text{Total population}} \times 52 \text{ weeks} = \text{Visits/person/year}$$

Number of consultations per clinician per day

Definition: Average number of total consultations (new and repeat cases) seen by each clinician per day.

Formula:

$$\frac{\text{Total number of consultations in one week}}{\text{Number FTE* clinicians in health facility}} \div \text{Number of days health facility open per week}$$

* FTE (full-time equivalent) refers to the equivalent number of clinicians working in a health facility. For example, if there are six clinicians working in the outpatient department but two of them work half-time, then the number of FTE clinicians = 4 full-time staff + 2 half-time staff = 5 FTE clinicians.

References and further reading

Sources

International legal instruments

The Right to the Highest Attainable Standard of Health (Article 12 of the International Covenant on Economic, Social and Cultural Rights), CESCR General Comment 14, 11 August 2000. UN Doc. E/C.12/2000/4. Committee on Economic, Social and Cultural Rights.

World Health Organization (WHO) (2002), 25 Questions & Answers on Health & Human Rights. Health & Human Rights Publication Issue No. 1. Geneva. http://whqlibdoc.who.int/hq/2002/9241545690.pdf

Health systems

Inter-Agency Network for Education in Emergencies (INEE) (2004), Minimum Standards for Education in Emergencies, Chronic Crises and Early Reconstruction. Geneva. www.exacteditions.com/exact/browse/436/494/2635/2/47?dps=on

Inter-Agency Steering Committee (IASC) Global Health Cluster (2009), Health Cluster Guide: A practical guide for country-level implementation of the Health Cluster. WHO. Geneva.

Management Sciences for Health (1997), Managing Drug Supply, 2nd edition. Kumarian Press. Bloomfield, CT, USA.

Office of the United Nations High Commissioner for Refugees (UNHCR) (2009), Emergency Health Information System. www.unhcr.org/pages/49c3646ce0.html

Pan American Health Organization (PAHO) (2000), Natural Disasters: protecting the public's health. Scientific Publication No. 575. Washington DC.

WHO (1994), Health Laboratory Facilities in Emergencies and Disaster Situations. Geneva.

WHO (1999), Guidelines for Drug Donations, 2nd edition. Geneva.

WHO (2000), World health report 2000 – Health systems: improving performance. Geneva. www.who.int/whr/2000/en/index.html

WHO (2001), Macroeconomics and health: Investing in health for economic development. Geneva.

WHO (2009), Model Lists of Essential Medicines. Geneva.
www.who.int/medicines/publications/essentialmedicines/en/index.html

WHO (2008), The Interagency Emergency Health Kit: Medicines and Medical Devices for 10,000 People for Approximately 3 Months, 4th edition. Geneva.

WHO and PAHO (2001), Health Library for Disasters. Geneva.
http://helid.desastres.net/

Control of communicable diseases

Heymann, David L (2008), Control of Communicable Diseases Manual, 19th edition. American Public Health Association. Washington DC.

WHO (2002), Guidelines for the Collection of Clinical Specimens During Field Investigation of Outbreaks. Geneva.

WHO (2005), Communicable disease control in emergencies. Geneva.

WHO (2005), Malaria Control in Complex Emergencies: An Interagency Field Handbook. Geneva.

WHO (2007), Tuberculosis Care and Control in Refugee and Displaced Populations: An Interagency Field Manual, 2nd edition.Geneva.

Child health

WHO (1997), Immunisation in Practice. A Guide for Health Workers Who Give Vaccines. Macmillan. London.

WHO (2005), IMCI Handbook (Integrated Management of Childhood Illness). Geneva.

WHO (2005), Pocket book of hospital care for children: Guidelines for the management of common illnesses with limited resources. Geneva.

WHO (2008), Manual for the health care of children in humanitarian emergencies. Geneva.

United Nations Children's Fund (UNICEF) (2009), The State of the World's Children 2009. New York. www.unicef.org/sowc09/docs/SOWC09-FullReport-EN.pdf

Sexual and reproductive health

IASC (2009), Guidelines for Addressing HIV in Humanitarian Settings.
www.aidsandemergencies.org/cms/documents/IASC_HIV_Guidelines_2009_En.pdf

Inter-Agency Working Group on Reproductive Health in Crises (2010 revision for field review), Inter-agency Field Manual on Reproductive Health in Humanitarian Settings.

Women's Commission for Refugee Women and Children (2006), Minimum Initial Service Package (MISP) for Reproductive Health: A Distance Learning Module. http://misp.rhrc.org/

WHO (2006), Pregnancy, Childbirth, Postpartum and Newborn Care: A guide for essential practice, 2nd edition. Geneva.
http://whqlibdoc.who.int/publications/2006/924159084X_eng.pdf

WHO and UNHCR (2004), Clinical Management of Rape Survivors: Developing Protocols for use with Refugees and Internally Displaced Persons. Geneva.

WHO, United Nations Population Fund (UNFPA) and Andalucia School of Public Health (2009), Granada Consensus on Sexual and Reproductive Health in Protracted Crises and Recovery. Granada, Spain.

Injury

Hayward-Karlsson, J et al (1998), Hospitals for War-Wounded: A Practical Guide for Setting Up and Running a Surgical Hospital in an Area of Armed Conflict. International Committee of the Red Cross (ICRC). Geneva.

PAHO (1995, reprint 2001), Establishing a Mass Casualty Management System. Washington DC. www.disasterpublications.info/english/viewtopic.php?topic=victimasmasa

WHO (2005), Integrated Management for Emergency and Essential Surgical Care tool kit: Disaster Management Guidelines. Geneva. www.who.int/surgery/publications/Disastermanagguide.pdf

Mental health

IASC (2007), IASC Guidelines on Mental Health and Psychosocial Support in Emergency Settings. Geneva. www.humanitarianinfo.org/iasc

IASC Reference Group on Mental Health and Psychosocial Support (2010), Mental Health and Psychosocial Support (MHPSS) In Humanitarian Emergencies: What Should Humanitarian Health Actors Know? Geneva.
www.who.int/mental_health/emergencies/en/

WHO (2010), mhGAP Intervention Guide for Mental, Neurological and Substance Use Disorders in Non-specialized Health Settings. Geneva.
www.who.int/mental_health/

WHO, World Vision International and War Trauma Foundation (forthcoming), Psychological First Aid Guide. Geneva.

Non-communicable diseases

Spiegel et al (2010), Health-care needs of people affected by conflict: future trends and changing frameworks. Lancet, Vol. 375, 23 January 2010.

WHO (2008), The Management of Cardiovascular Disease, Diabetes, Asthma and Chronic Obstructive Pulmonary Disease in Emergency and Humanitarian Settings. Draft, 28 February 2008. Geneva.

WHO (2009), WHO Package of Essential Non-communicable Disease Interventions (WHO PEN). Geneva.

Further reading

International legal instruments

Mann, J et al (eds) (1999), Health and Human Rights: A Reader. Routledge. New York.

Baccino-Astrada, A (1982), Manual on the Rights and Duties of Medical Personnel in Armed Conflicts. ICRC. Geneva.

Health systems

Beaglehole, R, Bonita, R and Kjellstrom, T (2006), Basic Epidemiology, 2nd edition. WHO. Geneva.

IASC Global Health Cluster (2010), GHC position paper: removing user fees for primary health care services during humanitarian crises. Geneva.

Johns Hopkins Bloomberg School of Public Health and International Federation of Red Cross and Red Crescent Societies (2008), Public health guide in emergencies. Geneva. www.ifrc.org/what/health/relief/guide.asp

Médecins sans Frontières (MSF) (1997), Refugee Health. An Approach to Emergency Situations. Macmillan. London.

Noji, E (ed) (1997), The Public Health Consequences of Disasters. Oxford University Press. New York.

Perrin, P (1996), Handbook on War and Public Health. ICRC. Geneva.

WHO (2006), The Interagency Emergency Health Kit 2006. Geneva.

Essential health services

Checchi, F and Roberts, L (2005), Interpreting and using mortality data in humanitarian emergencies. Humanitarian Practice Network. Overseas Development Institute. London. www.odihpn.org

MSF (2006), Rapid health assessment of refugee or displaced populations. Paris.

SMART (2006), Measuring Mortality, Nutritional Status and Food Security in Crisis Situations: Standardized Monitoring and Assessment of Relief and Transition. www.smartindicators.org

UNHCR (2009), UNHCR's Priniciples and Guidance for Referral Health Care for Refugees and Other Persons of Concern. Geneva. www.unhcr.org/cgi-bin/texis/vtx/search?page=search&docid=4b4c4fca9&query=referral%20guidelines

WHO (1999), Rapid Health Assessment Protocols for Emergencies. Geneva.

Control of communicable diseases

Cook, GC, Manson, P and Zumla, AI (2008), Manson's Tropical Diseases, 22nd edition. WB Saunders.

Connolly, MA et al (2004), Communicable diseases in complex emergencies: impact and challenges. The Lancet. London.

WHO (2004), Cholera outbreak, assessing the outbreak response and improving preparedness. Geneva.

WHO (2005), Guidelines for the control of shigellosis, including epidemics due to shigella dysenteriae type 1. Geneva.

Child health

WHO (2005), Guidelines for the management of common illnesses with limited resources. Geneva.

WHO, UNFPA, UNICEF and The World Bank Group (2003), Managing Newborn Problems: A guide for doctors, nurses, and midwives. Geneva. http://whqlibdoc.who.int/publications/2003/9241546220.pdf

Sexual and reproductive health

Inter-agency Standing Committee (2006), Guidelines for Gender-based Violence Interventions in Humanitarian Emergencies. Geneva.

International Rescue Committee (2003), Protecting the Future: HIV Prevention, Care and Support Among Displaced and War-Affected Populations. Kumarian Press. Bloomfield, CT, USA.

UNFPA and Inter-agency Working Group on Reproductive Health in Refugee Situations (2008), The Reproductive Health Kit for Emergency Situations.

UNHCR (2006), Note on HIV/AIDS and the Protection of Refugees, IDPs and Other Persons of Concern. Geneva. www.unhcr.org/444e20892.html

UNHCR (2007), Antiretroviral Medication Policy for Refugees. Geneva. www.unhcr.org/45b479642.html

UNHCR and Southern African Clinicians Society (2007), Clinical guide antiretroviral therapy management for displaced populations. www.unhcr.org/cgi-bin/texis/vtx/search?page=search&docid=46238d5f2&query=art%20guidelines

UNHCR, WHO and the Joint United Nations Programme on HIV/AIDS (UNAIDS) (2009), Policy Statement on HIV Testing and Counselling in Health Facilities for Refugees, Internally Displaced Persons and other Persons of Concern to UNHCR. Geneva. www.unhcr.org/4b508b9c9.html

WHO, UNFPA, UNICEF and The World Bank Group (2000, reprint 2007), Managing Complications in Pregnancy and Childbirth: A guide for midwives and doctors. Geneva. http://whqlibdoc.who.int/publications/2007/9241545879_eng.pdf

Injury

International Society for Prosthetics and Orthotics (ISPO) (2001), ISPO consensus conference on appropriate orthopaedic technology for low-income countries: conclusions and recommendations. Prosthetics Orthotics International. Vol. 25, pp 168–170.

ISPO Code of Conduct for International Non-Governmental Prosthetics, Orthotics, and Mobility Assistance: www.usispo.org/code.asp

Landmines Survivors Network (2007), Prosthetics and Orthotics Programme Guide: implementing P&O services in poor settings: guide for planners and providers of services for persons in need of orthopaedic devices. Geneva.

Landmine Survivors Network (2007), Prosthetics and Orthotics Project Guide: supporting P&O services in low-income settings a common approach for organizations implementing aid projects. Geneva.

MSF (1989), Minor Surgical Procedures in Remote Areas. Paris.

WHO (1991), Surgery at the District Hospital: Obstetrics, Gynaecology, Orthopaedics and Traumatology. Geneva.

Mental health

UNHCR and WHO (2008), Rapid Assessment of Alcohol and Other Substance Use in Conflict-affected and Displaced Populations: A Field Guide. Geneva. www.who.int/mental_health/emergencies/en/

WHO (2009), Pharmacological treatment of mental disorders in primary health care. Geneva. www.who.int/mental_health/

Non-communicable diseases

Fauci, AS et al (eds) (2008), Harrison's Principles of Internal Medicine, 15th edition. McGraw Hill Professional. New York.

Foster, C et al (eds), The Washington Manual of Medical Therapeutics, 33rd edition. Lippincott Williams & Wilkins Publishers. Philadelphia.

Tierny, LM, McPhee, SJ, Papadakis, MA (eds) (2003), Current Medical Diagnosis and Treatment, 42nd edition. McGraw-Hill/Appleton & Lange. New York.

Annexes

Annex 1

Key Documents that inform the Humanitarian Charter

The Humanitarian Charter sets out shared beliefs and common principles concerning humanitarian action and responsibilities in situations of disaster or conflict, and notes that these are reflected in international law. The following annotated list of key documents includes the most relevant international legal instruments relating to international human rights, international humanitarian law (IHL), refugee law and humanitarian action. It does not attempt to represent regional law and developments. The list also includes a number of other guidelines, principles, standards and frameworks that inform the Humanitarian Charter. As this is necessarily very selective, further resources and web links to these documents are available on the Sphere Project website (www.sphereproject.org). Owing to the limitations of space, notes are provided only for the documents which seemed to require introduction or special explanation, because they are newer or have specific sections concerning disaster or conflict.

The documents are listed thematically, under the headings of:

1. *Human rights, protection and vulnerability*
2. *Armed conflict and humanitarian assistance*
3. *Refugees and internally displaced persons (IDPs)*
4. *Disasters and humanitarian assistance*

To ensure clarity about the status of each document, they are each classified under sub-headings as:

1. *Treaties and customary law (where applicable)*
2. *UN and other formally adopted intergovernmental guidelines and principles*
3. *Humanitarian policy frameworks, guidelines and principles*

1. Human rights, protection and vulnerability

The following documents relate primarily to the human rights recognised in universal treaties and declarations. A number of key documents relating to age (children and older people), gender and disability are also included because these are some of the most common bases of vulnerability in disaster or conflict.

1.1. Treaties and customary law on human rights, protection and vulnerability

Human rights treaty law applies to states that are parties to the relevant treaty, but customary law (e.g. the prohibition on torture) applies to all states. Human rights law applies at all times, with two possible exceptions:

- Some limited civil and political rights may be suspended during declared national emergencies, consistent with Article 4 of the International Covenant on Civil and Political Rights ('derogation')
- During recognised armed conflicts, IHL applies first if there is any inconsistency with human rights law.

1.1.1. Universal human rights

The Universal Declaration of Human Rights 1948 (UDHR), adopted by UN General Assembly resolution 217 A(III) of 10 December 1948.
www.un.org/en/documents/udhr/index.shtml

Proclaimed by the UN General Assembly in 1948, the UDHR set out, for the first time, fundamental human rights to be universally protected. It is not a treaty but is generally agreed to have become part of customary international law. The first sentence of the preamble introduces the concept of the 'inherent dignity' of human beings as a fundamental basis for human rights, and the first Article states, 'All human beings are born free and equal in dignity and rights.'

International Covenant on Civil and Political Rights 1966 (ICCPR), adopted by UN General Assembly resolution 2200A (XXI) of 16 December 1966, entry into force 23 March 1976, United Nations, Treaty Series, vol. 999, p. 171 and vol. 1057, p. 407. www2.ohchr.org/english/law/ccpr.htm

Second Optional Protocol to ICCPR 1989 (aiming at the abolition of the death penalty), adopted by UN General Assembly resolution 44/128 of 15 December 1989, entry into force 11 July 1991, United Nations, Treaty Series, vol. 1642, p. 414. www2.ohchr.org/english/law/ccpr-death.htm

States parties to the ICCPR must respect and ensure the rights for all individuals within their territory or under their jurisdiction, while recognising the right of 'peoples' to self-determination and the equal rights of men and women. Some rights (marked with asterisk*) may never be suspended, even in the most dire national emergency.

Rights: right to life;* no torture or other cruel, inhuman or degrading treatment;* no slavery;* no arbitrary arrest or detention; humanity and dignity in detention; no imprisonment for breach of contract;* freedom of movement and residence; only lawful expulsion of aliens; equality before the law, fair trial and presumption of innocence in criminal trials; no retrospectivity in criminal offences;* equal recognition before the law;* private life; free thought, religion and conscience;* free opinion, expression and peaceful assembly; freedom of association; right to marriage and family life; protection of children; right to vote and participate in public affairs; minorities' right to enjoy their own culture, religion and language.*

International Covenant on Economic, Social and Cultural Rights 1966 (ICESCR), adopted by UN General Assembly resolution 2200A (XXI) of 16 December 1966, entry into force 3 January 1976, United Nations, Treaty Series, vol. 993, p. 3 www2.ohchr.org/english/law/cescr.htm

States parties agree to commit the maximum of their available resources to 'achieving progressively' the covenant rights, which are to be enjoyed equally by men and women.

Rights: to work; to receive just remuneration; to join trade unions; to have social security/insurance; to family life, including protection of mothers after childbirth and protection of children from exploitation; to an adequate standard of living, including food, clothing and housing; to physical and mental health; to education; and to participate in cultural life and enjoy the benefits of scientific and cultural progress.

International Convention on the Elimination of All Forms of Racial Discrimination 1969 (ICERD), adopted by UN General Assembly resolution 2106 (XX) of 21 December 1965, entry into force 4 January 1969, United Nations, Treaty Series, vol. 660, p. 195. www2.ohchr.org/english/law/cerd.htm

Convention on the Elimination of All Forms of Discrimination Against Women 1979 (CEDAW), adopted by UN General Assembly resolution 34/180 of 18 December 1979, entry into force 3 September 1981, United Nations, Treaty Series, vol. 1249, p. 13. www2.ohchr.org/english/law/cedaw.htm

Convention on the Rights of the Child 1989 (CRC), adopted by UN General Assembly resolution 44/25 of 20 November 1989, entry into force 2 September

1990, United Nations, Treaty Series, vol. 1577, p. 3.
www2.ohchr.org/english/law/crc.htm

Optional Protocol on the involvement of children in armed conflict 2000, adopted by UN General Assembly resolution A/RES/54/263 of 25 May 2000, entry into force 12 February 2002, United Nations, Treaty Series, vol. 2173, p. 222. www2.ohchr.org/english/law/crc-conflict.htm

Optional Protocol on the sale of children, child prostitution and child pornography 2000, adopted by UN General Assembly resolution A/RES/54/263 of 25 May 2000, entry into force 18 January 2002, United Nations, Treaty Series, vol. 2171, p. 227. www2.ohchr.org/english/law/crc-sale.htm

The CRC has almost universal state accession. It restates the basic human rights of children and identifies when they need special protection (e.g. when separated from their families). The protocols require positive action on specific child protection issues for states that are parties to them.

Convention on the Rights of Persons with Disabilities 2006 (CRPD), adopted by UN General Assembly resolution A/RES/61/106 of 13 December 2006, entry into force 3 May 2008, United Nations Treaty Collection, Chapter IV, 15. www2.ohchr.org/english/law/disabilities-convention.htm

The CRPD supports the rights of people with disabilities under all other human rights treaties, as well as dealing specifically with awareness-raising regarding persons with disabilities, non-discrimination and accessibility of services and facilities. There is also special mention of 'situations of risk and humanitarian emergencies' (Article 11).

1.1.2. Genocide, torture and other criminal abuse of rights

Convention on the Prevention and Punishment of the Crime of Genocide 1948, adopted by UN General Assembly Resolution 260 (III) of 9 December 1948, entry into force 12 January 1951, United Nations, Treaty Series, vol. 78, p. 277 www2.ohchr.org/english/law/genocide.htm

Convention against Torture and Other Cruel, Inhuman or Degrading Treatment or Punishment 1984, adopted by UN General Assembly resolution 39/46 of 10 December 1984, entry into force 26 June 1987, United Nations, Treaty Series, vol. 1465, p. 85. www2.ohchr.org/english/law/cat.htm

This convention has a very high number of states parties. The prohibition on torture is also now generally recognised as part of customary international law. No kind of public emergency or war may be invoked to justify torture. States must not return (*refouler*) anyone to a territory where the person has reasonable grounds to believe he or she would be in danger of torture.

Rome Statute of the International Criminal Court, adopted by the Diplomatic Conference in Rome, 17 July 1998, entry into force 1 July 2002, United Nations, Treaty Series, vol. 2187, p. 3. www.icrc.org/ihl.nsf/INTRO/585?OpenDocument

Article 9 of the Statue (Elements of Crimes), adopted by the International Criminal Court (ICC) in 2002, describes in detail war crimes, crimes against humanity and genocide, thus codifying much of customary international criminal law. The ICC can investigate and prosecute matters referred to it by the UN Security Council (even if the accused person's state is not a party to the treaty), as well as crimes allegedly committed by nationals of states parties to the treaty, or in their territory.

1.2. United Nations and other formally adopted intergovernmental principles and guidelines on human rights, protection and vulnerability

Madrid International Plan of Action on Ageing 2002, UN Second World Assembly on Ageing, Madrid, 2002, endorsed by UN General Assembly resolution 37/51 of 3 December 1982.
www.globalaging.org/agingwatch/events/CSD/mipaa+5.htm

United Nations Principles for Older Persons 1991, UN General Assembly Resolution 46/91 of 16 December 1991.
www2.ohchr.org/english/law/olderpersons.htm

1.3. Humanitarian policy frameworks, guidelines and principles on human rights, protection and vulnerability

Protecting Persons Affected by Natural Disasters: IASC Operational Guidelines on Human Rights and Natural Disasters 2006, Inter-Agency Standing Committee. www.humanitarianinfo.org/iasc/pageloader.aspx

International Law and Standards Applicable in Natural Disaster Situations (IDLO Legal Manual) 2009, International Development Law Organization (IDLO). www.idlo.int/DOCNews/352doc.pdf

Inter-agency guiding principles on unaccompanied and separated children 2002, developed by the ICRC, the Office of the UN High Commissioner for Refugees (UNHCR), the UN Children's Fund (UNICEF), World Vision International, Save the Children UK and the International Rescue Committee, 2009. www.icrc.org

Gender Handbook in Humanitarian Action 2006, Inter-Agency Standing Committee. www.humanitarianinfo.org/iasc/pageloader.aspx?page=content-subsidi-tf_gender-genderh

IASC Guidelines on Mental Health and Psychosocial Support in Emergency Settings 2007, Inter-Agency Standing Committee. www.humanitarianinfo.org/iasc/pageloader.aspx?page=content-subsidi-tf_mhps-default

INEE Minimum Standards for Education in Emergencies, Chronic Crises and Early Reconstruction 2007, as updated 2010, Inter-Agency Network for Education in Emergencies (INEE) (formally recognised as companion standards with Sphere since 2008).
www.ineesite.org/index.php/post/inee_minimum_standards_overview/

2. Armed conflict, international humanitarian law and humanitarian assistance

2.1. Treaties and customary law on armed conflict, international humanitarian law and humanitarian assistance

International humanitarian law (IHL) specifies the thresholds of when violent conflict becomes 'armed conflict' and thus makes this special legal regime applicable. The International Committee of the Red Cross (ICRC) is the official repository of the IHL treaties, and provides extensive information and resources on its website (www.icrc.org), including the official commentary on the Geneva Conventions and their Protocols, and the rules of the Customary International Humanitarian Law Study.

2.1.1. Core IHL treaties

The Four Geneva Conventions of 1949

Protocol Additional to the Geneva Conventions, Protection of Victims of International Armed Conflicts 1977 (Protocol I)

Protocol Additional to the Geneva Conventions, Protection of Victims of Non-International Armed Conflicts 1977 (Protocol II)
www.icrc.org/ihl.nsf/CONVPRES?OpenView

The four Geneva Conventions – to which all states are parties and which are also generally accepted as part of customary law – concern protection and treatment of the wounded and sick in land warfare (I) and at sea (II), treatment of prisoners of war (III) and protection of civilians during armed conflict (IV). They apply primarily to international armed conflicts, except for Article 3 common to the conventions which concerns non-international conflicts, and some other elements now accepted as customary law in non-international conflicts. The two 1977 protocols updated the conventions at that time, especially the definitions of combatants and codifying of non-international conflicts. A number of states have not acceded to the protocols.

2.1.2. Treaties on restricted or prohibited weapons and cultural property

In addition to the 'Geneva law' outlined above, there is also the body of law often described as the 'Hague law' on armed conflict. This includes the convention on protection of cultural property and a number of conventions on the types of weapons that are restricted or prohibited, including gases and other chemical and biological weapons, conventional weapons that are indiscriminate or cause unnecessary suffering, as well as anti-personnel landmines and cluster munitions. www.icrc.org/ihl.nsf

2.1.3. Customary IHL

Customary IHL refers to the law of armed conflict that is accepted by states, through their statements, policies and practices, as representing customary rules that apply to all states, regardless of their accession to the IHL treaties. There is no agreed list of customary rules, but the most authoritative interpretation is the study below.

Customary International Humanitarian Law (CIHL) Study, ICRC, Henckaerts, J-M and Doswald-Beck, L, Cambridge University Press, Cambridge & New York, 2005. www.icrc.org/ihl.nsf/INTRO/612?OpenDocument

The study covers almost the full ambit of the law of armed conflict. It lists 161 specific rules and whether each applies in international armed conflict and/or non-international armed conflict. While some legal commentators criticise its methodology, the CIHL study emerged from a broadly consultative and rigorous research process over ten years, and its authority as an interpretation of the customary rules is widely recognised.

2.2. UN and other formally adopted intergovernmental principles and guidelines on armed conflict, international humanitarian law and humanitarian assistance

UN Security Council 'Aide Memoire' on Protection 2002, as updated 2003 (S/PRST/2003/27). www.un.org/Docs/journal/asp/ws.asp?m=S/PRST/2003/27 This is not a resolution binding on states, but a guidance document for the UN Security Council relating to peacekeeping and urgent situations of conflict, resulting from consultations with a range of UN agencies and IASC.

UN Security Council resolutions on sexual violence and women in armed conflict, especially resolution numbers 1820 (2008), 1888 (2009) and 1889 (2009)
All UN Security Council resolutions by year and number:
www.un.org/documents/scres.htm

2.3. Humanitarian policy frameworks, guidelines and principles on armed conflict, international humanitarian law and humanitarian assistance

Professional standards for protection work carried out by humanitarian and human rights actors in armed conflict and other situations of violence 2009, ICRC. www.icrc.org

3. Refugees and internally displaced persons (IDPs)

UNHCR – the UN Refugee Agency – has a special legal mandate for the protection of refugees under the Refugee Convention and Protocol. It has also been mandated by the UN General Assembly to liaise with states for the protection of IDPs. UNHCR has extensive resources on its website.

3.1. Treaties on refugees and IDPs

In addition to the international treaty, this section includes two African Union (formerly Organization of African Unity, or OAU) treaties, because they both set historic precedents.

Convention relating to the Status of Refugees 1951 (as amended), adopted by United Nations Conference of Plenipotentiaries on the Status of Refugees and Stateless Persons, Geneva, 2 to 25 July 1951, entry into force 22 April 1954, United Nations, Treaty Series, vol. 189, p. 137.

Protocol relating to the Status of Refugees 1967, noted by the UN General Assembly, in resolution 2198 (XXI) 2 of 16 December 1966, United Nations, Treaty Series, vol. 606, p. 267. www.unhcr.org/protect/PROTECTION/3b66c2aa10.pdf

The first international agreement on refugees, the Convention defines a refugee as a person who, 'owing to a well-founded fear of being persecuted for reasons of race, religion, nationality, membership of a particular social group or political opinion, is outside the country of his nationality, and is unable to or, owing to such fear, is unwilling to avail himself of the protection of that country or return there because there is a fear of persecution...'

OAU Convention Governing the Specific Aspects of Refugee Problems in Africa 1969, adopted by the Assembly of Heads of State and Government at its Sixth Ordinary Session, Addis Ababa, 10 September 1969. www.unhcr.org/45dc1a682.html

This accepts and expands the 1951 Convention definition to include people who have been compelled to leave their country not only as a result of persecution but also owing to external aggression, occupation, foreign domination or events seriously disturbing public order. It also recognises non-state groups as perpetrators of persecution and it does not require that refugees show a direct link between themselves and the future danger.

African Union Convention for the Protection and Assistance of Internally Displaced Persons in Africa (Kampala Convention) 2009, adopted by a Special Summit of the African Union, held in Kampala, Uganda, on 22 October 2009, not yet in force as at October 2010. www.unhcr.org/4ae9bede9.html

This is the first multilateral convention concerning IDPs. It was initially signed by 17 African Union states in October 2009 but requires 15 formal accessions/ratifications to enter into force.

3.2. UN and other formally adopted intergovernmental principles and guidelines on refugees and IDPs

Guiding Principles on Internal Displacement 1998, recognised in September 2005 by heads of state and governments assembled at the World Summit in New York in UN General Assembly resolution 60/L.1 (132, UN Doc. A/60/L.1) as 'an important international framework for the protection of internally displaced persons'. www.idpguidingprinciples.org/

These principles are based on international humanitarian and human rights law and analogous refugee law, and are intended to serve as an international standard to guide governments, international organisations and all other relevant actors in providing assistance and protection to IDPs.

4. Disasters and humanitarian assistance

4.1. Treaties on disasters and humanitarian assistance

Convention on the Safety of United Nations and Associated Personnel 1994, adopted by UN General Assembly resolution 49/59 of 9 December 1994, entry into force 15 January 1999, United Nations, Treaty Series, vol. 2051, p. 363. www.un.org/law/cod/safety.htm

Optional Protocol to the Convention on the Safety of United Nations and Associated Personnel 2005, adopted by UN General Assembly resolution A/60/42 of 8 December 2005, entry into force 19 August 2010. www.ocha.unog.ch/drptoolkit/PNormativeGuidanceInternationalConventions. html#UNSpecificConventions

In the convention, protection is limited to UN peacekeeping, unless the UN has declared 'exceptional risk' – an impractical requirement. The protocol corrects this major flaw in the convention and expands the legal protection to all UN operations, from emergency humanitarian assistance to peacebuilding and the delivery of humanitarian, political and development assistance.

Food Aid Convention 1999, a separate legal instrument under the Grains Trade Convention 1995, administered by the Food Aid Committee through the Secretariat of the International Grains Council (IGC).

Tampere Convention on the Provision of Telecommunication Resources for Disaster Mitigation and Relief Operations 1998, approved by the Intergovernmental Conference on Emergency Telecommunications 1998, entry into force 8 January 2005, United Nations, Treaty Series, vol. 2296, p. 5. www.unhcr.org/refworld/publisher,ICET98,,,41dec59d4,0.html

UN Framework Convention on Climate Change 1992 (UNFCCC), adopted by the United Nations Conference on Environment and Development, Rio de Janeiro, 4 to 14 June 1992, welcomed by the UN General Assembly in resolution 47/195 of 22 December 1992, entry into force 21 March 1994, United Nations, Treaty Series, vol. 1771, p. 107. http://unfccc.int/essential_background/convention/items/2627.php

Kyoto Protocol to the UNFCC 1997, adopted at the third session of the Conference of the Parties to the Framework Convention, Kyoto, Japan on 11 December 1997, entry into force 16 February 2005, United Nations, Treaty Series, vol. 2303, p. 148. http://unfccc.int/essential_background/kyoto_protocol/items/1678.php

The UNFCCC and Kyoto Protocol address the urgent need for implementing climate change adaptation and risk reduction strategies, and building local capacity and resilience, especially in countries that are prone to natural disasters. It emphasises disaster reduction strategies and risk management, especially with regard to climate change.

4.2. UN and other formally adopted intergovernmental principles and guidelines on disasters and humanitarian assistance

Strengthening of the coordination of humanitarian emergency assistance of the United Nations, with Annex, Guiding Principles, General Assembly Resolution 46/182 of 19 December 1991.
www.reliefweb.int/ocha_ol/about/resol/resol_e.html

This led to the creation of the UN Department of Humanitarian Affairs, which became the UN Office for the Coordination of Humanitarian Affairs (OCHA) in 1998.

Hyogo Framework for Action 2005–2015: Building the resilience of nations and communities to disasters, adopted by the World Conference on Disaster Reduction 2005. www.unisdr.org/eng/hfa/hfa.htm
This sets out strategies for states and humanitarian agencies to incorporate disaster risk reduction in the implementation of emergency response, recovery and preparedness programmes, integrate it in sustainable development and build capacity for resilience.

Guidelines for the domestic facilitation and regulation of international disaster relief and initial recovery assistance, (IDRL Guidelines) 2007, adopted by the 30th International Conference of the Red Cross and Red Crescent (which includes states parties to the Geneva Conventions).
www.ifrc.org/what/disasters/idrl/index.asp

4.3. Humanitarian policy frameworks, guidelines and principles on disasters and humanitarian assistance

Code of Conduct for The International Red Cross and Red Crescent Movement and Non-Governmental Organisations (NGOs) in Disaster Relief (see Annex 2: Code of Conduct on page 368).

Fundamental Principles of the International Red Cross and Red Crescent Movement 1965, adopted by the 20th International Conference of the Red Cross. www.ifrc.org/what/values/principles/index.asp

HAP Standards in Humanitarian Accountability 2007, Humanitarian Accountability Partnership (an international self-regulatory body for the humanitarian sector, including certification). www.hapinternational.org

Principles and Good Practice of Humanitarian Donorship 2003, endorsed by the Stockholm conference of donor countries, UN agencies, NGOs and the International Red Cross and Red Crescent Movement, and signed by the European Commission and 16 states. www.goodhumanitariandonorship.org

Principles of Partnership: A Statement of Commitment 2007, endorsed at the July 2007 Global Humanitarian Platform meeting (a dialogue mechanism between UN and non-UN humanitarian organisations).
www.globalhumanitarianplatform.org/ghp.html

Annex 2

The Code of Conduct
for the International Red Cross and Red Crescent Movement and Non-Governmental Organisations (NGOs) in Disaster Relief

Prepared jointly by the International Federation of Red Cross and Red Crescent Societies and the International Committee of the Red Cross[1]

---

1   *Sponsored by: Caritas Internationalis,* Catholic Relief Services,* International Federation of Red Cross and Red Crescent Societies,* International Save the Children Alliance,* Lutheran World Federation,* Oxfam,* World Council of Churches,* International Committee of the Red Cross (* members of the Steering Committee for Humanitarian Response).*

Purpose

This Code of Conduct seeks to guard our standards of behaviour. It is not about operational details, such as how one should calculate food rations or set up a refugee camp. Rather, it seeks to maintain the high standards of independence, effectiveness and impact to which disaster response NGOs and the International Red Cross and Red Crescent Movement aspires. It is a voluntary code, enforced by the will of the organisation accepting it to maintain the standards laid down in the Code.

In the event of armed conflict, the present Code of Conduct will be interpreted and applied in conformity with international humanitarian law.

The Code of Conduct is presented first. Attached to it are three annexes, describing the working environment that we would like to see created by Host Governments, Donor Governments and Inter-governmental Organisations in order to facilitate the effective delivery of humanitarian assistance.

Definitions

NGOs: NGOs (Non-Governmental Organisations) refers here to organisations, both national and international, which are constituted separately from the government of the country in which they are founded.

NGHAs: For the purposes of this text, the term Non-Governmental Humanitarian Agencies (NGHAs) has been coined to encompass the components of the International Red Cross and Red Crescent Movement – The International Committee of the Red Cross, The International Federation of Red Cross and Red Crescent Societies and its member National Societies – and the NGOs as defined above. This code refers specifically to those NGHAs who are involved in disaster response.

IGOs: IGOs (Inter-Governmental Organisations) refers to organisations constituted by two or more governments. It thus includes all United Nations Agencies and regional organisations.

Disasters: A disaster is a calamitous event resulting in loss of life, great human suffering and distress, and large scale material damage.

The Code of Conduct
Principles of Conduct for The International Red Cross and Red Crescent Movement and NGOs in Disaster Response Programmes

1 The humanitarian imperative comes first

The right to receive humanitarian assistance, and to offer it, is a fundamental humanitarian principle which should be enjoyed by all citizens of all countries. As members of the international community, we recognise our obligation to provide humanitarian assistance wherever it is needed. Hence the need for unimpeded access to affected populations is of fundamental importance in exercising that responsibility. The prime motivation of our response to disaster is to alleviate human suffering amongst those least able to withstand the stress caused by disaster. When we give humanitarian aid it is not a partisan or political act and should not be viewed as such.

2 Aid is given regardless of the race, creed or nationality of the recipients and without adverse distinction of any kind. Aid priorities are calculated on the basis of need alone

Wherever possible, we will base the provision of relief aid upon a thorough assessment of the needs of the disaster victims and the local capacities already in place to meet those needs. Within the entirety of our programmes, we will reflect considerations of proportionality. Human suffering must be alleviated whenever it is found; life is as precious in one part of a country as another. Thus, our provision of aid will reflect the degree of suffering it seeks to alleviate. In implementing this approach, we recognise the crucial role played by women in disaster-prone communities and will ensure that this role is supported, not diminished, by our aid programmes. The implementation of such a universal, impartial and independent policy, can only be effective if we and our partners have access to the necessary resources to provide for such equitable relief, and have equal access to all disaster victims.

3 Aid will not be used to further a particular political or religious standpoint

Humanitarian aid will be given according to the need of individuals, families and communities. Not withstanding the right of NGHAs to espouse particular political or religious opinions, we affirm that assistance will not be dependent on the adherence of the recipients to those opinions. We will not tie the promise, delivery or distribution of assistance to the embracing or acceptance of a particular political or religious creed.

4 We shall endeavour not to act as instruments of government foreign policy

NGHAs are agencies which act independently from governments. We therefore formulate our own policies and implementation strategies and do not seek to implement the policy of any government, except in so far as it coincides with our own independent policy. We will never knowingly – or through negligence – allow ourselves, or our employees, to be used to gather information of a political, military or economically sensitive nature for governments or other bodies that may serve purposes other than those which are strictly humanitarian, nor will we act as instruments of foreign policy of donor governments. We will use the assistance we receive to respond to needs and this assistance should not be driven by the need to dispose of donor commodity surpluses, nor by the political interest of any particular donor. We value and promote the voluntary giving of labour and finances by concerned individuals to support our work and recognise the independence of action promoted by such voluntary motivation. In order to protect our independence we will seek to avoid dependence upon a single funding source.

5 We shall respect culture and custom

We will endeavour to respect the culture, structures and customs of the communities and countries we are working in.

6 We shall attempt to build disaster response on local capacities

All people and communities – even in disaster – possess capacities as well as vulnerabilities. Where possible, we will strengthen these capacities by employing local staff, purchasing local materials and trading with local companies. Where possible, we will work through local NGHAs as partners in planning and implementation, and co-operate with local government structures where appropriate. We will place a high priority on the proper co-ordination of our emergency responses. This is best done within the countries concerned by those most directly involved in the relief operations, and should include representatives of the relevant UN bodies.

7 Ways shall be found to involve programme beneficiaries in the management of relief aid

Disaster response assistance should never be imposed upon the beneficiaries. Effective relief and lasting rehabilitation can best be achieved where the intended beneficiaries are involved in the design, management and implementation of the assistance programme. We will strive to achieve full community participation in our relief and rehabilitation programmes.

8 Relief aid must strive to reduce future vulnerabilities to disaster as well as meeting basic needs

All relief actions affect the prospects for long-term development, either in a positive or a negative fashion. Recognising this, we will strive to implement relief programmes which actively reduce the beneficiaries' vulnerability to future disasters and help create sustainable lifestyles. We will pay particular attention to environmental concerns in the design and management of relief programmes. We will also endeavour to minimise the negative impact of humanitarian assistance, seeking to avoid long-term beneficiary dependence upon external aid.

9 We hold ourselves accountable to both those we seek to assist and those from whom we accept resources

We often act as an institutional link in the partnership between those who wish to assist and those who need assistance during disasters. We therefore hold ourselves accountable to both constituencies. All our dealings with donors and beneficiaries shall reflect an attitude of openness and transparency. We recognise the need to report on our activities, both from a financial perspective and the perspective of effectiveness. We recognise the obligation to ensure appropriate monitoring of aid distributions and to carry out regular assessments of the impact of disaster assistance. We will also seek to report, in an open fashion, upon the impact of our work, and the factors limiting or enhancing that impact. Our programmes will be based upon high standards of professionalism and expertise in order to minimise the wasting of valuable resources.

10 In our information, publicity and advertising activities, we shall recognise disaster victims as dignified humans, not hopeless objects

Respect for the disaster victim as an equal partner in action should never be lost. In our public information we shall portray an objective image of the disaster situation where the capacities and aspirations of disaster victims are highlighted, and not just their vulnerabilities and fears. While we will cooperate with the media in order to enhance public response, we will not allow external or internal demands for publicity to take precedence over the principle of maximising overall relief assistance. We will avoid competing with other disaster response agencies for media coverage in situations where such coverage may be to the detriment of the service provided to the beneficiaries or to the security of our staff or the beneficiaries.

The Working Environment

Having agreed unilaterally to strive to abide by the Code laid out above, we present below some indicative guidelines which describe the working environment we would like to see created by donor governments, host governments and the inter-governmental organisations – principally the agencies of the United Nations – in order to facilitate the effective participation of NGHAs in disaster response.

These guidelines are presented for guidance. They are not legally binding, nor do we expect governments and IGOs to indicate their acceptance of the guidelines through the signature of any document, although this may be a goal to work to in the future. They are presented in a spirit of openness and cooperation so that our partners will become aware of the ideal relationship we would seek with them.

Annex I: Recommendations to the governments of disaster affected countries

1 Governments should recognise and respect the independent, humanitarian and impartial actions of NGHAs

NGHAs are independent bodies. This independence and impartiality should be respected by host governments.

2 Host governments should facilitate rapid access to disaster victims for NGHAs

If NGHAs are to act in full compliance with their humanitarian principles, they should be granted rapid and impartial access to disaster victims, for the purpose of delivering humanitarian assistance. It is the duty of the host government, as part of the exercising of sovereign responsibility, not to block such assistance, and to accept the impartial and apolitical action of NGHAs. Host governments should facilitate the rapid entry of relief staff, particularly by waiving requirements for transit, entry and exit visas, or arranging that these are rapidly granted. Governments should grant over-flight permission and landing rights for aircraft transporting international relief supplies and personnel, for the duration of the emergency relief phase.

3 Governments should facilitate the timely flow of relief goods and information during disasters

Relief supplies and equipment are brought into a country solely for the purpose of alleviating human suffering, not for commercial benefit or gain. Such supplies should normally be allowed free and unrestricted passage and should not be subject to requirements for consular certificates of origin or invoices, import and/ or export licences or other restrictions, or to importation taxation, landing fees or port charges.

The temporary importation of necessary relief equipment, including vehicles, light aircraft and telecommunications equipment, should be facilitated by the receiving host government through the temporary waving of licence or registration restrictions. Equally, governments should not restrict the re-exportation of relief equipment at the end of a relief operation.

To facilitate disaster communications, host governments are encouraged to designate certain radio frequencies, which relief organisations may use in-country and for international communications for the purpose of disaster communications, and to make such frequencies known to the disaster response community prior to the disaster. They should authorise relief personnel to utilise all means of communication required for their relief operations.

4 Governments should seek to provide a coordinated disaster information and planning service

The overall planning and coordination of relief efforts is ultimately the responsibility of the host government. Planning and coordination can be greatly enhanced if NGHAs are provided with information on relief needs and government systems for planning and implementing relief efforts as well as information on potential security risks they may encounter. Governments are urged to provide such information to NGHAs.

To facilitate effective coordination and the efficient utilisation of relief efforts, host governments are urged to designate, prior to disaster, a single point-of-contact for incoming NGHAs to liaise with the national authorities.

5 Disaster relief in the event of armed conflict

In the event of armed conflict, relief actions are governed by the relevant provisions of international humanitarian law.

Annex II: Recommendations to donor governments

1 Donor governments should recognise and respect the independent, humanitarian and impartial actions of NGHAs

NGHAs are independent bodies whose independence and impartiality should be respected by donor governments. Donor governments should not use NGHAs to further any political or ideological aim.

2 Donor governments should provide funding with a guarantee of operational independence

NGHAs accept funding and material assistance from donor governments in the same spirit as they render it to disaster victims; one of humanity and independence of action. The implementation of relief actions is ultimately the responsibility of the NGHA and will be carried out according to the policies of that NGHA.

3 Donor governments should use their good offices to assist NGHAs in obtaining access to disaster victims

Donor governments should recognise the importance of accepting a level of responsibility for the security and freedom of access of NGHA staff to disaster sites. They should be prepared to exercise diplomacy with host governments on such issues if necessary.

Annex III: Recommendations to inter-governmental organisations

1 IGOs should recognise NGHAs, local and foreign, as valuable partners

NGHAs are willing to work with UN and other inter-governmental agencies to effect better disaster response. They do so in a spirit of partnership which respects the integrity and independence of all partners. Inter-governmental agencies must respect the independence and impartiality of the NGHAs. NGHAs should be consulted by UN agencies in the preparation of relief plans.

2 IGOs should assist host governments in providing an overall coordinating framework for international and local disaster relief

NGHAs do not usually have the mandate to provide the overall coordinating framework for disasters which require an international response. This responsibility falls to the host government and the relevant United Nations authorities. They are urged to provide this service in a timely and effective manner to serve the affected state and the national and international disaster response community. In any case, NGHAs should make all efforts to ensure the effective co-ordination of their own services.

In the event of armed conflict, relief actions are governed by the relevant provisions of international humanitarian law.

3 IGOs should extend security protection provided for UN organisations, to NGHAs

Where security services are provided for inter-governmental organisations, this service should be extended to their operational NGHA partners where it is so requested.

4 IGOs should provide NGHAs with the same access to relevant information as is granted to UN organisations

IGOs are urged to share all information, pertinent to the implementation of effective disaster response, with their operational NGHA partners.

Annex 3

Abbreviations and Acronyms

ACT	artemisinin-based combination therapy
ALNAP	Active Learning Network for Accountability and Performance in Humanitarian Action
ART	anti-retroviral therapy
ARV	anti-retroviral
BCPR	Bureau for Crisis Prevention and Recovery (UNDP)
BEmOC	basic emergency obstetric care
BMI	body mass index
BMS	breastmilk substitutes
BTS	blood transfusion service
CDC	Centers for Disease Control and Prevention
CE-DAT	Complex Emergency Database
CEDAW	Convention on the Elimination of All Forms of Discrimination Against Women
CEmOC	comprehensive emergency obstetric care
CFR	case fatality rate
CHW	Community Health Worker
CIHL	Customary International Humanitarian Law
cm	centimetre
CMR	crude mortality rate
CRC	Convention on the Rights of the Child
CRPD	Convention on the Rights of Persons with Disabilities
CRS	Catholic Relief Services

CTC	cholera treatment centre
DAC	Development Assistance Committee
DPT	diphtheria, pertussis and tetanus
ECB	Emergency Capacity Building (Project)
ENA	Emergency Nutrition Assessment
EPI	Expanded Programme on Immunization
ETAT	Emergency Triage, Assessment and Treatment
EWARN	early warning
FANTA	Food and Nutrition Technical Assistance
FAO	Food and Agriculture Organization of the United Nations
FTE	full-time equivalent
GMO	genetically modified organism
HAP	Humanitarian Accountability Partnership
HIS	health information system
IASC	Inter-Agency Standing Committee
ICC	International Criminal Court
ICCPR	International Covenant on Civil and Political Rights
ICERD	International Convention on the Elimination of All Forms of Racial Discrimination
ICESCR	International Covenant on Economic, Social and Cultural Rights
ICRC	International Committee of the Red Cross
ICVA	International Council of Voluntary Agencies
IDLO	International Development Law Organization
IDP	internally displaced person
IFE	infant feeding in emergencies
IFPRI	International Food Policy Research Institute
IFRC	International Federation of Red Cross and Red Crescent Societies
IGC	International Grains Council
IHL	international humanitarian law
IMAI	Integrated Management of Adult Illness
IMCI	Integrated Management of Childhood Illnesses
IMPAC	Integrated Management of Pregnancy and Childbirth
INEE	Inter-Agency Network for Education in Emergencies
IPC	infection prevention and control
IRC	International Rescue Committee
IRS	indoor residual spraying
ISPO	International Society for Prosthetics and Orthotics

IYCF	infant and young child feeding
km	kilometre
LBW	low birth weight
LEDS	light-emitting diodes
LEGS	Livestock Emergency Guidelines and Standards
LLIN	long-lasting insecticide-treated net
MISP	Minimum Initial Service Package
MOH	Ministry of Health
MSF	Médecins sans Frontières
MUAC	mid upper arm conference
NCDs	non-communicable diseases
NCHS	National Center for Health Statistics
NFI	non-food item
NGO	non-governmental organisation
NICS	Nutrition in Crisis Information System
NRC	Norwegian Refugee Council
NTU	nephelolometric turbidity units
OAU	Organization of African Unity (now African Union)
OCHA	United Nations Office for the Coordination of Humanitarian Affairs
OECD	Organisation for Economic Co-operation and Development
OHCHR	Office of the United Nations High Commissioner for Human Rights
ORS	oral rehydration salts
PAHO	Pan American Health Organization
PEP	post-exposure prophylaxis
PLHIV	people living with HIV
PLWHA	people living with HIV and AIDS
PMTCT	prevention of mother-to-child transmission (of HIV)
PoUWT	point-of-use water treatment
Q&A	quality and accountability
RH	reproductive health
RNI	reference nutrient intakes
SCM	supply chain management
SEEP	Small Enterprise Education and Promotion (Network)
SKAT	Swiss Centre for Appropriate Technology
SMART	Standardised Monitoring and Assessment of Relief and Transitions

STIs	sexually transmitted infections
TB	tuberculosis
TIG	tetanus immune globulin
U5MR	under-5 mortality rate
UDHR	Universal Declaration of Human Rights
UN	United Nations
UNAIDS	Joint United Nations Programme on HIV/AIDS
UN-DDR	United Nations Disarmament, Demobilization and Reintegration
UNDP	United Nations Development Programme
UNFCCC	United Nations Framework Convention on Climate Change
UNFPA	United Nations Population Fund
UN-Habitat	United Nations Human Settlements Programme
UNHCR	Office of the United Nations High Commissioner for Refugees (UN Refugee Agency)
UNICEF	United Nations Children's Fund
UNISDR	United Nations International Strategy for Disaster Reduction
USAID	United States Agency for International Development
VCA	vulnerability and capacity analysis
VIP	ventilated improved pit (latrine)
WASH	water supply, sanitation and hygiene promotion
WEDC	Water, Engineering and Development Centre
WFH	weight for height
WFP	World Food Programme
WHA	World Health Assembly
WHO	World Health Organization
WSP	water safety plan

Index

D

Visit the Sphere Project website

www.sphereproject.org

To order the Sphere Handbook please go to

www.practicalactionpublishing.org/sphere